BEHIND THE MIDDLE EAST CONFLICT
The Real Impasse Between Arab and Jew

BEHIND
THE MIDDLE EAST
CONFLICT

The Real Impasse Between
Arab and Jew

---

by Gil Carl AlRoy

Capricorn Books
G. P. PUTNAM'S SONS
NEW YORK

APR 29 1977

Copyright © 1975 by Gil Carl AlRoy

SBN: 399-11525-0
Library of Congress Catalog
Card Number: 75-7558

PRINTED IN THE UNITED STATES OF AMERICA

Because the transcription of Arabic and Hebrew varies widely among writers, slightly different versions of the same names may be found in this volume.

CONTENTS

1.
On the Sociology and Psychology of the
Knowledge of the Middle East in the West   11

2.
Zionist Perceptions   24

3.
Evolving Israeli Orientations   50

4.
Mirage in the Desert—Diplomats, Journalists,
and Other Strangers   81

5.
Dilemma, Double Meaning, and Dissonance   116

6.
What the Arabs Are Saying   141

7.
Arabs and Modern History   159

8.
Jews and Muslims   176

9.

A Variance of Arabs   202

10.

Imagining the Future   231

Notes   255

Bibliography   287

Index   309

BEHIND THE MIDDLE EAST CONFLICT
The Real Impasse Between Arab and Jew

1

ON THE SOCIOLOGY AND PSYCHOLOGY OF THE KNOWLEDGE OF THE MIDDLE EAST IN THE WEST

STUDENTS of international relations have in recent years become particularly aware of the uses—and misuses—of cognition in their field of study. Relations among nations now impress them as being often what people think they are, the gap between reality and imagination sometimes assuming great, even dangerous, proportions. Certainly when men carry their fictions into the global arena and respond to them rather than to the world outside, the chances for rational and pragmatic policies diminish. Misperceptions affect domestic politics as well, but they are for obvious reasons much more likely in international politics—and much more perilous there as well. Struggles among the most powerful nations in the contemporary world were found to have been conducted substantially in the realm of fantasy, further straining already great tension and obstructing avenues of accommodation.[1] Waged on the basis of unrealistic perceptions of adversaries and of self, struggles of powers endowed with enormously destructive capacities thus assumed a certain anomic, disorienting quality. Poor predictability generates hysteria and furthers rigidity, because the tendency to protect cherished beliefs makes for curious disregard for conflicting evidence.

Yet people never really respond to the "objective" facts of a situation, only to its images. Reality is in the last resort just what we believe it to be. "If our image of the world is in some sense 'wrong,' of course, we may be disappointed in our expectations, and we may therefore revise our image: if this revision is in the direction of 'truth' there is presumably a long-run tendency for the 'image' and the 'truth' to coincide."[2] There is just no acceptable substitute for trial and test and submission to the judgment of experience.

The Middle East conflict between Jews and Arabs, now in the second half of its century, is a classic case of misperceptions, yet very different from the usual. Ordinarily false cognition exaggerates the causes of conflict; in this case there is a lingering reluctance to accept them for what they are, for they are unpleasant and not inspiring of hope. This does not mean that the Middle East conflict is insoluble, but its protracted character alone must surely constitute a certain presumption against sanguine expectations. Yet after decades of unremitting frustration, not only is opinion shifting—only with great reluctance and with little conviction—toward a sober evaluation of the conflict, but it is always eager to believe against experience—most recently since the October War—that the end is just around the corner.

Adding puzzlement to the disbelief surrounding the Middle East conflict is its extraordinary advertisement. In few other conflicts has one side proclaimed unremitting hostility to the other, so consistently, so uniformly—virtually without dissent—and for so long, as the Arabs have toward Jewish political aims in the Middle East. Arabs admit to many sins of commission or omission, but the failure to oppose these aims is not among them; rather, they may deplore insufficient militancy in this endeavor. The very emergence of modern Arab nationalism, coincidental with the Jewish national renaissance, was already marked by vehement rejection of the latter by Palestinians and other Arabs. Palestinian Arab representatives in the Ottoman parliament strongly opposed the Zionist work at its very start; as early as 1905 the Christian Jerusalemite Neguib Azury alerted the barely beginning Arab national movement against Jewish designs on the land (and all other peoples against the "international Jewish peril"); the King-Crane Commission, investigating popular sentiment on the spot in the wake of World War One, encountered unyielding rejection of Zionist aspirations everywhere. Summing up the British Mandate of Palestine between the two world wars, one wonders indeed whether Arab attitudes toward the Jewish National Home could possibly have been more hostile; so hostile, in fact, that some historians despair that any Jewish concessions short of surrender could have made for less hostility. "In fact," one wrote in the 1950's "it has been there from the beginning while its strength and range have been steadily increasing with the rising nationalism throughout the Arab East."[3]

Yet the nature of Arab hostility to Israel remains a highly controversial and largely misunderstood phenomenon. After half a century of intermittent warfare, there is still insufficient appreciation of the Arabs' utter inability to be reconciled to Jewish statehood in what they regard as part of their homeland. If their rejection of Israel is finally common knowledge, few outsiders realize the depth, the intensity, indeed the obsessive quality of this feeling. To Arabs the Jewish state is *really* unacceptable; while some can accommodate themselves intellectually, they cannot do so emotionally at all. An Egyptian intellectual of Marxist leanings recently resolved to take "a cool look" at Israel in his book, *Confrontation with Israel.* Dedicated to the need for balanced thinking on Israel, he admitted that this is difficult "not only because of the accumulated rage, the surging pain and the burning resentment in the soul, but also because we are confronted by an alien phenomenon that is highly complex."[4]

Awareness of the intensity of hostility, moreover, does not necessarily mean a good grasp of its character; one may perceive all the sound and fury, but what really is at stake? The question is not paltry, for the prospects of war and peace in the Middle East are very closely connected with the answer. Conceptions of the character of Arab hostility must determine the views one holds on the possibilities and modalities of conciliation. To conceive of Arab hostility as a function mainly of agitation or manipulation of opinion is to point to political opportunists and demagogues not merely as the source of trouble, but also as the target of peacemaking—either for their removal or their pacification. A conception of Arab hostility as a genuine expression of popular feeling would lead to different conclusions. Equally, to identify the roots of these feelings in negotiable interests concerning land or water rights implies a different perspective on the conflict from seeing its roots in problems of identity and self-respect. To regard Arab hostility as a reactionary force is to place the hopes for peace upon modernity. To regard it as affecting the Cairene as Arab, but not as Egyptian, is to place these same hopes upon the strength of parochial nationalism in the Arab world and upon the weakness and decline of integral pan-Arabism. To regard these roots in a total rejection of Jewish statehood entails other perspectives altogether.

To dwell on the importance of the Arab's hostility in the Middle East conflict is crucial not in order to blame them, but rather because of the historical situation. Indeed, one may argue that, had not the Jewish side pressed for dominion in the Holy Land, no hostility as we now know it would have been forthcoming from the Arabs. Nor does the importance of Arab attitudes in any way render Jewish attitudes irrelevant, for they weigh no less in the scales of peace. Conceivably once the Arabs accommodate to the Jews' insistence on nationhood, the latter could still go to war with their neighbors for various different reasons, good or bad. But accommodation comes first—even though it need never come.

Serious students of Arab hostility to Israel like to explain it with images of regressing appearances. Thus, one might think of it as an iceberg—only a small part is above the surface, while the bulk, and presumably most ominous part, lies submerged in the deep.[5] Or one might compare it with an onion or cabbage, having layer after layer of manifestations covering the essential core. One might also use the imagery of the Dance of the Seven Veils, which had earlier been suggested in connection with racial attitudes in the United States. Local opposition to public housing of poor blacks has invariably taken the shape of protests on esthetic, sanitary, educational, and other grounds, but once the tax "veil" and the school "veil" and the sewer "veil"—to use the language of one economist—had been removed, there remained the reluctance simply to have poor blacks as neighbors.[6]

Professor Abba P. Lerner recounts such an experience with Arab and Jewish students at the University of California. A number of these students were assembled at Berkeley for a discussion of the possibilities of peace in the Middle East. They had been carefully picked for their coolheadedness and sophistication. The discussions turned into a search for the conditions under which these intellectuals could conceive of a peaceful settlement. The conversation very naturally took the form of this question being put to the Arab students.

"It was a very successful meeting in the sense that we were able to remove a whole series of red herrings that disguised the real issue. The Arab students at first said there cannot be a settlement because Israel is expansionist. With great effort we got them to assume that somehow Israeli expansion was prevented. Would they then be able to conceive of a peaceful settlement? Then they brought up the question of the refugees. We got them to suppose that this was solved somehow, and there was no problem of refugees. And so on through a whole list of apparent obstacles. Finally they were forced to admit that these were still not what was at the bottom of the matter. The solution of all these problems would still not permit them to conceive of a peace being reached. What was really required and seen as absolutely essential was one simple thing—that there shouldn't be any Israel in the Middle East!"[7]

Conventional discourse of the Middle East conflict invariably focuses on the more superficial "veils" or offers explanations, which, though gratifying, are plainly tautological. The most common explanations cite such factors as refugees, occupied territory, maritime rights, Jerusalem, usually in that order. The implication, often explicitly stated, is that the conflict would dissipate automatically with the resolution of these, presumably constituent, problems. In this mechanistic approach the Middle East conflict is the sum of several such building blocks, the removal of which leaves zero substance. (Of course, the conflict existed already before these problems arose.) This approach is bolstered by the equally popular belief in a previous Semitic amity between Jews and Arabs. Once these problems are solved, there would presumably be not just neutrality, but actually a resumption of fraternity. The belief in prior amity actually casts an aura of puzzlement on the entire conflict. A popular Quaker report on the Middle East described the present Arab-Jewish struggle as "one of the great ironies of history," for, after all, far from having shared ancient mutual animosities, Jews and Arabs are "Semitic cousins."[8] The same belief gives rise to exhortations to "restore harmony to the Middle East."[9] Where peace once reigned, the path to peace seems somehow less forbidding.

As with other problems, there are many pseudo-explanations, perhaps more because of the particularly puzzling nature of the Middle East conflict. The familiar practice of restating questions in other words produces the kinds of "answers" that help to minimize the real conflict. One such explanation holds that Arabs and Israelis (or Jews) "hate" each other, which in the narrow sense of the word is demonstrably false and in the broader one simply meaningless. (Such an explanation says only that conflict exists because the sides are in conflict.[10]) There are more sophisticated explanations of the same kind, such as the references to an "Arab psychology," not meaning the academic study of psychocultural dynamics peculiar to Islamic or Arab society (which, incidentally, inclines toward pessimism concerning the conflict), but rather as a commonsensical notion suggesting either that Arabs, unlike other persons, are inscrutable, or, like children, are capricious and unpredictable. Some theories explain that the unconscionable protraction of the conflict is a consequence of "Arab psychology" (the Arabs are that way) or that the canons of logic do not apply for the same reason. In this manner one is free to argue against evidence and logic for one's particular prejudice. One can claim that Arabs are implacably opposed to the Jewish state and at the same time ready to drop this opposition, which is absurd, but not among Arabs, who are presumably endowed with an exceptional "psychology." This proposition has been argued in the pages of *Foreign Affairs* by the head of the Jewish World Congress and on the floor of the U. S. Senate by the Chairman of its Foreign Relations Committee.[11]

Journalistic reporting sustains such beliefs by the sheer weight of repetition and advertisement. In the press, moreover, references to manifestations of hostility in the Middle East are offset by references to almost equally ubiquitous peacemaking. An Arab-Israeli armed clash is followed by some "resolution" at the United Nations; threats of war from the Middle East must compete with news of conciliation efforts, peace plans and diplomatic initiatives.

Writers on the long Middle East conflict have tended to endorse a "myth of the unredeemed solution," as J. Bowyer Bell called it.[12] Tracing the intricate course of a half a century of conflict, they are often impressed with narrowly missed opportunities for settlement. In one recent history we repeatedly read of almost consummated agreement, how very close the dispute came to solution.[13] If only the Israeli government had not procrastinated immediately after the 1948 war, when talks were in progress with King Abdallah; if only Dag Hammarskjöld's initiative in 1959 had been accorded more significance; if only Jerusalem had summoned enough courage for a direct bid to the Palestinian Arabs on the morrow of the 1967 war; if only the Israeli concessions over territory and refugees in 1954 had been made a littler earlier; if only Mohammed Neguib had pressed on with negotiations a while longer in 1953; and so on; this festering sore would have been over and done with. Different chroniclers have their different favorite missed chances: For Rony Gabbay the "golden opportunity" was missed in the wake of the war of 1948, when the Israelis let the "miracle" of their survival in the Arab invasion deter them from making appropriate concessions;[14] for Kennett Love and Maxime Rodinson it came later, when the Israelis spurned Egyptian overtures;[15] for Elmo Hutchison it came earlier, when the United Nations partition plan for Palestine was adopted, in 1947 (and yet another somewhat later);[16] for Arthur Lall it came much later, in the wake of the passage by the United Nations Security Council of Resolution 242, in November of 1967.[17] (Secretary Kissinger told a group of Jewish intellectuals soon after the October War that a "golden moment" had been missed by Israel immediately after the previous war and he was not about to let them miss another, just after this one.) In the histories of the conflict the very frequency of failure of conciliation thus curiously appears as proof of the eminently soluble nature of the dispute.

One cannot be sure whether opportunities for settlement indeed existed. But to cite these "failures" as evidence of the eminent solubility of the conflict is to assume the very thing one sets out to prove. Further weakening the thesis is the proponents' habitual cavalier regard for fact for often the critical evidence is dubious. Often it is simply tautology, with opportunities for settlement appearing only because the writer chooses to ignore the real nature of the conflict. One is in effect told that the conflict is soluble, if only there were a modicum of "goodwill." Yet if there were such will, would we not face a different conflict?

But the malaise in the understanding of the Middle East conflict goes deeper. The great sin of omission consists in the fact that professional students of that region and its culture long ago abandoned the public to the mercy of propagandists—when they themselves did not join them. The great emotion and controversy aroused for so long by the Arab-Jewish dispute has brought about a veritable invasion of partisan amateurs, which the professional students could not, or did not really desire to, check—so much, in fact, that even interested laymen often ignore the existence of work in the field other than purely partisan tracts. Having degenerated into sheer controversy, as if Middle Eastern reality could not be studied by the usual methods of analysis, the prevailing discourse assumes that it must instead be deduced on some fifty-fifty basis from the rhetoric of opposing advocates. Elsewhere events may be explored in the usual fashion; in the Middle East, however, the prudent observer will find Truth by homogenesis, or middlingness—presumably lying midway between the claims of antagonistic spokesmen. They will accuse each other of atrocities and deceptions, and we will deduce that they are equally guilty—the great irony being that in the Middle Eastern conflict the confrontation involves particularly unlike peoples and cultures. Hence rigid symmetry is imposed on a situation characterized by extraordinary asymmetrical relationships. There are no established propositions, no verifiable relations, for all is contention; the most appreciated skill is forensic (law professors abound among the popular experts) and the highest value is even-handedness (works are scrutinized especially for fair distribution of "blame"). Factualism is often tested by partisan advantage. Journalistic reports of acute hostility to the Jewish state from Arab lands in the 1950's were ignored by editors as Arab propaganda;[18] similar findings just one decade later were defined in the press as Israeli propaganda.[19]

The great sin of commission in the professional study of the Middle East consists in its responsiveness to the particular needs of narrow Western ecclesiastic interests in that part of the world. The situation is similar in Britain and in the United States. In a paper first published in 1958 Elie Kedourie exposed the corrupt version of recent Middle East history emanating from the prestigious and authoritative Royal Institute of International Affairs for three decades under the directorship of Arnold J. Toynbee. As an intellectual clearing center for businessmen, scholars, officials, and journalists; as a research center and publishing institution; and even temporarily an official arm of the Foreign Office, Chatham House (the name of the residence of the institute) wielded a dominant influence on public and even governmental thinking in Britain on the Middle East. Rooted in British Radicalism and the romanticism of English Orientalists, the Chatham House Version was characterized by an idealization of pristine Islam and guilt for the modern West's transgressions against the Arabs.

The Chatham House Version has its equivalent in this country in conceptions produced by American Protestant missionaries in the Middle East, which, though not identical, tend to the same conclusion. The missionaries first went to the region more than a century and a half ago, achieving few conversions, but establishing an American "interest" in the Arab world, long before petroleum, commerce, strategic considerations, and even Zionism, chiefly by patronizing and promoting Arabs and their causes. Their colleges became the nurseries of Arab nationalism; they themselves, their families, friends, and prestigious associates became the passionate advocates of their clients, dispensers of "paternalist sympathy," as a former Chatham House historian put it.[20] "Their case is curious," wrote Kedourie, "they went out to proselytise and have stayed to sympathise. To America they began, since some fifty years ago, to present a picture of Islam as a strict unitarian version of Protestantism, democratic and egalitarian. The task before Christians, they said, was not to make converts from Islam to Christianity, it was rather to lean over middle eastern society with compassion, to take it by the hand, and rescue it from centuries of superstition, corruption and tyranny. Essentially and basically, Islam was enlightened and progressive. The western education which they, the missionaries, provided, would serve to make Muslims aware of the true value of their religion and to inculcate in them a sense of brotherhood toward the Christians, who after all, worship—albeit in their own manner—the same true God as the Muslims. And in fact, it is asserted, this is what is more and more happening in the middle east. Enlightenment is spreading, the rulers are acquiring a public conscience, and democracy becomes stronger every day. To take recent instance of the attitudes of these missionaries: 'The time seems ripe,' writes the Reverend Erich W. Bethman, director of the Department of Research and Publications of the American Friends of the Middle East, 'to usher in the era of cooperation—a cooperation based on mutual respect for and esteem of the deep spiritual qualities inherent in both religions. These qualities are a part of every believing Muslim and every believing Christian, finding in each their deepest realisation in prayer.' "[21]

Ecclesiastic daydreams would be harmless were it not for their influence on the governmental, academic, and other institutional structures of the knowledge of the Middle East. For it is Protestant missionaries and their associates and relatives who colonized the appropriate sections of the Department of State; who established and ran the American research and study centers in the Middle East and the numerous corresponding institutes in American academies; who formed and directed the network of extra-academic centers, institutes, associations, and study groups that direct and control the substance and flow of research and output, in publication and public intervention, bearing the stamp of expertise. Official and private institutions thus tend to speak with one voice on the Middle East, a voice, moreover, identified in the public mind with *the* American voice, rather than as a narrowly sectarian opinion. Comparing the pronouncements of such institutions as the Department of State, the Middle East Institute, the Friends of the Middle East, the Holy Land Center, and many others, one is struck by their common adherence to the Missionary Version. Comparing the roster of these institutions, one is equally struck by certain sociological common denominators, particularly proximity to missionary Protestantism, sacred and lay, and the phenomenon of interlocking directorates. A biographical examination of the leadership of the Middle East Institute, which presumes in the establishment of Middle Eastern studies in this country to a position akin to that of the Académie française in its field, reveals it as extremely homogenous, though not in terms of scholarly prestige in the discipline, even though some among them are scholars. More than half are associated with the Department of

State; half show long residence in the Muslim world (at least three were born there). They share considerable and varied association with ecclesiastics and missionaries and some are actually ordained ministers and religious missionaries, while many more are associated with the lay missionary institutions in the Middle East.[22] Most leaders also direct the lesser institutions and control the Middle East sections of prestigious foreign affairs institutes (such as the Council on Foreign Relations).

The sociology of Middle Eastern studies in American academies is equally extraordinary.[23] There is, first, a relatively low percentage of Jews (9.4 percent; an additional 2.8 percent are Israeli Jews) in the ranks of teachers, a phenomenon not immediately apparent because they tend, as in other disciplines, to be concentrated in the more prestigious—hence more visible—universities. This fact is not remarkable for any intrinsic desirability of Jews in that particular field; there is merely the question, why American Jews, who appear in disproportionately large numbers (nearly 15 percent) in the related social sciences in general, should avoid this particular field? It is all the more puzzling, since Middle East studies would seem to be one field in which Jews may be presumed to have a particularly acute interest, not a lack of such attraction. Avoidance would seem rooted in perception of the discipline as unfriendly, regarding both discriminatory access to much of the region itself and the personnel and intellectual climate of the profession at home. The second extraordinary aspect of the social composition of the profession serves to clarify the latter anxiety: There is a prevalence in the profession of Arabs (particularly Palestinians) and other non-Jewish Middle Easterners. A conservative estimate puts their number at well over one-fourth, bearing out the observation frequently heard in universities that the teaching of Middle Eastern affairs in the typical "out of the way" small college is very often the function of an Arab instructor. This also applies to numerous large state and private universities. In addition a considerable number of non-Middle Easterners with missionary-diplomatic associations are also found in the professional ranks, besides dominating the leading nonteaching organizations.

From this extraordinary structure of the production and distribution of Middle Eastern knowledge in the United States flows a stream of consequences we have not yet really begun to fathom. When sectarian missionary patrons and their clients so influence this process in a vast and diverse nation, its foreign policy is likely to be

founded on narrow prejudice. Since distortion in the Missionary
- Version goes to the very roots of Muslim civilization and Arab culture, our diplomatic assumptions about the nature of Arab nationalism, orientations toward Western powers and capacities for modernization have unsurprisingly proved to be disastrous. (The irony
consists in the fact that the "learning" from past failures by the
Department of State has located the error in simple bias, not basic
conceptualization. Now, it is said, the prejudice of "Arabists" is recognized and countered in decision-making, but they remain the intellectual resource men of the government, because of recognized
expertise.[24])

Particularly pertinent to perceptions of Arab-Jewish conflict in the
Missionary Version is the deliberate ignorance of the politically aggressive nature of Islam. This trait of Muslim civilization is about as
controversial among Oriental scholars as Newtonian theory is
among physicists, but establishmentarian expertise treats its very
mention, particularly when relevant to political struggles, as defa-
mation unworthy of acknowledgment. The manner in which the
Middle East Institute, as authoritative national institution discharg-
ing a vital responsibility, explicates the nature of the Arab-Jewish
conflict to the public illustrates this avoidance. There is no mention
whatever of the extraordinary Muslim presumption to dominion,
particularly over so traditional a subject people as the Jews, with
which the study of Islamic civilization is consummately concerned;
instead, the exact opposite of this relationship is suggested as representing the consensus of serious students.[25]

A more sophisticated method of obscurantism is practiced by
some scholars, who use esoteric terms and code words familiar to
other experts, though not to laymen, to whom their writings are often directed. In doing this they may merely imitate the style of the
culture they study or actually seek to disguise and euphemize certain unpleasant aspects of it. Whatever the reason, popular enlightenment is not well served. In one such case a well-known academic
specialist in effect indicated that real acceptance by Arabs of Jewish
statehood is unlikely, yet the lay reader, not likely to know the
codes, may actually understand the essay to endorse conventional
expectations of peace in the Middle East. The writer emphatically
opens with, "Peace could come to the Middle East in the 1970s! It
could be imposed on Israel and the Arab states by the Soviet Union
and the United States," and indicates that the Arabs have already
accepted Israel. Yet at the end, as if by afterthought, he writes that

"lasting peace" could come only when "Israel will have . . . become a Middle Eastern rather than a European nation transplanted to the area with an ideology which bases national identity upon ethnic or religious exclusivity," which is a tortured, but thoroughly familiar, euphemism for an end to Jewish statehood.[26]

Yet at the root of the problem stands the reluctance and perhaps sheer inability in the cultivated and liberal circles in the Western world to acknowledge the vehemence and violent bitterness of the Arab rejection of Jewish political assertiveness in the Middle East. The "ugly" side of Arab hostility is usually shunned—the tendency, as has been said in another context, "to close one eye because the reality which breaks upon the sight of both eyes is too terrible to contemplate."[27] The bearers of "bad news" tend to meet with public displeasure—a familiar enough experience in this particular field of study—which may be one of the reasons for the above euphemizing and cosmetologic practices.

This repression is one variant of the larger phenomenon that accounts for the repeatedly noted understudy of political violence in the social sciences. Researchers for the National Commission of the Causes and Prevention of Violence have thus found that their subject does not rate an entry in the new *International Encyclopedia of the Social Sciences*.[28] "When today's social science has become intellectual history," writes Harry Eckstein, "one question will almost certainly be asked about it: Why did social science, which has produced so many studies of so many subjects, produce so few on violent political disorder—internal war? Here indeed will be a problem for future sociologists of knowledge, for by any common-sense reckoning the contemporary literature of social science should be brimming over with such studies."[29] He cites a recently published anthology of social theory, compiled by several notable contemporary social theorists, as an indicator of the neglect of the subject; though internal war is commonplace and interest in it has been intense, with hardly any considerable social thinker not holding the subject worthy of serious attention, no special section in that mammoth work was devoted to revolution and virtually no extensive reference to it can be found in it.

Insulated from the raw phenomenon itself, and lacking an appropriate conceptual framework for the occasional data which he encounters, the Western liberal copes with the troubling Middle East problem mainly by resort to some obvious psychological mechanisms. Nora Beloff has described the dynamics of what she termed the "Kiss-and-Make-Up Delusion" as follows: manifestations of Arab hostility are discounted and expressions of Arab goodwill are exaggerated; the causes of Arab hostility are placed on superficial, hence easily manageable, levels; the belief is tenaciously adhered to, "that, given sweetness and compassion from the physically superior Westernized side, the 'two wronged nations' could kiss and make up."[30] The typical syndrome (exemplified by an intervention in the House of Commons by Sir Dingle Foot, brother of Lord Caradon, the "father" of the famous Security Council Resolution No. 242) consists of admiration for Israel's humanitarian achievement and indignation at injustice suffered by the Arabs in the process, the latter taking forms intelligible to the liberal mind—such as refugees. Since the idea of eliminating an existing state altogether sounds absurd to the liberal (particularly the liberally minded left), it becomes indigestible and is resisted.

Since the practical effect of these dynamics is to generate pressure for Israeli concessions, Nora Beloff regards the liberal friends of Israel in the West as unwittingly encouraging Arab hopes for the elimination of Jewish statehood. When faced with the disagreeable truth about the conflict, such people turn panicky and argue that if there cannot be instant peace, there will certainly be disaster. Such panic justifies the international interventions in the Middle East conflict that Israel dreads. The Zionist movement and Israel would thus appear to have a stake in clarifying the true nature of Arab resistance to their work. Actually, however, they constitute perhaps the most serious source of mystification of the nature of Arab hostility in the long history of the conflict.

2

ZIONIST PERCEPTIONS

SYMPATHY for Zionism in the West was nourished by the belief that the Arabs would themselves be uplifted in the process of the re-generation of the Jewish people in their midst. Just emerging from the torpor of many centuries, the Arab was not always expected to be overly appreciative of this endeavor, but his sustained rejection might have impaired the faith. The Zionists certainly were reassur-ing. International diplomacy alone required as much. There had been pressure on the Zionists to evince a show of Arab acquies-cence, and even consent, in order to satisfy the Wilsonian principles of national self-determination even during the peace conference in Paris. If Wilson's King-Crane Commission reported great hostility among the Arabs of the Levante toward the Zionist movement, the latter was able to produce written testimonials warmly welcoming the Jews' return to Palestine by no less than Prince Faisal, the ac-knowledged head of the Arab national movement.

The need to show Arab acquiescence then arose in the seemingly interminable squabbles of mandatory politics, without abating in the world at large. It was characteristic of this triangular game—Arabs, British, Jews—for the London bureaucrats and politicians and their local proconsuls to justify their reluctance to honor the international commitment for a Jewish national home in terms of the resistance of the Arab inhabitants of Palestine (and later also of Arab govern-ments outside). The Zionists faced the task of explaining away to the British the increasingly more violent manifestations of that re-sistance; the reports of the several British inquiry commissions, in-variably called in the wake of the more violent instances, show the Zionist ingenuity in this pursuit to have been considerable, though not always convincing to the investigators. Political imperatives of foreign opinion and diplomacy thus imposed on the Zionist move-ment an optimistic appraisal of Arab attitudes toward its work.

Internal political needs only strengthened this evaluation. The extraordinary political system it is, Zionism possessed several "domestic" publics abroad—the Jewish diaspora—which together nurtured yet another, the authentically Zionist public, in Palestine. There existed a fundamental division of labor in the system: the poor and intolerant Eastern half of Europe supplied most of the manpower for Zionist settlement; the Jewry of affluent Western democracies provided the bulk of the material and political support. In the former the pressures of want and persecution could overcome the impact of Arab hostility in Palestine; but the hold of Zionism was only tenuous in the West and therefore more vulnerable to these manifestations, at least until the rise of Nazi power in Central Europe produced more compelling support for Zionism.

The greatest sensitivity to Arab resistance in the 1920's and early 1930's is therefore felt in London and New York, where special efforts at explanation by great Zionist leaders take place. Following three waves of anti-Jewish violence in Palestine in 1920–21, claiming at least fifty-four Jewish fatalities, we find the president of the World Zionist Organization, Professor Chaim Weizmann, announcing in New York that the conflict between Arabs and Jews "was gradually righting itself" and picturing the success of Zionism as "a bridge between the cultures of the East and the West."[1] One year later, at a fund-raising affair, he declared to the press in New York that "the trouble between Jew and Arab has been greatly exaggerated."[2] Earlier he had stated: "If left to themselves . . . the Arabs and Jews would have no difficulty in co-operating"; the troubles had been incited by the Bolsheviks and exaggerated by "crude, antisemitic propaganda."[3] Judge Julian W. Mack, president of the Palestine Development Council, told journalists in Berlin, en route from a visit to Palestine, "I am deeply convinced that the relations between the Jews and Arabs of Palestine can be established on a sound and peaceful basis. It is necessary only to emphasize the value of Jewish colonization to the Arabs. We must enlighten Arab opinion and understanding is sure to follow."[4] Back in New York the judge declared, "The Arabs and Jews are not naturally antagonistic. All through history they got along, not only well, but exceedingly well. There has been no conflict. I will not say there is not some conflict today, but I do say that conflict is highly exaggerated."[5] Few dissenting Jewish voices were heard; to Zionists it was not just that they might be wrong that mattered, so much as they resented publicized doubt as malicious, if not simply treasonable.

Though politically expedient, indeed imperative, the very discovery of Arabs in the Holy Land was a trauma of extraordinary dimension to the earliest settlers. The compelling picture of Zion that had cast its spell on the Jews in their dispersion for nearly two millennia was that of a home from which their forefathers had been expelled and that languished in desolation for their ultimate return. A dictum current in the early phases of Zionism expressed this notion concisely: "The land without people, for the people without land." The land then was indeed a miserable backwater in the corrupt and stagnant Ottoman Empire, so that reality lent some support to the image of desolation, even emptiness. But there existed a substantial population, most *Sunni* (orthodox Muslim) and virtually all Arabic-speaking, and the land and life reflected its culture and character. Arrival for Zionists from Eastern Europe thus involved a startled recognition of this fact; in some cases there was shock triggering crisis of conscience. For Ben-Yehuda, father of modern Hebrew, arriving in 1882, discovery led, in his own words, to a torture of the heart; he came "to this country as a proselyte, a stranger, the son of a foreign country and a foreign people; in this, the land of my forefathers, I have no political and no civil right. I am a foreigner. . . . I suddenly broke. Something like remorse rose in the depths of my soul. . . . My feet stood on the holy ground the land of the forefathers, and in my heart there was no joy. . . . I did not embrace the rocks. . . . I stood shocked. Dread! Dread!"[6] But Ben-Yehuda was unusually sensitive, and even he quickly enough overcame the crisis sufficiently to carry on the mission that possessed his soul; the warm hospitality of a Jewish innkeeper and the fluent Hebrew of a Jaffa moneychanger were enough to restore his spirits. Among the Zionists far away in Europe the news that "there are Arabs in Palestine" probably made a less severe personal impact; whether many serious candidates for immigration were deterred from going is not known; for the movement abroad the discovery was merely an intellectual problem, not an existential one, as it was for those who had already "gone up" to the land.

The discovery of the Arabs in the country was less of a problem than the discovery of their opposition to the Zionist work. Both ancient imagery and contemporary humanist ethos in Zionism could readily accommodate a passive indigenous non-Jewish people. In the first Arabs were a relic or squatters, the picturesque but derelict caretakers of the land (indeed, the more romantic among the settlers imagined them as the true Hebrews—still looking and living much like Abraham—upon whom conquerors had forced alien tongue and faith); the progressive, even generous, ethos imagined them as grateful beneficiaries of the fabulous transformation the Zionist movement was about to accomplish in the wretched, malaria-ridden land and their brutish lives as well. That these poor people should reject utopia was unthinkable.

The rejection, moreover, was not unequivocal, at first, at any rate. Violence, even collective violence, in a land of which so much was "the realm of insolence"—where the law and fiat of the Ottoman government was at best sporadic—did not necessarily signify political opposition. There had been conflict with simple *fellaheen,* Arab peasants, over the implementation of land acquisitions from absentee landlords from the earliest days of the new *Yishuv,* the Jewish community in Palestine. But the bad feeling, even physical violence, was natural enough wherever modern concepts of property and deed were imposed on traditional rights. Much marauding and looting could be seen as simply manifestations of the Arab nomads' tendency to plunder wherever the opportunity presented itself. Then there was communal hostility, so typical also of Middle Eastern culture; the Christian Arabs in particular appeared ready to incite the Muslim mass against another urban, literate group, the European Jews, a potential competitor in commerce, the professions, and other functions chiefly preempted by the Christians. The missionary connection to the Christian West also seemed to the *Yishuv* a channel for some ugly manifestations they thought they had left behind, in Europe. "The local Christian Arabs," wrote a Zionist official toward the end of 1907, "have formed an Anti-Semitic gang under the leadership of one Anton Cassar and they make every effort to harm the Jews at every turn."[7]

Nor did the Muslim mass appear to reject the Jews' modernity; they did not run from them, indeed flocked to them in a movement that was in later years to turn into large-scale Arab immigration into Palestine from surrounding regions.[8] As had been characteristic of Islam's encounter with the resurgent West from the first—in Egypt in the Napoleonic era and after and elsewhere—the former, far from rejecting, actually craved the artifact, material side of the modern culture, though the same cannot be said about grasping or accepting its moral foundation as well. It has indeed been one of the most remarkable aspects of the Arab-Jewish conflict throughout that the Arabs have sought the tangible fruits of Jewish modernity with unabashed enthusiasm in even the darkest days of war with the Jews—from access to their hospitals to clamor for their higher wages. If these people seemed to reject the Jew, they were surely, in Jewish eyes, not just a bit too savage yet, but probably also still slaves to feudal masters, who would rather have them wretched and reliable.

When an intensification of violence after the Young Turk Revolution of 1908 forced the Zionists to face up to "the Arab question," they responded by asserting existing explanations, only more emphatically than before. The animosity of the Christian Arabs and Arab landowners was affirmed as distinct from a presumed community of interests of the Jews and the Arab population as a whole. The theme was repeated in various forms at the Tenth Zionist Conference; for example, Ben-Zvi, the future second President of Israel, emphasized the benefit to the Arabs of the introduction into Palestine between Arabs and Jews, said they must not be exag- Thon, "likewise referring to the frequent outbreaks of violence in Palestine between Arabs and Jews, said they they must not be exaggerated in that they did not reflect popular Arab opinion. The disturbances were caused, according to Thon, by individual local officials and journalists. Like Kaplansky [a labor delegate] he was convinced that there was no discrepancy between the basic interests of Arabs and Jews, and the time would come when the Arab population would appreciate the benefits brought to them by the Jews as a cultural element and as the only group in Turkey which was free of the stigma of dissolution and disintegration. This was quite apart from the profit accruing to the country from the very existence of the Yishuv, a profit reaped for the most part by Palestine's Arab inhabitants."[9]

Awareness of political opposition was slowed also by the poor visibility of the Arab national movement; surreptitious, subterranean and weak, the movement entered the public arena in the wake of the putsch of the Young Turks. From then until the conclusion of the First World War the Zionist movement as a whole slowly, reluctantly, haltingly, but effectively just the same, came around to the realization that the Arabs they had, to their surprise, discovered in their ancient homeland also had a genuine national movement in opposition to their own.

An Israeli writer relates Ben-Gurion's recollection of his personal discovery. It happened in 1915, ten years after his first arrival in the country, as he strolled about in the courtyard of a Turkish fortress in Jerusalem, a prisoner of Djemel Ahmed Pasha, the Governor General, who intended to remove him forever from the country as a Zionist agitator and alleged advocate of the secession of Palestine from the empire. He encountered a young Arab, a former fellow student at the University of Istanbul, with whom he had been friendly and intimate. The Arab inquired about Ben-Gurion's condition and offered his help.

"I told him I was under arrest as a Zionist, that the Turks wanted to expel me from the country. He looked me up and down silently. *'As your friend,'* he said, *'I am deeply sorry. But as an Arab I am pleased.'*

"It came down on me like a blow," Ben-Gurion recollected. "I said to myself, 'so there *is* an Arab national movement *here'* (and not just in Lebanon and Syria). It hit me like a bomb. I was completely confounded. . . ."[10]

Jewish settlers were discovering the great depth of Arab hostility to their presence with remarkable candor in various places. Those in Rishon LeZion told a sympathetic British officer in 1917 that they had tried to befriend the Arab, "but no amount of kindness or humoring will make the Arab love them or even like them."[11] That it was the Arabs they would have to face politically was a notion that settled ever more deeply in the mind of the *Yishuv* as the British era began. But while some thought that the Jewish National Home could not be based on struggle with the Arabs—or was not worth building on such basis—and indeed required spontaneous Arab cooperation, to be sought by any means, most did not really desire to think about this matter; and when they did, they tended to feel that if anything was wrong, it was not that there had been too much Zionist ardor, but rather too little of it. The key to everything was in trying harder yet.[12]

This attitude is natural enough in "revolutions of saints," as in that of the English Puritans, with men obsessed with the vision of a new order for which they unhesitatingly deny their selves, and possessed, like the Zionist pioneers, by an intensely sacred fervor in pursuit of secular dreams of total personal and social transformation, with awesome self-righteousness and stunning asceticism. (Had these men been simply colonialists, as Arab spokesmen now aver, they would probably have removed themselves quickly in the face of local hostility and reluctant unreliable British protection, and utter commercial unprofitability—indeed, they might never have sought out such desolate region for settlement in the first place.)

Most Zionist leaders were largely insulated from the Arab reality in Palestine, which even to the settlers mostly meant only some personal contact with few Arabs and certain superficial generalizations.

Above all else, the settlers were powerfully motivated to carry on regardless of the real nature of Arab hostility, and at times the Zionist venture must have seemed impossible, quite apart from Arab feelings toward it. The sacrifice required to overcome daily difficulties in that country seemed to many foreign observers at odds with both normalcy and reason. The emphasis on the extrarational in the folklore of the otherwise exceedingly rationalized Israeli society reflects even now this desperate streak of the early phases of Zionist settlement. A considerable proportion of the highly selective population of settlers was indeed incapable of coping long with the strains and privations of daily life in the Jewish sector of Palestine and chose to leave the country.

It should not be too difficult to imagine that full consciousness of the real depth of Arab feelings would have added a perhaps unbearable strain to an already critical situation; nor is it surprising that psychological mechanics were brought into play to reduce this burden. Hence the split-perception of Arab hostility so characteristic of the Jewish settlers in Palestine—the ability, on the one hand, to recognize and cope with overt manifestations of Arab hostility; on the other, the denial that hostile behavior expresses any serious attitudes, orientations, or motivations among the Arabs. The euphemization of Arab intent was compensated in the *Yishuv* by excessive anxiety and concern with actual Arab violence. In this sense the Zionist movement in Palestine fought wars with the Arabs while denying that any real conflict existed between the belligerents.

A candid realization of the character of Arab hostility would have required knowledge of Arab society and culture that few of the Zionists possessed. The enormity of their ignorance was that their beliefs were drastically opposed to historical reality and that those among them who deplored the *Yishuv*'s indifference to things Arab themselves pleaded for unconditional reliance on such fantasy. For their belief in a fraternal historical relationship of Jews and Arabs actually furthered the euphemistic interpretation of the Arabs' behavior toward them. The long encounter of Jew and Arab has in reality been rather unhappy though punctuated by some symbiosis. But different historical perspectives have sharpened Jewish awareness of the different aspects of the long coexistence, and historians have reflected these needs in their work. It happened that modern Zionism emerged in an optimistic period of Judeo-Muslim historiography, one in which it was naturally thought of their past linkage essentially as the fruition of a glorious civilization. In that perspective contemporary Arab antagonisms seemed both pathological and curable.

Moreover, personal experience often confirmed the thesis of historical amity. For while some Jews, and sometimes quite a few, would be shot by strange Arabs, almost all Jews knew some Arabs with whom one could do business and even form warm relations. Contemporary historians of the Arab-Jewish conflict in Palestine sometimes perhaps unwittingly obscure the very considerable economic intercourse between the political antagonists, especially when they discuss the Zionist emphasis on Jewish labor in Jewish enterprises and the Arab boycott of Jewish goods. Throughout the period of the Mandate the Jews depended no less on Arab agricultural produce than the Arabs depended on Jewish medicine, and perhaps no fewer Arab establishments would have been economically unviable without Jewish patrons than Jewish ones without unskilled Arab labor. True, in the cultural and political realms there was virtually no collaboration; but there was more in the social realm than seems possible from the perspective of our own time. When so distinguished a Jerusalemite as Katy Antonius, widow of the author of *The Arab Awakening*, fondly recalled her Jewish antebellum acquaintances to an American journalist reporting the war of 1948, it was neither cant nor really exceptional.[13] The record of even catastrophic moments of Palestine history is not fully devoid of affective and even intimate relationships. We read in the diaries of the settlers of the doomed Etzion Bloc of Arab friendship and devotion, as the settlements lay isolated in the hostile Hills of Hebron in 1947–48; of the Arab friend of Haim M., in neighboring Bet Umar, who was asked to Haim's wedding and tried to protect his Jewish friend from the violence of fellow villagers; or of the Hazbouns, a Christian Arab family from Bethlehem, who lived and perished with their neighbors in Kfar Etzion.[14] The apparent contradiction between economic cooperation and political antagonism was largely resolved in the minds of Jewish settlers by questioning the authenticity of the latter.

"After forty years of living in this region," wrote a leading Israeli official, "I am convinced that Jews and Arabs have a great deal in common with each other, and that we can live at peace. I have never found among Moslems, who made up the great majority of the Arabs of Palestine, any trace of feeling against Jews comparable to anti-Semitism. As people, Jews and Arabs have always got along well and liked each other. When there was no political agitation or religious incitement by fanatics, we lived together on terms of amity.''[15] Foreign visitors, already in sympathy with Zionism, usually endorsed this view. ''After seeing Europe,'' wrote I.F. Stone shortly before the first Arab-Israeli war, ''I am more than ever convinced that Jews and Arabs can live together in peace. There is no ill feeling in Palestine between Jews and Arab as exists in Czechoslovakia between Czech and Slovak, or in Yugoslavia between Croat and Serb.''[16] He was especially impressed by Arab-Jewish collaboration in the municipality of Haifa.

To the common confusion of ordinary social relations with political relations was added the burden of utterly inconsistent political orientations. For the struggle pitted one of the world's most naturally political people against one of its least comfortable in any overt assertiveness for power—one of the celebrated ruling peoples of history against the people that has over two thousand years become the very epitome of political subjection everywhere. The Arabs' traditional conception of Jews conflicted with actual Jewish behavior in many ways. The fact that the Jews had been able to commit the world's great powers to a Jewish Palestine was consistent with their fabled prowess to run this world behind the screens; but when the putative new masters arrived (in fact, the Arabs had already seen their kind in the earlier immigration waves), they were not at all the Rothschilds of this world, but rather wretched men and women who peculiarly insisted on doing with their own hands all the work usually left only to the most abject strata in Middle Eastern society. Incoherence was further aggravated by the patronizing and contemptuous demeanor of this ''scum'' toward the natural masters of the land. The Islamic system prepares well for role playing in either arbitrary use of power or abject submission to it, without attaching moral stigma to either, as in the West (tradition-bound Muslims can thus be extraordinarily docile subjects of even infidel rulers); but it prepares poorly for acting in less unilateral authority relations—in contrast to systems which encourage and permit free bargaining among equals and the lawful exercise of authority.[17] Flexibility exists not in roles, but rather in the incumbency of roles, which is unstable, indeed highly volatile. Up today and down tomorrow. To political tension was thus added the psychological strain resulting from incoherence between the always particularly sensitive patterns of authority.[18]

On the Jewish side was lacking even an understanding of the traditional Arab-Jewish relations, much less a grasp of Islamic orientations toward politics. The reality of Jewish subjection in Islam, permanent and unchanging from the days of the Prophet, had been dissolved or obscured in the myth of brotherhood and partnership formulated and diffused by Jews, who in an earlier generation responded in this way to the predicament of imperfect emancipation in Western Christendom. The belief had been invented by Jews, endorsed by other Europeans, but not shared by Muslims, who never conceded the presumption of their superiority over all others, and the Jews in particular. Emancipation had failed to bring true equality and full acceptance to the Jew in Western society. "Told that he was a Semite or an Oriental, he looked to other Semites and other Orientals for comfort—just as the Czechs and Serbs looked to their Slavic big brothers in Russia. The obvious choice was Islam. . . ."[19] He romanticized it, became its ardent partisan, idealized it. He played so disproportionately great a role in Oriental studies as to have virtually founded this branch of scholarship in Europe by himself, and in the process distorted the past of his relations to Muslims to a dream. The Jew invented the golden age of equal rights, says Bernard Lewis, as a reproach to Christians, only to have the myth taken up in our own time by Muslims as a reproach to Jews, namely, that they have made their Arab brother in Palestine pay for Christian oppression of Jews in Europe.

Other than occasional references to religious kinship (as imperfect precursors of Islam, Christianity and Judaism stand in it above paganism, as "People of the Book") in certain greetings and rituals, there was little to nourish the myth of fraternity in the reality of the Middle East. From his vantage point on the spot, in intimate and intensive contact with Arab leaders, Dr. Lichtheim discovered even before the First World War that the Arabs "do not care a straw for the 'joint Semitic spirit,' just as they do not care a straw for Muslim solidarity. I can only warn urgently against a historical or cultural chimera that can cause us severe damage. The Arabs do not require a Semitic revival. They want orderly government, just taxes and political independence. The East of today aspires to no marvels other than American machinery and the Paris toilet. Of course, the Arabs want to preserve their nation and cultivate their culture. What they need for this, however, is specifically European: money, organization, machinery. The Jew for them is a competitor who threatens their predominance in Palestine. . . ."[20]

Insofar as the Jews could at all grasp the Arabs' utter insouciance to equality and partnership with themselves, they were still unable to go beyond imagining their conflict as one between two opposing national movements, both presumably alike in seeking to emancipate an oppressed people, which certainly applies to the Jews. But on the other side, the Muslims discovered Arab nationalism only after purely Turkish nationalism rebuked the notion of a common Muslim overlordship in the Ottoman Empire (Arabism was a virtually all-Christian movement before Turkish nationalism assumed strident forms.) The *Sunni* Muslim Arabs (*Sunni* Muslims are the overwhelming majority still among Palestinian Arabs) had actually been part of the ruling people before the destruction of the Ottoman Caliphate or Empire. As "Arabs" they appeared as an oppressed people (now enabled to blame all untoward aspects of their society on Turkish overlordship), and under Wilsonian national self-determination their movement asserted the old *Sunni* presumption of dominion over the whole Ottoman Empire, save the purely Turkish region itself. The fact that the Jews adopted the theory of two rising nationalisms as a self-conscious attempt at correcting their previous ignorance of the Arab, not only points up the real depth of that ignorance (which they share with others),[21] but also that exhortation to understanding and even sympathy does not necessarily broaden understanding. The result, rather, is that contemporary Israeli Jews think they demonstrate particular enlightenment in matters Arab by emphatically repenting their betrayal of a historical relationship with Muslims that had been invented out of thin air in the first place.[22]

Arabs must have thought it ironic and impudent that the Jews should presume to concede *them* a certain parity, but in Jewish eyes it must have seemed charitable, indeed. To those from even backward Eastern Europe the mass of Arabs loomed only as unwashed, illiterate, even savage people; if their forebears had indeed been conquerors and wielders of a great civilization, they themselves seemed rather degenerate. That these people should presume to rule the Jewish pioneers must have seemed incredible; that they should actually be ruled by them was unthinkable. Yet the Jews' patronizing attitude can be made to fit well with their myth of historical partnership and equal rights, as is illustrated by this summary of the Muslim era in a popular exposition of Jewish history: "Though the Mohammedan Empire is dead, the human element which shaped its grandeur is still living. The Arabic culture was not built on the plunder of other countries and the brains of other men. It sprang from deep wells of creativity within the people themselves. For seven hundred years Arab and Jew lived side by side in peace with mutual respect. If Jews today in the Arabic world live under the most squalid conditions, it is not because Arabs pushed them there. These conditions were created for Jew and Arab alike by subsequent conquerors. Today, the Arab world is arising from its slumber. If the Arabs can use the Jews to hoist themselves out of the abyss into which history hurled them, they can be blamed no more than other nations which are playing similar power politics. It is up to Jewish leaders, in their own national self-interest, to convince Arab leaders that the Arab world can achieve its legitimate aims with the friendship of the Jews, as in days past. Astute statesmanship can relax the present Israeli-Arab tensions, because they are not caused by deep-rooted racial and religious antagonisms but by temporary political expediencies. History has shown that Jew and Arab can live together without strife and with mutual profit."[23]

Where group relations are characterized by so much incoherence—between definitions and cognitions, roles and their performance—perhaps the remarkable thing is that there was so much decent interaction across the lines, not so little of it. By all accounts, however, the requisite of whatever decent Arab-Jewish interaction occurred (and still does) was anxious avoidance by all of political topics. In this sense the Arab-Jewish conflict is perhaps a study in noncommunication, or rather perverse communication, one side (Arabs) telling the other in the most polite possible manner that *it* alone among people on earth is unworthy of self-government, the other (Jews) equally straining for compliments for a people whom in their heart of hearts they regard somewhat less than human.

Utter incoherence characterized also the great controversy over Jewish immigration to Palestine, a prime political issue in mandatory politics. In the Arab perspective of stagnant agrarianism, an economy founded on land and cheap labor, the issue is clearly man versus man. The Arab version of the problem was thus population displacement, viewing Jewish immigrants as pushing the indigenous Arab population off the productive land.[24] Further strengthening this conception is the ancient Islamic practice of people farming, taking initially the form of the systematic conquest of alien populations to be left working in peace in order to support fully the community of ruling Arabs, and subsequently turning the latter into history's busiest slave-traders. On the other hand, Jewish and most Western accounts depict Jewish immigration to Palestine primarily in terms of adding productivity—as filling up empty spaces of sparsely settled land and focusing on the transformation of marshes and desert land

into flowering gardens. The struggle here is between man and nature, reflecting the future-oriented, dynamic, and scientific civilization of the modern West. A peculiarly Jewish anxiety over physical
violence may have further strengthened the displacement of struggle
from man to nature. It is interesting that the prophet of political
Zionism, Theodor Herzl, never envisaged the use of violence in furthering his *Judenstaat*, nor did he contemplate its use in opposition
to his vision. He was remarkably certain that purely peaceful means
would accomplish the national regeneration of one people in a land
occupied by another. Ludwig Gumplowicz, one of the founders of
modern sociology, had warned Herzl that his vision was illusory:
"You are endowed with political naïveté such as one can pardon
only in poets," he wrote to him. "You want to found a state without
bloodshed? Where have you ever seen such a thing? Without force
or cunning? Just like that, open and honest—by easy
instalments?"[25]

What must have strained especially the credibility of Arab hostility in the eyes of Palestine Jews was the proverbial venality of their
alleged antagonists. The proclivity of Arab landowners to thunder
against the alienation of native soil to the Jews only the better to sell
their own land was one of the open secrets of the land. "For years,"
recalled a Zionist leader, himself unconvinced after four decades of
life in Palestine that Arab antagonism was really serious, "one of
the Mufti's close relations prospered mightily by forcing Arab small-
holders to sell land, at niggardly prices, which he then resold to Jews
at a handsome profit."[26] Equally general was the awareness of the
ease with which Arab informers were purchased by Zionist intelligence agents. According to Lieutenant Colonel Netanel Lorch of
the Israel Defense Forces, one of the sources of the *Haganah*'s
weapons before 1948 was the enemy himself. "Arms were acquired
from Arabs, including some of those who were most hostile in their
public utterances, and soldiers of the Arab Legion."[27] If in the rather puritan community of settlers the professed antagonism of venal
Arabs was not very convincing, quite a few settlers knew that the
rare show of Arab conciliation was also not infrequently produced
with the help of *baksheesh*, or bribery.

Following the first serious wave of anti-Jewish outbreaks in
British-occupied Palestine, during the first week of May, 1921, the
governmental Commission of Inquiry into the Palestine Disturbances, the first in a series of many, discovered that hostility to Zionism was profound and widespread in the Arab population. Although

complex and varied, the gist of the animus was fear that the Jews aimed to establish their rule in the country. Some Arabs mentioned cultural friction, others fear of Bolshevism, imported by the Jews, yet all understood, in both town and country, that the basic question was who was to govern whom.[28] Such acute political sensitivity is natural in Islam, which reckons its beginning, not from the birth of the Prophet, nor from the moment of spiritual revelation, but from the conquest of power in Medina. The first British Commission of Inquiry discovered that even in the countryside, among barely literate rural folk, the chief topic of discussion was politics—an incredible phenomenon in most other rural societies. The grasp of the problem, incidentally, was better than that of the literate and sophisticated Jews who appeared before it.[29] As revealed to British intelligence, "disturbances"—the fateful *maoraot* that was to terrify and puzzle the *Yishuv* for many years to come—were to Arabs plainly and uncomplicatedly war, in which one had to kill and loot.[30]

These British reports were models of lucidity regarding the nature of the Arab-Jewish conflict. Echoing the Haycraft Commission of 1921, the Shaw Report, after the disturbances of 1929, denied that Arab hostility was superficial or artificial; its roots lay, it said, in utter rejection of the Jews' change from tolerated minority to rulers. The Peel Report, following the next great disturbances in the 1930's, saw Arab and Jewish positions "as incompatible."[31]

In all these hearings the Jews usually excelled in rationalizing and obscuring their ultimate political goal. Their references to it were shrouded in anxiety and vagueness (only in 1942 did the Zionist movement categorically demand statehood). Moreover, their interpretations of the Arabs' violence, while not wholly inaccurate or unimaginative, usually skirted the gist of the matter. Some argued that the Arabs merely lusted for loot; others suggested that the violence had been artfully stimulated, either by Arab reactionaries ("sheiks and moneylenders") or by foreigners ("French agents," in one version). Some saw the riots as directed really at the British, not themselves.[32] Some even saw them as actually demonstrating the falseness of the claim that the Arabs were opposed to the building of the Jewish homeland. All agreed that Zionism as such was blameless, though they conceded that not all its practical manifestations were perfect and that they had not perhaps tried hard enough to make the Arabs recognize its true and benign character.

In time a number of stock theories took root in the *Yishuv*, the several Zionist factions favoring some theories over others, though some were rather generally shared. The bourgeois and respectable center (known as General Zionists later) stressed the socioeconomic uplift of the Arab population by Jewish settlement. The Arab mass, who stood only to gain from this work, were the unwitting victims and tools of reactionary leaders doomed by Zionist-inspired progress. In Herzl's vision of the new Zion the Arabs were already shown to be grateful for their emancipation. Rashid Bey, a leader of the Arabs, in his major work rebuked a Prussian visitor who expressed puzzlement at such an attitude toward intruders: "Would you consider him a robber who takes nothing away from you but gives you something? The Jews have made us rich. Why should we be angry with them?"[33]

More closely in contact with the reality in the land than early visionaries, the settlers did indeed realize that the Arabs had something to lose; hence, uplift in their thoughts often assumed the character of compensation for the loss. This "thesis of attrition [of antagonism] by Arab social reform," as one writer termed it,[34] was premised on belief that Palestine may be the weakest link in the pan-Arab chain and progress the force the Arabs can least resist. Material and moral uplift of Palestinian Arabs and the achievement of political goals for the rest of the Arab nation would thus compensate it for the loss of Palestine.[35] The theory seemed cogent enough to the many enthusiasts of progress and cognoscenti of Arab venality, and only the rare Zionist had serious qualms; one, Henrietta Szold, felt that it was unrealistic to expect the Arabs to be bribed out of their patrimony in this fashion.[36] (The thesis has survived all disappointments. Almost on the eve of the establishment of Israel, President Roosevelt still envisaged winning Arab agreement to a peaceful settlement with the Zionists with *baksheesh*.[37] And it is difficult not to view even the most generous American offers of financial support in behalf of various peace initiatives in later years in a similar vein; the most recent offers after the October War were clearly understood by Congress in this way.)

In their painful ambivalence toward modernity, the Arabs voted for Jewish progress with their feet and hands and rejected it in their hearts and especially with their voices. While masses of Arabs from neighboring countries streamed into Palestine, attracted by higher wages and living standard and government services, financed essentially from Jewish sources but used almost exclusively for Arabs, Arab spokesmen invariably demeaned the Jewish-induced progress. They either denied there had been such progress or conceded its existence with the qualification that the Arabs would have achieved it themselves anyway, without the Jews. If the Jews were part of it, they wanted none of it, they said. Besides, the Jews had brought also social decay, immorality, and crime. One could plainly see on the streets of Tel Aviv that what most attracted the young men of Arab Jaffa were immodest Jewish women, not Bauhaus architecture.

Arab social structure and politics in British Palestine lends some credence to an uplift thesis. Arab politics was in essence intrigue among few cliques of landed clans and notables, chief among whom were the Husseinis, who had won control of the religious establishment and with the moral hold on the mass and the extensive patronage this yielded enforced conformity with extreme nationalism and noncooperation with both Jew and Briton, by means of terror and assassination, if necessary. Almost any criticism or independent action under these circumstances struck one as moderation and was so hailed on the Jewish side, if only as a relief from the unrelenting negativism of the Husseinis. In the 1920's there were some attempts at regional peasant parties, stressing bread-and-butter issues at the expense of national ones and pressing consequently for cooperation with Jewish and British elements. The slow emergence later of an Arab urban working class entailed similar orientations. Groups opposed to the Husseinis often stressed community of (economic and social) interests with the Jews and sometimes spoke in reassuring, though always vague, terms in matters political. The essential difference between the Husseinis and their main opponents, the Nashashibis, appears to have been over means, not ends, the latter preferring less belligerent tactics on the road to an Arab Palestine. The Nashashibis' milder manner was never really afforded a chance to prove itself perhaps amenable also on ultimate goals. As it happened, the Husseini tactics were apparently successful for Arabs, insofar as they forced the British to dismantle their commitment to Zionism, step by step, in tandem with the growth of Arab violence, until its virtual repudiation in 1939, with the White Paper that envisaged permanent minority status for the *Yishuv*.

The connection between Arab violence and British concessions was not lost on the Zionist center, but they were not inclined to regard the violence as a true expression of popular Arab sentiment, because of the authorities' shockingly permissive attitude. British laxity went far indeed toward explaining the rowdies' facility in manipulating the mass. Center spokesmen, however, usually refrained from imputing bad faith to the British.

The Zionist left deemphasized national differences between Arab and Jew, insisting instead on their proletarian alliance in the struggle against feudal and capitalist exploitation. The left thus adhered also to the uplift theory, but had authentic sources for its peculiar formulations. The extreme left (*Poalei Zion Smol,* and soon also the *Hashomer Hatzair*) tended toward proletarian internationalism in the conventional sense; the nationalist-Marxist left (*Poalei Zion,* later known as *Achdut Haavoda*) denigrated Arab nationalism, though affirming Jewish nationalism in militantly proletarian terms. Their Borochovism (named after the chief Marxist ideologue of Zionism, Ber Borochov) envisaged historical forces, as inevitable as those forcing the Jews out of Europe, making for their proletarization in Palestine, which, because it was desolate, would be free of imperialist meddling. The Arabs were thought to lack an authentic cultural and economic character and, hence, could not produce a national movement and would in time be assimilated into proletarian Jewish society.

The non-Marxist left (*Hapoel Hatzair*), mildly socialist and heavily Tolstoyan, opposed in particular economic exploitation of the indigenous population. Hence, they formulated the principle of Hebrew labor (*Avoda Ivrit*), according to which Jewish settlers were to perform themselves all work, no matter how menial, and won the more leftist *Poalei Zion* over to this position. In consequence there arose a self-reliant, "normally stratified" Jewish community, with its separate and substantially independent economy. While Arab workers bitterly resented denial of lucrative Jewish jobs, Hebrew labor was actually by its theoreticians to prevent national antagonism, for without exploitation of Arab labor the latter could not "objectively" be opposed to the Zionists.[38]

David Ben-Gurion gave expression to the general ethos of the Zionist left in 1931, saying, "the Arab laborer is our brother in fate, and our partner in the fatherland."[39] For him and the others in the nationalist majority of the left the fatherland was to be a Jewish commonwealth; as to the internationalist minority, they envisioned a binational state in Palestine. The nationalist majority promoted a particular strategy of social change for the attainment of Zionist ends, encouraging the rise of a unionized Arab working class, emancipated from Arab traditional leadership, but tied to its Jewish unionist patrons and sponsors. Their efforts at organizing workers in the still preindustrial Arab sector of Palestine met with only modest success, but the political proclivities of early Arab trade unions seemed promising enough.[40] If this approach to Arab-Jewish collaboration was selective and instrumental, that of the more militant and internationalist left was broad-gauged and idealistic; collaboration for the former was to take place at arm's length, through parallel institutions, so as not to impair the autonomy of the *Yishuv*; for the latter proximity, indeed intimacy, was always an ideological imperative. In their pursuit of this goal, one faction, the *Poalei Zion Smol*, focused on urban workers, the other, the *Hashomer Hatzair*, on the countryside. There was but a minute number of Arabs available for the compulsory and ritualistic presence in the internationalist left's activities.

Rationalizing Arab hostility to Zionism was a widely shared need in the entire *Yishuv*, but was accompanied by particularly dogmatic fervor in the internationalist left. One familiar ritual was experienced by a noted British Labourite, who visited the *Hashomer Hatzair* kibbutz Mishmar Haemek, near Haifa, in the aftermath of World War Two. "Just across a rivulet, on a hill two hundred yards away, was the stenchiest Arab village I have ever seen. They agreed that I should spend most of my time talking to the sheik to find out how the collective and the village got on. So Bentov, editor of the party paper, and the muhtar (each collective has one Arab expert for relations with Arabs outside) took me across, and we were soon seated on the floor of a filthy hovel drinking tea. Obviously the muhtar and the sheik got on well. I asked the sheik if he wasn't envious for his children of the life in the school on the farm one hundred yards away. He said 'No' in a way which showed that he couldn't comprehend the question. I was nearly convinced that Arab-Jewish co-operation was perfect when I asked 'What about immigration?' Suddenly the sheik's son leaped to his feet and delivered a full-length speech containing the whole Arab case including the return of the Mufti [then sought as a Nazi war criminal]. 'But you don't mind the Jews in this collective?' He fiercely replied that any more Jews in Palestine would ruin the country. The Jewish muhtar then said: 'But if you had had your way we shouldn't have been here and you like us, don't you?' At this point the sheik and his son answered nothing, and the muhtar turned to me and said in English: 'You see they really like us, and it's all propaganda from above on the Arab side.' "[41]

The great ideological fervor in the internationalist left of Zionism may well be a function of the strain between ideological imperative and reality. There was certainly great tension between dogmatic idealization of the Arab and the personal cognitions and fears of the believers, many of whom did not just distrust the Arab but also saw him as a primitive capable of unspeakable horrors. An account of a *Hashomer Hatzair* kibbutz under siege in 1948 reveals that the informal motto of the settlers was "Never trust an Arab" and their strategy was influenced by the fear that rape and mutilation were the lot of Jewish captives in Arab hands.[42] These cognitions were shared with the rest of the *Yishuv*, reflecting a communal experience which, insofar as the pattern of violence was concerned, was painfully realistic. (Primitive warfare, as anthropologists term it, is rather spontaneously practiced among Arabs and other Muslims.) In the internationalist left, however, these cognitions must be decried as false and defamatory.[43] It is ironic that members of this movement should claim special expertise in Arab affairs.

The position of the Zionist right ("revisionists") toward Arab hostility was somewhat ambivalent. Their own strong penchant for political and military action made for a certain empathy with the Arabs. They thus conceded that an Arab national movement could not help but oppose the intrusion of another. In this sense Arab antagonism and even violence against the Jews was quite natural. But their deprecation of the Arabs was so profound as to deny the possibility of a worthwhile or even genuine Arab national action. "True, theoretically the Arabs were opposed to any increase in the Jewish population," and other Zionist aims; but they were "not to be taken seriously."[44] The Arab struggle against the Jews was a paper tiger staged by the British for their own imperial needs. Without this interference the Arabs would meekly submit or easily be made to submit to the Jews. "All Arab opposition," said Menachem Begin, "was instigated by the British themselves."[45] The real conflict was between the dominant (Jewish) nationalist force in Palestine and the imperial power, not between Jews and Arabs. (In the extreme left the theme of British *divide et impera* assumed appropriately internationalist-proletarian overtones.)

The reality component of the revisionist theory was not insubstantial. British officialdom in Palestine was from the beginning generally anti-Jewish, and often violently so, and ended its tenure of a quarter of a century in waging barely disguised warfare on the nascent Jewish state. While few Jews in mandatory Palestine did not know some civilized and even friendly act of individual Britons, few Jews indeed did not know or allege to know of despicable behavior toward them by British institutions, rather than men, though men implemented policy and sometimes distorted it by excess. Regulations on the illegal possession of arms were thus implemented on a sharply discriminatory basis as between Jews and Arabs, the British conceding the traditional character of universal manhood armament among the latter. British discharge of police powers in "distur- bances" was invariably marked by: a. insufficient preparation before threatened Arab violence; b. belated and ineffectual intervention when it finally took place; c. disarmament and prosecution of Jewish defenders. (The British personnel of the Palestine Police was admit- tedly overwhelmingly anti-Jewish.)[46]

An encounter of Pierre van Paassen, then correspondent of the *Evening World* of New York, with Harry Luke, the highest-ranking British official in the country, at the outbreak of the 1929 riots, il- luminates the British approach. "The gentleman appeared to be in a blue funk in the first days of the rioting when I called on him at Gov- ernment House in Jerusalem. 'The situation has gotten out of hand,' he repeated over and over again, 'and just at a moment when there are no troops within easy call.' I asked him if there were no arms on hand either. 'Plenty,' he said. 'Well, then there is nothing to be afraid of,' I suggested. 'Give me a gun and give a few more British subjects a gun, and we can keep order. If need be, you can arm a few thousand Jews. They are being attacked by people who seem to have plenty of arms. It would be logical, in view of the fact that the government does not possess the means to protect them, that they be allowed to defend themselves.' 'But that would mean civil war,' objected Mr. Luke. 'Well, you pretty well have a civil war on your hands as it is.' 'We, the government, would merely become a third party of disorder if I carried out your suggestion,' he said. 'Disor- der? By suppressing disorder you do not become disorderly,' I re- marked. 'The Mufti's clique is the party of disorder. The Jews, whatever your objections to them may be, are the party of order. I have looked at the Arab rioters in Jerusalem, Hebron, Safad, and elsewhere. They are the lowest dregs of the population, uncouth hooligans, gangsters, and cutthroats. As against them the Jews rep- resent civilization here.' 'Ah,' he objected again, 'but you must keep in mind that the government is neutral, must be impartial in this quarrel between Jews and Arabs. We are the watchdog. . . .'" 'Neutral and impartial when it is a question of barbarism versus civi- lization, when it is a case of gangsters attacking peaceful, innocent citizens? . . . Isn't being neutral in such a case tantamount to tak- ing sides, if one leaves the way open for more attacks, more mur- ders of women and children?' 'By the way,' Mr. Luke broke in, 'are you Jewish?' "[47]

When shouting *dawla maana* ("the government is with us"), the rioting mobs probably exaggerated the extent of British involvement; it is understandable that the Jews who heard them also did. The allegation that high British officials in some cases actively encouraged Arab violence seems cogent enough;[48] but the shock of even a single instance more than suffices for the jumping at conclusions that overly deprecated the Arab national movement.

What the revisionists saw more clearly than the British was the pretense of the vaunted Muslim martial prowess. In actual fact, though often bloody and costly, Arab military performance in modern times was not impressive. But the British invariably appeared anxious to avoid, even at great cost, provoking the legendary wrath of the ferocious Muslims, probably because they were more genuinely captive of this myth of the Orient in Flames—which, incidentally still influences journalistic and diplomatic perceptions of the Middle East in our day—than the revisionists realized, which nourished their oversimplified conspiracy theory of Arab violence.

The revisionists' evaluation of Arab military capacity cannot fail to astonish the historian. In March of 1944 General George C. Marshall, Army Chief of Staff, advised the Senate Committee on Foreign Relations, then considering a pro-Zionist resolution, that he would not be responsible for the military consequences in the Muslim world if the resolution passed. Center and left Zionists in the United States deferred to his judgment, however much they resented its consequences; the revisionists alone demurred. In a sharp statement published in the New York *Post* of March 14 and in *New Republic* of March 27 they registered "astonishment and dismay" at Marshall's intervention. "What is that 'military expedience' so alarmingly proclaimed in opposition to the Palestine resolution? Wherein lies that threat of Arab resistance, so grave and enormous, that General Marshall is reported to have said he 'could not take the responsibility for certain consequences?' The Arabs are not a military factor," they insisted, "there is not the remotest possibility of Arab disturbances in the Middle East that may hamper the war effort or involve the loss of American lives."[49] (Later, on the very eve of the establishment of Israel, General Marshall warned the Zionist leadership that the Arabs would quickly overrun their new state.)

But the revisionists shared a common Western misconception of Arab violence patterns. While Arab military performance is sometimes seen as nearly burlesque, by the West's standards, it is usually ignored there that "backward" warfare represents the really spontaneous genuine ways of war (sporadic killings, ambushes, looting, mutilation, etc.) of Arab peoples. For far from being quiescent in Palestine, the Arabs were indeed waging war on the Jews as best they knew. Ignorance of the Muslim martial tradition made the ordinary Arab mode of mob mobilization appear suspect in the eyes of the *Yishuv*. Incitement mainly by means of religious hyperbole, though common in traditional Islam, merely strengthened Jewish beliefs that Arab hostility was only artificial or false. After all, the Jews *knew* they did not intend to raze Muslim holy shrines from the face of the earth, as the *ulema* claimed in the mosques, to ignite the faithful.

A strongly romantic biblicism in revisionism gave rise to two curious, yet seemingly contradictory, minor orientations toward the Arabs in the *Yishuv*, specifically a view of them as descendants of the ancient tribes from whom the Hebrews had conquered the land (Ammonites, Amorites, etc.). While some believers imagined themselves to be continuing the conquest in their day, others (in the so-called Canaanist fringe) yearned to be rejoined with these tribes in a pristine Semitic heathendom, rejecting latter-day Jewishness ("phylactery Judaism") with contempt. (Exponents of these two orientations have joined in the Land of Israel Movement, which advocates retention of all land conquered by Israel in the June war of 1967.

Since the center and left together dominated both the World Zionist Organization and the *Yishuv*, it was their particular perceptions of Arab hostility that influenced official Zionist policy and to a lesser degree state policy after the establishment of Israel. These perceptions thus influenced the formulation and practice of *havlagah*—the policy of utmost restraint in the face of violent provocation from the Arab side—over which, incidentally, occurred the fatal cleavage in the *Yishuv*'s defense organization in the 1930's, leading to the creation of the dissident National Military Organization (*Irgun*), and by a yet later split to the so-called Stern Gang (Freedom Fighters of Israel), the two terror organizations especially prominent in the last years of British rule. The rationale of *havlagah* was indeed a web of various doctrines based on center and left perceptions: the loss of innocent Jewish life was regrettable, even when viewed from the Arab marauder's own real welfare (doctrine of intrinsic compatibility); one could only compound the misunderstanding between fellow Semites by shedding innocent Arab blood in revenge (doctrine of unfortunate misconception and doctrine of the purity of Jewish arms [*tohar neshek*]); indiscriminate retaliation would merely play into the hands of the spoilers (doctrine of artificial stimulation, which the right also shared). *Havlagah* influenced security policy as late as the early 1950's but has been eclipsed by the stern policy of reprisal since.

The same perceptions have inspired attempts at getting across to the Arab mass—if only there were no Haj Amin al-Husseini (the *Mufti* of Jerusalem) or Nasser or other leaders who interpose their evil designs and poisoned relations with the Arab peoples![50] The desire to remove Nasser as a barrier to peace was probably part of the motivation to go to war in 1956. On the other hand, these perceptions moved Zionist leaders repeatedly to accept proposed solutions to the conflict, the implementation of which may well have entailed the liquidation, in part or in whole, of the Zionist program. Israel's acceptance of virtually indefensible armistice lines in 1949 was far from involuntary, but actually consistent with a doctrine ("good neighbors rather than good borders"), which naturally complemented the other doctrines founded on old Zionist perceptions of Arab hostility.

Perceptions of Arabs and attitudes toward them were affected by factors other than the above left-right variable, as is manifested by an influential, though numerically insignificant, segment of opinion in the *Yishuv,* known variously as *Brit Shalom* or (earlier) *Ichud.* The group of notables, many of German background and of academic distinction—Ruppin, Lichtheim, Bergmann, Magnes, Buber— while often regarded as opposing the mainstream of Zionism, was in fact an offshoot of the Zionist center, propagating its meliorist theory, though in extreme formulation. They displayed unusual awareness of, and anxiety over, the lack of Arab-Jewish communication and made an entente between these fellow Semites the keystone of the Zionist endeavor, indeed its absolute prerequisite. But it is obvious that these men were distinguished from the center by an extraordinary moral fervor, a religious pacifism, not unlike Quakerism; and it appears that they manifested in effect another variable (besides left-right) in Jewish political behavior, one shaped by the peculiar experiences of Jewish history.

There have from the origins of modern Zionism been certain differences in the approach to international politics, particularly from the inception of British rule in Palestine, and usually regarded as "tactical": the bulk of the movement endorsed "organic" (or evolutionary) Zionism, a minority espoused "monolithic" (or precipitate) Zionism.[51] The former, personified by Dr. Weizmann, stressed patient, piecemeal, building of an autonomous Jewish community in Palestine, through selective immigration of pioneers, steady rural settlement, with a "low profile" in diplomacy—defensive, pliant, inconspicuous and ambiguous about ultimate political aims. The latter, embodied by Vladimir Jabotinsky, sought maximal diplomatic assertiveness for the immediate achievement of sovereign requisites and the mass transfer of millions of Jews to Palestine, an impatient "shortcut" approach necessitating reliance in virtually all vital functions, defense included, on foreign powers, chiefly Britain—at least in the short run, but also exhibiting a tendency to accept foreign models for national institutions rather than nurturing autochthonous ones, as in the first approach. Under the catastrophic pressures of the years just prior to World War Two, there took place a fundamental shift. Time for patience having run out (because of the Nazi onslaught on Europe's Jews and the simultaneous deterioration of the British attitude toward Zionism) and a substantial autonomous national base having already been built, the bulk of the majority adopted in effect the "monolithic" position of the previous minority. With this force behind it the Biltmore Program was carried during the war, committing the Zionist movement finally to Jewish statehood. In the struggle for the state and after its achievement one could discern a certain diversity about assertiveness on sovereignty.

"Activism," as one tendency has been termed, was only imperfectly related to the left-right continuum in Zionist politics: the center was split pretty much in half and so was also the major labor party (Ben-Gurion as "activist"; Eliezer Kaplan as "moderate"). Still, the most moderate groups were found on the extreme left (*Hashomer Hatzair*) and in the center (*Ichud*) and the most activist on the right (revisionist)—but also in the moderate Marxist left (the new *Achdut Haavoda,* standing to the left of Ben-Gurion's dominant faction in *Mapai,* the major labor party). In a curious mixture sympathizers of red revolutionism joined religious zealots in forming the ultra-activist Stern Group (a precursor of anti-imperialist urban guerrillaism). As manifested then and in subsequent struggles over Israeli foreign policy, "activism" and "moderation" describe opposite postures on the following: the weight attached to foreign opinion (degree of anxiety over displeasure abroad with one's behavior; respect for foreign views as authoritative); the importance of foreign power (ease of intimidation by its threat and readiness to defy it—and here a tendency to be easily intimidated goes hand in hand with readiness to trust its justice, to throw oneself on the mercy of foreign power); the evaluation of one's own power (resisting foreign pressure in diplomacy; meeting military jeopardy from Arab neighbors; the utility of displays of power for altering Arab behavior).

The term "Weizmann School" continued to identify a particularly strong inclination toward foreign-policy concessions, or the militant moderates, so to speak. In some cases concessions were offered or suggested even before they were asked. Such an instance was recorded by Count Bernadotte, United Nations Mediator for Palestine, in his diaries: In his first meeting with an official agent of the provisional government of Israel, the latter (Nahum Goldmann) actually suggested to him such far-going territorial concessions and limitations on the just-proclaimed Jewish sovereignty that, when Bernadotte later incorporated them in his peace plans, the Jewish government fought them as a direct threat to its secure existence.[52] The concession was motivated by a pessimistic evaluation of Israel's military capacity, also a rather characteristic trait of the Weizmann School. (Goldmann and Shertok [later Sharett] had urged deferment of the proclamation of the state on similar grounds only some weeks before. As chief spokesman for what is left of the school since the 1967 war, Goldmann has argued for total withdrawal from conquered land and full reliance on international guarantees on the basis of his emphatic denial of Israel's capacity to resist Arab military pressure in the foreseeable future.)

Linked to the anxiety in confronting foreign powers and personalities (timidity to some, realism to others) with Jewish assertiveness, is great confidence in personal diplomacy. As Weizmann himself had counseled against challenging even the hostile White Paper policies of Whitehall and urging instead reliance on personal ties to British leaders, so Goldmann also argued when President Roosevelt later endorsed anti-Zionist moves. The defiance of Roosevelt by Rabbi Hillel Silver reminded Goldmann of Jabotinsky, "a great Zionist but his policies of antagonizing the powers that be—even though they were often unjust to Jewish people—would have led to catastrophe. . . . If this fight against the President and this policy of attacking the Administration is continued, it will lead us—and I choose my words very carefully—to complete political disaster."[53]

Seeking an imposition of an Arab-Jewish settlement by foreign powers also has been a persistent trait of the Weizmann School throughout the decades, beginning in the 1920's and 1930's, when the *Hashomer Hatzair* and the *Brit Shalom* wanted the British and other powers to impose on both Jews and Arabs a binational solution, and even in the present, when the remnants of the school form a conspicuous dissenting minority from Israel's strenuous opposition to foreign dictation of a settlement. *77-144*

Speakers for the opposing tendencies in foreign policy have accused each other as narrowly parochial (against the activists) and as reflecting a ghetto mentality (against their detractors)—and both are quite correct. For a profound distrust of the gentiles and a sense of total isolation in this world, pushing toward defiance of the world even to the brink of disaster, indeed reflect a particularistic Jewish tradition, which in some of its aspects is more popularly known as the Masada spirit. Yet just as authentically reflecting long historical experience is the ghetto-related phenomenon of *shtadlanut,* the institution of coping with a hostile environment—powerless Jewish communities surrounded by antagonistic and capricious gentiles— by means of personal representation, bargaining, pleading and bribing by professional fixers before the powerful of this world. *Shtadlanut* certainly attained great achievements for Zionism early on—the Balfour Declaration, for one—but the evolution of an actual national base in Palestine and the incidence of Holocaust in Europe's Jewry could not but make for an increasing shift away from it.

Activism implies a "hard" line toward Arabs besides the inclination to rely on Jewish power for the control of Arab belligerency, even confidence in winning acceptance by coercion, being pessimistic about a more spontaneous kind. The "soft" line of Weizmannism, while looking for practical compensations to the great powers, is inextricably tied to an expectation, that despite everything Arabs cannot but respond in kind to decency and finally accommodate the Jews. One's cognition of Arabs and one's temperamental inclination would seem to interact here: belief in the eminent solubility of the Arab-Jewish conflict may incline one toward cautionary tactics and concessions; on the other hand, one so inclined by temperament in the first place would probably feel attracted to optimistic evaluations of the solubility of the conflict anyway.

3

EVOLVING ISRAELI ORIENTATIONS

HOWEVER generous its spirit, the implementation of Zionism involved force with awesome dislocation, infringement of rights, continuous strife and bloodshed—yet another instance of "moral man-immoral society," or the familiar "price of revolution," though surely a lesser contradiction than in the case of other "true believers."[1] As in other cases of disappointed beliefs, here too many men were more inclined to rationalize history than to learn from it, particularly since history seemed to vindicate not merely views different from their own, but views of dubious moral quality as well. The actual course of history has been a particularly great disappointment to the extreme left, one made especially galling by the "I told you so" stance of those they consider "fascist" (revisionists). Many have concluded that what was wrong was history, not their convictions, and much historiographical effort goes into discovering just where it had gone astray, why it was deflected from its proper course, who had corrupted it.

The survival of older Zionist orientations toward Arabs has been nourished especially by a theory that explains the festering conflict in terms of insufficient efforts at settlement with the Arabs or the wrong kind of efforts. The Jews had not tried hard enough to come to terms with the Arabs or they handled them, when they did interact, with the wrong allure, the wrong approach. In one of the earlier versions of the theory, published at a particularly gloomy and ominous turn of Zionist history, Zionist leaders were accused of having misled their followers with the notion that it is not necessary to take into account seriously the opposition of the Arabs; they were urged to win the sympathy of the Arabs by all means; the compatibility of Arab and Jewish objectives was naturally taken for granted by the writer.[2] The argument has become more complex and sophisticated three decades later, but the postulate of compatibility persists.

An ambitious typology of Israeli perceptions of the Arabs has thus been suggested by a high Israeli Foreign Office official to a student of Israel's foreign policy, and accepted by him, according to which "Buberism" (named after the distinguished philosopher, member of the *Ichud*) represents a sense of contrition for injustices done to Arabs, a thrust always toward concessions for peace; "Shukairism" (named after the leader of the Palestine Liberation Organization before 1968, a popular symbol of Arab genocidal threats) represents the opposite pole, viewing the Arabs as malicious, unyielding, little better than other historical tormentors of the Jews, who deserve no concession, for it is only Jewish force that will produce a change of heart among them. "Sanity," on the other hand, represents the view that the Arab-Israeli conflict is a conventional one, amenable to the usual diplomatic means. The cogency of the last proposition is derived (apart from its name) from references to "Arab psychology" and speculations about what might have happened had Israel taken more initiatives for peace, sought more contacts, etc. To this "sane" proposition naturally is attached a sympathetic image category as well: "In the language of image analysis, Ben Gurion [alleged paragon of "Shukairism"] revealed an 'inherently bad faith' perception of 'the Arabs'; the 'Buberites' adhered to the 'inherently good faith' model, and Sharett's image ["sane"] was characterized by empathy and firmness without rigidity."[3]

The trouble with the theory of wasted opportunities is obvious, but even its factual basis is fallacious: The presumption that few or no contacts with Arabs were made or that the initiatives for agreement by the dissenting few had been promising, yet were spurned by Zionist officials, is simply not tenable. Certainly as far as the prestatehood period is concerned, there would seem few secrets of any import left uncovered and, at any rate, what has been reviewed and studied quite clearly denies the negligence thesis.

What actually impressed students of Arab-Zionist contacts most was the utter futility of political communication rather than its paucity, the latter probably reflecting the sense of uselessness engendered by such experiences. The small band of Jewish conciliators was indeed revealed as tireless in its efforts to bring together responsible or merely influential Arab and Jewish personalities, and there may well have been more face-to-face or direct negotiation between the antagonists at that phase than at any subsequent one in the long conflict. (In 1936 Dr. Magnes actually brought off a series of "summit" meetings involving, among others, Ben-Gurion, Musa Alami, and George Antonius, the leading Arab nationalist theoretician of his time.) Yet direct communication at such level merely sharpened the utter hopelessness of agreement. A steady stream of projects, plans, and proposals for conciliation was produced by the same source, flawed only by the absence of any significant support on the Arab side. "Both Magnes and Kalvarisky were constantly turning to the Jewish Agency with what they believed to be 'openings' for reaching an agreement with the Arabs. Dr. Magnes, who was greatly respected amongst the Zionist leaders [a leader in American Reform Judaism, he was president of Hebrew University in Jerusalem], was a great idealist and pacifist who truly believed that without agreement with the Arabs the Zionist endeavour would lose its moral force. Kalvarisky was an 'incurable optimist,' who firmly believed that reaching an agreement with the Arabs was simply a question of paying the right sums of money to the right persons. Both shared a dogged stubbornness in their efforts to bring about a binational solution to the Jewish-Arab problem. They failed because neither pure idealism nor money could bridge the growing gap between the two peoples."[4] On the rare occasion when even a glimmer of opening could be effected, assassins quickly saw to its closure: In 1946 the League for Jewish-Arab Rapprochement and Co-operation (a union of the extreme left and centrist pacifists) succeeded in interesting a leader of a small dissident Arab group in Jerusalem, Fauzi Darwish al-Husseini, in binationalism, only to mourn his violent death at the hands of Arab assassins soon afterward.

Faith makes failure itself the proof of rightness, as the historiography of the faithful amply demonstrates. But unbelievers draw the more conventional conclusion, as does this reviewer of a typical work, Aharon Cohen's *Israel and the Arab World*: "Mr. Cohen's massive book lists these missed opportunities, yet it leaves the reader unconvinced. The facts as given are not wrong, though they are regrettably incomplete, and the selection is often arbitrary. He rightly argues that the Zionist leaders should have given much greater attention to the Arab question, should have tried even harder to win friends among their neighbors. The catalogue of sins of commission and omission is substantial: the new immigrants should have been more tactful, they should have studied the language and customs of the Arabs, more could have been done to see that the Arabs shared the economic benefits of Jewish immigration. There were possibilities of influencing Arab public opinion, of explaining that the Jews did not intend to dominate the Arabs. Whether this would have dispelled Arab fears is more than doubtful. The trouble with Mr. Cohen is that, after all these years of studying Arab-Jewish relations, he seems not to have understood the basic character of the conflict; that, as in a Greek tragedy, each step follows the preceding one as its necessary consequence, with few surprises and no *peripeteia*. He is reluctant to acknowledge that politics is about power—a curious aberration in a Marxist."[5]

The judgment of the past seemingly more relevant to the experiences of most contemporary Israelis was that of the founder of *Brit Shalom* himself, Arthur Ruppin, whose involvement in the forward lines of conciliation spanned the virtually whole pre-state period of settlement, from 1907 until his death in 1942. (Since Moshe Dayan has repeatedly been cited as fairly representative of dominant views in post-1967 Israel on these issues, it is significant that he chose to endorse the Ruppin analysis in public and fully identify with its conclusion.) Ruppin came from Germany a truly humanist Zionist, unchauvinistic yet dedicated to the settlement and social experimentation on the land, himself a pioneer of the *kibbutz* conception of communal living, and became after the First World War chief manager of rural colonization in Palestine. His early exposure to Arab politicians in the Jaffa office of the Zionist Organization quickly immunized him against many romantic ideas congenial to other settlers, and he emerged from the experience with emphatic awareness of the need to face up to Arab opposition. His first phase of consciousness was dominated by the notion of a solution by Jewish integration with Arab peoples; but he soon realized the slender cultural and other grounds for such union, a supernational "civilized community," shifting by 1925 to a binational solution. He founded *Brit Shalom* to promote the idea of separate nations in one state, one rejected by most Jews and virtually all Arabs. The idea was revolutionary for his time, and he realized, also before other proponents, its failing as well, barely five years later.

As early as 1928, however, he was troubled by deeper doubts, as "it became clear how difficult it is to realize Zionism and still bring it continually into line with the demands of general ethics."[6] The terrible notion took hold, that the opposing interests were simply incompatible, not just misunderstood or misconceived: To accommodate Arab views Zionism would have to be abandoned; to insist on Zionism meant ineluctably struggling with Arabs. The problem from the Arab perspective, he put it to fellow Jews, was simply that "we were here." Ruppin parted ways with his companions, pleading against further evasion of the dilemma, certain that no magic formula could dissolve it. He had written at the end of 1931 to a friend, "What we can get from the Arabs we do not need [the status of a tolerated minority]; what we need [control of Jewish destiny—immigration, settlement, etc.] we cannot get."[7] By 1936, with Hitlerism on the ascendance in Europe and the Arab rebellion erupting in Palestine, Ruppin had reached the phase of resignation; he ceased believing in the possibility of persuading the Arabs to cooperate in the Zionist venture. His words were cited by Dayan thirty-two years later before senior military officers as stunningly prescient: "The Arabs do not agree to our venture. If we want to continue our work in Eretz Israel against their desires, there is no alternative but that lives should be lost. It is our destiny to be in a state of continual warfare with the Arabs. This situation may well be undesirable, but such is the reality."[8]

But the Jews *had* won agreement, had they not, from leading Arab figures, both at the start of the mandatory episode and later, upon the launching of their state. Unlike the dubious Arab messengers of peace—who would in true Levantine fashion fly in stealthily with their peace proposals, always from "most reliable sources," but soon to dissolve as mist—there had been substantial, monarchic figures—Hashemite brothers, reckoning their descent from the Prophet himself—who, in public or with little disguise, indicated acceptance of Zionism. The unfulfilled Weizmann-Faisal Agreement of 1918 and the stillborn agreement between Abdallah and the Israelis in the aftermath of the 1948–49 war have both had an extraordinary impact on Jewish thinking on their conflict with the Arabs and their spell still taunts the Jews' imagination.

The Faisal Agreement is certainly significant as precedent for public acknowledgment of Jewish nationalism in the Middle East by an Arab leader; the Arab attempts at representing it as fraudulent are unconvincing,[9] though Faisal might have harbored *arrières pensées* about the eventual political status of a Jewish entity in a larger Arab sovereignty. As leader of the Arab national movement, Faisal actually went beyond mere acquiescence, in that he acknowledged the legitimacy of Zionism by reference to Jewish historical claims and anticipated benefits for his own peoples. He obviously deemed this a price commensurate with what he asked in return, nothing less than the realization (with Jewish assistance) of all his other dreams of Arab grandeur. Since the bargain never materialized, it is idle to speculate whether it would indeed have been kept; it is certain, however, that the mass of Palestine Arabs bitterly rejected the deal and, knowing it, Faisal sought to hide it from them and, when the agreement was made public simply denied its existence. These facts do not augur well for the usually sanguine and expansive interpretations of the Faisal phenomenon in Zionist historiography.

It was Faisal's defeat at the hands of the French in Syria that led the British to ensconce his brother Abdallah on the Transjordanian territory of their Mandate in 1921. His openness to dealing with the Jews lent further strength to the romantic attachment in Zionist and Israeli lore to the Hashemites—one, incidentally, subsequently lavished upon King Hussein, Abdallah's grandson. What is clear is Abdallah's readiness to talk and bargain with Zionist leaders—particularly startling in contrast with the behavior of the dominant Arab party in Palestine. A critical scrutiny of the extended dealings must conclude, however, that nothing was ever really achieved in the way of formal agreement or even informal settlement of the Arab-Jewish dispute. Deals either failed to be consummated or were implemented in such fashion that if taken as a test of seriousness of purpose, augur less well than even the Faisal experience. Something of Abdallah's successful handling of the Jews is illuminated in this recollection by a Zionist leader. "In private conversations with representatives of the Jews, whom he trusted not to disclose the contents of his conversations, Abdullah had often professed his friendship and his concern for the welfare of the Jews. As with so many Arab leaders, an entire world separated his publicly declared views regarding the Jews from his private and confidential protestations of friendship to them made under circumstances which would leave him free to deny any Jewish leakage. For example, in 1933 this Arab patriot wandered so far from the accepted policy of Arab nationalism not to dispose of land to Jews that he agreed to rent a large area of his territory in Transjordan to the Jewish Agency. I drafted the lease agreement and met the Emir at his winter palace at Shuna. He was full of affability and good will, and hoped that the Jews would develop the land agriculturally so that it would be a model to Arab farmers in Transjordan. While he accepted his regular payments of rent, he managed to find all sorts of excuses to put off the date when we could take occupation of the land."[10]

Abdallah's ability to win the Jews' affection—while profiting materially from them as well—without actually giving anything substantial in return, certainly stands out as a more cogent aspect of his historical record than that cherished in Jewish lore: either the Scarlet Pimpernel of the Arab World, as a minority in the *Yishuv* saw him, or Redeemer of the Golden Age, in the eyes of most other Jews (and the English and Americans). As ruler of a desolate territory with no economic life worthy of mention, dependent entirely on the grace of the English and their money, it could be only diplomatic prowess that made an Emir of tribal nomads a central figure in Levantine politics. (According to his longtime English military aide, Glubb Pasha, Abdallah actually managed to wag the British dog, while ingratiating himself with the latter.) He went to war with the Jews without much impairing their affection for him (as Hussein did after him) and lavished such friendship on them as would not be acknowledged before the world. He was, of course, distrusted by other Arabs—but then distrust is modal in their interpersonal relations, except that as a particularly adept practitioner of conventional Arab politics he was particularly much distrusted.

The real significance of the Abdallah phenomenon for the Arab-Jewish confrontation is in its manifestations of the limits and complexities of Arab moderation in this context. For whatever else he might have been, Abdallah certainly was a paragon of moderation in that conflict; for this reason alone the Israelis' fondness for him is understandable and, in a certain sense, justified. The painful ambiguities about Arab moderation concerning Israel, which Westerners habitually confuse with moderation in consensual politics, may be appreciated from this: A sober appreciation of Abdallah diplomacy might have led to the conclusion that he could not be taken seriously; but, representing moderation such as it is among Arabs of any consequence vis-à-vis Zionism, how could the Jews not take it seriously? This means, among others, seeking agreements that are quite one-sided and otherwise unfulfilled from leaders who feel free to translate private statements of affection into open warfare. The predicament is bad enough even when one understands Arab culture and disorienting in the extreme when—as with Israelis and Westerners generally—it is superficial or entirely absent. Thus, against the background of Islamic tradition the wheeling and dealing with the Jews suggests an instrumental relationship, for the Jews are a competent and able group, whom the wise Muslim ruler uses for his own aggrandizement. (Abdallah's great dream was dominion over the "Fertile Crescent"—a well-watered region north of the Arab Desert, flanked by the great river systems of the Nile and the Euphrates-Tigris.) The Jews, in return, are entitled to decent (personal) treatment and generous protection (as a semiautonomous religious group). It is false to read into such dealings recognition as sovereign equals, as say, between the French and the Germans.

In the British period the peace strategy founded on Arab moderates was extremely popular in the *Yishuv*. If only the British would encourage the Arab moderates to reach agreement with likeminded Zionists and firmly impose it on all, was a recurrent theme. The Whitehall inquiry commissions could not fail to acknowledge the theory—and reject it. Their analysis (as in the Peel Report) was persuasive enough: The theory was dubious in its assumption that Arab nationalism was weak and artificial and in overrating the capacity and willingness of the Arab moderates to help such policy. "First, Arab 'moderation' has never extended to the higher plane of politics. Willingness to co-operate with Jews in municipal government is unhappily no evidence at all of willingness to co-operate on a national scale. . . . Secondly, the will to co-operate has never been strong enough to survive a crisis. When race-feeling was aroused, when an outbreak became imminent, then, if ever, was the time for the moderates to cling to the principle of co-operation, to seek for common ground, to use all their influence to avert the storm. But in public at any rate, whatever may have happened in private, they were never strong enough to take the line of compromise and conciliation. . . . Another reason for questioning the wisdom of trying to base a settlement on moderate Arab opinion is the difficulty of finding anyone now to profess it. The moderates have always been nationalists. They have been exposed like other Arabs to the pressure of events and influences which have operated, as has been pointed out, to inflame and intensify their nationalism. . . . Our last reason is drawn from experience. As we pointed out in discussing the situation in 1925, the extremist has usually kept the lead, the moderate has rarely counted, in a struggle for national independence. We see no reason why the history of nationalism in Ireland, India, Egypt—to mention only countries with which Britain has been concerned—should not repeat itself in Palestine."[11]

Yet the partition scheme of the Peel Commission itself seemed, at least for a short while and perhaps even then only deceptively, not totally unacceptable to both sides. There was a certain hesitation in some Arab quarters in Palestine and abroad before the general chorus of negativism erupted, a pause interpreted by some as amenability, even if very reluctant amenability, to going along. The German *Auswärtiges Amt,* quite alert to matters Jewish-Arab-British just prior to World War Two, "considered that the decisive political circles in the Arab countries desired to avoid a serious conflict with Great Britain despite the prevailing aversion in the Arab world to the emergence of a Jewish state. Thus, [Otto] von Hentig [senior counselor of the Middle East Division of the Ministry] maintained that the Arabs 'are well aware that England considers the question important enough to impose her point of view by force of arms without restrictions.' This viewpoint predominated, at least immediately after the publication of the Peel Commission report. And when the opposition of the Arab leaders became more definite many German officials did not hide their surprise."[12] British hesitation deprived the theory of peace with the moderates of a test. In the end the Arabs rejected emphatically and in unison the scheme the British never really pushed with conviction.

What if partition had been accepted in 1937? How effective could Abdallah's nonagression pact with Israel have been, if concluded, a decade and a half later? (Abdallah was assassinated for it as a traitor to the Palestine cause in Jerusalem in 1951.) While one can always hope for the best, the actual record of Arab-Jewish agreements points to the opposite, for they tended to die before being born and to rest unfulfilled even when born. The weight of Islamic international law presses mightily against a lasting treaty obligation toward non-Muslim powers and the actual practice of contemporary Arab diplomacy inspires little confidence in startling changes toward other norms. A witness before the following British commission of inquiry (the Woodhead Commission), when asked whether the Arabs would acquiesce in the partition of Palestine into Jewish and Arab states (under so-called Plan C, envisioning an even smaller territory for the former than the original Peel scheme, actually just 490 square miles of the 10,435 square miles of Palestine), assuming one could forcibly impose it on them, said, "It is just like pressing down a rubber ball; when you take the pressure off, the rubber ball resumes its natural shape."[13] The series of armistice agreements concluded some ten years later, in 1949, between Israel and four neighboring Arab states tended rather to validate this proposition. The tendency of the latter was to bounce back to old postures once pressure diminished; as Bilby reported, the armistice was barely concluded and talk of a "second round" already filled the air in the Arab world. The Arab tendency "to turn the clock back" was already asserting itself.

Despite the extraordinary preoccupation of the Western press with Israel, awareness in the West and elsewhere of attitudes toward Arabs in the Jewish state is generally poor. Much of what is widely believed is mainly false. Leaving aside such patently foolish beliefs as those holding that Israeli Jews "hate" their Arab antagonists, one discerns supposedly some presumably informed opinion, which upon little scrutiny appears as more false than the first. Two such views have been diffused widely in the post-1967 period, when the problem of settlement of the Arab-Israeli dispute, particularly the disposition of conquered territories, was frequently in the center of international discussion. One view holds that the firm ("intransigent") position on peacemaking and territories of the Jerusalem government exaggerates both the real position of governmental leaders and of the population at large; in this view the formal Israeli position is merely a bargaining forward position, or first position, from which negotiators would quickly withdraw to a more realistic one, which presumably also conforms more to actual popular opinion. The other view holds that the less intransigent position in the population at large is also the growing position; identifying "hawkishness" with the older generation and a "dovish" position with the young, it perceives the latter as the wave of the future.

The falseness of these propositions was apparent from any but utterly superficial impressions gained on the spot, not to speak of a mass of survey data collected in Israel that consistently denied the views prevailing abroad. Nearly four years into the controversy, *Time* commissioned a Louis Harris poll, which concluded that the outside world was indeed in error. Regarding Jerusalem's "tough and hypercautious" position on peacemaking, the "poll indicates that this stance enjoys overwhelming support among Israelis. If any U.S., Soviet or Arab policymakers assume that there is a significant dove faction in Israel, they appear sorely mistaken. . . . The poll upsets the assumption that young Israelis are considerably less rigid than their elders. Under some circumstances they are: those aged 18 to 29, for instance, appear more amenable to increased social relations with Israeli Arabs than do older groups. More of the young think the government has been too rigid in its approach toward peace than do other groups (14% *v.* 2% among those aged 40 to 59). But the young are also more insistent than the older Israelis on holding direct talks with the Arabs rather than the indirect discussions being conducted through United Nations Mediator Gunnar Jarring. When it comes to surrendering territory captured from the Arabs during the 1967 Six-Day War, the 18-to-29s are most hawkish: 28% want to retain all territory or expand Israel's borders, *v.* 21% in the overall sample.''[14] The survey found that 85% of Jewish Israelis thought the government was doing all it should to negotiate a peace treaty; 73% felt that some conquered territory should be returned for peace and only 4% that all land should be returned; only 3% thought that the Golan Heights should be given back to Syria; less than 0.5% that East Jerusalem be returned to Jordan; and 4% that Sharm al-Sheikh be returned to Egypt; the readiness to return areas in the Gaza Strip and particularly in the West Bank, as well as in Sinai, was substantially more pronounced.

What accounts for such extraordinary distortion of reality on such an intensely ''covered'' area of concern? The previously indicated role of journalism and diplomacy is apparent here, for the stubborn Israeli attitudes are so disturbing to conventional diplomatic conceptualization of Middle Eastern war and peace as to be almost inconceivable. Indeed, the diplomatic and journalistic discourse proceeded long on the assumption that they do not exist (or that they must not exist, if indeed they do). A diplomatic and journalistic expert on the Middle East, who, in the Nixon administration, had been involved in endeavors for a settlement in the area, thus reassured his readers that Israeli positions were not what they patently were.[15]

The role of Israeli and other Jewish factors appears equally significant. Briefly put, the Israeli voices reaching foreign publics, as well as Jewish channels abroad mediating them, are likely to mislead, sometimes deliberately, the foreign—including Jewish—publics. In the first place the Israelis who represent only a minute section of public opinion at home are vastly overrepresented in the nongovernmental ''messages'' reaching foreign public. This is due chiefly to the zealous information work of the New Outlook group, consisting of *Mapam* leaders and assorted journalists and academics, as well as some Jewish and Arab public figures and related groups, by means of speakers and periodicals (*New Outlook, Tadmit Newsletter*), reaching numerous opinion-makers, academics, and others abroad. Israelis of similarly unrepresentative views form also a large part of the speakers brought in through other channels, Jewish or other. In part at least this seems a consequence of the fact that their views are more congenial to Western audiences than the harder, official Israeli position.

The leadership of American Jewish organizations, reflecting in this respect perhaps not too inaccurately the orientations of American Jews generally, tends toward views that are clearly less firm than those of Israel's Jews and their leaders, though these leaders are usually supportive of Israeli policy in a general way. Their rostrums and journals are open to unrepresentative Israeli voices to a substantial degree. Young Israeli literati and artists, usually voicing dissenting views, speak often to Western publics through these channels, passing themselves off as spokesmen of their generation, and tend to be accepted as such by foreign literati and others.[16]

There is something of a lag between orientations of Israel's Jews and those in America in this respect. The shift to pessimism regarding Arab hostility proceeded at a much slower rate among the latter. While the 1967 war is widely regarded as the watershed for Israelis, as the decisive turning point to pessimism, the shift would seem to have been long under way; indeed, to have been consummated in essence before the war.

The realization that the Arabs of Palestine and other Arabs rejected Zionism simply as Arabs naturally dawned on many Jews early on, but ignorance of the structure and strength of Arab opposition lingered. Occasional early Jewish opinion is impressive in its lucidity, as when an unnamed Jewish witness, referring to Arab opposition, told the Peel Commission in 1937, "*The* underlying cause is that we exist."[17] Ruppin had articulated this proposition in 1936 and even earlier in terms that only few Jews in Palestine and elsewhere could endorse.

The process of erosion of early doctrines under exposure to persisting Arab hostility probably occurred in spurts—up and down —rather than uniformly. There seems to be a peculiarly erratic quality about the public mood of Israelis, which Elon described in connection with their characteristic alertness to news: "The habit of following the news so often and so closely partly explains the sudden shifts in the public mood, which can be as sharp as they are frequent. Israelis easily fall from heights of exhilaration to dark abysses of gloom; from glowing hope for imminent peace to bleak depression that the war will never end and that they may be crushed by it. One morning there is a hopeful report that the Arab position is softening; a few hours later the morning's hopes are crushed by a subsequent newscast."[18] (A cross-national study indeed revealed the Israelis as most intensely concerned, or "worried," of all nations.)[19] In the British period the old doctrines would usually reappear with new life following periods of "disturbances" and were sometimes even nourished by the course of the violence, as when the reluctance of some Arabs to take part in it was noted.

It appears that the immediate aftermath of the first major Arab-Israeli war coincided with a significant shift in attitudes toward peace. The period, usually depicted in histories as the most propitious wasted opportunity for peace, was characterized by sanguine hopes for imminent peace, certainly in Israel, the unrealization of which led to a particularly potent disillusionment as well. Before the middle 1950's Ben-Gurion, who had managed to ignore his own earlier realizations of the true nature of Arab resistance to Zionism, was shifting (again only temporarily) to a pessimistic perception of the chances for peace with the Arabs, saying that he had "no illusions" in this respect.[20] The failure of peace again to materialize in the wake of the next major war, in 1956, probably deepened this pessimism. Opinion surveys in late 1961 and early 1962 revealed "a pervasive fear of war with the Arabs" among Israelis; a high percentage (12, as opposed to 1 in Egypt) cited "peace" as a personal aspiration, and 26% (as opposed to 4% in Egypt) cited "war" as a personal fear; 55% cited "peace" as a national aspiration (9% in Egypt) and 49% cited "war" as a fear for the country (31% in Egypt).[21] The views of Golda Meir, expressed in a *Knesset* debate in November of 1961, would seem to be the same as those she aired one decade later as Prime Minister, describing the Arabs as implacably opposed to the very existence of the Jewish state (the conflict thus not being simply over refugees or territory); as not divertable from their objective by tokens of goodwill or concessions; as treacherous in their approach to bargaining with Israel; and as ultimately amenable to coexistence with the latter only because of the sheer inability to remove it. A perceptive foreign observer somewhat later presented the Israeli positions on peace as essentially the above.[22] A distinct hardening of public sentiment took place between 1962 and 1966.[23]

The noted Arabist, S. D. Goitein, reported as follows in the beginning of the 1960's: "The average Israeli is very eager to learn what is going on in the Arab countries; however, he has become somehow apathetic to discussing the possibilities of a peace settlement. Too many and too mighty forces are at work at present in the Middle East to render such a prospect futile for the immediately foreseeable future. In addition, the Israelis are fully aware of the fact that an anti-Israel obsession, a mass psychosis, has been created among their neighbors . . . [and] the attitude of the average Israeli towards his future is: Be prepared, be alert for any emergency; otherwise, wait and see. Last summer, when I was in Israel, the subject of a settlement with the Arabs was hardly touched."[24] Israelis believed the chief obstacles to peace to be meddling of foreign powers, socioeconomic backwardness in the Arab world, authoritarianism and aggressiveness in Arab nationalism, and acrimonious disunity among Arab rulers. (The courageous and secure Arab ruler presumably would make peace with Israel, putting his people's needs ahead of "political" pressures.[25]) What seems striking about these beliefs is that they remind one of the old doctrines, appearing to be updated versions of the latter; there is, as in the old days, more than a grain of truth in what they affirm but, as before, also no suggestion that something genuinely Arab, or inherent in the historic relationship to Arabs, generates this opposition.

The survival of old doctrines in their pristine form was naturally largely limited to the older Jews; one finds them even in the post-1967 period, as when a veteran diplomat invokes again the Golden Era of Islamic-Jewish history and other familiar arguments.[26] This is particularly likely still in the dogmatic left; thus, Peretz Merhav, restating the old faith in untarnished form: "This writer, and many others in the Jewish Zionist camp and among the Israeli Arabs, believe in the second choice: that *there is no real conflict* and rather even a complementarity and symbiosis. We don't see any objective and inherent conflict, despite the misunderstandings, the mistakes and subjective involvements on both sides between the historic aspirations of Arab nationalism—unity, independence, renaissance, development and progress—and Jewish nationalism—the return to Zion, ingathering of exiles, independence, renaissance, a healthy social and economic structure, development and progress. Any deviation from this assumption turns Jewish (or Arab) nationalism into reactionary and militaristic chauvinism and threatens the fulfillment of both sides' genuine aspirations."[27] One finds the old faith surviving among Zionist old-timers abroad and, because of their insulation from Middle Eastern reality, even among the younger Jews there.[28]

The existence of generational differences in attitudes toward Arabs and peace is additional reason for thinking of the erosion of old doctrines in Israel as discontinuous, rather than proceeding in measured, uniform doses. Pragmatic and anti-ideological, the native young in Israel seem to have resisted these doctrines by and large, often clearly repudiating them. Thus, Amos Oz, a writer who is not otherwise representative of the political orientations of his generation: "It is a gross mistake and an oversimplification to believe that the dispute is based on a misunderstanding. It is based on full and complete understanding: we returned and offered the Arabs goodwill, good neighbourliness and co-operation, but that was not what they wanted from us. They wanted us to abandon the establishment of the Jewish State in the Land of Israel, and that is a concession we could not make and shall never be able to make. It is the utmost of naivety to believe that but for the quarrelmongering of foreign elements and the backwardness of reactionary regimes, the Arabs would be able to realize the positive sides of Zionism and straightaway fall on our necks in brotherly love.

"The Arabs did not oppose Zionism because they failed to understand Zionism, but because they understood it only too well. And that is the tragedy: the mutual understanding *does* exist. We want to exist as a nation, as a Jewish State. They do not want that State. This cannot be glossed over with phrases. High-minded loving-kindness of the Brit Shalom style will not help, as little as the political acrobatics of the Semitic Action; and Arab tactics such as claiming to be satisfied if the refugees are given their rights will not either. Any search for a way out must start from the open-eyed realisation of the full extent of the dispute: a tragic conflict of tragic power."[29]

Because of the traumatic quality of the war of 1967, and especially the crisis leading up to it, one might expect it to have influenced perhaps even more than previous wars Israeli attitudes on Arabs and peace. We know that the crisis and war found Israelis emotionally unprepared, despite their acquiescence in a lingering condition of no peace; above all, the rapid succession of diplomatic and military events, beginning in mid-May of 1967, destroying within a few days popular premises concerning international guarantees and other props of security, plunged masses of Israelis into a state of emotional disarmament, in which the spectacle of abandonment by the gentiles coupled with the mounting frenzy in Arab countries produced a so-called Holocaust mentality. Israelis (and Jews in the Diaspora) believed they faced a situation similar to that of Europe's exposed and deserted Jewry in World War Two.[30] The trauma did result in much more affective attitudes toward Jews abroad, even among the previously unsympathetic native young; a deepening of the Jewish identity among the secular native young also followed; and there have been other significant changes in Israeli attitudes in its wake.[31]

Whether or not the 1967 war had a greater impact on attitudes in Israel toward Arabs and peace than the first major war, in 1948, is uncertain, but the June war formed a watershed of sorts without question. If the essential structure of attitudes was already set before the war—indeed, even the political institutionalization of the so-called hawk-dove controversy has not much changed after the 1967 war[32]—what impact did the war itself have on attitudes toward Arabs and peace? There is no question that hard and pessimistic attitudes had become only more so in the postwar era and that more individuals shared them. While surveys fail to show a measurable widening in the ranks of adherents to a policy of firmness toward the Arab states soon after the war, at least not until 1970 (see below), there are indications of a deepening sense of pessimism concerning chances for peace occurring sooner; the failure of peace to materialize on the morrow of the Arabs' greatest debacle snuffed out some illusions that had long lurked beneath the sense of resignation.

"In the first few weeks after the war," wrote Yael Dayan, "came a realization of the most horrible of facts—war does not automatically terminate in a peace treaty. People who were sure this was their last war were shocked into the admission that this may not be so, that a country that fought in order to obtain peace found itself as far from it as before."[33] A university student offered another version, saying that "in the circumstances of the present day, there are only two ways to attain peace—both through violence and destruction, not through creative effort. The one way is annihilation of the Jewish State. . . . The second way to peace, was, in my opinion, wide open to us in the Six Day War. We missed it. It was a destructive path to peace. We could have squeezed the enemy until he cried: 'Enough.' " Another student, from a pro-Communist family, averred on the same occasion that the war had changed his mind on the possibilities of peace: "For many years, and especially during the 1956 Sinai campaign, I thought that Israel's whole foreign policy was misguided, that our attitude to the Arabs was all wrong. Up to the Six Day War I believed we weren't doing enough to win the goodwill of the Arabs, we weren't ready to make enough concessions to bring peace closer. If you ask me today whether I see a way to peace, my answer will be very pessimistic. I see no way—not with the Arabs screaming day in, day out, dawn and dusk, that Israel has no right to exist. No right!"[34] These views were quite representative of the native young Jews in Israel.

With deepening pessimism regarding peace, the 1967 war also brought, especially to the native young in Israel, an unprecedented sense of confidence and security, primarily because of their performance in the war and the radical change in Israel's strategic position (new borders) the war produced. The implications of this change for peacemaking and relations to Arabs are immediately apparent. As for the first, Yael Dayan accurately defined the fateful consequence within a year of the war: "The 1967 victory did not give us peace but it gave us security. More, it elevated security to a level that if one is asked to choose between it and peace, we'd rather have security. In other words, 'Peace at any price' does not exist anymore. Peace without secure borders is out of the question and full security without peace is a possible way of life in this area for us.

"The war gave us confidence. The [Arab] cartoons which show us drowning in the sea hang in Israeli homes while bikini-clad girls stretch out on our beaches and tourists photograph the burnt hulks of Egyptian tanks in the Sinai. We know we did it alone, we know that short of the help of the Jews in the Western world, we cannot count on others doing the job for us—be it war or peace—and for once isolation is not associated with brave suicide but a brave, possible survival."[35]

As for relations to Arabs, personal security had, as usually happens, enhanced toleration of differences, of the alienness of the latter. A more relaxed attitude toward Arabs as individuals had already distinguished the *sabra* (native) from the immigrant before the war of 1967. An elaborate experiment in intergroup relations has suggested the same conclusion that more informal observation also indicates: the *sabra* appears self-confident yet eager to conciliate the Arab. "The Jewish participants had gained enormously in self-confidence from military confrontations with the Arabs. Nevertheless, the moral and ideological components of Zionist settlement of the country did not permit casual indifference to the hardships created for Arabs in the country. The themes were reiterated—'How to be just while remaining strong?' 'How to diminish personal suffering which stems from the "tragic conflict" of interests and aspirations?' The aims of accommodation, of easing restrictions, of reducing suspicion was a major preoccupation."[36] It would be interesting to compare the treatment of Arabs caught on the Israeli side of the ceasefire lines in 1967 with the situation after 1948: openness and freedom of movement, with deliberate risk-taking, for Arabs on both sides of the lines in the more recent case (Dayan's "open bridges" policy) *versus* confinement and anxious control of Israeli Arabs within small pockets ("military rule") following the first major war. The fact that then the Israelis' exhilaration was tempered by disbelief in their triumph (many termed it miraculous) may help explain the contrasting policies toward Arabs.

The structure of Israeli (Jewish) attitudes concerning the crucial problems of peacemaking and perceptions of Arab hostility has been revealed by systematic surveys since the 1967 war as follows: the overwhelming majority tends toward very pessimistic evaluations of the chances for peace with all or part of the Arab world in the near future;[37] an equally high percent (over 70%) believe, however, that important factors in the Arab world indeed desire peace with Israel on terms the latter could live with;[38] despite the pervasive pessimism (nearly 90% believe the Arab states are not now ready to talk about real peace),[39] two-thirds felt Israel must reply affirmatively to every Arab initiative for direct or indirect negotiations.[40] This cautious yet skeptical *attentisme* was reflected in a determination to hold onto occupied territories, without jeopardizing conceivable avenues of peacemaking by premature Jewish settlement in some territories; after the summer of 1969 there was actually a significant rise in cautionary attitudes in this respect.[41]

Regarding the disposition of territories conquered in the 1967 war, the surveys clearly conflict with foreign beliefs. Ranking Israeli Jews in the order of readiness for territorial concessions, a survey put 6% in "extreme concession"; 21% in "moderate concession"; 52% in "slight concession"; and 21% in "categorical no concession."[42] (The so-called Rogers Plan of 1969, envisioning only insubstantial alterations in the 1949 armistice lines, thus satisfied only some 6% of Israeli Jews.) Ranking specific territories in order of popular determination to retain, there was first, as expected, East Jerusalem, followed by Golan, then Sharm al-Sheikh, Sinai, the Gaza Strip, and lastly the West Bank.[43] The contingency of heavy American pressure made little, if any, difference; where it had a certain effect (concerning the last three territories), there was a markedly weak attachment to begin with anyway. In sum, Israeli Jews were not prepared to surrender East Jerusalem, the Golan Heights, and Sharm al-Sheikh even for peace, but inclined toward moderate concessions in the areas of the Gaza Strip, the West Bank, and Sinai, even when envisaging heavy American pressure.[44] There seemed to be no appreciable correlation between one's optimism on peace and readiness to withdraw from occupied territories.[45]

Israeli Jewish perceptions of chances for peace with the Arabs were unrelated to sex; only weak differences obtained according to age, the youngest (up to twenty-nine) and some of the old (fifty to sixty) displaying somewhat more pessimism than the rest; a weak linkage existed between pessimism and the degree of religiosity (identification with Jewish orthodoxy); education seemed unrelated on the whole to pessimism; ethnic background was somewhat significant, with *sabras* of Afro-Asian descent being a little more pessimistic on peace than all others.[46] There were virtually no differences with respect to sex, age, or ethnic background, concerning readiness to withdraw from occupied territories, either in principle or in respect to particular territories.[47] Religiosity and education made for some interesting differences regarding specific aspects of the withdrawal issue: the university-educated were most willing to make extreme territorial concessions, while the least educated seemed almost totally unprepared for such concessions;[48] the higher the educational achievement, the greater the willingness to abandon the West Bank rather than the Gaza Strip;[49] religiosity produced the opposite inclination.[50] Concerning support for a policy of firmness toward Arab states, ethnic background seemed significant: *sabras* of Afro-Asian descent were more supportive (80%) among *sabras* in general (72%); the least supportive (65%) were those born in Europe and America; a major increase in popular support for the policy came nearly three years after the war.[51]

Additional insight into the structure of Israeli attitudes in the same period may be gained from impressionistic, albeit imaginative, analyses, notably the study of "annexationism" by Georges R. Tamarin.[52] He identified one variable as the left-right political spectrum (see Table I). While not all anti-annexationists in Israel were dogmatic leftists, virtually all dogmatic leftists there were vigorous anti-annexationists. The role of dogmatic leftism in molding orientations toward peace and Arabs had been discussed by Merlin even before the 1967 war and the ensuing annexationism controversy. He found left-wing leaders and writers treating "the problem of peace with Arabs not only on the merits of the issue and from the exclusive point of view of Israeli interests but also from ideological considerations."[53] This entailed dichotomizing the Arab world into progressive-revolutionary and reactionary camps and putting hopes for peace almost entirely on the former, whereas in reality what moderation there is vis-à-vis Israel in the Arab world is more congenial to such conservative and pro-Western regimes as the Lebanese, Jordanian, or Tunisian. This makes for ambivalence and for additional complication of an already overly complicated matter; peace in the Middle East is elusive enough, even without adding to it special doctrinaire (pro-Soviet, neutralist, socialist) desiderata. *Mapam*, the most rigidly dogmatic political movement in Zionism, which belongs overwhelmingly in the decidedly anti-annexationist

TABLE I

Anti-annexationists (Doves)	Moderate Annexationists	Unconditional Annexationists (Hawks)
Movement for Peace and Security		Land of Israel Movement
Mapam		Eldad's Circle
Independent Liberals		Herut-Liberal Bloc (Gahal)
Haolam Haze		Free Center
Israel Communist Party (Maki)	Canaanites	
Israel New Left	National Religious Party	
New Communist List (Rakah)	Agudat Yisrael (?)	
Mazpen		Etatistic List
Labor Party (Mapai-Ahdut Avoda-Rafi)		

(Reproduced by permission: Tamarin, *The Leap Forwards—Into the Past*, p. 21)

camp, may serve to illustrate some intellectual processes rather typical of the whole camp. Basic ideological tenets concerning Arab-Jewish fraternity, inherent harmony, etc., have been preserved over the years, as if events in the real world could not possibly affect their verity, as was the case with dogma concerning the Soviet Union.

"The idealization of the Soviet Union as a whole," wrote a social scientific investigator of a *kibbutz* affiliated with *Hashomer Hatzair* (since 1954 practically identical with *Mapam*), "is equalled only by the glorified picture of its leaders. The author heard chaverim [members] discussing Stalin—his personality, his achievements, his brilliance, the miracles he had wrought in Russia—in the same glowing terms and with the same awe that a *chassid* [a follower of a wonder-working rabbi, or rebbe] would speak of a *rebbe*. For many chaverim, Stalin was more than a charismatic leader—he was a semidivine father, all-good and all-wise, whose every decision was to be accepted as true and good.

"This idealization of the Soviet Union and its leadership stands in marked contradiction to the *kibbutz* ideals of liberty, and great intellectual effort is required to reconcile this obvious contradiction. As is true in any theological system, such an effort can succeed only if it is based on a profound faith or on an intense 'will to believe.' The chaverim, like Tertullian, must be willing to assert, ultimately, that they believe because 'it is absurd.' For it is absurd that a society which is so passionately devoted to the cause of freedom should believe in a dictatorship, and it is absurd for Zionists to place their faith in a country which has been consistently anti-Zionist. . . . It has banned Hebrew culture, imprisoned Zionist leaders, and refused permission to Jews to migrate to Israel or to have any contact with world Jewry. But, say the chaverim, this *apparent* anti-Zionist behavior is not *really* anti-Zionist; it only appears that way to those who do not understand its true motivations. . . ."[54]

This "will to believe" makes Arab-Jewish harmony true and indisputable; if it does not *appear* to be, the failure must be due to extraneous malignancy, the Israeli government usually being the most likely source, probably because it is close at hand and often in the hands of another party anyway. While that government is far from immune to criticism, what characterizes the behavior of *Mapam* and related groups is the fact that their criticism of the government in matters of war and peace is actually a premise rather than some conclusion: The absence of peace—sadly a permanent condition in contemporary history—means that the Jerusalem government is doing *something* wrong. This position curiously aligns *Mapam* and related groups with the ideological devil—the imperial powers, the religious missionaries, the capitalist press abroad, and others also rigidly faulting the Jerusalem government for troubles in its part of the world. Thus obtains the rare spectacle of journalistic organs, otherwise alive with the spirit of proletarian international revolutionism, warmly featuring pronouncements by spokesmen for foreign churches, oil lobbies, and establishmentarian types of other stripes.

Dogmatic leftism tends to preserve doctrines concerning Arab-Jewish relations that have become obsolete or have entirely disappeared in other segments of Israeli society. While the mass of Israelis has abandoned the old doctrine, "Good neighbors rather than good borders," in the assumption that the Arabs do not now, nor are they likely in the foreseeable future to, qualify as such neighbors, the doctrine persisted undaunted in *Mapam* and related groups. "Cannot Israel be defended better within more limited borders by the intensive use of modern technology?"[55] was a typical argument in these circles in the debate on territories after 1967. What is distinctive about such arguments from the doctrinaire left is not that they questioned the military worth of particular borders, which others often did, but that a special moral valuation was placed on living dangerously, preserving virtue, however grotesque the security conditions.

A particular dilemma of the doctrinaire left, the self-styled peace movement's core, was produced by undesirable trends both abroad and at home. At home the "wave of the future" has been steadily engulfed in a rising tide of right-leaning sentiments;[56] not only have socialist partners in the labor movement adopted the "fascist" policies of revisionism, in their shift to a hard line toward Arabs, but orientations of the major likely group of immigrants to Israel promised to deepen that trend still further. All indications pointed to a strong rightward tendency by recently arrived Soviet Jews in Israel; even those affiliating with moderate labor groups endorsed "hawkish" positions on peace and the Arabs.[57] The left's disappointment here was all the more painful, for its cherished hope that precisely this Jewry, nurtured in the Country of Socialism, would ultimately help redeem Israel from reactionary failings.

Since the right wing of *Mapam* (with Yacov Hazan) had also developed moderately annexationist tendencies, some militant pacifists faulted *Mapam*'s standing in the peace movement. Uri Avneri thus excluded *Mapam* from the "active" peace movement, including instead *Rakah* (the Arab communist party of Israel), a part of the nationalist Jewish communist party *(Maki)*, the *Siah* (Israeli new left: left-wingers who have bolted *Mapam*), his own *Haolam Haze* (radical, nonleftist), and diverse bourgeois and other notables grouped in the peace list.[58] The electoral strength of this movement was put at about five percent (Arab voters included). The "passive" peace movement, comprising professors, artists, leftist and centrist politicians, journalists, and others was more diffuse and more broadly based, yet even so the whole movement was under normal circumstances only a small minority in Israel. Looking abroad, the doctrinaire left component of the peace movement was particularly embittered by the militant anti-Zionism of doctrinaire leftists the world over. Their isolation abroad was yet another burden placed on the already strained "will to believe."

The mere mention of nonsocialists in the peace movement suggests that the left-right variable alone would not do. (An interesting deviation from it is the leftist *Achdut Haavoda* [formerly united with *Mapam*, lately reunited with *Mapai* and *Rafi* in the new Labor Party], whose leaders favor firmness toward Arabs and resist territorial concessions, in some cases as strenuously as the extreme right.) The fact that many political parties were internally divided on just these issues has impressed Tamarin with the importance of ethnic background and age group as more important variables than left-right. His classification (see Table II) was supported by systematic opinion surveys as far as the younger *Sephardi* and Oriental group and possibly also the younger Orthodox were concerned. Concerning the old *Sephardi* "aristocracy" (scions of old, prestigious *Sephardi* families) and the German and other Central European immigrants, substantial casual observation would seem to support Tamarin as well. As far as the latter are concerned, a "German" name indeed made for a fair presumption that the person tended toward dovish positions; such names were frequently found among academic pacifists and the bourgeois notables in such groups as New Outlook; the relatively few militant anti-annexationists in the religious camp were almost exclusively "German." The Independent Liberals, mostly of Central European and German descent, were firmly dovish for the most part; the Progressive Party, their previous institutional formation, and the *Aliya Hadasha*, the original—and virtually all-"German"—version of the party were each, along with the doctrinaire leftist *Hashomer Hatzair,* the most faithful supporters among all parties of *Weizmannism,* and of the man himself, during his active political life. (It is of some interest in this connection that the German Jews in America were deemed—unlike the *Sephardis,* who preceded them here, and the Eastern European wave that followed—particularly nonaggressive in matters Jewish on the American scene. Their attitude was described as "a blend of defensiveness, apology, and anxiety—a condition expressed by the Yiddish word *tsitter,* whose very sound suggested trembling and uncertainty. . . . In the case of American Jews *tsitterdik* signified edg-

TABLE II

Non-annexationists and Anti-annexationists	Annexationists
German and other Central European immigrants (regardless of age)	East-European veteran immigrants (60 and over) and their elder (40 and over) Sabra sons (this group includes also the "Canaanites")
Old Sepharadi "aristrocracy" (over 55 years)	
Young secular Sabras (below 35 years) and especially the youngest of this group	Younger Sepharadi and Oriental (immigrants and Sabras; below 50 years)
	Younger Orthodox (except the fanatically anti-Zionists); while the older NRP establishment, 45 and over are mostly moderate annexationists

(Reproduced by permission: Tamarin, *The Leap Forwards—Into the Past*, p. 24)

iness about any Jew's behavior which might through glib generalization reflect badly on the position of all American Jews." German Jews were known to the East European Jews as *Yahudim*, a somewhat derisive term signifying economic success, acculturation, and anxiety lest one's Americanism be compromised or questioned because of other Jews' assertiveness. Their reaction to Zionism was negative, almost violently so; the idea of Jewish nationhood anywhere elicited sharp denunciations and remarks, such as the one from Dr. Isaac Mayer Wise, that Russian Jews loved to deride: "We want no Jewish princes or government. We prefer President Hayes to a Jewish prince."[59] (The militantly anti-Zionist American Council for Judaism, incidentally, is still alluded to by American Jews as the *Yahudim*.)

The young secular (*Ashkenazi*, or Europe-descended) *sabras* were categorized as non-annexationists and anti-annexationists with reservations. While they revealed a marked indifference to "historical rights" (they *know* that Tel Aviv is theirs but doubt that Hebron is), they also tended toward an unemotional and pessimistic view of

Arabs and a marked reliance on power. Thus, a much greater percentage of *sabras* (50%) than of veterans endorsed the possibility of a Palestinian state for Arabs; yet more than 70% only shortly before backed Jewish settlement in Hebron, situated in the area envisaged for just such a state.[60] Secular *sabras* displayed more empathy for Arabs than veterans, as well as more toughness toward them; they believed the Arab opposition to them to be genuine and justified, in Arab terms—if they were Arab, many said, they would feel and act as *fedayeen*—and precisely because of this they were determined to leave the Arabs as few options as possible for hostile acts. A unit of reservists, mainly of this group, recounts Tamarin, camping near Ramallah (a town on the West Bank), was engaged in small talk, when one soldier pointed to the town and asked whether it was "ours"; the others agreed it was Arab, purely Arab. Should it, therefore, be returned to Arab rule? Not at all, they concluded; security demanded that the town be retained.[61] Their epitome was Moshe Dayan, with whom, Tamarin felt, as did many others, "the Sabra generation [as a whole] identifies as with nobody else."[62]

The secular *Ashkenazi sabras*, unlike the religious and *Sephardi* native young, would not feel a great loss if Hebron were returned; but nationalism and security-mindedness aligned them with the latter in backing settlement in that "town of the patriarchs." They would, like most Israelis, insist that everything be done to explore possibilities of peace, and perhaps more than many others reiterate also that "one cannot trust an Arab."

Most Israeli Jews had little personal contact with Arabs and knew little of them and of Islam, which has molded the Arabs. They thought not well of them, as cruel, cowardly, dishonest, though a substantial minority felt that Arabs were not less diligent than Israeli Jews;[63] the epithet *Arabush* expressed widespread lack of appreciation for the traits these Jews saw in Arabs. Some Israeli Jews shunned personal proximity to Arabs, however brief; about half did not want to live next door to Arabs; most objected to intermarriage with them. Afro-Asian Jews, though sharing in the Arabs' Middle Eastern culture and frequently engaging in social intercourse with Arabs in Israel, were more antagonistic to them; *sabras* were least antagonistic.[64] For the latter, it seems, the veterans' sense of awe, envy, and humility of the alien toward the Arab rooted in the soil of the country was *passé*, as were their dreams of socialist brotherhood. A survey of contemporary Israeli writers suggests that Arabs had ceased to be a moral problem, turning instead after 1948 into a claustrophobic, nightmarish situation.[65] Judging from the more recent literary output of the young, there has emerged among them a fashion of romanticizing Arab characters, heroic yet demonic, and envisioned as vengefully abusing Israeli Jewish characters.[66] Among them and other groups, especially the youngest sons and daughters of the secular *Ashkenazi* elite, the Arabs are indeed a moral problem.

Israeli conceptualization of their conflict with Arabs remained even after 1967 curiously unconcerned with their identity prior to the disintegration of the Ottoman Empire. Even among members of Israel's educated class, the Arabs of the region were at that point not recognized as *Sunni* Muslims in a *Sunni* Muslim dominion, but rather some adventitious element of as yet undetermined status. The dispute thus sprang for them full-blown, like Athena from Zeus' head, with the juxtaposition of two yet untried nationalisms, Arab and Jewish. Discourse on Arabs in an intellectual climate that ignored or understated their Islamic matrix was naturally enough marked by a tendency to exaggerate perceptions of variability among them regarding hostility to Jewish statehood (both the differences among Arabs in this respect and their significance were overstated) and by another tendency to exaggerate the role of the leaders' manipulation of the masses against Israel and the role of economic rationality in the structure of Arab motivations in the struggle with Israel. Hence, an inclination to mock generalizations about Arabs in respect to hostility to Israel; the variation of attitudes to Israel among them presumably is too wide to speak of "the Arabs"—a familiar form of sarcasm in the literature. (The real irony lies in the fact that it is precisely in a Middle Easterner's identification with "the Arabs" that we find a crucial variable in hostility to Israel.) In view of the Israeli conceptualization of the conflict as political in a narrow sense (nationalism, indoctrination, manipulation, failure of leadership, etc.), the severity of Arab antagonism naturally puzzled many Israelis, who resorted in consequence to explanations of Arabs as somehow extrahuman. (Hence, the appeal among them, says one Israeli Arabist, of the thesis of a peculiar, "Arab," psychology, which "implies that, when God distributed reason to mankind, the Arabs were absent.")[67] Many intellectuals in Israel tried to make sense of the conflict by straining hard for "balance" (Arabs have hallucinations, but so have Israelis, etc.),[68] thus obscuring real differences between the antagonists,which are quite extraordinary in some respects, after all (in relation to violence and war, for instance).

There was little new in all this, for Jews in Palestine had all along been better at coping with actual manifestations of Arab hostility than at theorizing about its roots. Even after 1967 most were more concerned with the hardship of carrying on in the face of seeming hopelessness of their relationship to the Arab world than with intellectual exercise. The curious lack of correlation between optimism on peace and willingness to withdraw from occupied territory revealed in opinion surveys[69] apparently reflected the willingness of certain Israelis to abandon strategic territory despite any lack of conviction in the peaceable intent of Arabs, in some cases because of moral considerations. This applied to part of Israel's artistic and academic communities. Their personal estimate of Arab intentions toward Israel may be gathered from their earlier pessimistic insistence that the war of 1967 was fought to avert annihilation; but as the postwar deadlock lingered, and hopes for a settlement appeared to vanish, their reading of Arab attitudes toward Israel became increasingly more hopeful. In at least some cases it is quite obvious that this shift expressed willingness to accept the risks inherent in territorial and other arrangements premised on overstated Arab moderation, in preference to the feared decay of Israel's moral fiber in a continued domination of hostile populations.[70] "The loss of hope chills the heart, and there are those in embattled Israel who fear their state may become a modern Sparta, and that Israelis may forget the Torah's essential teaching: 'That which is hateful to you, do not unto others.' "[71] The deviant position of many Israeli artists and intellectuals may be explained also by the fact that an important reference group for their political attitudes was located outside the country, among leftist Jewish artists and intellectuals in the West, invariably critical of majority Israeli positions on vital political matters.[72]

An exchange between Israeli Jewish students at a university symposium delineated the cleavage over "hope." The pessimism and dogged determination to persist among his peers struck one student as sheer despair, which he simply refused to accept. "My own general attitude to the issue of peace is, or has become, ambivalent. On the one side, in the light of all that is being written and said in the Arab world, I tell myself in all sobriety that peace lies way over the horizon, out of reach. As against that, I am body and soul with our possibly naïve doves in Israel who cherish peace above all things and who assure us that it is within our grasp, if only we unbend enough." (The speaker added that he would not wish to live in Israel if indeed there were no hope for peace.) "I wish to endorse nearly everything Zvi has said with such beautiful lucidity," replied another. "But while I think as he does, I cannot follow his final reasoning. Myself I am pessimistic about peace. Zvi sees peace somewhere in the offing. From an identical assessment of the situation we arrive at different conclusions. Perhaps Zvi can explain why he thinks there is a prospect of peace." Zvi replied: "He doesn't think, he is certain, because war cannot last forever. War solves nothing, and people are in the last resort rational."[73]

There was little new even in the majority's manner of coping with "hopelessness," however. The process of Jewish renaissance in Palestine had been studded with apparently insoluble problems from its beginning, so much so that virtually all early Zionist theorists, Herzl and others, were thought, even by close friends, to be insane for proposing their plans. The settlers themselves never really faced up to the dilemma of living with the Arabs in one country, much less a Jewish state with possibly more Arabs than Jews; they built their castles on what the world saw as mere sand, yet with single-minded purposefulness. Then history seemed to take care of hopeless problems: Rabid anti-Semitism in Europe brought hitherto scarce manpower; the world war weakened the increasingly hostile British and greatly strengthened the *Yishuv*, economically and militarily above all else; the Soviet Union suddenly jettisoned implacable opposition to Zionism, not merely supporting Jewish statehood diplomatically, but also with vital arms, in the face of active British and Arab belligerence and an American embargo. (They again seemed to produce the incredible, by letting their Jews emigrate to Israel after the June war.) The Arabs of Palestine, just as suddenly and incredibly, emptied large areas of the country in 1948. From the Jewish perspective Zionist history thus appeared as an erratic and catastrophic problem-solver; nothing was really impossible so long as Jews did their work: "It is not important what the *goyim* (gentiles) say; what is important is what the Jews do."[74] In the aftermath of the June war they just pushed on with their work in the face of seeming hopelessness as before, settling in the Golan, building in East Jerusalem, laying a highway to Sharm el Sheik, firm in the belief that peace would eventually come pretty much on their terms, after all. The world may seem to line up against them, but they felt that history was on their side.

The October war has shaken that confidence. The gloom and even despondency that was soon obvious has been attributed by foreign observers to a number of upsetting events. The Arabs were not helpless, as they had seemed, and their surprising attack demonstrated an unsuspected organizational and even combat efficiency. But this was exaggerated abroad, as was the impact of Israel's casualties. While heavy for such a small country, these were in fact only about one-tenth the ratio suffered in the first major war, from which Israel emerged jubilant. Besides, the gloom had set in before the real extent of these losses was known. That the roots of the malaise went deeper was suggested by some of these observers, but the real feelings of Israelis remained mainly unknown to the world outside.

The urge to break with Jewish history had been a powerful drive behind resurgent Jewish nationalism in the last century. Powerlessness and lack of control over one's own fate were to be transcended by the "normalization" of the Jews and their achievement of sovereignty in their land. The reality of Israel among the nations never quite matched the ideal, but Jews could do things in their own country that were unthinkable elsewhere and even in the international arena they had a measure of influence disproportionate to their meager numbers and resources and could act in behalf of Jews abroad in terms of power rather than traditional appeals to charity. Their military ascendancy triggered after 1967 an unprecedentedly independent political posture, and successful defiance of their American ally (and the other superpower) for several years induced a triumphant sense of assertiveness in a hostile world.

For the Israelis there is no doubt about when the gloom set in. Thus, one "said that a 'mood of depression' set in when the people realized that neither Washington nor Moscow would ever allow Israel to achieve a decisive victory over the Arab states."[75] Another: "I think the traumatic experience of the Israelis was not the sudden unexpected attack on October 6, but the Russian-American ultimatum on October 22. Namely, you are not allowed to win any war anymore. This war, this game, is over. We can help you not to be defeated, but you are not allowed to end the war and defeat the enemy."[76] Standing alone in a hostile world, opting for Arab oil over Jewish blood, was an essentially familiar and even inspiring condition. But having the gentiles also tie one's hands before one's tormentors was to be back in the ghetto, to what had been "normal" for Jews for centuries. "When my parents came here in 1935, 38 years ago," recounted Amos Oz, "they didn't come here because they, God knows, because they wanted to renew the glory of the past. They came simply because they were rejected by every single country in Europe. I was nine years old in 1948, which was obviously much more desperate than this war, much more desperate. I remember my father saying to me that if Zionism doesn't prove to be a better way of life for a Jew, at least it is a better way of death. Now I wouldn't like to be misunderstood. I don't have the feeling that we are doomed, that the whole thing is lost or something. But basically I feel that Zionism in 1973 is just what it was in 1903, a desperate attempt to survive. That's the first thing beyond everything else."[77]

Whatever the intent of Kissinger's actions in the war—denying urgent supplies then denying victory—the result was injury at the very roots of Israeli morale and consciousness. The mixture of bitterness and despair could make for meek submission to foreign dictation or catastrophic outburst or both. The history of the *Yishuv* and the state has been characterized by alternating periods of emotional depression and exultation, the transitions often being markedly the outcome of wars. In the more recent past the triumphant War of Independence initiated a "fat" period lasting through the 1950's. The Sinai campaign of 1956, after which military success was transformed by the superpowers into Arab diplomatic triumph, was followed, after brief excitement, by a depressed period. On the eve of the stunning June war, which turned Israel sharply toward optimism, their country was seen by Israelis as actually regressing into some dead end.

The new period of depression has all the earmarks of the previous ones. As before, the mood is reflected in the national economy, now greatly troubled and down from the exhilarating growth rates of the previous interwar period. Furthermore, immigration to Israel is down (as much as 33% in the first six months of 1974)[78] while interest in emigration has risen. (Even the level of mental health appears to have dropped immediately after the war.)[79] There is a marked tendency toward privatism and apathy in the population and almost nausea at the thought of still more war, but also a certain resignation that the Arabs' new aggressiveness would lead to just that.

Despite some brief fluctuations in the war and immediately afterward—first in a hawkish direction, then back—the essential attitudes on peace and territory have been remarkably unaffected by the war some said had changed everything. Soon after the war 84% of Israelis expressed the belief that the Arabs intended to destroy their state, substantially the same proportion as before. At the height of the war only 19% were willing to return parts of the Sinai to Egypt, but the ratio soon returned to the more normal 52%.[80] (The figure some six months before the war was actually 59%.)[81] Israeli attitudes on retention of territory appear altered by the war only in a tactical sense, in that portions of occupied land deemed anyway unessential for security or other reasons are more likely to be traded for periods of nonbelligerency. Otherwise little change has taken place. "The attitudes and views which developed in Israel between the June 1967 and October 1973 wars," concluded a recent study, "provide the basis for post-1973 war negotiations for an Arab-Israeli settlement."[82] Noting the persistence of these and other political orientations on the eve of the first postwar national elections (which the voting confirmed), despite the shock of war, the Tel Aviv *Middle East Intelligence Survey* was moved to aver, "The More It Changes the More It Is the Same."[83] One year after the war, the major change in domestic politics appears to have been in the personnel at the top, chiefly in that younger men replace some older leaders.

4

MIRAGE IN THE DESERT— DIPLOMATS, JOURNALISTS, AND OTHER STRANGERS

THE nature of the Arab-Israeli conflict is obscured in wide circles by a popular conception of the struggle in terms of a simple general model of conflicts, rather than through the particular facts of the Middle Eastern confrontation. In this familiar view the conflict arises from opposing, but adjustable, claims, the proper balancing of which would yield a solution. To strike this balance between the sides is the job of diplomacy; since there surely exists an appropriate formula, it just must be discovered. The fact that the conflict has resisted the application of an apparently endless series of ingenious and esoteric formulations for so long—far from undermining the theory—only elicits greater determination to press on with the search, which has already produced two Nobel Peace laureates (Bunche and Pearson). The elusive nature of the right formula is all the more challenge to the imagination and ambition of diplomats. Naturally one must not confuse a mere conflict of interests between mutually tolerating contestants, where a "balancing of claims" applies, with one in which the very existence of one side is the issue— and after many years of exposure to the particular facts of the Arab-Jewish confrontation, who could have missed this point? So the tendency has been to "transform" the conflict into an ordinary one, by disclaimer, by asking one of the sides to deny that it seeks the elimination of the other. Thus, the proffered formulas invariably insist that the Arabs simply stop feeling the way they feel about Israel. Left once more with an ordinary political conflict through this maneuver, the search for the appropriately ambiguous phrasing of the felicitous compromise continues.

Success actually has already been proclaimed by fiat of the high council of the nations in the weary search for the elusive formula. The essential elements of the happy ending, say the believers (indeed, virtually all the world's statesmen), are to be discovered in the vaunted November Resolution of the Security Council. A virtual potpourri of clichés on the Middle East conflict, stated so ambiguously as to allow absolutely contradictory interpretations with ease, Resolution 242 may, indeed, be said to contain the solution to the conflict, much the same way as the perfect novel can be said to inhere in the alphabet.

It is obvious why the world of diplomacy should be particularly inclined toward such perception of the Arab-Israeli struggle. The disputes usually handled by diplomats are, indeed, ordinary conflicts and the craft of diplomacy emphasizes bargaining, rationality, and semantic mastery. Hence an inherent tendency to "conventionalize" their subject matter, further strengthened by the greater facility to handling tangible interests than elusive attitudes. A series of interviews with representatives of five African states at the United Nations conducted in the late spring of 1969 supports this proposition; it discloses that the African diplomats view the Arab-Israeli conflict as a conventional international conflict; it shows that they do not identify Arab claims in terms of Jewish statehood, but in connection with derivative issues, such as the impairment of personal rights of previous Arab inhabitants in the area.

A certain lack of sensitivity to the nature of the conflict may derive from the need of policy—where cognition follows "national interest," a form of "psycho-logic," disturbing cues being filtered out to fit with policy or other needs of the observer. Nadav Safran has called attention to such instance in the memoirs attributed to Nikita Khrushchev, "when, towards the end of his visit to Egypt in 1964, Nasser talks to him about the wounds that would never heal that were inflicted on the Arab people by the creation of Israel, he does not understand that Nasser is pleading for a change in the Soviet position supporting the *existence* of Israel and goes on to say that he certainly sympathised with Nasser's position and, before retiring, made speeches from time to time against Israel's aggressive policy."[1] A statesman to whom the alleged naïveté of the Russian cannot readily be attributed, Senator Fulbright, when championing policy presuming the existence already of a conventional conflict in the Middle East, likened the latter to no less than the relationship between the United States and Canada.[2] Westerners, Americans in particular, tend toward overly optimistic perceptions in conflict resolution anyway.[3]

The methodology of diplomacy itself desensitizes to the particular character of the conflict in the Middle East; diplomacy may be an honorable function, but it is not, to paraphrase Daniel Patrick Moynihan, a process of scientific inquiry. Diplomats mainly talk to other diplomats, exposing them to primary sources on *positions* over problems, not necessarily on the latter. The overconcern with what diplomats say and do leaves precious little concern for what it is they talk about. As a result, diplomats tend to be well informed on maneuvering over the Middle East conflict and are in this sense truly "insiders" and experts, along with some journalists; the things they frequently say about the conflict as such, however, even on the highest level, simply borders on the preposterous.[4] It is instructive that as an academic analyst Henry Kissinger pleaded with vigor against the common confusion of conventional conflicts with those involving "unlimited" objectives but as diplomat presents the most egregious latter case—in the Middle East—as perfectly amenable to solution by compromise.

The diplomatic process was illustrated in the work of an illustrious Indian practitioner of the art, Arthur Lall, an expert in the affairs of the United Nations, on the handling in the U.N. of the Middle East crisis in 1967.[5] The considerable analytical prowess of this observer is focused on diplomatic activity: He quantifies and classifies speeches, interventions, positions on issues, hints, etc.; references to the Middle East as such are few and vague. Achievement is measured in resolutions, votes, and other diplomatic output; there is much interest in pattern of semantics, yet diplomatic activity throwing light on the reality in the region under discussion passes unnoticed. This diplomatic analyst faces the sharp contrast between the prewar period—when, despite the alarming news from the region, it seemed virtually impossible to engage the United Nations in the crisis (the Arabs appeared to be in the ascendance)—with the almost incessant, frantic activity in that organization, from the moment the fact of Arab debacle becomes apparent. But he sees no lesson, no implications for the conflict or its handling in the United Nations. There simply prevails an assumption of the inherent desirability of diplomatic intervention—a not surprising bias among diplomats—and the possibility, voiced by some, that the United Nations may actually aggravate the conflict is shut out completely, as blasphemy. Within such conceptual framework there is, indeed, relevance for rhetorical interventions of statesmen, whose contribution in either brain or brawn to the conflict is dubious. The confusion of conflict with maneuvering over conflict obviously leads to the illusion of solution to the former when only diplomatic gaming is composed in resolutions. The realization of incoherence between diplomatic achievement and undiminished conflict—that despite the passage of resolutions, the conflict lingers as before—produces despondency in the writer, as in other diplomats, the resulting frantic behavior diminishing still further rationality in approaching the conflict.

What renders even the positions of the antagonists themselves uncertain sources of information on the conflict in Lall's diplomatic perspective is a characteristic worldliness of the profession; for not only is the significance of antagonists reduced by the injection of other diplomatic actors—the positions of Arabs and Israelis are ranged by the writer along with other opinions, rather than opposed in isolation, for more clarity—but, as diplomats, their positions are assumed also not to be genuine expressions of the conflict, the expectation being that exaggerated, extreme versions will be put out for tactical, bargaining reasons, at least initially. This may be true enough in general, but when genuine "extreme" positions are involved, as in nonconventional conflicts, the tendency is to discount them, thus distorting the true character of the dispute. The diplomat Lall thus perceives, on the one hand, Arabs retreating from the extreme position, destruction of the Jewish state, and, on the other, refuses strenuously to acknowledge or take seriously Israel's hard posture on secure borders.

On a deeper level worldliness assumes a particularly disingenuous character; for in the last resort Lall really expects the international "realities" to prevail, whatever the peculiar facts of the matter. The rhetorical solution of the conflict may or may not be captious, for he expects that superior power will impose it, making it real regardless. The writer thus extols the fairness and wisdom of Resolution 242, but really relies on pressure by great powers to actualize its virtue—without, with some delicacy belaboring the vulgar fact that the direction of such coercive effort is predictably one-sided in this conflict. The general inclinations of the craft thus combine with the particular Arab-Jewish power ratio in international politics to produce diplomatic perceptions of an unusually refractory conflict as an eminently soluble one. As an Indian national, therefore involved in a conflict (with Pakistan) similarly at variance with the conventional model of confrontations, the writer might be expected to look more closely at the particular facts of the Arab-Israeli conflict for explanation of the lingering absence of solution; he looks instead to the great powers to do what is expected of them, as do other diplomats, in an environment in which resources, wealth, alliances, numbers, and desirability are almost all on the side of the Arabs.

The diplomatic Middle East specialist does not usually transcend the limitations of other diplomats, for the customary acquisition of diplomatic expertise in this field itself enhances misperceptions of the conflict. Exceptions may be more apparent than real, as the interesting case of Charles W. Yost, formerly United States Permanent Representative to the United Nations, suggests. In an article in the January, 1968, issue of *Foreign Affairs* Yost acknowledged the irrational roots of the Middle East conflict, referring to the Arabs' inability emotionally to face up to Israel and to the traumatized Israeli reaction to them;[6] and in a book published later that year he stressed the imperative need in foreign affairs "to take account in both leaders and peoples of the factors of passion, frustration, and habit which spring from deep instincts and emotions, which are not subject to rational rebuttal. . . ."[7] Yet several months later he dismissed the Arabs' rejection of Israel as some erroneous conviction, as a "myth" that, once unmasked, can be made to vanish—one merely had to convince the Arabs of the error of their belief. And on this basis he advocated the policy, subsequently followed by the Nixon administration, of actively seeking a great-power solution to the Middle East conflict.[8]

It is difficult to explain how Middle Eastern "factors of passion" became "subject to rational rebuttal" so suddenly, but some answers may be suggested. Perhaps the awareness of the irrational factors in the Middle East was superficial in the first place; perhaps pressures to "settle" the conflict, if only to bring temporary relief from that part of the world, produced perceptions of the obstacle appropriate to the need; perhaps the greatly disproportionate weight of the Arabs in international politics demanded just such an outcome in any case. The last factor is the main reason for assuming that the resources of international diplomacy are not likely to be mustered or applied effectively against the Arabs even if the Arab-Israeli conflict would be recognized as "imperialistic," that is, involving the overthrow of the status quo, rather than seeking adjustments with the existing order.[9]

But actual diplomatic formulations assume the opposite, that Arab opposition to Israel is only secondary to, or derivative from, disputes over "adjustments" in water, borders, refugees, holy sites, etc. Acceptance of Israel presumably would follow automatically from the settlement of these disputes—to which, in consequence, serious efforts must be devoted—or is even attainable beforehand, by some semantic exercise. Thus, the essential ingredient in the diplomatic formulations at the United Nations and elsewhere since the June war, coupled with the demand that Israel evacuate captured territories, is the demand that the Arabs *renounce* their belligerency toward Israel.

The diplomatic perspective on the Arab-Israeli conflict seems naturally congenial to the profession of international law, whence comes not merely support for the diplomats' approach to the problem but actually special efforts at creative contributions toward solution, in the form of esoteric legalistic formulations.[10] Other foreign policy professionals tend to be guided by diplomatic specialists in this field as well. The place of the press is particularly important.

Journalism disseminates the diplomatic definitions of the Arab-Israeli conflict to wider audiences but also tends to propagate the same perspective by its editorial comment. A systematic analysis of the New York *Times* editorials since May, 1967, supports Robert Alter's allegation that this influential voice of American journalism presents the Arab-Israeli conflict as just another ordinary political conflict.[11] The *Times* strains for parity in its conception of the opposing sides and for striking a balance between them as policy. The opponents are generically equal, "nations" that wage "war," except that there are more of them on one side, while the other is temporarily better at waging war. There are at best hints at such disparities as may exist in culture, religious tradition, economic development, or social structure. There is no real reason why the two sides should not be able to compromise on the outstanding issues between them (borders, refugees, water, holy sites), given a modicum of reasonableness and some diplomatic ingenuity. Hence, peace is prevented by such factors as Soviet incitement of the Arabs or demagogic aspirations of Arab leaders, Nasser in particular, although the *Times* expressed disbelief that even he—unlike "an irresponsible Arab minority"—sought the elimination of the Jewish state.[12] The Israelis are by definition peaceful, and especially reasonable, although sometimes misguided, particularly when not heeding the advice of their "friends" (presumably Britain, the United States, the *Times*, and others). The stated positions of the antagonists are systematically euphemized, the best possible construction being put on their motives or actions. To illustrate, on March 15, 1972, King Hussein of Jordan stated his intention to convert his kingdom into a federated state, in which an autonomous Palestinian region would "consist of the West Bank and any other Palestinian territories to be liberated,"[13] the latter being the usual Arab reference to the dismantlement of Israel, which foreign observers in this case took to mean the Gaza Strip, also under Israeli rule. The *Times* editorially interpreted the statement as "a readiness to accept Israel and to abandon the extremist demand for the recovery of all Palestine"—certainly the opposite of what Hussein ostensibly said; and, if a true evaluation of royal intent, the Hussein statement would actually be a particularly inept manifestation of moderation being worded in rather ostentatious antagonism to the Jewish state. Perhaps there are good grounds for the editorial opposite assumption, but they are not revealed—a curious lapse for journalism, yet a natural enough step in statecraft. There would, indeed, seem to occur some confusion of roles in the editorial writing of this pivotal journal between observer of the diplomatic process and actual participant in it.

Whatever they say, the Arabs really want peace; if not, they ought to want it; the editorial writer consequently assumes such readiness regardless. When the *Times* avers in the above commentary that a truncated Palestine "should" satisfy Arab aspirations, it assumes that it "will." Extraordinary belligerency sometimes raises the *Times'* doubts in this respect, but they invariably fade quickly: A Sadat speech had such effect in June of 1971, the *Times* feeling reassured just a month later that he really sought peace with Israel, after all, only to utter new doubts about "the sincerity of President Sadat's expressed desire to reach a lasting peace with the Israelis," many months later, yet surely not for long, as always.[14] For Arab hostility to the Jewish state in the *Times* partakes of the character of plumbing: Like running water, it can be turned on and off at will.

Euphemizing the Israeli position involves utter refusal even to acknowledge undesired features, probably because the level of toleration of unreasonableness is much lower for Jews than for Arabs. A case in point was the sharp Israeli rejection of Ambassador Jarring's demand, in line with great power and other diplomatic pressure, for a commitment to total withdrawal from occupied territory prior to negotiations. The *Times* repeatedly represented the position as unserious, merely a bargaining ploy, explaining that it meant the opposite of what it said it meant, even that it was fully consistent with Jarring's own. (The *Times* here as diplomatic actor, supported an offensive in the United Nations and elsewhere for breaking the deadlock by optical illusion or semantic artifice.[15])

For the *Times* the long search for the elusive formula for the final resolution of the Arab-Israel conflict appeared to come to an end on November 22, 1967, with the adoption by the Security Council of Resolution 242. That the conflict should linger so long after this epochal achievement fills its editorials with ominous thoughts on the future of mankind. (When liberals come face to face with the intractability of the Arab-Israeli conflict, observed Nora Beloff, they turn panicky and argue that if there cannot be instant peace, there will be disaster.)[16] This has added the strength of despair to the already powerful trust the *Times* has placed all along in diplomacy, and especially in the United Nations. After the October war, the long search again appeared to come to an end with the "magic" of Kissingerian diplomacy, the *Times* announcing the existence even of a radically "new" Middle East.

For despite putting its best foot forward for the Middle East antagonists, the *Times'* editorial thinking deeply distrusts both sides as irresponsible, Balkan-type firebrands from whom the enlightened self-interest of the great powers must save themselves and all others. The editorials constantly evoke awesome visions of global holocaust, initiated by the compulsive arsonism of Arabs and Jews, dragging behind them helpless superpower patrons into the abyss. Hence, the incessant campaign for great power talks, agreement, enforcement, intervention, initiatives, proposals, etc. The *Times* propagates imagery that Bernard Lewis exposed and rejected before a Congressional committee in these words:

"Contrary to the general impressions which prevails [*sic*], the Arab-Israel dispute is not the main world issue in the Middle East. It is basically a local issue, a conflict between local interests. Left alone, the participants would no doubt eventually reach some *modus vivendi* and, even if they did not, it would not constitute a major menace to world peace. Neither side is capable of inflicting mortal wounds on the other. Without a settlement, the quarrel might smoulder on, like Cyprus or Kashmir, troublesome but not critical for the participants, and a minor nuisance to the rest of the world.

"In the Middle East as elsewhere, it is not small quarrels which inflame great power conflict, but rather the reverse. The major issue and the major threat in the Middle East is the encounter between the U.S.A. and the Soviet Union, to which perhaps China may soon be added. It is this global confrontation which affects and transforms local conflicts, otherwise trivial, making them both more difficult and more dangerous.

"In this age of mass media, it has become common practice to see and even to think in simplified images. Many of these are both false and dangerous.

"One which enjoys great popularity is the legal or forensic image, in which the great powers are seen as participants in a law suit, sometimes as judges, sometimes as advocates, with Israel and the Arab states in the role of clients or litigants.

"Both versions are inappropriate. The great powers are not sitting in judgment to administer the law or to dispense justice, but are there to protect and advance their own interests. All have basically this same purpose but pursue it with varying degrees of wisdom, decency, perseverance and ruthlessness. This fact is well known to the small powers.

"The role of the great powers is not that of advocacy either. Great power negotiation is not a courtroom. There is no judge, little law and the adversary runs no risk of disbarment for breaking the rules. And as for the client, if at all, he is so in the Roman not the modern sense of the word.

"Forensic imagery, though attractive to lawyers accustomed to the contentious procedures of Anglo-Saxon law and to viewers weaned on television courtroom drama, is profoundly irrelevant.

"Another such image derives from school and the nursery and depicts relations between powers in terms of big boys and small boys or teachers and pupils. The absurdity of this image of international relations is obvious once it is formulated. Large countries may possibly have wiser leaders than small countries, but this is not a necessary consequence of their size."[17]

One could explain the adoption by journalists of the diplomats' perspective on the Arab-Israeli conflict by citing the symbiotic relationship between them. The result, for whatever reason, is that two politically sophisticated groups tend toward superficial conceptualization of a problem, in at least one basic aspect of which the mass of Americans shows, ironically, a better grasp by sheer intuition. The condition is neither recent nor exclusive to the United States. A British observer wondered more than fifteen years ago "why no newspaper that I have seen has yet described the intensity of feeling in the Arab world against Israel. For some reason, none of the correspondents or any of our politicians seem to have appreciated what some of my colleagues and myself have found to be our most striking impression on visiting the Arab world today."[18]

This failure has not ceased to outrage and puzzle the Arabs and their friends in the West. Citing some instances of pressure and recrimination by offended Jewish individuals or organizations, they invariably suspect that vast conspiratorial networks systematically deny the public access to the truth as they see it. At times the sense of persecution is acute, as when the difficulty in tracing a certain volume, or the discovery of a vandalized tome—a common enough occurrence in public libraries—is adduced as serious evidence of a national or international book-burning campaign.[19] But Arab dismay is real enough; it is not difficult to imagine how one would react if one's feelings were denied or termed unworthy of serious attention. Besides, conspiratorial explanations appeal anywhere to the mass, and literate Arabs seem rather fond of the idea that the Jews really run things in this world, appearances to the contrary notwithstanding, a suspicion shared with many foreign sympathizers. (The notorious *Protocols of the Elders of Zion* is in several editions one of the most popular books in the Arab world.)

While certainly widespread enough abroad to suggest some occult manipulation on a grand scale, the misrepresentation of the Arabs' feelings is a more complex phenomenon than they and others realize, and surely less sinister. The earlier cited IPI Survey thus hinted at Zionist pressure in this connection, but the fact is that the press has consistently tended to misrepresent Arab feelings, whether or not it suited Zionism. On the Middle East conflict generally the Western press has leaned toward Zionism up to the June war in 1967 and away from it afterward—often involving the same journals published in the same locales with the same substantial Jewish populations. If Western editors simply suppressed true reports as offensive to Jewish readers and advertisers before, why do they fail to do so now? Their celebration of the Palestinian *fedayeen* has in recent years fallen little short of ecstasy. One gathers rather that the press responds to its own compulsions rather than to Jewish threats; the side that appeals more to Western prejudice and sympathy wins journalistic support. When Little David uttered pleasant sounds, one joined with him against "Arab propaganda." Now that he is rather Goliath and obdurate, one is alerted against "Israeli propaganda." Realistic appreciation of the conflict is resisted both before and after, though for different and, indeed, contradictory reasons. More sympathy for the Arab cause has not much sharpened journalistic sensitivity to Arab feeling; Arab readers now respond more effectively to editorial comment, and their letters hint as clearly as good manners allow that the real trouble with Israel lies much deeper than the editor surmises,[20] but the latter still is not listening.

Journalistic misrepresentation of the Middle East conflict extends beyond editorial comment into "straight" reporting. The slant in reportage has inclined heavily in recent years toward euphemization of antagonism. One pattern is the representation of code words of antagonism as expressions of moderation. The New York *Times* thus reports from Beirut a speech by the President of Syria calling for a "popular war of liberation to regain Arab land and rights," in which the Arabs should seek to recover territory lost in the 1967 war and the "re-establishment of the rights of the Palestinian people"[21]—the usual references to the disappearance of the Jewish state. The report goes on to explain this is *not* calling for the destruction of Israel. The press equally accepted current euphemisms even where that destruction was emphatically and explicitly asserted, as with the Palestinian *fedayeen*. In one such case it was explained that the latter should seek to replace Israel with "a secular state in Palestine, in which Moslems, Christians and Jews can live together"— without quotation marks, as if its meaning were perfectly obvious.[22] Another pattern is selective perception of news events, with a high visibility for "positive" developments. The reporting from Cairo by the *Times* thus followed closely for many months the Friday columns in *Al-Ahram* of its editor, Mr. Haikal, widely regarded as the alter ego of President Nasser; readers were acquainted repeatedly with Haikal's preference for a political settlement of the post-June war crisis with Israel; yet his candid discussion in the same columns of his position as a clever deception was omitted. Once the *Times* featured on its front page the news that Saudi Arabia had finally abandoned its ban on pilgrims to Muslim holy sites from Israel, explaining this act as additional indication that the Arabs are indeed moving toward accepting the Jewish state.[23] The news was a hoax. Misrepresentation of the ubiquitous Security Council Resolution 242 was systematic.

Particularly interesting is the fact that the Arabs themselves have made real contributions to the general unenlightenment concerning their position toward Israel. If diplomats and journalists tend to make light of Arab hostility, this is due in no small measure to their privileged access to Arab leaders, an experience which often induces cynicism about the leaders' public pronouncements and Arab politics in general. First, there is the notorious hyperbole of Arabic, a language rich in exquisite expression and seductive poesy, which has often been cited as proof that the Arabs do not really mean what they say against Israel. Many Westerners, particularly those claiming expertise because of some sojourn in the Middle East, when confronted with expressions of extreme hostility by Arabs assume a stance of knowing bemusement, as if in the presence of benign naughtiness. The argument is curious, for men tend to dream of things they crave, rather than things that are paltry; and particularly so in that the narcotic qualities of Arabic are invoked to dismiss Arab hostility, when loss of touch with reality may actually aggravate hostility.

Still, add to the bombast the more than usual corruption and mendacity in Levantine politics and the transparent manipulation of its mobs, and the worldly outsider finds it difficult to believe public statements in the Arab world. After only a few years on the spot, a high United Nations official described the formation of a military alliance of three Arab states surrounding Israel just prior to the Sinai war of 1956 as follows: "The alliance had been celebrated with the usual fantastical Arab oratory, whose theme was the recovery of the Arab homeland in Palestine and the extirpation of the State of Israel."[24] He did not say this to justify Israel's decision to go to war; it was actually part of his denunciation of Israel's action as cynical for citing the Arab alliance's threats as reason for taking action. Uttered by politicians who act like buffoons, dire threats at Israel often strike the worldly journalist or diplomat as pranks. The credibility of Ahmed Shukairi's blood-curdling threats in the pre-June war crisis could thus be ridiculed by those privileged to observe some time earlier that he was so willing to ingratiate himself with reporters as to offer two radically different versions of his statement on some matter to suit their fancy. (Western and Arab sociologists recognize such behavior as a typical plot in the culture for control of the situation; but a French journalist, Rouleau, who, because he was born there, speaks with authority on the Middle East, takes this to mean that nothing the man says is worth taking seriously.)[25]

It ought to be particularly interesting to ask why the practitioners of such rhetorical plasticity should find it so difficult to utter exactly those words that indicate unambiguous acceptance of the Jewish state. Apparently verbiage is not unrelated to attitude among Arabs; just that judgments are made abroad on inadequate knowledge of the nature of that relationship. The popular Arabists have been exposed by a serious scholar as really ignorant of Arabic. "Arabic," writes Bernard Lewis, "is one of the noblest instruments that the human race has ever forged for the expression of its thoughts. It is indeed a language of poetry and eloquence, two arts the practitioners of which are not always to be taken as saying exactly what they mean or meaning exactly what they say. But that is only one side of Arabic. It is also a language of remarkable clarity and precision. As a medium of philosophical and scientific literature, its only peer is Greek. At once poetic and accurate, Arabic was for a very long time one of the major languages of civilization. To offer such excuses for the utterances of individual Arabs is an expression not of sympathy but rather of ignorance and, ultimately, of contempt."[26]

Why one should take blood-curdling threats as odd, as requiring special explanation, in Middle Eastern culture is curious, indeed; after all, they are perfectly consistent with both the conceptualization and practice of violence in the culture. As among other practitioners of primitive warfare, the mutilation, dismemberment, and ritualistic uses of slain enemies are widespread among Arab peoples.[27] Although a common aspect of the Arab-Jewish conflict, these practices have been suppressed abroad by both the Jews, reluctant to advertise this particular facet of life in Palestine, and the Arabs, who deeply resent any intimation of their backwardness. While only rare references to this aspect are made by Jewish sources abroad, it is actually Arab allegations which call some attention to it there, such as the claim by the mother of Sirhan B. Sirhan to have seen with her young son in Jerusalem a Jewish display of mutilated Arab women. Since such allegations are unsubstantiated, and even more importantly inconsistent with the pattern of Jewish violence, while quite consistent with the Arab pattern, they probably resulted from the common mechanism of projection.

The nature of blood-curdling threats is thus quite authentic, as is, incidentally, the limited capacity to execute them against a dynamic, industrial society, though it is precisely that limited capacity that inspires disbelief in the authenticity of Arab threats against Israel. A biographer of Lawrence tells of an interesting incident in the early British period in Palestine, when Churchill and Samuel (first High Commissioner of Palestine) met in 1921 on their way to Jerusalem, for the conference with Abdallah that gave Transjordan to the latter. "Large Arab crowds at Gaza greeted the two statesmen with shouts of enthusiasm bordering on frenzy. The great men stood bowing and smiling their acknowledgment, though, according to Captain Coote, Lawrence whispered to him that they were shouting in Arabic, not with enthusiasm for the statesmen but for the murder of the Jews."[28] The event can serve as a veritable paradigm of Western-Arab communication.

The gap between Arab words and deeds in the realm of regular warfare has led some observers to doubt that the Arabs ever really meant seriously to harm their foe. Astonished by the poor Arab military performance, they concluded that the Arabs just have not got their heart in fighting Israel, assuming, of course that they could wage modern war effectively, provided they wished to do so. In reality, a general discrepancy exists in Arab society between verbalized intent and collective performance—for instance, as a serious difficulty in generating "practical" ideologies, as distinct from merely "expressive" ones—the social scientists seeking explanations not in volition, but in social and cultural characteristics in the Arab world.[29] In military matters no Arab society has ever been able to wage modern war, except on a very limited scale or ineffectually. But they are capable, indeed, of waging sporadic and sedentary warfare, which in the irregular variant assumes the familiar forms of brigandage, tribal raids, ritualized murder, and *fedayeen* violence as we have long known it; and in the regular armies is expressed in artillery barrages (and reliance on missile delivery from relatively safe distances generally), sieges, small-scale raids, and hit-and-run attacks on land, sea, and in the air. This naturally produces wars of attrition, which in combination with economic and especially diplomatic leverage can be exceedingly effective. The war of the irregulars prior to the Arab military invasion in 1948, for instance, proved nearly fatal for the nascent Jewish state in March of that year. The Arabs thus produce spontaneously forms of war that do not quite fit the warfare concepts common in the modern West. As a result, they are not very "visible" there, as the experience of the United Nations truce and armistice supervisory personnel in the Middle East has shown. These men regarded economic boycotts and waterway closures as purely diplomatic matters; they conceived of marauding and other irregular warfare as ordinary civil police business; and looking for "real" warfare, they found the Arabs passive and halfhearted, while the Israelis, eminent practitioners of modern war, looked aggressive and deadly.[30] The projection of modern Western warfare patterns, capacities, and concepts on the Arabs thus impairs the credibility of their avowed intentions toward the Jewish enemy.

Of similar consequence is the great personal charm of the men alleged to harbor unpalatable designs against the Jews. Even the casual reader of the European or American press could discover that Nasser was a "charmer," though few Westerners are aware that this trait is rather modal in Arab society, so that even the notorious

Shukairi could impress foreign correspondents as a jolly fellow. The evidence amply shows that in their meetings with Arabs of the cultivated class, Westerners find them gracious, accommodating, even indulgent, impeccable hosts, and thoroughly ingratiating;[31] the ordinary folk captivates them with its quaint, romantic aura;[32] their retainers display a personal attachment and submissiveness rarely found in the West;[33] albeit genteel Anglo-Saxons find little charm in the urbanized, modernizing mass.[34] On the Israeli side, "Good manners and politeness are suspect. On the other hand, the whole social life of the Arabs is dominated by a carefully observed etiquette. An Arab would address you politely, even if he wished you to go to hell, while the young men of Israel are sometimes rude, even where they have every reason to be polite."[35] Some Westerners with marked liberal-cosmopolitan inclinations may feel comfortable in the egalitarian, unglamorous, unesthetic milieu of dynamic Israel, but most other Westerners prefer the other side. United Nations officers in Palestine, Bilby discovered more than twenty years ago, "liked the Arabs because, they frankly conceded, they were treated with more respect and with more social courtesies. In Israel they were treated with reserve, with suspicion, and at times with open hostility."[36] An American lieutenant, an old acquaintance, recalls Bilby, greeted him as he crossed into Arab Jerusalem: " 'You'll like it better over here,' he confided before I had opened my mouth. 'These people know how to treat you decently.' "[37]

The story of the involvement of Westerners in the Arab-Jewish struggle has all along indeed been captivation with the Jews' case abroad and with the Arabs' graciousness on the spot. The early epitome was the journalist Vincent Sheean, who went to Palestine with a commission to write for the New York Zionist weekly the *New Palestine*. There he fell so deeply under the spell of George Antonius and Haj Amin al-Husseini, the *Mufti* of Jerusalem, and the beauty of Arab scenery that he thought the latter man a paragon of peaceful reasonableness. (Haj Amin some years later became an active collaborator in Hitler's Final Solution for the Jewish Problem.[38]) Bilby later contrasted the milieus in which Westerners moved: "The Arabs were wonderfully hospitable people. They entertained beautifully and they received you as a gentleman. But those Jews scowled at you in the street, greeted you curtly and suspiciously, and talked in mystical terms of messiahs and redemption and suchlike."[39] The journalist in war especially, though both sides did not much facilitate his work, found the Arabs at least accessible and affective, as humans, said Bilby.[40] The earlier cited IPI Survey found the Israeli press services in the 1950's much better organized than the Arab, yet foreign correspondents still commended the affective personal services of the overall ineffectual Arab information bureaus. In the first war a foreign journalist, Bertram C., confided to a Jewish colleague why he favored the Arabs: "Their gracious movements and gestures, the flowing lines of their clothes, give him a sense of repose. The Jews make him nervous; he finds them furtive and ungainly."[41]

Western Jews, even Zionists, have similar experiences, particularly with younger Israelis, as in the case of the American Hadassah delegation to the recent Twenty-sixth Zionist Congress in Jerusalem. The Hadassah women, declared one of their leaders, found "only insults and rudeness and ugliness," particularly from the *sabra,* native Israeli, contingent.[42] An Israeli writer has described the speaking manner of the latter as "often inordinately stark, divested of all ornament and elegance, without nuance, and delivered in harsh staccato sequences."[43] Rudeness, like unadorned frankness, seems a tantalizing value in Israeli culture; in 1965 a study of bureaucratic behavior at a large Israeli enterprise disclosed that more than 60% of officials in contact with the public did not believe in greeting a visitor, nor would they reply to his greeting, while an even higher percentage would not offer him a chair, simply letting him stand during the interview.[44] American Jewish sympathizers who have resided in Israel frequently tell of discourtesy as marking its way of life.[45]

Westerners resident in the Middle East tend to identify with the Arabs against Israel to the point of passion. Colonel Meinertzhagen, a rare Zionist sympathizer in colonial officialdom, whose involvement in the area dates from the arrival of the British in Palestine, described the characteristic encounter: "I have met many Jews; being oriental, their looks are often repugnant to the insular British; I have met many nasty Jews and just as many nasty Christians and Mohammedans. One outstanding Jewish characteristic is persistence; they will not take No for an answer and that was our main trouble in Palestine during the Mandate; the officers of the Administration found Jews troublesome because they were intellectually superior; I have often been present at interviews when the Jews got the better of an argument much to the British official's annoyance. Most Europeans find Jews unattractive owing to some little oriental mannerism in speech or deportment; I have heard it said that we English drink in hebraphobia with our mothers' milk; there is certainly a sign of inherited contempt and I often wonder if Jewish insistence on the crucification of Jesus may not lay at the root of dislike of Jews by Christians, forgetting that Pilate sentenced Jesus who was himself a pure Jew. The Arab with his picturesque clothes and romantic surroundings has always appealed to Englishmen; his simple mind often a cloak for stupidity, and his dignity, usually a cloak for lack of humour, has always appealed to those who administer him. It is remarkable how many English men and women have fallen in love with Arabs and the Desert and how many eccentrics, ancient and modern, have sprung from those two influences."[46] Another high British official in Jerusalem in this early phase of British rule recorded his reaction to the Jews, with an "ill-mannered smile" and "arrogance," being appalled at "the squalor, the foulness, the meanness, the lying, the sneaking furtiveness of this purely Jewish Society," in the quarter of the orthodox Jews in Jerusalem. The whole lot was "even worse than their brethren of Whitechapel [the poor Jews' quarter in London];" the young Zionists especially: "The behaviour shocks the Moslem aristocrat and the English gentleman, such young cubs!"[47]

For the resident Westerner—official, missionary, businessman— the Arab fits in his place; the Jew is an offense, among others, also to his self-worth, his psychological balance, indeed his very stance— his "burden"—in backward lands. Arthur Koestler has depicted the dilemma of British proconsuls from personal experience in his novel *Thieves in the Night* and earlier in *Promise and Fulfillment;* the Jew was not only ill-mannered, but actually outraged their every sensibility. They were secure in handling colonials, but the Jews were impossible, particularly in contrast with Arabs. And another writer: "On the one hand, the British saw a bunch of agitated Utopians; on the other, vast crowds of calm, proud, dignified traditionalists. On the one hand they were confronted with continuous demands for change [they shocked the first British governor of Jerusalem with the suggestion for building tramways in the Holy City], with acid but often unjust criticism, with boring and irritating moral arguments. On the other they met with outward appreciation, respect, and understanding, especially from the pro-British Arab notables. The Jews were garrulous, over-educated, and lacking in charm and manners. The Arabs were perhaps pompous, mainly illiterate (as colonial natives should be), and gracefully mannered. Thus the British lived in a state of perpetual psychological defence where the Zionists were concerned. . . ."[48]

The strong anti-Jewish sentiment in the British community in Palestine was taken for granted, even officially acknowledged;[49] what remained controversial was just how overwhelming it was. Captain Orde Wingate, an extraordinary dissenter, thought the British administrators of Palestine and Transjordan were "to a man anti-Jew and pro-Arab." (They like the Arab, "who, although he shoots at them, toadies to them and takes care to flatter their sense of importance."[50]) Bartley Crum wrote "that fully seventy per cent of the colonial officials whom I met in Palestine either were, at worst, openly anti-Semitic, or at best, completely unsympathetic and even resentful toward Jewish hopes in Palestine."[51] Crossman thought the anti-Jewish bias particularly strong among the British Army and the Palestine Police, citing Weizmann's estimate in the initial occupying forces as nine-tenths of the officers being anti-Zionist, "and a high proportion of them were anti-Semitic as well. Throughout the Mandate the average British soldier and policeman, very soon after his arrival in Palestine, became pro-Arab and anti-Jew. As for the tiny minority who evinced Zionist convictions, one could usually trace their eccentricity to a female connection—and this was especially true of Palestine police. If a soldier or policeman didn't have a Jewish girl, he was nearly always on the side of the 'poor old Arab.' "[52]

The impact of these attitudes is extended by the symbiotic relationship between British and American and other Western residential colonies in the region, by the socialization of Western newcomers and visitors to the area and other feedback effects into the mother countries, and by the input of foreign officials into policy making in their respective home governments and their interpretation of policy through implementation on the spot. By all accounts the British orientations toward the Arab-Jewish dispute in Palestine mirrored pretty correctly both those in the American colony in the Holy Land and the Anglo-Saxon orientations throughout the Middle East as a whole. The American colony in Jerusalem, replete with ecclesiastic personages, like all other Western colonies in the region, was justly famous for many decades for shielding American Protestant visitors from Jewish influence and indoctrinating them in the "Christian" approach to the conflict. The Western journalist, diplomat, or businessman would soon enough adopt the colonies' outlook as his own anyway but tends to adopt it already on arrival as part of his acceptance by a colony, without which he would be totally isolated in alien land. Bilby's exposure to various resident Anglo-American groups in the Levante produced the following observations:[53] A British diplomat in Damascus expresses regret that the Nazis failed to exterminate all the Jews; his opposite number in the American embassy, a former missionary, expresses similar sentiments in less violent terms—both men, incidentally, were press attachés, who guide, inform, and otherwise assist incoming Western journalists; around some dinner tables resident Westerners express hostility in a manner so acute as to lose self-control, one Britisher actually inflicting violence on his own person in sheer frustration. "Everywhere in the Arab world I found the so-called neutrals as partisanly Arab as the Arabs themselves." American and British diplomats everywhere delivered themselves of the "bitterest indictment of American and British policy in the Middle East," when American policy merely wavered between support and denial of support for Jewish statehood, while the British veered from open hostility toward some actual direct military intervention against Israel and back again to merely cold negativism.

Men like these advise their governments on the Middle East and interpret policy to their Arab hosts with the predictable slant now known widely. What may be less well known is the sometime fantastic imagery of the conflict held by the statesmen they advise. In his dealings with Whitehall top decision-makers, leaders of his own Labour Party, Crossman discovered that the thinking on the Arab-Jewish conflict in the minds of Prime Minister Attlee and Foreign Secretary Bevin was colored by the notion that the Jews were merely a religious group, hence the idea of a Jewish nation amounted to an absurdity they resisted with vigor. (President Truman seems also to have been troubled on this score.)[54] Ernest Bevin, when faced with a difficult international problem, sought solutions based on his own trade-union experience, as did Clement Attlee, whose early political experience had been in the East End of London. The promotion of working-class solidarity in that district of feuding Jews and Catholics involved the imperative of discounting religious differences. "As a result, both men got it firmly into their heads that the Jews of Palestine should be treated as a religious group, on a par with the Christians and the Moslems. The Arabs, in their view, had a right to national self-determination, because they were a nation. But the principle did not apply to the Jews, since they were only a religious community."[55]

Crossman's personal testimony about the factual situation in Palestine—"But, Ernie, I've seen it for myself. The Palestine Jews have grown into a nation, and if you refuse them partition, they will fight for their lives"—only embittered the leaders still more; irritation quickly turned into "cold anger" and, in Bevin, who had marked anti-Semitic leanings, into "violent passion." Without much personal experience with Arabs, Bevin absorbed the imagery of diplomatic specialists: "The Arabs were a simple, straightforward people with a deep liking for the British and respect for their leadership." When reality clashed with illusion, the leaders of the great power retreated into various states of dementia, reacting increasingly to delusions of international conspiracy: the Jews were in league with the Americans and others (shades of the *Protocols of the Elders of Zion*), even with the Bolsheviks; the Foreign Office advised Bevin in 1947 that the Russians had massed an army of Jews at Odessa for the attack on British Palestine.

It is in the setting of foreign colonies in the region that diplomatic Arabists acquire their expertise, as do all others who, on return to the mother country, identify as members of a special in-group, "those who know" the Middle East, instructing their compatriots, correcting what they regard as misguided conceptions of the conflict at home. This expertise usually consists of only some linguistic skill and the sort of trivial knowledge common to all Western residents in exotic countries, such as how to handle natives in ordinary situations (they haggle; they are emotional; they cheat; etc.). Arnold Hottinger has produced a penetrating study of one form of such expertise, the "Mandate Mentality" of the French in the Levante, showing how the special knowledge of the people on the spot actually reflected their own peculiar social and psychological needs among the Arabs, rather than the reality of the Arabs.[56] In the case of Anglo-American colonies in the Middle East, distortion is particularly likely because of considerable personal attachment, which, incidentally, vitiates the work of even the rare serious students in their midst.

Anglo-Americans in the Arab world may be divided into pro-Arabs and proconsuls: the former being particularly attracted to the Westernized Arab intelligentsia (educated Englishmen, found Crossman, were strongly attracted to the latter, whom he described as having "a French elegance of mind and of expression and are a fascinating mixture of immmense interest and charm");[57] the proconsuls carry all the prejudices and conventions of their countries with them wherever they go.The Arab expert (British or American) is not unlike the pro-Arab; he is in love with the Arabs, who "have given him a contact with ultimate values which he missed at home. There he would have remained an unfulfilled personality; in the Middle East he has found himself. He is determined somehow—he does not yet know the way—to harmonize Western civilization with Arab culture. . . . He rejects the British and American belief that the Arabs are natives with everything to take from us and nothing to give. He himself has learned from the Arabs the most valuable things in life. But he knows their weaknesses: He is frustrated by their indolence, the corruption of their upper classes, and above all by the bogus Western civilization which the educated Arab often assumes in defiance of his own traditions. He is indeed the sharpest critic of the Arabs because he understands them; but his criticism is that of someone who has identified himself with their cause."[58] The Americans, like the Australians and South Africans, among the Anglo-Saxon residents in the Arab world, can at least temper their dislike for Zionism with some empathy, because of their own pioneering background. The English identify strongly with the long-settled, traditional community with roots in the ancestral soil, rallying temperamentally even more strongly to the Arabs, whom they see engulfed in their own historical trauma, fighting off an alien conqueror.[59]

The traditional attitudes were merely carried over into new formal settings following the political changes in 1948: The Israelis now brought to their relations with United Nations officials the distrust and deception they had learned under the British, though a richer variation in attitudes was now manifested as well. Latins and Catholics thus generally followed the American pattern: Unlike the British, they were friendly toward Zionists abroad; in the area itself they tended toward the British pattern.[60] Whatever it might have been in New York or in theory, the relationship of Israel and United Nations in the area itself was one of merely occasionally relieved hostility from the first. United Nations personnel, like other Westerners in the Levante, spontaneously formed social links with Arab society wherever possible; contacts with Jews were chiefly limited to business, with a considerable carryover from home of stereotypical imagery on the Jews. It is ironic that many of them complained bitterly of the underhandedness of the Israeli method of penetrating United Nations ranks by means of feminine lures, when the resort to ruse itself bespoke their own corruption of the international organization's rule of impartiality.

A systematic examination of the published accounts of leading Western diplomats and military representatives of the United Nations in the Middle East discloses an almost uniform fascination with their Arab opposites and near repugnance with personalities on the other side. The characterizations of his interlocutors, which the first United Nations mediator for Palestine, Count Bernadotte, confided to his diary (*To Jerusalem*) in 1948 are a good example. With the exception of Doctors Joseph and Cohn, of the Jewish Agency in Jerusalem, who received him "in the most delightful manner" (p. 86), Bernadotte's encounters with Jewish officials were invariably bitter and distasteful throughout his mission. Even the Paris meeting with Dr. Goldmann, in which the latter suggested to Bernadotte considerable—and apparently unauthorized—Israeli concessions with a view to facilitate his mission, was just "a very interesting conversation" (p. 8). Of his several Arab contacts, his impressions were just as invariably affective. Thus, Azzam Pasha "attracted me strongly; I felt an instinctive liking for him" (p. 32); Molki Pasha "was as charming as could be" (p. 41); Abdallah, "a decidedly fascinating personality" (p. 42); Lebanese Foreign Minister Hamid Frangieh "made an extremely pleasing impression" (p. 57); and so forth. In Amman he records: "I was to be the guest of a high Arab pasha, one of the richest men in Transjordan. I had never before stayed in an Arab home, and I was pleasantly surprised at the extraordinarily charming way we were received. The true Oriental hospitality shown by our host knew no bounds" (p. 195). In Israel the leaders of the government had taken the Swedish aristocrat "to a concert given by the Tel-Aviv Philharmonic Orchestra by an American Jew" (p. 39). The sole warm and charming encounter with Jews occurs in Jerusalem, when a deputation of "venerable white-bearded Rabbis" come to urge the internationalization of the city, eliciting his comment that "the orthodox Jews are nothing like as fanatical as, for example, the extreme Zionists" (p. 142). An early reviewer of his book suggested that Bernadotte felt comfortable with Jews fitting the stereotype in Old Europe, "a bearded Jew who came to plead," yet "unconsciously irritated by the military prowess and independent attitude of the brash Israelis."[61] The memoirs of other high United Nations officials in the Middle East reflect equally the fascination with Arabs and the repugnance for Jews.[62] And testimony to this fascination has been forthcoming from a long succession of American diplomats, not the least of whom is Henry Kissinger, whose effusive response to the Arabs' treatment of him as "family" strikes all observers as genuine.

With such gracious and hospitable interlocutors Western journalists and diplomats may broach the subject of Arab relations with Israel with understandable anxiety, only to find their hosts disarmingly open, very cooperative, and surprisingly reasonable and agreeable. Their excessive politeness, which is a typical alternate-substitute of the equally excessive hostility in Arab interpersonal relations, thus appears to negate the existence of hostility, in this instance toward Israel. The pattern is as familiar to both Arab foreign sociologists as it is disorienting for the layman, whether diplomat or journalist, or the conventional expert, for the various reasons indicated earlier.

Problems of cross-cultural political dialogue have not gone unnoticed among diplomats and academic students of international relations and were in fact publicly discussed by even the former. In a recent article a former Department of State official thus analyzed some hazards of "summitry" in particular: "Besides giving excessive play to the element of personal compatibility in international relations, summitry often tends to create an illusion of understanding that can be quite dangerous. Americans with a common heritage of ideas and national experience are normally able to appraise one another with fair precision, so that understanding can often be advanced by face-to-face discussion. But when leaders have quite different backgrounds, customs and language and, in many cases, ethical attitudes and ideology, summitry is more likely to produce mistaken and misleading impressions than a clear meeting of the minds. . . . Few myths have done more harm than the sentimental conceit that men of different countries can understand one another better through direct conversation than when their exchange of views and ideas is filtered through experts sensitive to the nuances that derive from different cultures. Such a fanciful belief becomes particularly misleading when cultural differences reflect quite disparate habits of thought—as, for example, between Americans and Orientals."[63] Indeed, some of his colleagues have shown particular alertness to this case, with China, and perhaps no less to American-Soviet communication.[64]

Yet little attention is devoted to the substantial disparity between

American (or other Western) and Arab (or other Islamic) cultures, since the drifts of the official science of the area and policy for the area are together pulling toward assumptions of homogeneity. Both the pressure for "evenhandedness" in policy-making and public discussion of the Middle East conflict and the peculiar interpretation of Islam as merely a corrupted version of Protestantism in the establishmentarian Anglo-American knowledge of the Middle East (the Chatham House and Missionary Versions) tend toward the illusion of commonality and comparability. Little wonder that the "filtering" of Western-Islamic messages through official or officious experts in this country, particularly as they relate to the Arab-Jewish conflict, has proved to be rather a laundering of untoward assertions.

Radically different relationships between politics and religion in Christendom and Islam have thus been homogenized in conventional commentary on Middle Eastern events. Father Haughey has called attention before the October war to President Sadat's repeated calls for war and the "does he or doesn't he?" game played by Western analysts. "Most observers think he doesn't mean it because they interpret him from within their own secular, political frame of reference rather than his Moslem one. . . . For a Moslem, the will of Allah comes to realization in the political order. The arena wherein salvation is worked out and God's sovereignty is made manifest is the state. The acquiescence in temporal defeats such as the loss of Moslem lands to non-Moslems is tantamount to faithlessness. To engage the enemies of Islam is religious action and victory a vindication of the truth of Islam. . . . [Sadat's] speeches teem with Islamic allusions, something that the Western press is negligent in communicating, either because it doesn't consider them significant or doesn't understand them.[65] Though his was a rare dissenting view in the pages of America's leading liberal newspaper, Father Haughey's assertion of the profound fusion of the political and the religious in Islam is about as controversial in the serious study of Islam as the multiplication table. (Even some of the romantic-missionary-diplomatic school join the essential scholarly consensus in this and other respects, once they transcend the "phase of paternalistic sympathy for the Arabs," as one former Chatham House historian recently said of himself.)[66] Behavior patterns and culture in the Arab world present the same problem; conventional political analysts are puzzled by the relationships in it of politeness to aggression, hostility to ingratiation, or manipulation to affability; yet these are not much of a mystery to Arab sociologists and their Western colleagues. Insofar as an "Arab psychology" emerges from their work, it is not a rationalization of incoherences perceived from afar in narrowly parochial perspectives, but rather coherence as in all autonomous systems; not a corrupt or infantile version of Western culture, but rather an authentic culture, with a logic and rationality of its own.

On the hospitality-hostility polarity one American sociologist has written: "There are special reasons why such a pattern should develop among desert nomads but, like so many other of their values, it has permeated the rest of Arab life. In the desert, hospitality comes about as a means of overcoming the individual's helplessness in so harsh an environment. In the villages and cities, it has a different function; it reduces the tendency of the ever-present hostility to burst into violence at every moment. Exaggerated hospitality and politeness are reactions to exaggerated hostility, at least in part. . . . Hospitality and generosity are means of demonstrating friendliness; they ward off expected aggression. One has the feeling, indeed, that the hostility that becomes overt aggression is so uncontrollable that such measures as excessive politeness (a form of avoidance) or hospitality (a form of ingratiation in a situation where intimacy cannot be avoided) are at times absolutely necessary if social life is to be maintained at all. . . . Conflict is so much on the verge of breaking out that interpersonal relations seem to be largely directed at avoiding or covering up the slightest tendency toward the expression of difference. There are few informal mechanisms for the serious discussion of opposing beliefs without a display of intense animosity. . . ."[67]

Some Western subcultures actually approximate the Arab pattern. "The simple skills necessary merely to survive," Barzini has written of his native land, "are not difficult to learn. They are, after all, not exclusively Italian but roughly common to all insecure societies, with, however, untold local refinements and subtleties which cannot be matched elsewhere. Italians become such deft masters, so early in life, in these arts, that they are usually unaware of their existence. As a result, life flows smoothly, conflicts are concealed or attenuated to the point that foreigners once believed they lived here in a heavenly country, almost the best in the world, an Arcadia where nothing harsh ever happened, where people were happy, cheerful and friendly. Some still believe it today."[68] The parallel with the Arab world may be drawn further in the familiar fascination of foreigners with the "charm" of Italy. "Very few travellers see the ugliness underneath, the humiliation, the suffering. Not one in a hundred perceives the fundamental dreariness of everything under the glittering ormolu, the bitter fate of men who are condemned perennially to amuse themselves and the world, to hide their innermost feelings, to be *simpatici* at all cost in order to make a living."[69] And further still: "Foreigners are automatically promoted to be honorary members of the ruling class," and there are other emotional and psychological satisfactions, here too, particularly for men from disciplined, efficient societies to the north and west, who, says Barzini, "take a holiday from their national virtues"[70] among lovable bunglers. Naturally the men from "trust" societies are particularly vulnerable to the virtuosi of "the art of being obliging and *simpatico* at all times and at all costs."[71] Barzini recalls an encounter in World War Two with a German captain that reminded him "how thoroughly Italian I was, in spite of my foreign travels and education, since I was able, practically without speaking, to convince a poor, guileless, candid Nazi that I was openly and firmly on the side of the Axis."[72]

An American writer has been struck in the Arab world by patterns reminiscent of his own native Southland: intense religiosity, "miasmal sexuality," violence, "delirious sentimentality, a quick combustibility of temperament and a sense of identity and loyalty beginning with one's immediate neighborhood and then proceeding in ever-diminishing priorities outward. . . . 'They have a way of maintaining this appearance for the outside world of an extraordinary courtesy and graciousness, but they still don't have any larger sense of community than that of a tribe. They only cohere in a crisis'—a condition reminiscent of the states of the Confederacy. Nevertheless, they cultivate civility of a gallantry, sometimes almost intimidating, that approaches the heroic. . . ."[73] Even so, he felt overwhelmed, being an "innocent" in more ways than even he realized. Egyptians (and the ubiquitous "official in one Western embassy") convinced him of their basic harmlessness. According to the Western diplomat, "Egyptians do not like to kill. There's no way to understand them unless you understand that."[74] Even more ironic than the fact that Egypt has one of the highest homicide rates in the world and was involved in virtually every war in Western Asia and Africa in the last quarter century, is the diplomat's mention of Egypt's use of poison gas in Yemen as evidence of the Egyptian's alleged revulsion from violence.

The Islamic system, in which power and submission were almost always at stake and relevant resources scarce, demanded manipulative rather than managerial skills, tactical flexibility rather than strategic planning; self-confidence in it is usually not the result of sustained productivity, but rather of nourished egocentricity, which feeds mostly on flattery and hospitality. Flattery is not simply corruption in this context; it is rather a vital style of communication allowing for subtle, yet acceptable, movement in human affairs marked by the intense anxiety surrounding highly unstable and crass authority relations, in which the demand for total submission may arise at virtually every turn. With personality so much at stake so often, impersonality of language is invaluable. The performance of tension-management by this style of communication would seem of equal worth; it is, of course, an excellent vehicle for persuasion and dissimulation without giving offense.

A social scientist of Arab birth has discussed the characteristic prowess in ingratiation: "The Arab changes his identity with little reluctance. With the Asiatics he is an oriental, with people from the West he is an occidental, with the old societies he is a traditional man, with the new a modern. The Arab is ready and able to form an in-group on relatively meagre bases for identification. He always manages to find some common ground and hastens to create the atmosphere of an in-group necessary for the success of conducting a business, carrying out a plan or obtaining a favor."[75] She terms the two modes of obtaining favor of others as *tadlis* (deluding) and *tamliq* (wheedling), and flattery, for Arabs, "an art."[76]

The Egyptian social anthropologist, Hamed Ammar, has defined the chief characteristic of the Egyptian personality pattern (the *fahlawi* is its epitome) as quick adaptability, involving the capacity of promptly grasping the kind of response expected of one, and of producing it as well. The positive side to this trait is a flexibility in meeting novelty and adjusting to change; the negative side consists of superficial responsiveness and passing courtesy in order to evade facing real issues and hide one's real feelings; the *fahlawi*'s words and acts in this role are devoid of commitment. Another distinguishing trait of the *fahlawi* is a marked egocentrism and a persistent tendency to "show off," a drive to demonstrate unsurpassable ability to dominate situations and excel in general. Dr. Ammar insists that this trait, though suggesting self-confidence, actually manifests lack of security and the refusal to evaluate situations objectively; egocentric assertions tend toward sheer flippancy and lack of caution; they always involve trying for the difficult or impossible by mere gesture.[77] The influence of both ingratiation and the "show-off" compulsion on Arab communication has recently been grasped by a perceptive writer, who discovered among the Palestine *fedayeen* "the interviews to journalists [as] not necessarily representative of policy, motivated often by politeness and studded with spur-of-the-moment policy 'revelations.' "[78]

The course of Arab-Western tête-à-têtes touching on relations to Israel tends to follow a fairly distinct model, even though the sequential order varies and components are sometimes omitted, while others are added. The Westerner approaches the leader with apprehension, only to be put at ease by the gracious host. An American journalist-diplomat recalls that when going to see the Libyan ruler, Colonel Qadhafi, "I half expected to meet a wild man, and that half of me is vastly disappointed." Qadhafi is disarmingly winning, "sitting in a leather chair, jiggling his leg as John F. Kennedy used to do, gazing heavenward and rubbing his head against the back of the chair as if his neck were causing him discomfort. He chuckles at each question, particularly at those which concern himself, and speaks in a voice exemplary for its calmness."[79] What about the fierce military junta, the Revolutionary Command Council, which rules Libya with absolute power? Why, "they look like nothing so much as a band of chubby Boy Scouts. They are relaxed and comradely with Qadhafi, but when they glance at him they betray their adoration."[80]

Nasser, writes another American journalist, "was an engaging man to meet. He was equally endowed with natural charm and natural cunning, and he used his charm advantageously. His visitors were immediately at their ease. He was the incorruptible puritan revolutionary who never lost the simplicity of his tastes or the naturalness of his manners; the autocrat who disliked elaborate formalities and used the relaxed approach of democracy."[81] When his successor, Sadat, met Secretary Rogers, representing a power then assailed systematically by Egypt as the archenemy, he recalled, "We felt at ease in each other's company"; he constantly referred to Rogers, whom he had met for the first time, and to Assistant Secretary Sisco as "Bill" and "Joe."[82] (Rogers' visit with the leaders of "friendly" Israel on the same tour was marked by acute acrimony, shouting matches, and calculated insults.) When Secretary Kissinger replaced Rogers, he became "dear Henry" just as quickly.

Western interlocutors tend to identify broad cultural traits as peculiarly personal ones. While Nasser lived, he impressed them as exceedingly reasonable and personally devoid of hostility (the Russians, too); when Sadat succeeded him, his moderation was first missed and its passing deplored pending acquaintance with Sadat; when the latter began giving the usual performance, *he* was hailed as a moderate, indeed a marked change from Nasser, whom many now remembered only as belligerent, while Sadat's belligerent speeches were now explained away as political necessities of a basically peaceful man. The same analysts who had pleaded for arrangements based on Nasserite reasonableness now promoted his successor as reasonable, presumably unlike his predecessor.

Usually the Arab leader's sense of injury by Israel is emphatically vented, but aggressive intent toward it is firmly denied. Winston Burdett writes of Nasser, "when the conversation touched some old wound or grievance (chiefly, the stubborn indifference of 'the West' to the rights and justice of the Arab cause), his sentences would meander without apparent beginning or end, moving back and forth over the same ground with obsessive repetitions."[83] The anxious handling of the ugly topic was one manifested by another Arab speaker, "with an almost painful delicacy, indeed with the same self-abashment with which Nasser, in a television interview some weeks later, would seem to smile in sheepish embarrassment whenever he came to the slightest suggestion of any unmannerly, not to mention perhaps violent possibilities in Egypt's relationship with Israel."[84] Indications to the contrary, in word or deed, are explained as simply domestic or inter-Arab political necessities, which the worldly diplomat or journalist would surely appreciate.[85] For good measure, it is sometimes argued that the excitable, passionate mobs to be pandered to are actually harmless; to show that Arab violence is mainly verbal, one usually adduces the *dowsha*—the characteristic Cairene street incident, involving much shouting and fury and almost no physical contact—or, more disarmingly still, asserts that, as everyone knows, Egyptians (or other Arabs) make the worst soldiers.[86] The fact that Egypt (and other Arab countries) has one of the world's highest homicide rates and has rarely ceased waging wars or intervening in others' wars (Palestine, Yemen, Algeria and Morocco, Biafra, etc.) in the contemporary period seems not to have vitiated the argument in many instances. Journalists and diplomats have gone on to espouse it as their own personal revelation in subsequent interventions in private and public discussion, just as they have sought all along to make Israeli leaders believe that Arab threats were only "for domestic consumption,"[87] and Western publics that just "political reasons" of an internal nature are chiefly responsible for the leaders' refusal to make peace with Israel.[88]

That the Arab leader himself is personally free of popular passion and misconception is indicated to Western interlocutors, usually by some kind of discreet admission, in private only, that Israel does exist, after all. With many Westerners this turn in the conversation constitutes the *pièce de résistance*—they are awed by a historical revelation and feel suddenly part of a small circle privileged in sharing a momentous secret—the event becoming the chief determinant of their thinking on the conflict. It is an experience they greatly cherish and cite with pride as their conclusive argument in favor of plans for settlement based on discreet understandings with Arab leaders.[89] The more imaginative Arab leaders produce veritable bombshells on such occasions: In the spring of 1971 the Deputy Foreign Minister of Egypt, Salah Gohar, revealed to foreign journalists that the great ambition of his life has long been to serve as the first ambassador of his country to the Jewish state. Apparently innocent of the finer points of Levantine humor, these journalists were so impressed as to rush over to the other side to convey this revelation.[90] In the course of the diplomatic campaign to regain territories lost in the 1967 war the discreet acceptance of Israel has gone public, in that almost all Egyptian or Jordanian spokesmen would explicitly aver to foreigners that they implicitly accept Israel. "As one Egyptian official explained, 'I know that we have said at times in the past things about driving people into seas, such things, but of course you understand that in a situation of grave crisis and danger, you have to say certain things just to keep up the morale, the confidence of your people. But truthfully now—of *course*, we have accepted the existence of the Jewish state. I mean, after all, twenty years have passed: whether we may like it or not, Israel is a fact. Check our statements since 1967, and you will find there is nothing in our recipe about pushing Israel into the sea, any such business as that. Why, by our acceptance simply of the '67 U. N. resolution, which itself presumes the fact of the state of Israel, we have already tacitly recognized and accepted Israel's existence. No, that is not the problem. You must understand that the problem is simply Israel occupying the territory of Egypt, which she took from Egypt in war—and of course, the problem, the original problem of the Palestinians; think of this entire dispossessed people and you will see what we are talking about. . . .'"[91]

The leader often expresses consternation at other people's insistence that so unnatural or artificial a state as Israel be maintained at Arab expense (see above, at the cost of dispossessing another nation), especially in view of the traditional tolerance toward Jews in Islam, adding ingratitude to injury. The more or less veiled appeal to Western guilt, for both persecution of Jews and the alleged atonement of the sin at Arab expense, is curiously accompanied in some cases by a more or less transparent appeal to the Western interlocutor's presumed dislike of Jews. A common enough experience of Western visitors in Arab countries, it proves particularly embarrassing for German visitors, for obvious reasons, who are also perhaps more likely than others to publicize this experience. Colonel Meinertzhagen, in a tour of Arab countries following the 1948–49 war, "found that all Arabs when discussing Israel presumed that one disapproved of Jews."[92] In his tours in the Arab countries Bilby found resident Westerners generally anti-Jewish, often rabidly so.[93] Public appeals to Western anti-Jewish prejudice have been made repeatedly in the United Nations speeches by Arab diplomats. The November-December, 1967, issue of *Arab World,* published by the Arab Information Center in North America, was almost entirely dedicated to establishing a Muslim-Christian partnership in victim self-identification against Jewish dominion in the Holy Land. "The handsome, six-foot Nasser," recalls an American writer, "resembled the strikingly plain five-foot, five-inch Khrushchev in yet another way [besides domestic political skills]. He, too, was able to convince the West he was a moderate man. Nasser could tell the editor of a neo-Nazi West German weekly that he meant to crush Israel and add for good measure: 'Our sympathies were with the Germans in the second world war. Nobody seriously believes the lie that six million Jews were murdered.' Then, Nasser could talk so reasonably to the editor of the pro-Israel *Manchester Guardian* that the editor would go away convinced that Nasser was an enlightened socialist who didn't intend his threats against Israel's Jews to be taken seriously. A British correspondent, James Morris, described how Nasser projected the image of the moderate man. 'Sensible liberalism oozes from his manner,' the correspondent wrote. 'Nasser will be in his shirtsleeves, his shirt showing between his vest buttons, and he will talk pleasantly and intelligently for as long as you like. And what will he tell you? That all he wants for Egypt is peace and prosperity. The West has constantly thwarted him—he will say with an air of letting bygones be bygones—by supporting the intruder state of Israel, by refusing him arms to defend Egypt against Israeli attacks.

The hours will slip by easily as he expounds these persuasive theories, compounded of understandable patriotism and kindly reproach. The coffee cups will come and go, and when the President rises from his table to see you to the door, his sandals flip-flopping across the linoleum, you may well walk out into the night a warm believer in the liberalism of Col. Nasser.' ''[94]

In the end the leader shows himself resigned to the unhappy condition with Israel, provided that an "equitable solution" is obtained or that the "rights of the Palestinians" are restored or that simply "justice" is done or that some similar agreeably phrased vague condition is met. Yet should this be denied, the leader warns, there will follow unspecified but catastrophic consequences for the rest of the world, and particularly for the visitor's own country. Diplomats leave much encouraged in their search for Middle Eastern peace;[95] for the journalist there can be "scoops" of the first order of magnitude in the semantic exercises; and for the ordinary traveler, revelation. In June of 1970, Nasser's words to an American law professor were interpreted in one popular newsmagazine as "a new and intriguing offer"—that withdrawal from all occupied land and restoration of "Palestinian rights" would lead to acceptance of Israel.[96] (There was a rare note of caution, in that the latter phrase was qualified as "meaning presumably" only personal rights; the more representative reaction was that of the journalist who termed the statement "a boggling profession which, for the rest of that show and the weeks that followed, was simply left in the air, as if it simply could not be assimilated."[97])

It is common knowledge that mendacity and deception are especially prominent in Arab life—a fact foreign observers discover as unfailingly as Arabs themselves decry it—but Western interviewers of Arab leaders do not allow this datum to intrude upon their intimate appraisals of the latter. Rather, if any lying is being done, they deduce that it is the Arab public—not they—who are being manipulated. Confronting them with belligerent public postures of Arab leaders seems to have the curious result of convincing them still more of the nonbelligerency and reasonableness of these same leaders. Careful comparisons of the public and private, as well as the domestic and foreign, versions of Arab statements on Israel indicate that prevailing beliefs concerning the nature of mendacity in this connection may have to be revised. While there exist discrepancies between different versions of the same statement, these do not appear excessive in view of the understandably different functions the different versions are meant to perform. Different publics and different settings may everywhere produce different versions of the same message. What is particularly striking about Arab statements concerning Israel is actually the essential similarity of the different versions; the foreign and private versions merely being more vague, the domestic and public versions tending to be more explicit. Insofar as there is manipulation, it is not limited to the home audience, who actually seem to get more fully articulated versions than foreigners, and not necessarily less candid versions, particularly concerning Israel. While Arab deception of other Arabs concerning Israel exists, it is not likely to be as bold a deception as it can be to outsiders. In an interview with the editors of a German publication, the Secretary-General of the Arab League thus denied not only that the familiar threats to destroy Israel were made in earnest—which denial is rather common—but actually that these threats had ever been made.[98] Usually, however, a much greater similarity exists between domestic and foreign, and private and public, versions of Arab statements on Israel, a phenomenon that is both surprising and significant; surprising because one would expect such notorious plastic rhetoricians to produce strikingly different versions; significant because the essential sameness between these versions indicates how strongly they feel in this particular matter, concerning Israel. In view of this it appears that the Arabs have been quite gratuitously maligned by many of their friends, who argue that the Arabs are simply not to be believed, especially when it is Israel they threaten. In this patronizing view the Arab is to be excused because of his playful immaturity, alluring quaintness, and charm—and like a child, not to be taken seriously.

The serious student of Arab rhetoric must be impressed rather by the substantial coherence among different versions of statements on Israel. One appreciates especially the tightly argued and meticulously articulated phraseology, which strains to insure consistency, without producing jeopardy to the essential values, between what Arabs say among themselves regarding Israel and what they have to say to the world outside. Far from the conventional notion of looseness with words, there is actually—as Lewis suggested[99] and as one might expect in so markedly oral a civilization—a painfully scrupulous choice of language on this anxious issue. Burdett has perceptively observed of Nasser's English, that he "handled it ably, always making his thought clear, often with grace and irony and never tricked by the foreign syntax or vocabulary into saying something he did not intend to say."[100] One can observe in conversation with even ordinary Arabs the extraordinary length to which vagueness must be preserved around ultimate aims.

The chief instrumentality in this endeavor is semantic vagueness in general, and specific semantic formulations, or "codes," in particular. To illustrate, compare the different versions of an interview with President Nasser, one appearing in *Time*, on May 16, 1969, the other broadcast over Radio Cairo in Arabic three days earlier.[101] To the question, by *Time* editors, whether Nasser would sign a nonaggression pact with Israel, if a solution to the conflict were somehow achieved, the *Time* version records his answer as follows: "If there were a solution to all problems, this would be something to think about." The Radio Cairo version is less evasive and abounds in categorical negatives, beginning with, "No one has the right to forget history," and concluding with the assertion that there are two basic problems—"land and people"—which must be solved if peace is to return. In the *Time* version the phrase is explained as withdrawal from occupied territory and "the Palestinians must have the choice of returning to their homes"; in the Arab context the phrase is used to denote the so-called two-phase solution: first, liberation of territory lost in 1967, then liberation of Palestine—reducing Israel to precarious territorial shape ("land") and filling it with as large a number of Arab refugees as possible ("people"). In this shape Jewish sovereignty is expected to be untenable, either against internal pressure or external ones. In reply to another question Nasser gave this seemingly newsworthy, if not sensational, reply: "I accept the reality of Israel, and so will my people, if there is a humanitarian solution. Call it Israel, or whatever you want to call it, and I will recognize it." The Cairo Radio version explains that "humanitarian solution" means the same as "land and people."

Other popular code words are "equitable solution," "Palestinian resolve," "restoration of rights," "de-Zionization," "restoration of Palestine's Arab character," and many others. One can have quite a sport "translating" various Arab pronouncements into the inevitable logical absurdity, that the Jewish state is acceptable provided it ceases to be. For the amateur cryptographer the key is sometimes liberally provided, as the following case shows. In a widely publicized book Jordan's King Hussein recalls that there was considerable interest at his appearance before the National Press Club in Washington, in 1959, in the possibility of peaceful coexistence with Israel. "To this type of question I could only state what I have stated so often—that we all hope for a *just solution* to the Palestine question one day, adding, 'Maybe it will come sooner, once people all over the world actually look at the question and understand it properly and work for a solution.' "[102] The meaning of "just solution" becomes clearer presently (p. 271), as requiring "complete restoration of the rights of the Arab people of Palestine"; and clearer still, when the King asserts (p. 276) "that Jordan was never reconciled to the creation of Israel, imposed *de facto* on the Arab states in 1948. Jordan and the other Arab states firmly believed, as they do today, that a situation so starkly unjust could never last—and believed passionately and still believe that the world's conscience would sooner or later rectify the wrong by a just and satisfactory solution." Since amateur cryptographers and professional Orientalists only rarely form the King's audiences, his usual references to "injustice" as the root of the trouble elicit different and contradictory images in the speaker and in his public.

5

DILEMMA, DOUBLE MEANING, AND DISSONANCE

IN 1946 some members of the Anglo-American Committee of Inquiry traveled to Saudi Arabia for an interview with King Saud; in their meeting with the venerable monarch they were told of his utter repugnance for the Jews' enterprise in Palestine and of the Arabs' ancient enmity for that people. An American member subsequently reassured another that the King's words were not meant to be taken seriously, since he spoke merely for the record—"Arab shorthand men took down what was said during the audience, and that 'the King would have pooh-poohed the idea of violent resistance to large-scale Jewish immigration.' "[1] A quarter of a century of intermittent war later an American Secretary of State is told in similar terms by another Saudi monarch that Israel is an abomination. His advisers subsequently explained that the King is reconciled to Israel; only the details of coexistence are yet to be hammered out.[2]

It was perhaps inevitable that any approach grounded in missionary experience, as in the official American approach to the Middle East, should be marked by such mixture of disdain and affection, the patronizing attitude of missionaries toward their charges everywhere. That Arabs encourage the honeyed contempt toward them is understandable; few would much resist the temptation of the abandonment of responsibility for one's actions that goes with it. The world has often indeed been very good to the Arabs—perhaps too much for their own good, said John Bagot Glubb, in respect to their stupendous early conquests[3]—and this solicitude to apologize for them, even when they speak bluntly, must be intoxicating.

But the question of Israel provokes in the Arab world terrible pain and awesome dilemma. It is curious that their more usual resort to codes, which only strengthens abroad the impression of their ephemeral emotionalism in this respect, may actually betray the real depth of their quandary and anxiety; for codes form an old Islamic intellectual tradition for coping precisely with similar distress.

In the early phases of Islam, almost one thousand years ago, a fateful struggle raged on for many generations over the acceptance or exclusion of the Hellenic spirit in the new civilization. Orthodoxy emerged victorious, as revelatory theology, rejecting the philosophic and humanistic tradition, founded on human experience and reason and speculating from these premises. The triumph was not total, in that some of the best minds were, despite fearful repression, prepared still to espouse humanistic heresy. There evolved under these circumstances what Leo Strauss has shown to be a "double style." "In their writings they keep one meaning uppermost for the mass of their readers while concealing a second meaning in these same works for the chosen few who can read between the lines. From time to time they throw out hints about the inner, deeper meaning of their writings by logical breaks in the line of thought; their true meaning is concealed in 'repetition' of the views which were severally held. In secret the philosophers esteem truths arrived at by abstract trains of thought higher than those revealed by the Koran."[4] The people were not completely deceived; nor was the method exceptional, but rather a cultural pattern manifested in similar ways elsewhere. The *Ismaili* heretics thus overcame a similar dilemma by introducing the idea of *batin,* or hidden meaning: the Koran was something "external" and only the initiated could recognize its inner meaning.

The contemporary resort to codes thus appears as an ancient, honored skill in the culture, rather than some merely clever adjunct to foreign policy. One demonstrates prowess in its use inside the Arab world and particularly clever, subtle formulations meet with special appreciation by the cognoscenti. Two examples from the late Nasser are noteworthy: In one case, in 1962, when talking of the production of new long-range rockets in Egypt, he said they would reach even "south of Beirut" (Israel lies there);[5] when addressing troops several days before the outbreak of the June war in 1967, he indicated that his expulsion of the UNEF from Sinai and the ordered blockade of Eilat had turned the clock back to the eve of 1956 (when the blockade had been broken by Israel's campaign); now, he said, one must similarly turn the clock back to 1948 (the year of the establishment of Israel).[6] "Land and people," "the Palestinian resolve," "restoration of rights," and other more current codes are equally fine specimens of the subtle craft.

But like the traditional double meaning, the contemporary codes denote also a certain tactical flexibility within the bounds of rigidity; they are, after all, a symptom of dilemma, of a clash of imperatives. They denote strain, and it is illuminating that the incidence of codes, resort to codes, and proliferation of codes is in the history of the Arab-Jewish conflict in the Middle East a function clearly of rising complexity, difficulty and aggravation of the Arab position. They were scarcely present in the early phases of the conflict in Palestine; yet there came a veritable boom after setbacks in 1948; and following the worst Arab debacle, in 1967, one was virtually overrun by them. The Palestine ideal was as compelling as ever, but the gap between the ideal and the real had taken on frightening proportions for Arabs. In the beginning and until rather late Arabs confidently urged foreign powers to leave them and the Jews alone, so that the "natural" outcome might be consummated; later the very idea of being left by the world face to face with the Jewish juggernaut became a nightmare. There have accrued layers upon layers of unhappy reality to the ideal; the hands of the clock might have to be moved many times, indeed, before zero hour is reached again. The events of October, 1973, and after inspired Arabs with enormous confidence once more, but the road back remains long just the same, perhaps one whole generation long.

The nature of the moral imperative certainly is clear beyond a shadow of doubt in the Arab world: Jewish dominion in the heartland of the Arab homeland is an outrage. One may have to acknowledge it like other cruel facts of nature, but physical existence cannot legitimize it, as in the case of cancer, a favorite analogy in the Arab world. Even though some may reluctantly concede that some legal basis may be claimed for this phenomenon—the 1947 partition resolution in the United Nations—such claim is declared to be fraudulent, illegal, or to have been invalidated by Israel itself, and in any case to be illegitimate anyway. The whole mass of the incredibly vast outpouring of speech and writing in the Arab world strains to prove in every conceivable manner that there is no moral, ethical, humanistic, legal, or any other consideration that invalidates the imperative of the evil's elimination.[7] Thus, it is acknowledged that international law obliges Arab nations, as other nations, to refrain from certain acts against other states; but since Israel is not a real state, the restraint cannot apply to it; or injunctions against aggression do not apply to Israel, because Israel *is* aggression. For the same reason peace is meaningless so long as the aggression exists;

hence, "peace" connotes the elimination of Israel, or should designate this condition, if one is serious about it. And so on. As basic creed, the pinwheel of Arab ideology, the imperative of the elimination of the evil is duly inscribed in Arab constitutional documents, declarations of union or federations.

When one understands that the elimination of the Jewish state is the moral imperative in the Arab world, the virtually endless stream of invective and threats can correctly be assessed. Viewed from abroad, it may appear as some delinquency, as if some Arabs may want to give way to some immoral temptation, yet the more decent among them surely won't let them. Yes, avowed Cecil A. Hourani, in the aftermath of the terrible debacle in 1967, the Arab objective has, indeed, been all along the destruction of Israel. Addressing himself to fellow Arabs in a "moment of truth," even he, paragon of moderation in the Arab world, could find no justification for that outrage, merely arguing that methods used heretofore for its elimination had simply redounded to its benefit, not the Arabs'.[8] The issue is means, not the end.

The sort of concession to Jewish dominion that has occasionally been mooted as possibly compatible with justice envisages some specially secured religious enclave. When the invasion of Arab armies failed to topple the new Jewish state, the Secretary-General of the Arab League suggested to the United Nations Mediator for Palestine that "it might be possible to provide for the Jews along the same lines as for the followers of the Roman Catholic faith—to form a sort of Vatican State that would be symbolic of the Jewish idea and would be entitled to send out its ambassadors and ministers to various countries. This 'Vatican State' would be empowered to act as a mouthpiece for Jewish interests in various quarters and to deal with any complaints that might arise with regard to the treatment of the Jews."[9] In the Arab context it was not an ungenerous offer; the more common sentiment was given expression by Major Salah Salem, a member of the Egyptian cabinet: "Egypt will endeavor to erase the shame of the Palestine war even if Israel implemented the UN resolutions. It will sign no peace treaty with Israel, even if Israel consisted only of Tel Aviv."[10] More recently the influential Cairene *Al-Ahram* suggested the recognized permanent borders for Israel as "one Jewish synagogue in the heart of Tel-Aviv and an additional ten metres around it."[11]

Military weakness leaves the outrage intact and the vital political support abroad is unlikely to be obtained on explicitly maximalist claims (except from Peking and several other sources). The issues that emerge are thus simultaneously substantive and instrumental, a prime example of which after the first Arab-Israeli war was the refugee problem. The problem encompassed hundreds of thousands of Palestinian Arabs dislocated by the war, questions of their return and resettlement, real property losses and compensation, blocked bank accounts, the feeding and care of multitudes in many camps, etc. In this sense there are "real" matters at issue capable of objective handling and bargaining; within the Arab context, however, the issue is tied to a larger objective. Time and again this is reasserted in almost endless variations: "The return we seek is for return to Palestine, not Israel; not to live in Israel but on its ruins, in a country the sovereignty of which is only ours," in the words of a Cairene newspaper.[12] The theme is proclaimed with dulling sameness on the highest levels of government and is voiced in the squalor in their camps by the refugees themselves, who utter it in unison to the stream of foreigners who come to look and listen over the many years.

To issues debated abroad is thus added in the Arabs' context yet another option, but this wider range curiously diminishes flexibility, rather than the other way around. As they move on issues on two disparate levels, their tactical posture improves, but their capacity to advance on hard, substantive issues is impaired; since settlement of such issues must be handled with a view toward not jeopardizing the ultimate option (Arab Palestine), the Arab position on them assumes an otherwise unwarranted stickiness. And since substantive matters are not unimportant, sometimes involving particularly tantalizing values for individuals directly involved, the resulting frustration is considerable. In the wake of the first war Bilby encountered two American University of Beirut graduates, Palestine refugee leaders, in that city; they had prepared for his consideration a claim for lost properties in Israel for "astronomical sums," apparently in full confidence of immediate satisfaction, "as though they expected remittances in the next mail," he thought. "Would they, I asked, be prepared if the opportunity came to return to their houses and live under Israeli rule? 'Yes,' responded one. 'I would do anything to get my family's business and citrus grove back again.' " Bilby then asked, "Would you then concede that Israel is here to stay? 'Only temporarily,' he said after a thoughtful pause. And then he loosened his emotional floodgates. 'You don't know how fortunate you are to be an American. You come from a strong country. You don't have to endure this shame and this treachery. Today, the worst thing in the world is to be a Palestine Arab!' "[13]

The greater flexibility of the moderates in the Arab world is a function of the higher priority they attach to substantive matters. For the more distant, North African, President Bourguiba of Tunisia, the abstractions of the Palestine conflict assumed an appalling intimacy when he personally experienced the squalor of refugee camps in the Arab East in his great tour of 1965. He had little regard for Arab military capacities and was prepared to grant high priority to the human tragedy, even if it tended to obscure somewhat the ultimate objective. Bourguiba saw it as creative risk-taking. "What I proposed," he explained, "is the application of the United Nations resolutions; that is, the one about partition which would permit restoring to an Arab Palestinian State an important part of the territories now occupied by [Israel], and the one concerning the return of the refugees. . . . It will be difficult to escape or to hide any longer, once Israel agrees to negotiate on the basis I have indicated. If such negotiations actually take place they would make it possible not only to restore a vast portion of the Palestinian territory and bring the refugees back to their homes but also to diminish the present atmosphere of war, allay the hatreds, and reduce tensions. Everyone will then be able to breathe more freely and find himself in a plainly better situation than now. Things will not just stop there, but will take a turn in which both the Arabs and the Jews will modify their respective ways of seeing things, and a climate of cooperation will be established for the mutual benefit of both parties."[14] On another occasion Bourguiba argued that if Israel would make these concessions in territory and refugees, the basic situation would change greatly in favor of the Arabs, and then, "new possibilities will be opened for a permanent solution."[15] And this, as Bourguiba and other moderates invariably assert, means the return of the Jews to their "normal" or "natural" condition.

Moderation on the issue of Israel thus constitutes not a categorical departure from militancy in the Arab world, or an essentially different phenomenon, as is usually assumed; it indicates rather degrees of flexibility in the tension between a moral imperative and an intractable reality. Moderation is tactics. The all-Arab position after the first war with Israel was thus simultaneously militant and moderate, indeed a new version of the venerable double meaning. As one Orientalist put it: "The official Arab demand is no longer for the immediate destruction of Israel, but for its reduction to the frontiers laid down in the 1947 partition proposals—obviously as a first step towards its ultimate disappearance. Since Israel, clearly, would not submit voluntarily to such a truncation, and since the Arab states alone are unable to enforce it, this amounts in effect to a demand for an imposed settlement by the great powers—a kind of compulsory surgery on the conference table, in which, perhaps, Soviet arms would wield the knife, while Western diplomacy administered the anaesthetic."[16] This explains the eellike nature of Arab policy stands that puzzles Western editorialists and diplomats: the militant Nasser embraces moderate positions, only to revert to militant stands, and so on; even the notorious Syrians, popular epitome of ir-rational militancy, can surprise Western audiences. Thus, from a leader of the *Baath* Party quite a few years ago: "We do not think that an armed conflict with Israel is, from a short point of view, pos-sible or even desirable. Besides, we do not know what the future has in store for us. Nor do we know whether the Palestine problem will be solved by force of arms or not, taking into consideration the changes which may occur in the meantime both in the world and in Israel itself. On the other hand, we know that we cannot accept the existence of a Zionist state."[17] Almost exactly the same wording in recent statements is cited as evidence for the alleged radical change of Syria's position toward Israel credited to Kissingerian diplomacy in the wake of the 1973 war.

The projection of the Western conception of "moderate" pro-duces puzzles or gives rise to fallacious certainties which one main-tains by a selective misperception of facts. Thus, regarding King Hussein and his regime as moderate in our sense means dismissing his earlier cited exercises in double meaning as irrelevant semantics, and explaining away even more direct indications of intent or ignor-ing them entirely. Indeed, so massive a repression of factual reality is required to support the Western image, that Jordanian behavior in the June war, of the sort commonly derided as Shukairist antics, has already been expunged from the conventional, popular recollection of the past—as if it were the subject of Stalinist rewriting of history.

The outcome of the June war of 1967, widening very much the dis-parity between justice and reality, gave great scope for double meaning and tactical flexibility. For the defeat added more layers to those already disfiguring the ideal: More Palestinian territories were lost (Gaza Strip, West Bank) over and above those lost in 1948–49; the Arab part of Jerusalem was added to the part the Jews had held since; the Golan Heights of Syria and Egypt's Sinai were lost. The

Israelis now sat on the Suez Canal, on the Jordan, having radically reversed the strategic relationship—now huge areas buffered their vital population centers, while their armies were poised close to those of their enemies; oil fields were lost; etc. After the war the Arab world rallied to the cry for "the elimination of the traces of aggression"—of course the initial aggression was there still, but the last was closer in time, in space, in the heart, and certainly in the mind of the international community. As before, the latter quickly endorsed the Arabs' claim for lost land, which in their context, just as predictably, was at once a substantive issue and an instrumental one. For the claim, which the world understood in its obvious sense, is tightly connected among Arabs to the ultimate goal, in both practical and symbolic terms. Withdrawal from "occupied territory" means in the Arab context also withdrawal from Israel proper. The term "occupied territory" is not novel United Nations rhetoric in the Arab world at all, where it has popularly designated Israeli territory long before Resolution 242 was conceived.

An American writer in Arab Jerusalem in 1966 explained to the manager of Hotel Petra that he had just been to Israel. "The manager's face contorted as if I had jabbed him in the stomach. He no longer looked comfortable—or safe. 'From where have you come?' he asked. I tried to make the answer sound nonchalant, but it wouldn't come out that way. 'Israel,' I said, my voice cracking. 'Ah,' said the manager, 'you've been over in Jewish-held territory.' 'I guess I have,' I said." Asked whence he came to Jordan by the military governor of Bethlehem, he once more gave the unacceptable answer. " 'No!' he shouted again, and I began to wonder if the Arabs had borrowed some brainwashing experts as well as technicians from their new Eastern friends. But it turned out to be only a question of semantics. 'You mean you come from *Occupied Territory*,' the governor said."[18]

The greater scope for tactical flexibility was demonstrated clearly immediately after the catastrophic war of 1967. The worse the strategic situation got, the greater became the dependency on foreign opinion; and the more imperative the need to court it, the greater the reliance on codes. There was general agreement soon after the war that the talk of pushing the foe into the sea had harmed the Arabs most of all; as one Cairo weekly, *Al-Mussawar*, put it, the genocidal slogans "made it easy for Israel to win the propaganda war against us";[19] others suggested that the threats merely enhanced the morale of the foe's armed forces. Explicit language did not disappear in the Arab world, but the West now heard much less of it than before.

Bourguiba's two-step tactics, previously suspect in the Arab East as unduly jeopardizing "Palestinian rights," was forced now unequivocally on the most powerful of Arab nations. The defeat had suddenly given Egypt an important immediate goal. What the wretchedness of Palestine refugees was to the Tunisian, the loss of the Sinai now was to Egyptians. Whatever may happen later, this had to be succored first, and fast.

It is characteristic of the conventional discourse of Middle Eastern affairs that the two-step tactics are ignored by most foreign observers. Actually, the tactics were discussed as candidly in the Arab world as when Bourguiba in 1965 first urged the Arabs to pursue them without the usual hesitation. The Tunisian spoke openly: "The rights which have been taken away can be restored gradually, by stages," as in the case of his own country. One must realistically evaluate the relative forces the foe and one's own side can muster for the struggle, not fear flexibility, even "to appease imperialism, or to make concessions to it, even though this may expose [one] to murder." Never humiliate the foe. ("I succeeded in liberating myself from France, without having beaten the French Army—it is thus that I triumphed over imperialism. It is thus that France did not feel that it lost completely.") And above all else, "Take what is offered and ask for more later." The notion of one fell swoop was but a noble dream; in the reality of this struggle obstacles must be overcome "one by one. It cannot be done all at once."[20] The war two years later had sadly vindicated him, Bourguiba thought.

Now Cairo argued the two steps as persuasively and candidly as Tunis had before. The diplomatic campaign, with the Soviet bloc and other allies, immediately after the war, was frankly waged for the recovery of the lost territory. Security Council Resolution 242, which crowned the offensive, was immediately understood as addressing chiefly the first phase of a struggle that in the words of the authoritative *Al-Ahram* (December 29, 1967), "aims at liquidating the results of the June '67 aggression without losing sight of the aim of liquidating the results of the aggression of May '48 [the establishment of the Jewish state]."[21] (When outsiders affirmed the same thing, Egyptians and "Western specialists" in Cairo became indignant, reported a correspondent of the *Times*: "Egyptians, whenever questioned about their attitude toward Israel, emphasize that Cairo implicitly recognized Israel's existence by accepting the United Nations Security [Council] Resolution of Nov. 22, 1967. . . .")[22] The two-step policy was repeatedly enunciated in public by President Nasser. In one instance: "The Arab nation has decided to embark on the path of struggle and war. . . . We will move on to the containment of Israel, and after that to . . . its eradication."[23] On another occasion he insisted that there "is no alternative to the evacuation of all occupation forces from all occupied land," and that there "can be no bargains at the expense of Palestine's land or people. . . . We do not renounce a single inch of Arab land in any Arab country. . . ."[24] Speaking before the National Assembly of the United Arab Republic, on January 20, 1969, Nasser referred to the *fedayeen:* "They are entitled to reject this resolution [No. 242], which may serve the purpose of eliminating the consequences of the aggression carried out in June, 1967, but is inadequate for determining the Palestine fate."[25] There were some compensations in Egypt's worsened position: Egyptians now gloried in the newfound tactical flexibility in terms reminiscent of Bourguiba's earlier pleas. "Egypt risks nothing," argued Haikal, "by attempting first of all to solve the first phase by political means. The same does not apply to Israel. If the Arabs wish to retract their agreement to the Security Council resolution, it is easy for them to do so by a single word. But if Israel should wish to retract the implementation of this resolution—it will have to fight a new war in order to occupy again the territories it will have evacuated in accordance with that resolution."[26]

The extraordinary impact of even some semantic daring was best demonstrated by the stunning effect on the world of the wording of the Egyptian *aide-mémoire* of February 15, 1971, to Ambassador Jarring. That an Egyptian government should speak of readiness to enter into "a peace agreement with Israel" pushed Israel into a quandary, excited sympathies for Arabs all over, elicited powerful diplomatic support, wrested the initiative from the foe, exposing him finally as the real warmonger in the Middle East. As usual the offer was made contingent on the achievement of a "just" settlement for the Palestinians and the "full and scrupulous" implementation of United Nations desiderata, among others; the words "peace" and "agreement" are in the Arab context absurdities when associated with Jewish statehood, and "Israel" itself is not necessarily unacceptable, if cleansed of that evil. (As Nasser said two years earlier, concerning what might be left of Israel after a "humanitarian solution" was consummated: "Call it Israel, or whatever you want to call it, and I will recognize it.") The overture to Jarring was explained in the Arab world as a maneuver to deepen Israel's isolation in the international community, and the point was made repeatedly that the final option was not closed, though Egypt may have to make some temporary concessions to win back the Sinai.

Soon after the *aide-mémoire* was delivered, Haikal explained (February 26) that no material change had taken place in Egypt's basic aims: elimination of the traces of the aggression of 1967, followed by the elimination of Israel itself; the latter aim was unattainable under present conditions, he argued, but that did not mean that Egypt has abandoned it as a fundamental principle of its foreign policy. Some Arabs, he said pointedly to the *fedayeen*, "sometimes commit the error of starting with the second step instead of with the first."[27] Speaking on February 28 before the National Council of Palestine, Sadat said: "It is your right to oppose the decision of the Security Council. The just solution must be based on all the decisions of the United Nations until today. . . . The liberation of the territories is what we have chosen for this stage. Revolutionary Arab thought must define the stages of a consistent and diligent policy out of the necessity that all the various strategies used in the confrontation with the enemy should flow out of one grand strategy. This will assure the victory of the Arab will." He has repeatedly asserted since that the Security Council resolution and Jarring are a key to this problem: "The problem is the occupied territory and the rights of the Palestinian people."[28] On another occasion Sadat explained that contacts with Jarring and the United Nations must be based on two principles: "No surrender of one inch of Arab land. No bargaining on the rights of the Palestinians."[29]

The more distant objective is obscured for foreigners, but usually they themselves do this quite spontaneously when confronted by conventional codes. For instance, when the newly formed Federation of Arab Republics solemnly vowed that there will be "no bargaining on the Palestinian cause" (also "no peace or negotiation with the Zionist enemy, no yielding an inch of Arab territory"), the Cairo correspondent for the *Times* assumed that it meant no bargaining over personal property rights of refugees.[30] When Sadat mentioned the imperative of "a just solution to the Palestine problem," on which his readiness for peace hinges, to an American journalist, the latter just as spontaneously understood the phrase only in a limited sense (financial compensation, autonomy in only part of Palestine), asking was this what Sadat meant. Sadat replied quite agreeably: "I'm not in a position to decide for the Palestinians but this sounds like a reasonable way to solve the problem—compensation and referendum. They must decide for themselves."[31] When King Hussein announced his plans for a future United Arab Kingdom, which to Westerners at least appeared to move precisely in this moderate direction, Sadat broke relations with Jordan and vowed to the Palestinian National Council assembled in Cairo: "Egypt will not allow anyone to liquidate the rights of the Palestinian people. Palestine will not be lost and the political rights of the Palestinian people will not be a point of bargaining."[32] The assent of the main body of the *fedayeen* to Egypt's policy was founded on the frank understanding that the former will cooperate in Egypt's retrieval of territories lost in 1967 and the latter in the Palestinians' retrieval of their patrimony. Egypt insisted on the obvious (for Egyptians) order of priorities and most *fedayeen*, including the chief leader, Arafat, demurred, perhaps reluctantly. As for the time lag between the phases, such hints as were dropped abroad suggested something more than a decade, though more sanguine and more dilatory notions also existed.[33]

The impact of the policy on Western opinion may be gauged from the following samples. In the pages of the *Times* diplomatic and intelligence experts emphatically asserted that the Arabs had already made their peace with Israel,[34] as did a foreign policy leader, J. W. Fulbright, on the floor of the U.S. Senate;[35] the chief editorial writer of another influential newspaper asserted "a visible readiness among the top Arab leaders for a reconciliation" unmatched on the other side;[36] readers of a Jewish journal were informed from Cairo by another journalist that expert observers there, "witnessing Sadat's soft-spoken tactics and his offer to Israel of a peace treaty, believe Sadat genuinely wants to have a settlement with Israel."[37] The *Times* correspondent in Cairo reported: "'Sadat and the Egyptians want peace,' a European diplomat commented last week. 'But the irony is that they are beginning to believe they will have to go to war to get it.'"[38] Another Western specialist in Cairo had been reported as saying even before the *aide-mémoire* to Jarring that the Egyptians "have done everything except to run up the Israeli flag and salute it to make it clear that the annihilation of Israel is no longer their objective."[39] Perhaps the most remarkable fact was the absence of discussion in this country, indeed any reference in even serious journals, of the policy of phases, discussed with such openness and elaboration in the Arab world, including organs of expression, such as *Al-Ahram,* usually scrutinized by Western sources for political developments in that part of the world.

With the Arab mainsteam now poised on gradualism, the articulation of dissent fell chiefly to the Marxist fringe in the Palestine movement and its allies in Iraq, Algeria, Libya, and elsewhere. Their critique of gradualism, like the critique of the newly converted gradualists earlier against Bourguiba, expressed distrust in diplomacy and fear for the essential Arab stake in Palestine inherent in the method and the suspicion that the protagonists of moderation were actually not averse to liquidating all for a mess of lentils. Given the mercurial character of moderation in the Arab context and the characteristic free-floating distrust within it, one must expect quickly shifting confrontations of this kind even within the mainstream. A good example was furnished early in 1972, when King Hussein, having reportedly harbored the suspicion that the Egyptians intended to ignore other Arab claims for perhaps many years if the United States succeeded in effecting a partial Israeli withdrawal from the Suez Canal, seized the diplomatic initiative with a proposal for a Palestinian entity in a future United Arab Kingdom; the Egyptians and others, suspecting that Hussein was in league with the Americans and the Israelis, now joined all *fedayeen,* Iraq, and Algeria in accusing *him* of selling out the Arab cause.

The *fedayeen,* or Palestine guerrillas, free to assert their determination to destroy Israel unequivocally abroad as at home, were trapped in a dilemma of their own making. For them the basic problem was assuring the ultimate option—the Arab character of all Palestine following Israel's demise—while winning international support on the basis of a nonchauvinistic formulation. For the more avowedly progressive segments of the *fedayeen* movement, such a formulation was important also for their credibility as revolutionaries. The slogan that emerged from the search for nongenocidal language vis-à-vis Israel after the June war debacle was the now-familiar call for a "democratic Palestine in which Arabs and Jews will live in peace," which has appeared since in many variants. (Frequently the reference is to religious groups only, Muslims, Jews, and Christians, and often the term "secular state" is added.) As a public-relations maneuver the new slogan has been a great success, having been endorsed by new-left groups, ecclesiastic organizations, and others, with even liberal journals disseminating the slogan at face value, as if self-explanatory. While some sources would probably endorse the liquidation of the Jewish state in even other formulations, there is obvious appeal for many more in this particular vision of the removal of narrow, religious, even racist dominion in favor of a nonchauvinistic society in which all are equal.

In the Arab context the Democratic Palestine naturally means an Arab Palestine. The anxiety to assure beyond doubt this fact is reflected in a number of constitutional provisions embodied in the Palestinian National Covenant, the basic document of the Palestine Liberation Movement, the embryonic basic law of the state-to-be. Article 1 of the Covenant asserts that "Palestine is the homeland of the Palestinian Arab people and an integral part of the great Arab homeland, and the people of Palestine is a part of the Arab nation."[40] Article 3 reads: "The Palestinian Arab people possesses the legal right to its homeland, and when the liberation of its homeland is completed it will exercise self-determination solely according to its own will and choice." The exclusively Arab national character of the state-to-be following the demise of the Jewish state, asserted variously through the covenant, is assured explicitly further by the categorical assertion that Jews cannot possibly be viewed as forming a national group, merely a religious one (Article 20); having denied any legal, historical, national, or other tie between Jews and Palestine, it asserts that "Judaism, in its character as a religion of revelation, is not a nationality with an independent existence. Likewise, the Jews are not one people with an independent personality. They are rather citizens of the states to which they belong." Occasional references to the future Palestine as a "binational" state and to Jews as a "nationality" are meant to designate the Jewish part in this sense. The covenant insists (Article 20) that Jewish claims to Palestine are devoid of "the constituents of statehood in their real sense." The most avowedly progressive component of the *fedayeen* movement, the Popular Democratic Front for the Liberation of Palestine (PDFLP), has rejected on these grounds the binational formula of the *Matzpen,* a fringe group of Israeli Marxists; in presuming national parity of the two, Jewish and Arab, components of the future state, the *Matzpen* was not sufficiently progressive (since any Jewish national rights constitute Zionism, the liquidation of Zionism requires merely minority status for Jews in Palestine, though with full civil rights as citizens of an Arab state).[41]

Some implications of the slogan have produced anxiety and confusion in the ranks of the *fedayeen.* Were Jewish statehood to dissipate overnight, a democratically reconstituted Palestinian state might once more become a Jewish state simply because there would be more Jews than Arabs in it, even if all expatriates returned. The Covenant provides for this eventuality in Article 6, which lays down that only "Jews who were living permanently in Palestine until the beginning of the Zionist invasion will be considered Palestinians." In the Arab context the watershed is commonly and even formally placed at the Balfour Declaration of 1917, when fewer than 100,000 Jews were in the country. The matter is obviously embarrassing, for implementation would imply forced elimination of nearly 97% of the Jews of the country, and Arab spokesmen abroad have engaged in various semantic acrobatics, including outright distortion, in the attempt to parry questions touching on this painful problem.[42] A real moral and existential dilemma persists, however, among the *fedayeen* themselves, since the public-relations techniques do not actually remove the distracting likelihood of having to cope with a huge mass of Jews, who have in the past proved to be tough subjects to handle. Some pronouncements of the *fedayeen* have consequently implied obviously genocidal solutions, particularly in hinting at the extreme destructiveness of the people's war they claim to be waging. Harkabi, who has made careful studies of the *fedayeen*'s position, explained that the expression (*ifna*) used in this connection literally means reduction to "absolute nothingness," the distinction between formal military forces and civilians not being as fastidious in a people's war as in Frederician eighteenth-century warfare.[43] There are not going to be too many Jews left after victory, regardless, seems to be the message here.[44] But the PDFLR, taking their progressiveness seriously, are troubled by such reversion to what they decry as Shukairism and opt instead for the humane equivalent of reduction: The Jews would themselves wish to leave Palestine, once they have been freed from the shackles of the Zionist clique, above all the Jews lured to Israel from Arab states, now forming half the Jewish community in Israel. Efforts have been devoted to preparing the future return of these Jews to their previous homes by the PDFLR in particular, and promising announcements have been made in this regard. Still, the dilemma has lingered, the slogans were heatedly debated in Palestinian circles, special studies were initiated, and quite a few *fedayeen*, particularly in the more traditional *Fatah*, have opted for abandonment of slogans, which, albeit invaluable on the front of international propaganda, tend to be a source of anxiety for the Palestine Liberation Movement, if not a real threat to the ultimate aspiration itself.

In a post-June war survey of the Arab world, the Swiss Orientalist-journalist, Arnold Hottinger, suggested that the familiar codes, while serving Arab diplomacy in the struggle with Israel, actually betray the real—to him meta-rational—Arab position toward that state.[45] The insistence on indirect dealings with Israel has been officially explained as a reluctance to negotiate from weakness, to preserve honor ("capitulation"), and accepted as such abroad even at the highest levels. But in the Arab context, where Israel is an abomination that should never have been and with which one does not have dealings, indirect contact, though unpleasant, means just conceding to third parties that the evil exists, after all, and shows readiness to make arrangements concerning it for so long as political and military circumstances make more forthright action impossible. The ultimate option for "justice" is thus preserved, even if papers are signed, the Arabs insisting that, whatever the form of agreement, they are really addressing themselves to third parties—the United Nations, the great powers—in whatever they appear to be pledging to Israel. This stance is acceptable to Arab statesmen and their peoples as a "war ruse" well worth the territories won back from the foe, with a mental reservation: "Someday we will settle accounts. The reality of the, only temporary, existence of the state of the Jews must be conceded, meanwhile, by us; but we cannot and will not betray our right to Palestine or deny the fact that our country was unjustly taken from us."[46] If the Arabs could be assured in advance that all territories may be recovered in return for some face-to-face exposure to the foe, the triumph might justify even such step. (Even though claiming confidence in, and American promises for, full recovery of territories after the subsequent war, the Egyptians still insisted that all dealings, described abroad as finally direct negotiations, were nothing of the sort. At Geneva, they sat in a United Nations forum, as always; at Kilometer 101, their military officers met with Israeli military officers, as many times before, also under United Nations aegis; as for Kissinger's "shuttling" diplomacy, why they are always ready to talk to an American Secretary of State, or any other mediator.)

In a situation in which the Arabs could not hope to recoup all their losses, even if they agreed to direct negotiations, they risked compromising "justice," without the redeeming virtues of successful cunning. The issue before them, explained Hottinger, was thus not bargaining but "victory" (recouping the last losses while maintaining the integrity of the initial claim) or "defeat," which posture may explain their categorical insistence since the June war on total Israeli

withdrawal arranged under United Nations or great-power auspices
("political solution") pending recovery of losses by military
means.[47]

It was difficult to see in the West's intellectual climate, dominated
by diplomatic and journalistic perceptions, that the Arab insistence—categorical, repetitive and unchanged, almost ritualistic—on
total Israeli withdrawal represented insistence on ultimate Israeli
withdrawal from the Middle East altogether. It was successfully rationalized by several factors, such as the conditioned linkage of
"withdrawal" to "peace" or reference to irrelevant principles of international law on the acquisition of territory by aggression. The
words of Haikal, confidant of Egyptian rulers, explicating this insistence with clarity, thus merit citation at some length. The question
put to him by Edmund Ghareeb referred to the Rogers plan, envisioning total (or virtually total) Israeli withdrawal from conquered
territory; Haikal replied:

A. "The initiative came from America; the half per cent chance
for success, however, depended on Israel. Abdul Nasser could not
hope for a positive response from Israel, for he knew that Israel
would never accept total withdrawal. I believe that Abdul Nasser
viewed the issue of withdrawal as the testing ground which would
transform the issue into being purely one of territory. Would Israel
withdraw from all the occupied territories or would it refuse to do
so? That was the crucial question; he regarded everything else as
secondary at that stage.

"Abdul Nasser was certain, nevertheless, that Israel would not
accept total withdrawal, otherwise everything it had hoped to gain
through what it did in 1967 would be lost, all the objectives of the
campaign would remain unrealized."

Q. "Could you elaborate a little more on this? Are you saying
that, if Israel were to withdraw, all its objectives would remain unrealized?"

A. "Right. Why did Israel carry out the 1967 aggression? For two
obvious reasons; in the first place, to prove that it has the upper
hand as far as military strength is concerned—for military strength
is its trump card; secondly, to acquire new territory and at the same
time to undermine Arab claims to formerly occupied territories. It
would, in this way, be superimposing the peremptory demands of
one state of affairs on top of the peremptory demands of another.

"Once again, total Israeli withdrawal, if it were to take place,
would be tantamount to showing that military strength is irrelevant

to the outcome of the conflict, that the military factor is not decisive in the Middle East conflict, that it is perhaps capable of producing spectacular tactical results, but that their results will be shortlived.

"All the realities of the situation are against such a turn of events. If you could succeed in bringing it about, you would have passed sentence on the entire state of Israel. The survival of the entire state of Israel is contingent on its ability to force its presence. . . ."[48]

Repeating their truth in an environment of disbelief abroad, to so great an extent of their own making, the Arabs were not merely embittered, but often actually filled with doubt about the sincerity, intelligence, and sanity of others. This condition has fired some Westerners with a sense of mission to enlighten the deceived, in a crusade in which a little band of men and women, styling themselves as insiders ("those who had lived in the area" or "those who know the Middle East"[49]), dare to confront Zionist corruption and intimidation of the press and politics.

Yet these people, though zealously insisting on the gravity of the outrage suffered by the Arabs, themselves negated it by suggesting that relatively superficial concessions would actually satisfy the Arabs. Typical of the influence of this group is John H. Davis, who as Commissioner-General of the United Nations Relief and Works Agency, advised the General Assembly (in 1962) of the depth of Arab outrage, declaring that it is "the Arab people as a whole, and not just the million-odd displaced refugees, who feel deeply that an injustice has been committed against the Arabs of Palestine. As they view the situation, they see a country obliterated and a people uprooted and dispossessed. . . ."[50] Yet, he intimated, this proud people, known to practice elaborate systems of vengeance and retribution, merely desired the implementation of United Nations resolutions concerning the return of refugees. The refugees were the root of the problem.

Another popular nostrum is territorial adjustment. Commander Hutchinson, who returned to the United States from his duties as chief military officer of the United Nations in the Middle East, determined to convey to his compatriots the intensity of Arab bitterness, stressed the centrality of territorial adjustment. He suggested that the Arabs really wanted just "a more equitable division of the land."[51] The very men who felt that the world did not sufficiently appreciate the depth of Arab outrage thus made common cause, albeit perhaps unwittingly, with those who argued that Arab outrage was mostly superficial. Both concluded that the key to the conflict lay in repatriation and border adjustment. The existence of the Jewish state was not the issue, presumably.

Such incoherent perception of Arab attitudes may be explained by either pro-Arab or simply anti-Jewish sentiments. Since the open expression of anti-Jewish sentiments offends norms of decency in some classes in the West, particularly in the upper middle class and upper class in English-speaking countries, the Palestine conflict provided a convenient opportunity to be anti-Jewish with a good conscience. Bernard Lewis has suggested that the merely anti-Jewish may be distinguished from the pro-Arab essentially in that they show no interest in the Arabs or sympathy for them except as Jews are involved. They care little for wrongs suffered by Arabs at the hands of anyone but Jews; they show little interest in the history and culture of Arabs and their great achievements; indeed, they speak of Arabs disparagingly. They might style themselves as Arabists without seriously studying Arabic or Arabs; an expression of their demeanor toward Arabs is the manner in which they explain away the more extreme statements by Arabs, as if the latter are less than human, need not be taken seriously, and their language—actually a source of great pride to Arabs—not worth listening to, like random noise.[52]

Genuinely pro-Arab sentiment may lead to similar behavior through the psychological mechanism in opinion-influence situations thought to be a "strain toward consistency" among various cognitions.[53] This idea asserts that people tend to agree with people they like and tend to like people who agree with them. Under these circumstances, three sets of cognitions are "consonant," or consistent with each other: one's own opinion, one's evaluation of the source, and one's judgment of the source's position (which does not always correspond to the position actually held by the source). A conflict between a positive evaluation of the source and a negative evaluation of the position he holds (or vice versa) yields "cognitive dissonance," a state of psychological tension that produces efforts to restore these cognitions to a consistent state. One common outcome is misperception of the source's position. When one's highly positive feeling toward Arabs conflicts with unsavory intentions attributed to them, the resulting strain could be resolved by bringing these intentions in line with one's high regard for Arabs.[54] For instance, if the unsavory intention is merely alleged, one is likely to cast doubt upon the veracity of the message; if the statement has been personally witnessed, or is conveyed by an unimputable medium, one is likely to cast doubt on the seriousness of the statement —in the first case, "the Arabs did not say that," in the second, "the Arabs do not mean what they are saying." To Commander Hutchison, for instance, threats against the life of Israel is just so much verbiage uttered "in political heat."[55] Grant Butler, who displayed great attachment to the Arabs, handled these threats somewhat differently; according to him, "*Intelligent* Arabs do not want Israel destroyed."[56] Some writers thus concede that contemptible types (and which society does not have some?) indeed do such things; they often go on to challenge others to come up with but one instance implicating a man like Nasser in the same manner. (He was, frequently.) In the entourage of President Tito of Yugoslavia, whose great personal affection for Nasser was widely known, the latter's intent toward Israel was perceived in an extraordinary manner: Far from wanting to harm Israel, explained a high Yugoslav personage, Nasser was in fact vitally concerned for the security and prosperity of the Jewish state, for he believed it secured Egypt's own well-being.[57]

An interesting illustration was provided at a public debate in Washington. Christopher Mayhew, a leader in Arab-British amity, cited an Arab poem (Nashashibi's *Return Ticket*) as proof of the depth of feeling for the lost land, quoting:

"Every year I shall say to my little son, 'We shall return, my son, and you will be with me; we shall return to our land and walk there barefoot. We will remove our shoes so that we may feel the holiness of the ground beneath us. . . . Do you not remember Jaffa and its delightful shore, Haifa and its lofty mountain . . . the streets of Jerusalem, my dear Jerusalem, Tiberias and its peaceful shore with the golden waves. . . ?'

"And so on," concluded Mr. Mayhew. But another participant proceeded to quote from the poem later, as follows:

"I shall see the hatred in the eyes of my son and your sons. I want them to be callous and to be ruthless. I want them to enter their lairs . . . we will enter their lairs in Tel Aviv. We will smash Tel Aviv with axes, guns, fingernails and teeth."[58]

That it is great affection for Arabs that produces the view of them as simultaneously bitterly outraged yet curiously devoid of hostility must be evident from the extremely flattering conception of Arab character consistent with such a view; for one would have to possess a near angelic nature in order to muster such restraint. It is doubtful that even Scandinavian cultures would fit this model, despite their extraordinary normative restraints; yet the same model is asserted to function in Arab culture, in which the norms actually pull in the opposite direction. But it is equally apparent that this resolution of dissonance is facilitated by a weak commitment to the target of Arab bitterness, Israel. According to the "weakest link" hypothesis in influence theory, very intense opinions are not usually the "easiest" cognitions to change. If these writers had really a strong commitment to Israel, source derogation (i.e., bad opinion of the Arabs), rather than opinion change or misperception of the source's position, would more likely be selected as the mode of dissonance-resolution. In fact, protestations to the contrary notwithstanding, writers in this category manifest a weak commitment to the continued survival of the Jewish state, which probably constitutes the "weakest link" in the structure of their cognitions in the conflict.

It is thus characteristic of Western sympathizers of the Arabs to argue that the Jewish state compromises its justification for being by the wrongs it inflicts on the Arabs; but it is clear that many of them question its legitimacy on grounds not necessarily connected with Arab-Jewish relations. For the historian Arnold J. Toynbee, for one, Jewish nationhood anywhere in the world constitutes an historical anachronism at best;[59] for the theologian Millar Burrows, it suggests historical vindication of the Jews' rejection of Jesus.[60] Of particular interest are the traditional (as opposed to new-left) Jewish Western sympathizers of the Arabs; for Rabbi Elmer Berger, for instance, Jewish statehood constitutes a threat to his Judaism.[61]

When expressing a correct, and even solicitous, attitude toward the Jewish state, these and other writers betray little real concern for its continued existence. This is not to say what they ought to do; just what they actually do. Virtually all of them make practical suggestions for settling the Arab-Israeli conflict, invariably involving substantial concessions by Israel in return for its acceptance by the Arabs. This usually involves radical territorial changes, massive repatriation of refugees, and other concessions. Whether the resulting entity would at all be viable or long persist as a Jewish state, is not a question with which these writers are concerned. A rare exception actually furnishes a textbook illustration of the "weakest link" hypothesis presented earlier. "Will the Arabs, once they have received territorial concessions, keep asking for more and more?" wondered Alfred Lilienthal, who urged them. He continued: "It is true that no one can say with certainty whether any settlement of the

Palestine case, short of the destruction of Israel, would be satisfactory to the Arabs, *but President Nasser has indicated that he still wishes to direct his efforts in other directions and is concerned about Egypt's growing reliance on the Soviet Union. . . .*"[62]

In the wake of the Arab debacle in the June war many Western advocates of the Arabs have shown a markedly greater readiness to support openly the destruction of Jewish statehood. That this should happen just when Arabs themselves were muting their own pronouncements need not be a puzzle at all, for the dissonance theory actually requires the change. The outcome of the war and the resulting improvement in Arab public relations had sharply reduced the previous tension between evaluation of the source and judgment of the source's position: Whatever the Arabs might say, one now felt reassured that they really did not mean it, either because they did not want to or because they were incorrigible bunglers. With the ugly, genocidal cloud out as irritant, Arab aims could be acknowledged with less hesitation than before.

The exultation in the Arab world over the beginning demise of the Jewish state in the October war was celebrated in the West as its final accommodation with it in nearly hysterical terms. However spectacular, the sources of perception were familiar. To begin with, a revolutionary shift in the Arab attitude was proclaimed by America's most celebrated diplomat and his principal, a team credited with epochal foreign policy achievements. The press was even less inquisitive of Henry Kissinger in this area than in any other (though not of Richard Nixon) and treated the claim as fact. Besides, the journalists on the spot gave little reason for doubt, reporting the historic shift from various Arab capitals. Algeria, it was asserted one day, has drastically changed its position, and is now for a "negotiated peace with Israel," as are the *fedayeen* and others. Egypt had just accomplished an "astonishing shift of position," endorsed by the other Arab states, one read another day. Soon Syria followed. And so on. Yet on scrutiny the reports appeared dubious in the extreme, many being simply spurious inferences. In the New York *Times* Henry Tanner thus reported from Cairo that the acquiescence by Arab states in Egypt's participation in the Geneva conference "implies" recognition of Israel.[63] A summary of the Algiers summit announced "that Arab states for the first time *tacitly* recognized the right of Israel to exist as a state."[64] If such inferences, which some Arabs encourage, were a valid indication of the Arabs' intent, they would already have made their peace with Israel a quarter of a century ago, when their failure to leave the United Nations at Israel's admission was said to signify as much.

Other "evidence" for journalistic claims were the disengagement pacts, the military agreements that skirted completely outstanding political issues. "The [Syrian] accord, once concluded," read a typical evaluation, "can be taken as a firm repudiation of the old Arab ideology. . . ."[65] Another, for the *Times* man in Cairo, was the fact that Arab newspapers referred to Israeli official spokesmen in writing about Kissinger's disengagement talks. This would surely result in millions of Arabs thinking of Israel as a normal state, he thought, hence they were "accepting Israel."[66] The Arab press had of course been referring to and citing leading Israelis for many years before.

The Secretary himself, now international folk hero and "miracle" man in even the respectable press, steadily provided support at home and abroad, speaking of Egypt's "bold decision to move from confrontation to negotiation" and announcing to the Israelis their "friendly" acceptance by the Arabs.[67] As for *his* sources, they appeared from talks with Kissinger's aides to be words exchanged with Arab leaders and a certain idiosyncratic conviction that the antagonists' suffering and pain in the recent war must incline them to peace. (In reality his interventions in the war—first, denying the resupply of Israeli forces for one week of grave losses at the start, then forcing them to accept a cease-fire when the Arabs tottered on the brink of disaster, could only "brutalize" one side, giving the other exultation.[68]) And, having, indeed, said he believed the Arabs were ready for peace even before the war,[69] the "tilt" in these interventions appears not to have been just chance.

As for words passed between Arabs and Westerners, they are in the recent period no less tricky than before. Though Western excitement is stirred by frequent Arab resort to the term "peace" in connection with Israel, the usage in the original context denotes not what the term means to us. The term the Arabs are using is *salaam,* meaning less than full peace, and is more closely equivalent to our notion of an armistice. *Sulh,* or real peace, has been emphatically ruled out in this connection. Soon after the October war (December 7, 1973), the editor of Egypt's leading weekly magazine, *Al-Mussawar,* spelled out the difference between *salaam* and *sulh:*

"The Arab language has been called the mother of languages, because it is the richest language of all. For example, the English word 'peace' can be translated into Arabic as both 'sulh' and 'salaam' whereas in Arabic there is a difference between the two. Sulh is one thing. Salaam another.

"The conference that everyone is talking about, the one to be held in Geneva to solve the problems of the Middle East, is liable to confuse these two words because of their single meaning in the European languages, and as a result, the meaning of the conference might not be clear to others."

The article goes on to explain that Israel can have *salaam* in return for submission to all Arab demands at this time. "But sulh is another thing altogether. Sulh means that the Jews of Palestine— and I repeat and emphasize the expression 'Jews of Palestine'— will return to their senses and will dwell under one roof and under one flag with the Arabs of Palestine, in a secular state devoid of any bigotry or racialism, proportional to their respective numerical ratio in 1948.

"By this I mean that the original Palestinian Jews and their children and grandchildren shall remain on the Palestinian soil and will live there with the original Palestinian Arabs. The Jews who came from abroad will return to their countries of origin, where they lived as did their fathers and forefathers before 1948—for these countries bear them no ill-will."

In view of the painfully scrupulous choice of words the anxiety not to abandon the Arab cause even in rhetoric, it is often sheer carelessness and presumptuousness by Westerners that manages to sustain delusion. For sometimes just a hint of inquisitiveness clears the air. In an interview on the CBS program *Sixty Minutes on February 27, 1972*, Libya's Qadhafi was asked what he would do if Sadat were to sign a peace agreement with Israel. When the Libyan answered, "Sadat will not make peace with Israel," the interviewer would not let go and insisted that Sadat was talking as though he did want peace. Qadhafi explained: "It is not peace as peace, as we all know what it means. It is armistice."

Thus, the celebration of the historic shift could take place in our diplomacy and journalism while the familiar denigration of the foe, including the demeaning of Jews as such, continued unabated in the Arab communications media. The stream of invective is well epitomized in a cartoon in *Al-Ahram* (April 7, 1974), the leading newspaper of the Arab nation presumably leading the new departure, showing a line of figures queuing in front of a guillotine, the inscriptions on the figures reading in this order: "Moshe Dayan," "the government of Israel," "the Israeli political system," and finally "Zionism" itself. (Egypt's second-largest newspaper, *Al-Akhbar* [August 19, 1974], vindicated Hitler's genocide of the Jews, "the enemies of mankind." The Syrian leadership, newly converted to the new direction in the Arab world, was reported in Beirut's *Al-Bairak* [June 26, 1974] as commemorating Hitler in a meeting with Lebanese visitors.)

Having managed to ignore the strategy of phases earlier, our correspondents in the Arab world did as well on its projection after the October war onto Palestine itself. The apparent success of the strategy for Egypt (which endorsed it publicly soon after signing the disengagement pact)[70] combined with new opportunities and fears to incline the *fedayeen* toward it as their own approach to the final objective. Since there no longer existed doubts among Arabs about Israeli retreats, merely doubts about their rate, the *fedayeen* decided to prevent restoration of Hussein's rule in any territory vacated by Israel by taking it themselves. The rationale was clearly stated in their public organs (*Shuun Filastiniya* and others) and discussed elsewhere. When the Palestine National Council adopted its "phased political program," it repeatedly insisted on the meaning of accepting vacated territory. Thus, Point 8: "The Palestinian national authority, after its establishment, will struggle for the unity of the confrontation states for the sake of completing the liberation of all Palestinian soil and as a step on the path of comprehensive Arab unity."[71] *Fedayeen* spokesmen have usually been as explicit in talking with Westerners. Thus, Naif Hawatmeh, when asked by a German journalist (*Deutsche Zeitung,* April 19, 1974) whether the goal would still be the liquidation of Israel after a Palestinian state was established on the West Bank and the Gaza Strip, replied: "Yes. We shall not relent on this goal because our purpose is the establishment of a democratic state in all of Palestine. A state in the occupied territories is not an obstacle, it is a starting point."[72]

Western correspondents invariably translate "national authority" into "state," and the *fedayeen* sometimes indulge them but rigidly adhere among themselves to the crucial distinction, since the latter concept has a stable, terminal rather than a dynamic, struggling connotation. The *fedayeen* insistence is invariably dismissed for one reason or another. For Flora Lewis, writing from Paris, "there is no doubt that for the Palestinians negotiation would mean accepting the permanent existence of Israel as a Jewish state implanted in the Middle East."[73] Henry Tanner reports from Cairo: "The moderates that have a majority in the movement concede privately that this goal ('secular democratic state') is no longer realistic, but will not say so publicly."[74] The issue, as conveyed by our press, is only whether Israel will concede to the Palestinians once and for all their state in parts of occupied territory as a homeland for the refugees.

6

WHAT THE ARABS ARE SAYING

LIKE afflicted people everywhere, the Arabs have expressed their pain better than they have been able to explain it, possibly because they did not wholly understand it themselves. Of course they knew all along that their affliction was "Zionism," which is not inaccurate, but neither is it very enlightening. What exactly is there about this particular "ism" that fills them with such pain and bitterness?

There exists variability in feelings toward Israel in the Arab world, in terms of geography, class, and other factors; but to judge from what one hears, reads, or sees daily in its communication media, Arabs seem almost universally preoccupied with Israel to the point of obsession. This preoccupation saturates broadcasting and printed journalism and is reflected in an immense output of books and pamphlets, and also in casual conversations. The consuming concern has deepened since the 1967 war, but the media seemed hardly less obsessed with Israel before, though periods of relative calm alternated with periods of near paroxysm. Impressions gathered by acute observers some twenty years ago could easily be mistaken for contemporary reporting. One wrote in 1956: "The Arabs hate Israel with an intensity that surpasses measurement and description. The quantity of time, energy and passion devoted in the Arab countries to railing against, brooding over, and just hating Israel has to be seen on the spot to be believed."[1] Another had written earlier, in 1952: "Rarely a day passes that some aspect of the Palestine conflict between the Arabs and the Zionists fails to appear on the front pages of every newspaper in the Arab world, and rare indeed are conversations in which Palestine does not play a significant part."[2] Still earlier, soon after the first major Arab-Israeli war, another observer, who repeatedly crossed the lines between the combatants, found that the talk of peace heard outside the Arab countries seemed like a pipedream in the reality prevailing in all classes, save the royal palace in Amman; still dazed by the recent failure to conquer the foe, Arabs already spoke of the next attempt as merely a question of time.[3] The manner in which even ordinary Arabs use almost any exchange of views to vent their grievance, often in unrestrainable and violent fashion, suggests the depth of feeling on this matter.[4]

A measure of the Arabs' trauma with Israel is their conception of this predicament in extreme, even cosmic, terms. Israel's existence is habitually described in corresponding language, for instance, as "a cancer in the body of the Arab Nation, which ought to be exterminated,"[5] if that nation is to survive. Hence, also the customary reference to the "battle of destiny," in which it will be decided whether the Arabs "are either worthy of living or not,"[6] the test being Israel's removal, the existence of which is portrayed as the greatest outrage in human history and other catastrophic terms.

How do the Arabs explain their profound sense of outrage? They view themselves as the absolutely innocent victims of a particularly heinous crime, perpetrated by people who, far from being provoked, actually owed them an immense debt of gratitude. The "asp in our bosom" conception of Jews fits with traditional Islamic views of them as inherently depraved, treacherous people; the Prophet himself is said to have been betrayed (and murdered) by them. To foreign publics pre-Zionist Arab-Jewish history is presented in idyllic terms to make the same point of ingratitude and betrayal. The Prophet's spiritual kinship to Judaism is stressed (but not his denigration and massacre of the Jews); the protection of Jews in Islam is cited (but not their political subjection within it); much emphasis is given to the friendship existing among many Arabs and Jews before Zionism (the term itself connotes a challenge to an order in which everyone "knew" his place, without making this anxious idea too explicit). The posture is not uncharacteristic of challenged masters, as in our own Southland, where supposedly universal contentment was said to have been spoiled by outside agitation; or in industrial relations, when patronal paternalism is challenged by trade-unionism.

The aggression against the Arabs is portrayed as underhanded, rather than manly and direct. What the Jewish side regards as a long and desperate struggle to return a victimized people to its ancestral home, the Arabs see as a series of international deceptions and conspiracies for their despoilment, from the diplomatic duplicities of the Allies in the First World War to the alleged Anglo-American complicity with Israel in the 1967 war. There is no value or capacity inherent in Israel as such, which constitutes merely an instrumentality of international tormentors of the Arabs (and others); it is artificial and incapable of existence except as an extension of these factors. Israel is thus a horrifying irrelevancy, but an irrelevancy just the same; one does not really address oneself to, or treat with, a plague (or "running dogs," in leftist parlance). Even when one must talk to Israel, one sees oneself as speaking only to third parties; even at the height of the peace offensive to recoup lost territories after the June war, the President of Egypt held that Israel was irrelevant; what mattered was what the other powers and the United Nations said and did.[7] When not citing the inevitability of the Arabs' future military ascendancy over Israel, they base the certainty of their eventual salvation on the proposition that "imperialism," having been defeated or won over sooner or later, Israel will automatically wither and shrink into nothingness. (While, as part of that campaign, many influential visitors to Cairo were sent on to impress Jerusalem with Egypt's desire for peace, influential Cairenes paused to "speculate that Israel might in the foreseeable future be forced to go the way of Taiwan, claiming that there is an analogy between the two situations. They maintain that the Americans artificially upheld the existence of 12 million Formosans in the face of 800 million Chinese, but finally realised that this was not only unrealistic, but contrary to American interests. Similarly, these Arab leaders argue, the Americans will accept that it is more rational, and in line with their own interests, to support 100 million Arabs and leave 3,000,000 Israelis to their fate."[8])

Richard W. Cottam has sketched an integrated picture of reality that leads many Arabs to view events very differently from the way they are viewed in the West or in Israel. The historical lesson learned from the frustration of Arab hopes in the First World War for immediate dominion in the Arab East was that the British wanted to hold the area for themselves. For modernizing Arabs in particular the picture was one of British rule, in alliance with traditionalist elites, over raw-material-producing areas for British industry and outlets for British capital. Zionism was a natural adjunct to this picture: Jewish banking interests were at the heart of the capitalist system, and the Zionist settlers in Palestine were the instrument for perpetuating imperial control of the area. This adds up to a picture of an unholy alliance of three elements: Western (in particular British) imperialism; Zionism; and the traditional Arab elites. International and domestic events are seen through this perceptual filter and their interpretation reflects this view of reality. "To call such an interpretation irrational simply reflects an inability to comprehend the world as these Arabs see it."[9] The world view appears in variation but is tightly consistent and rigidly ideologized in respect to the Jewish state, so as to exclude any justification for its being. Some *fedayeen* leaders were said to approve of the humanistic, Marxist and democratic features of the Zionist idea, only to damn the Jewish state later for betraying them.

Although lacking a Hobson-Lenin overlay the more popular picture portrays essentially the same vision. Israel appears, as in leftist cosmogonies, as the tool of various imperial and colonial circles, except that the Jewish tail here wags the dog as well. The imperialists behind Israel are themselves the dupes of occult Jewish powers, conspiring to rule the whole world, not just some land in the Middle East. A typical literary product, *The Conspiracy and the Battle of Destiny*, credits Jewish conspirators with the following achievements: a. forcing American entry into World War One and the resultant German defeat; b. engineering the Russian revolution; c. putting across the hoax that the Nazis killed six million Jews; d. assuming control of the Soviet government; e. assassinating Presidents McKinley and Kennedy; f. inciting American blacks against whites; g. controlling the major television networks in the United States; and many more. The author, Saad Jumaa, Premier and Defense Minister of Jordan during the June war, and university educated, spent twenty-six years in the Jordanian civil service and was Jordan's chief censor and director of press and publicity, a minister at the royal court, and ambassador to Damascus and Washington.

How else is one to explain the puzzling defiance of the Arab nation, the equal, if not more, of all Christendom, by a contemptible mob, without painful reevaluation of self-worth? Through the direct language of political cartoons Arabs project a rather surprising image of their foe: where one might expect him to appear fierce and vicious, as in Soviet caricatures of Nazilike Tel Aviv militarists, he emerges as a defenseless nag trembling under the butcher's knife, as a *Stürmer*-type caricature of hook-nosed ghetto scum laughably playing at soldier or as some cringing vermin under the Arab boot. There would just have to be some resort to the ahistorical to make sense of the progress of such unlikely conquerors even to the gates of Amman, Damascus, and Beirüt.

It is by reference to this phenomenon, usually termed "expansionism," that the Arabs justify their repeated rejection of proposals to come to terms with the Jewish state, as with the *Yishuv* before. As one Syrian journalist put it to his Iraqi colleague: "Let us be practical and return to history. The method which Israel has followed since June 11 [1967] is an old 'tactic' which she always succeeded in using. It is summarized in drawing the Arabs—by negotiations, war and the threat of war—to accept new relinquishments, then she will herself retreat from being content with these relinquishments and impose new terms or new situations."[10] One can hardly exaggerate how widely diffused and deeply rooted this theory is in the Arab world. In a popular version the Israelis push on with deliberation and planning, with a view toward fulfilling a biblical vision of Hebrew dominion, from the Nile to the Euphrates; this is believed to be the official Zionist program enshrined in a map in Israel's parliament, the *Knesset.* Captured Egyptian officers taken into the *Knesset* in 1956 to see for themselves that there was no such map, concluded that the Israelis had merely hidden it; another group of Egyptian officers came to the same conclusion in 1967. There is evidence that even Anglo-American residents in the Arab world believe in the existence of this pictorial blueprint.[11]

When reassured that there is indeed no such map, another one takes its place in the minds of even highly educated Arabs. An Arab student told a Hebrew University symposium: "A foreign diplomat came and said to Ben-Gurion: 'Nasser tells me you have in the Knesset [Parliament] a map painted on the wall showing the future State of Israel stretching from the Nile to the Euphrates.' Ben-Gurion took the diplomat on a tour of the Knesset and said: 'Look, no map! What do you think of Nasser now?' The diplomat said: 'Nasser is a liar,' Ben-Gurion held up his hand: 'Take it easy! Nasser isn't far out. We don't have a map painted on the wall. We carry our map around in our heads. So next time you quote Nasser's threats, don't forget the words of Ben-Gurion.' "[12]

Ben-Gurion as the village trickster in Arab folklore, the biblical "river of Egypt" as Nile (it is actually the Wadi al-Arish), and other nonsense notwithstanding, the Jewish advance is real enough, entailing further explanation and justification. Starting as a tolerated religious community of some 50,000, mainly in Jerusalem and in a handful of old towns and settlements, at the turn of the century, the Jews already numbered by mid-century almost a million in a state of their own in more than half of Cisjordania. They were nearing three million, with four times as much territory, in 1972. The industrial and military dimensions of this expansion are even more impressive, especially in relation to the Arabs' own growth, but the latter usually refer to the Jewish advance in terms of demography and especially in terms of geography. Usually an exposition of the insidious nature of Zionism is achieved by direct, graphic means—presenting a succession of maps with progressively wider territorial outlines (planned or actual) of Jewish settlement and dominion. One such demonstration, entitled "Palestine 1919–1967," starts with the demarcations of mandatory Cisjordania, followed by: the outlines of the abortive 1947 partition plan; the armistice demarcation lines of 1949; the lines of the temporarily expanded area held by Israel in the winter of 1956; the cease-fire lines following the war of 1967; and a "Zionist Plan, 1919," involving altogether less territory than the previous outline, but included in the series possibly because it indicates further Jewish expansion into Transjordan, Syria, and Lebanon.[13] Another graphic demonstration, entitled "Zionist Colonialism," culminates in a map of uncertain origin described as "Zionist Empire from the Nile to the Euphrates???"[14]

Sophisticated variants of the expansionism theory substitute various forms of compulsion for Israel's alleged deliberation (or combine the two). Thus, some necessity inherent in the Israeli condition compels expansionism regardless of conscious intent. The compulsion can be a "mystique" or a spiritual drive or a financial and political dependency on the West and world Jewry, which motivates crises productive of foreign support or the need for internal cohesion by means of stimulated external hostility. There would seem rather complicated expressions of the folkore belief in the essential depravity of the Jew.

A particularly ambitious version of the expansionism theory argues that Israel bases its strategy on the principle of total preparedness and total force, on the assumption that the all-consuming passion of the Arabs is to destroy it. Rooted in the movement of colonization and lacking defensible borders (before 1967), Israel can only have an aggressive policy; since the other side denies it any legitimacy whatsoever, settlement for Israel has to be enforced by it up to the point where it can feel secure. Eventually a *Pax Judaica* imposed on the region would give Israel the land from the Suez Canal to the Litani River (in Lebanon) and the Jebel Druz in the North; from the Mediterranean to the eastern boundaries of Jordan; and further surround these borders with a string of weak buffer states, Maronite, Druze, Kurdish, and other non-Arab or anti-Arab entities. This strategy is said to be geared to protracting the conflict, not resolving it, for resolution would require concessions and the relinquishment of gains, which would undermine the strategy. For this reason attitudes of compromise on the Arab side are said to be a source of embarrassment and profound discomfort to Israel's leadership. The theory intimates that an acceptable alternative exists to Israel's "hard strategy," but does not define it; nor is Israel's basic assumption concerning Arab hostility explicitly denied; on the other hand, Israel's actual rejection by the Arabs at each step of its development is justified by its resort to force—which the theory assumes to be a response to rejection in the first place. There is no indication on what grounds the Jewish state can be legitimized at all, except for some vague suggestion that a return to an early stage of its development is required for even a search in that direction to be contemplated.[15] It all seems a particularly circuitous way of saying that between elimination and assertion Israel consistently opts for the latter.

The language of Colonel Qadhafi, the Libyan ruler, is more direct: He asserts that nothing but total liquidation of Israel is conceivable and accuses it of expansionism. Could the latter be explained by the former? No, it is just additional reason for liquidation; Israel is accursed and evil; having been born "in war and bloodshed," it is destined to perpetuate the same.[16]

Many observers have long regarded the perennial Arab rejection of increasingly less palatable dimensions of the Jewish presence in the Middle East as itself constituting the mainspring of the Jewish expansion. Already in the first major war, 1948–49, it seemed to an American "that the Arab world was secretly assisting in the growth of Israel. How else explain the obdurate refusal of Arab politicians to negotiate a peace settlement? Their armies were squabbling among themselves or were retreating pell-mell before the enemy. As the politicians procrastinated and issued bombastic threats of reprisal, the Jews were carving large chunks out of that half of Palestine allocated to the Arabs. The Arabs would not accept partition, so they lost the partitioned area. The Arabs would not accept the Bernadotte Plan, which gave them the Negeb, so they lost the Negeb."[17] Since the pattern goes back to the earliest proposals for settlement, even in the British period, the familiar Arab graphic expositions of Israeli expansionism represent maps that had actually been rejected by the Arab side. This did not go unnoticed among some Arabs and their friends. King Hussein once said that the "third pillar" of Zionism was the "Arab extremists who will not accept any solution but only weep and wail while they appeal to those who will never help them."[18] Speaking of the Palestine Arabs, Glubb Pasha was more explicit still: "Many opportunities for compromise were offered them and might, if accepted, have saved them. But they were utterly intransigent, and, as a result, they were destroyed."[19] In a widely publicized article in the wake of the June war Cecil Hourani discerned this pattern throughout the entire Arab-Jewish conflict.[20] "Foolish and daring to the end, the Arabs had thrown away those few but nevertheless real opportunities to settle for half a loaf," wrote Anthony Nutting. "If they were left with a dry and bitter crust, some of the blame must be attached to the false prophets who misled them and whose blind extremism demanded the rejection of any compromise."[21]

But the popular postulate of the inevitable eventual Arab ascendancy blunts the obvious implications of this judgment. Elmer Berger thus acknowledged that "Arab stubbornness and inflexibility have, without doubt, contributed mightily to the constant Zionist/Israeli escalation of force. This ingredient of international relations has been to the constant advantage of the Israelis and, accordingly, it can be said—by the pragmatists—that the Arabs have been their own worst enemies. But that judgment, all too frequently inserted as a consideration for a 'just peace,' is irrelevant. One of Israel's most mature and distinguished academics, Jacob Talmon," continued Berger, "put it bluntly to his own countrymen: 'Israel may be able to win and win and go on winning till its last breath, win itself to death, thereby demonstrating the truth of Hegel's aphorism about the "impotence of victory."'"[22]

Initially stunned by the windfalls from the bitter intransigence of their opponents, the Israelis seem later to have come to rely on it as some last-resort escape hatch in tight diplomatic situations. Although the Zionist movement had accepted the principle of partition in the 1930's, its rejection by the other side deprived the *Yishuv* of even a minuscule area on which to base independent efforts at salvaging the jeopardized Jewry of Europe. Jewish dominion envisaged in the various plans encompassed but a thin strip of coastal area south of Haifa and the northernmost part of Palestine in some of them: 490 square miles in the minimal plan (Woodhead Commission Plan C) and 2,955 square miles in the maximal plan (Peel Plan). The Morrison-Grady Plan of 1946 allocated the Jews some 1,500 square miles—a "ghetto in attenuated form," the American chairman of the Anglo-American Committee of Inquiry later termed it.[23]

While the blessing was not unmixed, because of the missed opportunity to save at least some of the victims of the Holocaust in World War Two, the larger area allocated to the Jews later, under the United Nations partition plan of 1947 (5,572 square miles), made the earlier Arab rejections appear as a godsend. The Arab rejection of that plan, too, resulting in the first major war between Arabs and Israelis, produced still wider borders for Israel, some 8,020 square miles. Moreover, the war disposed of a vast share of the Arab population that had been earmarked for Israel under the 1947 plan (nearly forty percent of its projected total). One of the few incontestible aspects of the otherwise acrimoniously contentious controversy over the creation of the Arab refugee problem is that in the initial phase the exodus was not staged by the Jews, however they may have welcomed and even "helped" its flow in later stages. The Jews at first reacted to the sudden departure from some areas of virtually all Arabs (as from Haifa) with a mixture of awe, stupor, and even anxiety, such as normally accompanies natural calamities, many interpreting it later as divine intervention.

They soon learned to anticipate the Arab pattern of rigid defiance and to exploit it. Operation Yoab in the Negev, in October of 1948, resulting in the capture of Beersheba, was thus premised on the assumption that the Egyptians could not restrain themselves and would fire on Israeli convoys traveling under the United Nations aegis. It is possible that the Israelis would have sought another justification for this operation, had the Egyptians not obliged them, as they did; but it is difficult to exaggerate the value to them of the Egyptian "collaboration" in the face of a cease-fire order issued by the United Nations Security Council. The subsequent repetition of the pattern—staged or unstaged (after all, the Israelis could not really have prevented the other side from accepting the Bernadotte Plan, to cite one instance, which sought to reduce Israel to an area even smaller than envisaged in the Peel Plan, to 2,470 square miles) —strengthened among Israelis the belief that, as many of them put it, in the last resort, Israel can always rely on the Arabs. They even conceive of their young nation's history as a sequence of Arab defiances and challenges from which the Jews have emerged stronger every time.

What seems to happen in this phenomenon, which both sides perceive in different lights, is the repeated rejection by the Arabs of situations they subsequently seek to restore. At every stage of the conflict so far, they have rejected offers, only to clamor for them after these were superseded by more onerous conditions.[24] Following the June war, the penultimate situation sought was the *status quo ante bellum*, or return to the armistice lines of 1949; before the war, however, the penultimate situation sought was the earlier Partition Plan of 1947, which had been rejected when available at that time; and so on. When the penultimate condition is retrieved, as after the restoration of the Sinai and the Gaza Strip to Egypt in 1957, by the Israeli victors in the 1956 war, under international pressure, the dynamics of the penultimate merely continue from the lower level to a yet earlier set of conditions. Israel's narrow borders of 1949 were presumably available for the asking, for nearly two decades.[25] Why were they not accepted? "We did once," exclaimed a Palestinian Arab publicist, "have those very same borders of June 4 [1957, established in 1949] for which we are now asking: Was the conflict then any less acute, or a solution any nearer to realisation?"[26] No, he suggested, since the Arabs wanted no Israel whatsoever, and the Israelis craved much wider borders anyway.

We cannot really say whether the Jews would have expanded anyway, even had the Arabs accepted them at any stage, for the simple reason that the Arabs have never allowed such a test. We can only speculate. It may be that the Arabs adhere to the expansionism theory for several compelling reasons: a. it confirms their conviction in the despicable nature of their Jewish foe; b. it expresses in a manner acceptable to self-esteem their genuine fear of him; c. it absolves them of guilt for the disastrous consequences of their policy (i.e., the Jews would have done it anyway), and given the marked predisposition toward the shifting of responsibility onto others in their culture, the function of the theory in this sense may indeed be invaluable; d. it enhances the effectiveness of their public-relations and diplomatic campaigns, since the theory of Israeli expansionism neutralizes accusations of Arab intransigence and serves to generate international pressure for recouping Arab losses in unsuccessful wars. American official policy pronouncements in recent years have repeatedly backed resistance to Israel's expansionism, most notably by Secretary Rogers, on December 9, 1969.

The case of Lebanon suggests that the theory serves internal Arab needs better than furthering knowledge of the behavior of Israelis.

A border strip of Lebanese territory, with several villages, occupied by the Israelis in the process of pushing Arab forces from the Galilee, was thus quickly vacated by them upon the conclusion of the Israel-Lebanon armistice agreement in 1949. Although none doubted Israel's capacity to sweep all Lebanon at any time since, there was no reoccupation of Lebanese territory until the aftermath of the June war. Repeated Lebanese warnings that Israel aimed to expand up to the Litani River seemed therefore puzzling in light of this record. These visions were closely tied to difficulties with the Palestinian *fedayeen:* As their activity spread in Lebanon, so also did the forebodings of Israeli annexationism, and they were loudest always when Lebanese relations with the *fedayeen* became particularly critical. The Lebanese dilemma is fear for the country's integrity both if stern action is taken against the *fedayeen*—who with the protection of Syria and other Arab states use Lebanese territory to wage war on Israel—and if no such action is taken—since the Israelis would then do the job themselves. The warnings thus seem to predict such an outcome, while exculpating the Lebanese in advance for their fate. The Israelis indeed repeatedly enter and depart Lebanon in pursuit of the *fedayeen*, but have not so far displayed any inclination to stay.

A writer recently suggested that the theory of expansionism has among the Arabs the trappings of a full-fledged myth. "The special quality of myth is not that it is false but that it is true for those who believe in it. Myths express unconscious wishes or fears which are somehow inconsistent with conscious experience and thus pervaded with contradictions. Sometimes that which the myth affirms only makes sense in terms of its opposite, that which is denied."[27] He cited the Arabs' insistence on total submission to their demands, rooted in the either-or dichotomy in Islamic political thinking, and their characteristic predisposition to assume verbal images of solutions confronting them rather than practical images of these solutions. Bourguiba discussed the phenomenon on March 3, 1965, in the same terms, saying that "the policy of 'all or nothing' brought us only defeat in Palestine and to the sad situation in which we find ourselves today."[28]

And Cecil Hourani: "Another consequence of our unwillingness to accept as real what we do not like is that *when reality catches up with us, it is always too late.* At every *débâcle* we regret that we did not accept a situation which no longer exists. In 1948 we regretted that we had not accepted the 1947 U. N. plea for partition. In May

1967 we were trying to go back to pre-Suez [1956]. Today we would be happy—and are actually demanding the U. N.—to go back to things as they were before 5 June [1967]. From every defeat we reap a new regret and a new nostalgia, but never seem to learn a new lesson."[29]

A Palestinian Arab writer has recently argued that life under Israeli rule has taught a lesson to which the Arab leadership outside may be oblivious, thus risking "the loss of everything, should they persist in their refusal to act in the light of the new circumstances. . . . This is the view of the overwhelming majority of our people who live in the occupied territories, and who are able to see what people living outside these territories cannot see. They are able to see the *faits accomplis* whose establishment goes on day after day, and which may give birth to developments similar to those that resulted from the rejection by the Arabs of the U. N. Partition Plan in 1947. The history of other peoples has shown that wisdom in such circumstances demands speedy action aimed at saving what can be saved."[30]

This tension between conquest and submission was apparent also in the encounter earlier of Islamic peoples with Western intruders in Africa and Asia, when the British and the French from time to time found themselves in possession of large territories they did not wish to govern, yet from which they could not withdraw because of the intractable character of Islam. "The hapless policy-makers of Paris had designed no more than a vague paramountcy over [the Muslim theocracies of inner Africa]. It was bad luck that, like the Egyptians, the Mahdists and southern Tunisians, the theocrats preferred the *jihad* to working with the French and so dragged them into vast imperial conquests instead. The paper partition had set the French army to grips with a reviving and recalcitrant Islam. In subjugating it, the paper empire had to be occupied."[31]

On the other hand, the assumption that Israeli expansion may be independent of Arab rejection could be based on the dynamic character of Israeli society: the Israelis' conviction that they exist in that part of the world by right, not sufferance; and the "factist" approach to Jewish settlement in the Holy Land inherited from an earlier period. The Arabs would surely be correct in assuming that the energetic Israeli society will not cease growing just because Arab acceptance has been won (though many Arabs expect it to dissolve in the absence of the integrative pressures of war), that acceptance would "freeze" Israeli strength at the level at which conciliation takes place. But whether further growth, especially by immigration, would also require territorial expansion is questionable; the Arabs' assumption that it must is understandable, for among them, as in other preindustrial cultures, wealth, political power, and social status are closely linked to land. Anxieties among the more Westernized Arabs, concerning the Israeli penetration of the region by science, technology, and commerce are more attuned to the authentic Israeli ambitions. For in Israel visions of the future growth of the country at peace are precisely vertical, growth within the borders, with expectations of leadership in collaborating with the Arabs outside for the development of the region.

Of course the Israelis believe they have rights in the whole of their ancestral homeland. Since the Arabs concede no right whatever, expressions of a feeling that is natural enough among Israelis assume a sinister quality on the other side, where they are cited as proof of criminal intent. In connecting expansionism to the religious (biblical) factor, the Arabs are quite correct, in the sense that orthodoxy in Israel indeed predisposes toward holding onto territories conquered in the June war; but a large majority of Israelis is not guided by religion in thinking of the territories; instead the criteria are rather pragmatic for the most part (especially security considerations), with Jerusalem the obvious exception. When Arabs envision Israelis as pursuing a biblical injunction in respect to borders, they seem rather to project their own basic religiosity, as well as their seeming inability to accept Zionism as an authentic nationalism, since Jews in their eyes can constitute only a *religious* community. In reality, while religion is tightly connected with modern Jewish nationalism, the latter is essentially a secular and political movement.

The grand, romantic visions of extended Jewish dominion have from the beginning concerned just a minority in the worldwide Zionist movement; in essence, the revisionist movement and the military groups *(Etzel, Lehi)* and political parties *(Herut, Gahal)* to which it later gave birth. While segments of other movements (the religious *Mizrahi* and the socialist *Ahdut Avoda*) have shown affinities for this orientation, the balance of Zionism was decidedly wedded to "factism," a pragmatic, cautious approach, seeking only that which was attainable at each stage of its development, leaving both the ultimate political status of the renascent Jewish community and its borders only vaguely defined, with options open in the light of changing circumstances.[32]

Purely Jewish sovereignty in even just the whole of Cisjordania was until recently (and for many even now) something of a pipe-dream. What was well organized and systematically practiced with clarity of purpose at all times was the production of "facts"—enlarging immigration, the economic base of the community, its military potential, the network of rural settlements, etc. While quite obviously an expression of the pioneer culture anyway, the ideological justification for factism held that the ultimate political-territorial shape of the community would be influenced by its tangible, real proportions when the reckoning arrived. (The analogy with the Protestant ethic is clear in the case of this equally austere, Calvinist-type movement: Calvinists believed that people could not interfere with predestined salvation or damnation of their souls; but their material achievements on earth were taken to be a reasonable clue to their eternal fate beyond.) Even now the Israeli government speaks of "secure and agreed borders," without being specific and at the same time creating new facts in the conquered territories, many observers suggesting that the placement of "facts" may reveal which territories Jerusalem really intends to return in future bargaining with the Arabs and which are not likely to be given up even then.[33]

Some have spoken of an Israeli *fait accompli* diplomacy as a source of permanent aggression: accepting half a loaf, then jumping on the rest, only repeating the sequence, perhaps until exhaustion or destruction. What is the actual relation of the Israeli sense of legitimacy to effective claims by Israel for territory? While it has been difficult, and perhaps impossible, to demonstrate that Israel goes to war in order to conquer, it is certainly obvious that it conquers once it is at war. In the October war, even though the Arabs admittedly surprised the Israelis, the latter still came out of it with large new conquests. Moreover, it is clear that Israel does not conquer all the land it could. In the latter phases of the 1948–49 war, for example, the Israelis could have advanced in various directions, to fulfill the alleged biblical blueprint, after smashing the invading Arab armies, but failed to do so. That the Israelis could have quickly overrun the Arab Legion at the conclusion of the various armistice agreements in 1949 is not seriously disputed by any source; though the Legion held Old Jerusalem, with the so-called Wailing Wall, and Hebron, Jericho, and other biblical sites, Israel asked merely for slight adjustments in the truce lines and ceded to Jordan some territory in the southern region in return. If the Israelis are expansionists, they certainly are very inept ones, to judge by this experience.

The Israelis put forward effective claims to territory once they are in its possession and are (or were, in the past) relatively ineffectual in realizing these claims, either because they do not assign to them the highest priority or because they fail to resist international pressures for withdrawal. Thus, they vacated their conquests in Sinai, the Gaza Strip, and many Lebanese villages in the process of concluding the armistice agreements in 1949. (After rectifying their lines with Jordan, they left the "waist" of Israel barely nine miles wide on a coastal strip devoid of any natural obstacles to military invasion.) The Israelis again vacated the Sinai and the Gaza Strip under international pressure in 1957; then, quite spontaneously, they vacated their conquests on the Egyptian and Syrian fronts in 1973, and then even land won earlier, in 1967. In view of this record one could select a series of appropriate maps and juxtapose them to the usual graphic demonstrations of Israeli expansionism to "prove" the existence of something called Israeli "withdrawalism." The ease with which Israel gives up, or can be made to abandon, territory conquered in war is surely unique among nations in the contemporary world. The fact that the hardening of Israeli attitudes in this respect in recent years represents frustration with, and a reaction to, this unusual record is obvious to the observer of the Israeli scene. Israelis frequently ask why would yet another withdrawal from Sinai and elsewhere affect Arab attitudes toward them, when this has repeatedly failed to happen before.

While the Arabs portray the Israelis as ogling their prey and systematically raping it, the latter appear rather much restrained, though potent. Many Israelis do, however, get romantic notions when thrown in with nostalgic places, Hebron for instance. But the importance of war itself as matchmaker cannot easily be overstated. "While in the period preceding the war [of 1967]," wrote an Israeli social scientist known for his stern anti-annexationist views, "there was truly no desire for territorial expansionism on the part of most of the population and perhaps none of the Herut ideologists seriously meant to realize the traditional slogans of that party concerning the 'historical frontiers,' following the conquest the slogan, 'not one inch of the liberated land should be surrendered,' has gained momentum."[34] Indeed, he pointed out elsewhere, that, in the new conditions on the morrow of the war, with the several Jewish venerated sites suddenly under Jewish dominion, some ultra-Orthodox circles, previously militantly anti-Zionist, just as suddenly emerged as ardent promoters of a Greater Israel.[35]

But is there a phase at which the "dynamics of the penultimate" come to rest—other than the logical conclusion, phase zero? In other words, is there any territorial shape in which Jewish statehood is really acceptable to the Arabs? There are many speculations invariably involving conceivable forms, but *actual* Jewish statehood has never yet been acceptable to them; it has been rejected in all its real forms, from a county-sized entity to its present large shape. The sheer inability to accept *actual* statehood has reduced Arab thinking about it to manipulation of either the past or the future—seeking to reconstruct earlier or never-existing historical conditions as points of departure for obscure and uncharted paths of conciliation, or envisaging the future denouement of the Jewish state, by inevitable historical forces, martial or pacific. This does not mean that suggestions to start anew at, say, the United Nations partition plan stage of 1947 or another earlier stage are necessarily insincere, though they frequently are, as Arabs themselves admit.[36] But it means that speaking of a hypothetical Jewish state is one thing, and being able to face up to an actual one quite another. Arabs have often been able to do the former but not the latter, certainly not in any appreciable number or in some politically effective manner. Yet even *that* much—asserting a readiness to accept a Jewish state, at least for a time, in a shape other than the real one—has been the distinctive trait of moderation in the Arab world. The point is significant, for claims to realism notwithstanding, moderation there still puts forward just verbal images of solutions to the problem with Israel, not really practical ones (which, after all, conforms to characteristic compulsions in Arab culture).

The familiar expressions of Arab outrage at Israel in terms of a theft of a country and the dispossession of its people share both in the strengths and weaknesses of the expansionism theory. They are genuinely representative of Arab feeling and possess a certain kind of *prima facie* cogency—after all, one can see that the Jews *have* taken over Palestine. (Where is it now, incidentally? "I Remember When Palestine Was on the Map. Do You?" asked an Arab Information Center advertisement.)[37] One can see that masses of Arabs *are* dispossessed exiles. The theft of a country theory portrays the Palestinian Arab in the sympathetic light of victim and clear him of responsibility for his fate, as does the expansionism theory. Above all else, the theory obscures a vital aspect of the phenomenon it purports to explain, namely, the struggle for political ascendancy.

In the real world new sovereignties are frequently accompanied by bloodshed, deprivation, sorrow, and infringement of rights. The Arabs certainly know this to be true; their gloried past consisted, after all, of the systematic deprivation of other peoples' lands and rights, often with toleration and magnanimity, but deprivation nevertheless. The contemporary attempt at restoring past grandeur involves the same messy business: of the Kurds in Iraq (besides the subjection in that country of the *Shiite* [sectarian Muslim] majority by the *Sunnis*); of the Christian and pagan (animist) blacks in the Sudan; of the Berber peoples by the Arabic-speaking peoples in North Africa; etc. The talk of the deprivation (though real indeed) of the people of Palestine puts the cart before the horse, so to say, as it assumes the original existence of such a political unit, when it actually was carved out by the British and French victors of the Ottoman Empire in the process of disposing of its ethnically, linguistically, and otherwise heterogenous remains into various arbitrary units.

As usual, the outcome was unfair, the *Sunni* Arabs winning overlordship over vast lands with large alien populations (though by reference to their mastery over a larger area many centuries ago they felt cheated); large peoples, such as the Christian Armenians or the Muslim Kurds, were entirely deprived of self-determination, in favor of the Turks and the Arabs, as were many other peoples, among them the Arabs (mostly *Sunni*) in the newly formed Palestine, in favor of the Jews. In plain language in the new Palestine and the new Turkey (and in Persia) some Arabs were placed in the same position of subordination in which many other groups found themselves under Arabs in several other new states in the Middle East following the First World War. The suppression of these groups in the new Arab sovereignties entailed sometimes genocidal measures. In Iraq the Assyrians (Nestorian Christians), who had fought for the Allies in the war and had repeatedly sought to win independence, were massacred in large numbers in 1932, most of their villages being totally wiped out or almost wholly destroyed by the Iraqi army; the Kurds in the same Arab country, numbering more than one million in contiguous territory around Kirkuk, have fought an almost interminable war with the army, in which the latter has used aircraft in "systematic reduction of Kurdish villages,"[38] by bombing, strafing (and the use of napalm and gas), repeatedly within the framework of vast offensives on the Kurdish region; also in Iraq, the forced removal *en masse* of Kurdish villagers in the 1960's and 1970's, and the settlement of Arabs on their lands, has also been applied to the large Persian minority, as tens of thousands were expelled from the country during tension with Iran over territorial rights in the Shatt el Arab and the Gulf. In the Sudan the coerced Arabization of the blacks in the southern third of the country resulted in nearly twenty years of incessant bloodshed (the Anyanya rebellion), with even conservative estimates of casualties ranging in the hundreds of thousands of mainly blacks, indiscriminately killed.[39]

With so much practice in deprivation overlordship, the very ingenuous might argue, the Arabs should be particularly understanding of the relatively minor exercise in the same in Palestine— although it is probably just such background of overlordship that makes it particularly difficult for them to acquiesce in subordination to others, and especially to Jews. Arab land has been alienated before (the Alexandretta region has been taken by Turkey from Syria), but the world has not heard much about it lately. Many tens of millions of Muslims came under Hindu control in 1947, and in the process of India's partition and later, more Muslims were killed and dispossessed than in the struggle with the Jews in Palestine; more Muslim refugees were created in this struggle than are held in all the United Nations Relief and World Agency camps in and around Palestine. Yet Muslim leaders assembled in Morocco in September of 1969 to consider *jihad* against the Jewish state welcomed governmental delegates from India, as hundreds of Muslims were being massacred by Hindus in Indian towns and villages.[40] Since they are not particularly fastidious or squeamish about such matters generally, why then have such relatively small losses (and in earlier phases of the conflict with the Jews they were practically minute in objective terms) as the Arabs have suffered in Palestine been accompanied by so much bitterness, despair, obsession, and calamity? In a world so thoroughly accustomed to frequent and large transfers of territory, why has the struggle over a mere sliver of land assumed cosmic proportions for Arab peoples?

7

ARABS AND MODERN HISTORY

ARAB bitterness is a compound of certain grievances deeply rooted in the past, in collective efforts at coming to terms with the present, and in individual attempts at coming to terms with themselves. The most profound grievance perhaps is dismay over the disastrous course of Muslim power in conflict with the West in modern history. Even if the Jewish identity of the foe were irrelevant (and it is not) and there were no prehistory of successive humiliations at the hands of the Western powers in the last several centuries (which obviously exists), the defeat in Palestine would still have repercussions more profound than those accompanying defeat of peoples other than Muslims. Secular misfortunes in Islam have terrible implications for individual faith and self-esteem as have perhaps never been experienced by Christians, with their Augustinian conception of the City of Man separated from the City of God. To Muslims—and Arabs regard themselves as purest Muslims—the rightness of their faith is reflected in the affairs of this world. Islam and the world were exhilaratingly right while its sword conquered; but since the rise of the West, history has brought mainly malaise, disorientation, and humiliation.

As Wilfred Cantwell Smith explained, Islam is not merely religion; it is a particular religion, stressing submission to a pattern of behavior rather than intellectual creeds, and power in this world rather than ethereal transactions. The beginning of the Islamic era is reckoned not from Mohammed's birth (as would parallel the Christian case), nor even from the time of divine revelation, but from the time when the nascent Muslim community came to political power (in Medina, A.D. 622). The test of Islam was to be in this world, and in its early history success was overwhelming. Islam, he said, ''has been characteristically a religion of triumph in success, of salvation through victory and achievement and power. . . . God told men how to live; those who accepted this and set out to live so were visibly receiving His blessing. . . . History confirmed faith."[1] Within a few decades Muslims had carved out an immense empire, conquering numerous peoples, a *Herrenvolk* out to destroy those who stood up to it in arms, but protective of the meek and submissive, who labored to support this elite in a style to which the bedouin had hardly been accustomed before Islam. Unlike other civilizations, which "discovered" the resurgent West only as backward peoples, Islam arose virtually within Christendom and, consuming it with lightning speed, challenged its very existence, not just as equal but as master and conqueror, for almost a millenium.

In founding a political community as faith the Prophet merely followed a tradition of hoary antiquity in the Near East, dominated by this conception from Sumerian times onward, which men in Western Christendom grasp only with difficulty.[2] "It is important to realize at the very beginning," cautions Hottinger, "that the link existing in Islam between worldly power and religion in no way smacks of hypocrisy. The Christian religion was born into a situation in which it had to separate the kingdom of Caesar from the Kingdom of God. Western thought is so used to this separation that we automatically suspect falsity, the conscious exploitation of religious motives to achieve worldly aims, as soon as we detect either in our own or in another religious tradition any co-operation between the two aspirations. In the Muslim world there is no separation between Caesar and God in Heaven. Muhammad lived in a town in which there was no government. One factor which led to the success of his mission was that he offered leadership just at that moment when the social system could no longer be contained within the narrow family and tribal system. He demanded and received this leadership in the name of God and all the sources we know of confirm that he honestly felt himself 'sent' and inspired for that purpose. What he did as Messenger of God seems to us to separate into either religious or political activities. In his eyes such a division would have been nonsense; he received messages and he acted according to these commands of God."[3] While Western Christianity has come to interpret the idea of a Kingdom of God as a spiritual kingdom, Jeffery explains that Oriental Christianity, much like Islam, still finds it difficult to dissociate religion from law, from personal status in the realm, from civic duties, from things political generally.[4]

This profoundly sociopolitical character of Islam accounts for the fact that men regard themselves as Muslims even though they may violently reject Islam as religion; no longer performing a single cult practice of the faith, they nonetheless feel part of the community of Islam. The particular affinity for the political in the civilization is manifested among illiterate rural people in a manner startling to Westerners. "In [Arab coffeehouses] nonliterate men can sit and listen to someone read the daily press, or all can listen to the radio and use the news of the day as a starting point for discussions. And because the Arab world is so much affected by foreign affairs, everyone has his attention drawn to world news. In the coffeehouses one can hear some remarkably well-informed discussions of current developments, and even when the information is of dubious accuracy, it is impressively full. Many Arab students have remarked that when they studied in the United States they were amazed at how uninterested and uninformed many American college students seemed about world affairs."[5] The Arab press devotes a high percentage of space to foreign news; the coverage to a large extent of all news is political in nature.[6] The production of books in the Arab world betrays the same bias. (A census of British Palestine reveals not merely a striking bias but also the spectacular disparity in this respect between the Arab and Jewish communities.) Arabs, much like Southern Italians, think mainly in political (not economic) terms and, like them, understand politics best as confrontations of pure power, not as a balancing of rights;[7] in Islam the focus is on naked power, poorly institutionalized, shifting, uncertain, unstable, erratic, unrestrained; power and submission are almost always at stake in social and other interactions in that system; free bargaining among equals and the lawful exercise of authority are uncongenial to it.[8]

As Arabs submitted to Islam, so the world was to submit to Muslims. The Arabs constituted themselves, in the words of Bernard Lewis, as a "*conquistador* aristocracy claiming both ethnic and social superiority"[9] even to new converts, supposedly equal to them in the Muslim community of rulers. In practice, as Hottinger points out, newly converted Muslims had to attach themselves to one of the Arab tribes as so-called clients *(mawali);* their struggle for equal rights marked the first two centuries of Islam, marked by almost incessant uprisings and wars that took on the coloration of religious heresy.[10] (The *Sunna* vs. *Shia* split reflects the pristine power struggle.) Toward non-Muslims the presumption to dominion was categorical; Jews and Christians were tolerated and protected in return for special taxation in an inferior, humiliated position; even this not by rights inherent in them, but at the pleasure of Muslim masters. "Unlike the Judaic-Christian growth in adversity, suffering and persecution, Islam was almost from the beginning a religion of rulers and of visible worldly success."[11] The Muslim conquerors "farmed" many more advanced peoples than they, though these had to provide them not only with economic sustenance and even surplus, but also with the very instrumentalities of management of themselves. "If the Arab could not conceive or construct an administrative machine, he could use one which another had made, and he could impose and maintain himself in supreme place at great distance from his home and for long ages, supported by surprisingly few men of his own race. Except in the history of the later Roman Empire, there has been nothing like that unquestioning and frank acceptance of one race as born to power, which was conceded to the Arab from Persia to Spain. It was not only that Arabs were installed and treated as God's noblemen, but that all sorts and conditions of men of other races Arabised themselves in name and speech."[12] However wretched later on, Arabs have drawn from history a sense of their superiority ("It is the nature of Islam to rule and not to be ruled . . ."),[13] manifesting both a sense of insufficiency in the modern world and such presumption as has suggested to observers a "superiority complex" ("Überwertigkeitskomplex der Araber").[14]

While the Arab-dominated phase of Islam was its classic and pristine era, it was relatively brief, and was followed by Turkish dominance; and the decay of the Arabs was marked already during Christendom's High Middle Ages. For some centuries thereafter, the Arabs could at least share vicariously the Muslim glory of the Turks; but by the eighteenth century the decay of all Islam before resurgent Christendom became progressively more difficult to disguise. Muslims were increasingly becoming impotent subjects of the powerful and contemptuous (also contemptible) Western nations; their cities were bombarded with impunity; their armies were humiliated; their lands became zones of occupation and colonies; their customs and faith became the butt of Western contempt and even of the Westernized men in their own ranks.

As purest Muslims, the malaise of the Arabs has been more profound, their response more frantic and perhaps also more futile and destructive of self and others, than the malaise of other Muslims and their attempts at "righting the world" once again. The humiliation of the power of Islam in its heartland, in Palestine, is thus felt as a cosmic disorder, not just rhetoric; in the Muslim context the ordeal is personal: disorientation, feeling of insufficiency and depravity, a state of utter disgrace. To acquiesce in the outrage is tantamount to faithlessness in a faith that encompasses one's very being[15]—hence, it is similar to nonbeing and a vindication of faith is becoming oneself again. As an American writer listened, a *Fatah* harangued Palestinians in a Jordanian camp: " 'Since the Zionists, the Arab people have always been divided. The Western world has continuously worked against the people of Muh-hammmmut—' the name was uttered in a kind of long broken moan, '—but it was in Muh-hammm-mut! that the Arab peoples created a great empire. We were masters then, while now we are slaves and servants. But, brethren, we are still the children of Muh-hammm-mut! The way is clear. It is armed struggle for the liberation of our Palestine.' "[16] Overcoming the state of the Jews means restoring Islam to its Truth; the end of Israel would be the vindication of Islam.[17]

Arab efforts at thorough Westernization have been frustrating, as the raw power of modernity was craved, but its intellectual and moral underpinnings were summarily rejected, and all too alien to be understood anyway. The atavistic fascination with power had produced a fatal equation of modernity with sheer technology, or technique, leading even intellectuals to conceptions of modernization as a gimmick. However heroic the rhetoric of drastic change in the Arab world, the actual deeds tend toward self-indulgence. The frustrations with becoming modern only intensify the malaise, and with it the resort to fatuous, but emotionally gratifying, means of coping with the trouble. Especially prevalent is escape from reality by means of nostalgia, apologetics, and other forms of self-delusion, and the mendacity so characteristic of contemporary Arab life, both private and public.

As for nostalgia, explains Fayez A. Sayegh, "The glories of the past often suggest themselves as a comfortable compensation for the humiliations of today, a convenient avenue of escape from the travails of the present and the arduous tasks of the future." The Arab sees in the past both escape from an unbearable present and guidance for future redemption, but is more likely to find paralysis. "It is because of the Arab's rejection of the West and what it stands for, that his self-assertion assumes the exclusive character that it does: and, obversely, the more the Arab furthers his rather pathological inclination to seek in himself—that is to say, in his past—the sole basis for his present awakening and future self-determination, the more hopelessly imprisoned within the narrow cell of himself he becomes, and the more hostile to any form of creative interaction with the Western spirit he grows to be."[18]

Apologetics, the resort to which is massive and constant, explains

Wilfred Cantwell Smith, "is the attempt to develop a system of ideas that will serve as protection against insecurity."[19] A frustrated and resentful people, the Arabs tend to perceive modern history as a series of insults and aggressions, and their sensitivity to even intimations of backwardness and inferiority borders on the pathological. They are forever defending utterly unrealistic self-perceptions, expressing deep resentment at indications to the contrary. The experience of the German journalist Erik Verg is rather typical. After a visit to Cairo, Verg reported in the *Hamburger Abendblatt* on the swindles and deceptions with which Cairenes prey on ingenuous visitors ("Kairoer Gaunerkomödie," or Caro Comedy of Rogues, he termed it). He was promptly taken to task by the Bonn Office of the Arab League and was angrily accused of calumny, although the shady practices in question are common knowledge among virtually all who have visited Cairo or resided there.[20] The press in this country has been indicted for similar reasons; in one review of its alleged calumnies, "the worst example" cited is Thomas Thompson's diary of the molestation and abuse of United States citizens in hysteria-gripped Cairo during the June war, an experience shared by many hundreds and witnessed by many thousands.[21] Kermit Roosevelt once wrote an article for *Harper's* magazine in which, while praising Egypt for progress achieved in health, indicated the enormous dimensions of illness in the country, citing statistics. "But the Egyptians," he recalls, "hit the ceiling. They called the article prejudiced, full of inaccuracies if not downright lies, written just to vilify Egypt. 'That man says 90 per cent of us have trachoma, but everyone knows that not more than 80 or 85 per cent actually do,' they complained."[22]

In general apologetics explains why Arab historiography is concerned more with cosmetics than exposition; why Western writings on the Arabs are appraised by them not in terms of accuracy so much as whether or not the author praises them. Although productive of emotional satisfaction, apologetics plays its practitioners false in two ways, according to Smith. "The attempt to glorify rather than to understand of course fails to understand. Further, it succeeds in glorifying only temporarily and on very costly terms. Both matters have serious consequences in perpetuating the situation out of which they arise. . . . One's self-esteem which the world of reality threatens to undermine is made to rest increasingly on what is in effect the work of one's imagination. . . . One therefore becomes afraid of the facts, since they have the power to undermine one's version of the facts. The very endeavour to overcome one's insecurity in the objective world by glorification, ends by making one the more insecure."[23]

Troubled by questions of power, not truth, and seeking not revision of doctrine but a redressing of history, Arabs envisioned a glorified past reconstituted as a mighty nation, once more on the rise, the West once more shrinking before it in panic. The dying West resorts to every trick and abomination to prevent the ascent of the Arab nation, and if it fails, whenever it fails, the West is behind the failure. The primary school "first reader" that most Arab children learn by heart contains a sentence that sums up one of the most pervasive sentiments among Arabs: "Our division is the cause of our weakness."[24] Since the West appears at the root of disunity, the West equals Arab weakness.[25]

But Arab resurrection was not to be denied; for despite its plotting and sabotage, the West began to retreat and was soon on the run. The Arab awakening, starting in the last century and moving increasingly faster in the twentieth, held out the promise of righting the world once again. Perhaps Arabs resent Israel so bitterly because it arose just as their cosmic vindication seemed within their grasp. "When imperialism collapsed in the first half of this century, thanks to the armed resistance and the new Muslim tide," said a Muslim scholar, "manifesting itself particularly in solidarity with Muslim liberation movements from Mostafa Kamal to the Algerian war, the cursed imperialists had no alternative—after full calculation and deliberation—but to drive the rotten wedge of Zionism in the heart of the Muslim world. This is in an endeavour to impede Muslim unity, hinder the process of independence in Muslim states and humiliate Muslims by having them subjugated by the basest race and people in the view of imperialism, while at the same time satisfying the grudge of remnants of the crusaders, whom nothing could satisfy but to see the Muslims attacked in the main part of their countries. This explains the enormous donations pouring into Israel from all parts of Europe and America, which constitute Christian aid by the fanatic enemies of Islam to the descendants of the Jews who crucified Christ in Christian belief. . . ."[26] On the verge of their triumph the West humiliated the Arabs once more.

In another version of this pervasive theme an Iraqi commentator speaks to his imaginary interlocutor, "Dear man of the west:

"I am not sure whether you agree with me that the West's civilisation has already become superannuated and is one foot in the grave.

I hasten to add that this is not my own view alone but also the view of many an eminent European thinker such as Schpingler [*sic*] and Sartre.

"In its state of superannuation, the European society is becoming increasingly fearful of death as is usually the case with men advanced in age. Accordingly the western society resorts to every method for asserting its vitality and virility.

"Sensing the nearness of the demise of its civilisation, the European society conceived the idea of setting up an alter ego to be planted in another continent where European society hopes to assert itself in a rejuvenated manner. Palestine became the guinea-pig in this experiment. The West transferred, or thought it did, the sum of its civilisation and experiment to the East pursuading [*sic*] itself that in addition to atoning for sins, it was setting up a new society which would be a model to others in the area. Needless to say the Zionists did everything to create this impression in the minds of the western people for whom they created the image of an outstanding branch of European civilisation burgeoning on the eastern shores of the Mediterranean. In so doing, the Zionists acted like a doctor giving his dying patient sedative doses."[27]

Viewing themselves as no less than destined to lead humanity and craving the humiliation of the West, Arabs find in Israel's being the symbol and very challenge of their real insufficiency. In Arab textbooks, "The Zionists and the imperialists are condemned not only because of their help to each other but because they constantly remind the Arab world of its failures and loss of glory."[28] In them "Israelis are described as either cruel or cowardly, and their success is attributed to foreign assistance. But the typical theme of all the stories is the feeling of dismay and humiliation at the Arab fate and the yearning not for a solution to the problem but for revenge and a return to the former situation." As for the Palestine refugees, Bilby wrote soon after the first war with Israel: "Their mere presence constitutes a symbol of defeat by a despised minority, a sneering proof that the so-called Arab awakening was little more than a myth. They rankle, they hurt, they humiliate; they give the lie to all communiqués which told of glorious victories and conquests."[29] Israel is visible reminder of the Arabs' failure to live up to their grandiose expectations; the symptom of failure is seen as the cause of failure; hence, the fondest expectations hinge on Israel's elimination. Israel blocks mere self-respect.[30]

The Arabs' peculiar perceptions are confirmed by various leftist dogmas, viewing contemporary history in parallel images: moribund Forces of Evil (imperialism, colonialism, capitalism, etc.) resist emerging Forces of Good (colonized, anti-Western, socialist, revolutionary, "Third World," groups, etc.), using despicable Instruments ("puppets," "running dogs," "tools," etc.) in futile attempts to prevent their collective Doom. The inherent attractions for Arabs are considerable: Islamic atavism emerges as a progressive force; the West is damned; the Jewish state appears as a noxious and doomed artifact. It has been pointed out that both Marxism and modern political Arabism share historical determinism (in the latter, as belief in the historical inevitability of the Arab national revival in our time) and in both the state of the Jews and possibly the Jews themselves are viewed as reactionary, antihistorical, as in other deterministic historicisms, incidentally. "Zionism is an insult, worse, a heresy, to the deterministic logic of a Lenin or a Toynbee and is treated as an historical abnormality by both."[31] (Also remarkable is the parallel dichotomy in Marxist and Islamic international law between the World of Strife and the World of Socialism [Peace] in the former and between the Realm of War [dar al-charb] and the Realm of Islam [dar al-Islam] or Realm of Peace, in the latter.)

Arabs draw a particularly painful analogy in the perspective of global decolonization in our age. They resent greatly their lingering inability to rid themselves of colonialism (Israel as a colonial outpost, as a "settler state"), while other oppressed peoples already have been, or are in the process of, shedding this curse. At the apex of the movement of decolonization only the Arabs—once rulers of half the world, now aspiring to similar glories—seem unable to accomplish what the humblest of colonized peoples can. This implication would seem amply balanced by the gratifying aspects of the analogy, the denial of an authentically Israeli nation (as merely a colony of other, real nations) and by other satisfactions.

Accustomed as we are to tracing our own difficulties with the Arabs to Israel, we easily ignore that Israel itself suffers from the Arabs' realization of how much Israel is like ourselves. Israel is a successfully modernizing society amidst peoples as yet painfully unable to modernize, notwithstanding rhetoric, good intentions, and hopeful theorizing by Western social scientists. The torments of transition to modernity easily turn into despair by invidious comparisons that Arabs simply cannot help making. Thus, their contention that Israel's very existence is an unbearable aggression has subtle and intimate meaning.

The relation of modernization to Arab hostility toward Israel is intricate. While it is true that the success of Israel emphasizes the Arab failure, the perceptions and their implications can vary substantially. Knowledge of Israel in the Arab world is generally poor, and serious deficiencies exist precisely in the critical areas of Israel's success with modernization. While Israel has been able to generate its authentic modern systems of action, within which the masses of Oriental ("Arab") Jews can be fitted with little jeopardy to their Jewish identity, the pressures of ideology foster on the Arabs a vision of Israel as an artificial conglomerate of uprooted refugees, precariously held together by Western injections of aid and Zionist coercion and propaganda. The fashionable theorizing among Arab intellectuals on Israel's "de-Zionization" and ultimate absorption by Arab culture are premised on disregard for the real nexus between dynamism and authentic culture in Israeli society. Yet the Arabs, and their intellectuals above all, themselves experience the strains of their own failure to blend culture and material progress in their own dynamic modes of life, rather than seeking to fit themselves in alien models, as in the military and other spheres of activity.

"The fundamental fact of the situation here," wrote Philip Windsor, "is that Israel's own development closely parallels that which the Arabs are willy-nilly attempting to undertake. After an extraordinary history, even more ancient than that of the Arabs, the Jews remained for centuries a scattered and subject people. Throughout, they maintained their own identity by their attachment to a powerful religion, regarding themselves as its true (and in this case unique) custodians. Like the Arabs, they inherited a rich and powerful language, but in their case the language was associated with an even more remote past and more closely bound to religious purposes. Indeed, Hebrew survived only because of its religious function. And in the return to Palestine the myth of the Jewish nation, linked to language and religion, overcame a multiplicity of social, sectarian, and national differences. But, today, the myth of the Jewish nation has become distinct from that of the state of Israel. In Israel, while antagonisms are still powerful, they are transcended by the appeal of the new state. (Insofar as the myth of the nation is an important force, it probably helps us to maintain the antagonisms by preserving emotional and cultural links with different national communities.) In effect, then, Israeli nationalism has created an authentic revolution of identity.

"The consequence is that the Hebrew language has become a vehicle for the development of a modern state; that it permits the Israelis to engage in fundamental scientific research and technological development; that Israel has been able to reconcile Jewish culture with a contemporary literature and with experiment in social ethics. Equally, the Jewish religion has become less of a determinant of 'belonging' in Israel than a loyalty to the conception of the Israeli state; and though the status of a Jew becomes more confused every day, and though it is still impossible to claim Jewish nationality without being officially affiliated to the Jewish religion, Israel has become in many respects a secular state. (Like many Moslem states, it also permits citizenship to those of a different religion.) Finally, the distinctions of class and sex which still bedevil most Arab societies have been overcome in Israel, at least to the extent of most countries in the West.

"In other words, Israel has already arrived—at least in the terms which are important to the revolutionary movements of Arab nationalism. In contrast, the great majority of Arab countries have begun a revolution in education without challenging the hold of the established religion over immense areas of personal life which are bound to be influenced by a modern education. Only one Arab country has dared to try to abolish polygyny—and that one (Tunisia) is the only one which is not interested in the struggle against Israel. In other countries, revolution has been accompanied by a partial reversion to traditional *mores*. In Iraq, for instance, the Kassem regime officially re-affirmed the right of a husband, father or brother, to execute a woman for bad behavior. But clearly, a rising generation of young Arabs finds the traditional *mores*, and the areas of life which have been most ruled by tradition, inadequate for their own lives, or else downright repugnant. They rebel against them: and in doing so, they experience a positively greater need to assert their own identity as Arabs. In this respect, Israel fills a required role. It is both a minatory example against the rejection of their own culture, and a common cause which enables them to remain Arabs while changing the nature of being Arab."[32]

Breaking away from traditional Islam has meant rootlessness, alienation, and this craving for a secular Arab identity that has yet to prove constructive. The nihilistic tendencies of the process so far may be a consequence of the fact that unlike the Christian West, where secularization uncovered deeper Hellenist humanism, in Islam the stripping of tradition leaves nothing of the kind. And becoming Arab in a modern sense only takes one back to the previous millenium of Arab history, intensifying nostalgia for global grandeur. Whether or not the above is an accurate explanation why so-called transitionals are particularly hostile to Israel, it is true that the rejection of the Jewish state is indeed greater among the younger and more educated than their more traditional elders.[33]

An interesting explanation for this phenomenon has been offered by Amnon Rubinstein, who suggested that modernizing Arabs under Israeli rule are subject to the particular strains of a love-hate relationship with their enviably modern rulers. "Added to defeat is frustration; it is simple to hate the enemy, it is much more demanding to have mixed feelings about him."[34] Another observer suggested that the accelerated modernization of Arabs under Israeli aegis is likely to produce resentment for the alien modernizer, as their exclusion from Israeli culture and identity would leave them psychologically crippled, though mentally competent.[35] Modernization does indeed increase the resemblance between Jews and Arabs of the younger generation in Israel. They are drawn together on the personal and professional levels. (Relations between Jews and traditional Arabs are restricted to a mixture of polite gestures and economic or political interests.) But modernization simultaneously repels them on the political and ideological level; nationalist ideology serves Arabs to guard against attempts at assimilation into the Jewish majority, which are inevitably doomed to failure anyway.[36]

Awareness of Israel's mastery of the modernity they crave stirs invidiousness and aggravates ambivalence toward modernization in the Arab world at large. Models to be emulated are tinged with repugnance for a particularly contemptible foe. The dedication to duty and work that the Jordanian newspaper *Ad-Difaa* contrasts with the sloth and hedonism of Arab civil servants is, after all, that of a despicable people;[37] or the exemplary organizational techniques for settlement, defense, and the absorption of refugees, cited by Cairo's *Al-Mussawar*;[38] and numerous other aspects of Israeli society deemed worthy of emulation in the Arab world. These experiences have implications greatly transcending the magnitude of things ostensibly compared. Eric Pace discovered that Aqaba, once a symbol of Lawrence's Revolt in the Desert, had become "A Symbol of Arabs' Anger": "The Arabs here are bitter because they feel that the hope and pride fostered by the Arab revolt are ridiculed now by the existence of Israel, for which they blame Britain and other Western countries. Israel's existence is particularly galling here because the flourishing Israeli port of Elath is visible across the Jordanian-Israeli border, only a few miles away . . .[from] less modern"[39] Aqaba. The Jews' competence symbolizes one's shortcoming. "To overcome them would allow one honestly to say that one can finally manage the modern world, that one really has arrived."[40]

Israel, experienced from within, often repels, offends, and disorients the Arab. The different levels of material development are matched by radically different cultures: One is characterized by familism, personal contact, aesthetics, and religion; the other is overwhelmingly secular, utilitarian, the life of the average individuals taking place within interlocking large organizational frameworks, which emphasize interchangeability and abstraction.[41] The disruptive impact of the second culture on the first has not been lost on observers from the start of Zionist settlement. In the beginning of British rule in Palestine the dynamism and ideas of the Jews were seen to be disturbing and frightening the Arabs, the latter frequently complaining to the British about the "bolshevism" of the Jews. (The term both denoted modernity and served to frighten the British.)

"With every year that passes," declared a British inquiry commission, "the contrast between this intensely democratic and highly organized modern community and the old-fashioned Arab world around it grows sharper, and in nothing, perhaps, more markedly than on its cultural side. . . . Anyone who attended the Toscanini Concerts at Jerusalem might have imagined, if he closed his eyes, that he was in Paris, London, or New York. Yet, almost within earshot was the Old City, the *Haram-esh-Sharif,* and the headquarters of the Arab Higher Committee. It is the same with science. The Daniel Sieff Research Institute at Rehovot is equipped with the most delicate modern instruments; the experiments conducted there are watched by chemists all over the world: yet from its windows can be seen the hills inhabited by a backward peasantry who regard it only as the demonstration of a power they hate and fear and who would like, no doubt, when their blood is up, to destroy it."[42]

Indications that, as Gerson Cohen said, "much of the Arab intransigence to the state of Israel is a transference of its keen hostility to the modern Western world,"[43] have not been lacking in more recent times. Consider this remark by a member of East Jerusalem's social elite in the aftermath of the first major war: "If our fellahin are content and happy sitting under a tree eating an apple, why do you have to change them?" Katy Antonius reproached an American journalist: "Why does America insist that the fallahin must have refrigerators to put their apples in? They've been happy for centuries without refrigerators, and now you Americans come along and try to change our way of life. Why don't you leave us alone? You insist on shoving an alien group of Jews in our midst and then you try to compensate for it with refrigerators."[44]

Before the war the substantial insulation of the *Yishuv* from the Arab community (by residence, education, employment, etc.) held down cultural friction to a relatively low level; from 1948 to 1967 there was only a small Arab minority in Israel existing in relative isolation inside and substantially cut off from Arab societies outside. Yet with more than one million Arabs suddenly brought into contact with Israelis in the conquered areas in 1967, one could observe anew cultural friction in relation to hostility in the various classes of Arab society. Very hostile on cultural grounds appear to be Arabs in the upper classes—merchants, bankers, professional men—threatened by the markedly egalitarian, nondeferential, and nondecorous aspects of Israeli society. Typical of reactions in these classes is an episode reported by Harvey Swados, who interviewed a prominent banker in East Jerusalem. After accusing the Israelis of strong-arm tactics in commercial competition, the banker exploded with what impressed Swados as his real grievance. "Trembling as he spoke, drawing himself up in his excellently cut English worsted, he burst out angrily: 'I tell you, those people are coarse and vulgar. They come into my office without jackets or ties—they would never be allowed in an English club or restaurant. . . . If they wish to cut my living standard 10 per cent, or even 20 per cent, all right—but 100 per cent? Not me. Never! Do they think we can live like them, huddled in their kibbutzim? A doctor friend of mine was visited by an Israeli colleague who looked around with his mouth gaping [for compared with his small apartment, the Arab doctor's home looked like 'a palace']. Can you imagine, a doctor in two small rooms? I tell you, my dear sir, they send their children into the streets filthy, even their beggars do not know how to conduct themselves like ours. They have no manners, no decency, no shame, no respect for my bank. They walk in with their arms around each other, the men and the women in their little skirts, they eat out on the street, they spit. . . .' He stopped speechless. 'No, no, never! We can never live with those people!' " The miserable mass of Arab humanity just outside the banker's door gave the reporter the feeling that he "had been a witness to some scene out of a tragicomedy about the dispossessed nobility of old Russia, or the baffled patricians of the old

South.'' But he admits not being certain that these passions were not shared by the less fortunate as well.[45]

The large mass of peasants seems inert, though they might respond violently—if free to—anti-Jewish appeals by traditional leaders; thus, to the grievance by Muslim religious authorities on ''the introduction by the Israeli occupation forces of vice and prostitution into the Holy City''[46] they certainly have done so in the past. Respect for Israeli power and the material uplift they experience under its sway are possibly affecting village attitudes toward Israel; the first certainly affects overt hostility. As for the Arab proletariat and clerical workers, living conditions under Israeli rule have in some respects been revolutionized, where, as in Jerusalem, they were suddenly included into advanced welfare-state structures dominated by the powerful Israeli trade unions; in wages this meant for some a sevenfold increase. They are gradually beginning to adjust also to such concomitants as high taxation and emotionally demanding role-segregation in waging bloodless labor conflict, for instance. They seem to develop an ambiguous relationship to Israel along opposing pulls of class and nation; there is resentment at Israeli rule but also sharper Arab intrasocietal tension, perhaps.[47] (The intelligentsia, of course, deserve special attention in another place.)

The interview, in revealing something of the (in the American context) ''Southern'' quality of Arab society, puts in doubt the imagery of Arabs promoted in the West by Protestant missionaries and romantics. Even when one's acquaintance with Arabic literature goes no further than *The Thousand and One Nights,* as Lewis has pointed out, one may feel some doubt about the myth they promote. ''King Shahzamān and King Shahriyār were clearly southern gentlemen, with sexual fantasies, or rather nightmares, of an Alabama-like quality. This southern impression in *The Arabian Nights* is confirmed if we look more closely into that work. Blacks appear frequently in the stories that make up *The Arabian Nights.* Where they do, it is almost invariably in a menial role—as porters, household servants, slaves, cooks, bath attendants and the like, rarely if ever rising above this level in society. Perhaps even more revealing in its way is the story of the good black slave who lived a life of virtue and piety, for which he was rewarded by turning white at the moment of his death. We thus have two quite contradictory pictures before us—the first contained in the *Study of History,* the second reflected in that other great imaginative construction, *The Thousand and One Nights.* The one depicts a radically egalitarian society free from prejudice or discrimination; the other reveals a familiar pattern of sexual fantasy, social and occupational discrimination, and an unthinking identification of lighter with better and darker with worse."[48]

Frady, from our own Southland, immediately felt at home in the Arab world, recalling the thesis put forward by A. J. Liebling in *The Earl of Louisiana*, "that the states of Deepest Dixie—Louisiana, Mississippi, a bit of Alabama, and a bit of Texas—are merely a continuation of a single long cultural littoral which also encompasses such Mediterranean societies as Egypt and Algeria and Lebanon; that the Mediterranean and Caribbean and Gulf of Mexico 'form a homogenous, though interrupted, sea.' There had always seemed a certain style of voluptuousness among the Texas baronies that reminded him [Frady] of oil sheikdoms along the Persian Gulf, as if there is some common efflorescence to societies that dwell on the marge of enclosed seas. Beyond so much obsessive coffee drinking (Turkish coffee, which is both sipped and gently chewed) in so much heat, he felt himself in a culture which, like the South until recently at least, still belonged more to the earth than to machines (it occurred to him he had even taken the same inoculations that probably would have been necessary if he had been traveling back to the South before the New Deal, when it was still largely a gullied land of pellagra and trichinosis and malaria), a people who had remained in a kind of historical ennui, a society fundamentally and abidingly inert rather than kinetic, but in which there is a feverish and lavish private play of energies, a delirious sentimentality, a quick combustibility of temperament and a sense of identity and loyalty beginning with one's immediate neighborhood and then proceeding in ever-diminishing priorities outward."[49]

The Jews have arrived in the Middle East in recent history as the Arabs were in the grips of a painful transformation, from the traditional to a more dynamic way of life, the former even furthering and quickening the process undergone by the latter. Their revolution and modernism offends a still deeply traditional and inert culture; their success at forging a dynamic culture with an ancient identity only rankles even more, highlighting the Arabs' failure in seeking the same achievement; their modernity attracts, for it is real and available, yet repels since it can never be the Arabs' own. Meanwhile the Arabs live neither in a really traditional society, now irrevocably broken up, nor in truly modern ones. In the nightmare of transition the idea of the Jews' demise signifies both the good old days before the trouble and the successful overcoming of the present travail.

The sheer existence of their state, manifesting the success of the Jews' assertiveness, permits the Arabs neither slumber on disintegrating or new laurels nor the delusion that they have really arrived; it tells those, who feel superior to others, that they are still insufficient. Little wonder that aspects of their behavior in this situation have led observers to use such terms of description as "paranoia," some suggesting that this particular conflict may lend itself better to the treatment of psychiatrists than to that of diplomats.

The Arabs are finally savoring a foretaste of the righting of history through power over the West. The petroleum in the depths of their deserts appears at last to restore the world to order and confirm the truth of the faith once more. They have risen suddenly from the contempt of the West to its humiliation, and only the very ingenuous will miss the atavistic exultation. As in the pristine glory, once again now simple nomads imperiously dictate to the most advanced and productive peoples on earth, who seem incapable to muster their enormous power or even to close ranks to avert disaster. And if the parallel holds further, the Arab masters will not desire to slay the cow that feeds them, though milk her of the last drop. With the enormous wealth, accumulated by the West since industrialization, in Arab hands the West may yield also its loyalties and arms and finally abandon its latter-day Crusader fortress in the Holy Land, as they now fondly expect, as "a political luxury the world could do without," in the words of an Egyptian diplomat at the United Nations. For "the day is closer than many people think," he warned, when "the steady current of history will be and justice will be done and peoples' right will emerge triumphant and the crazy dream would have faded and everyone would realize that crimes against humanity like any other crime does not pay. . . . Since October, Israel has lost its sex appeal and cancer in the area has turned into septic focus which will eventually be removed. . . ."[50]

8

JEWS AND MUSLIMS

THE extent to which Israel is not Western does not necessarily alleviate hostility to it in the Arab world. While we like to think of Jew and Arab together as fellow Semites, the mutual denigration of Jews practiced in both Islam and Christendom constitutes the more practically relevant alignment. In their sense of outraged righteousness, the Arabs insist that they have been more tolerant of Jews than the Christians. But the difference is only one of degree; the claim itself avers that both have been master to the Jew.

The fact is that the Jews have indeed lived as a *subject* people, at the mercy of rulers and the occasional excesses of mobs, among both Christians and Muslims. Nothing like the Nazi Holocaust ever visited the Jews in Arab lands,[1] but indignities and even bloodshed were permanent parts of their lives. The Muslim record of Jewish persecution looks good only by comparison with the even more devastating Christian record. The intent here is not to indict the Arabs but to make it clear that their denigration of the Jews is not essentially different from the Christians', at least regarding their political subjection. Thus, we can better understand Arab rejection of Jewish statehood if we imagine how Poles or Austrians might feel in a similarly absolute reversal of traditional relationships with "their" Jews. Many Christians need not even engage in this exercise in empathy, since they are offended by Jewish dominion in the Holy Land on theological grounds.[2]

The reason that this elementary proposition must be emphatically stated is that it has been both obscured and explicitly denied by all sides. Several reasons explain this curious consensus in a conflict otherwise marked by extreme controversy. As is known, Arab spokesmen invariably protest that their quarrel is not with the Jews at all, but with Zionism. While these terms are freely interchangeable among Arabs, who do it spontaneously and naturally, their spokesmen in the West are greatly disturbed when others do likewise.[3] They prefer the use abroad of code words: "Jewish" denotes acquiescence in the "natural" condition of that people, as a protected minority; "Zionist" denotes the pejorative quality of Jewish sovereignty but obscures it; "Israel" thus need not be absolutely unacceptable in every case, for if "de-Zionized" (read "no longer a Jewish state"), it might become acceptable. The usual claim—that Jews are fine but Zionism an outrage—thus avers that those people are fit to be subjects only, yet makes it seem a compliment. More recent variants of the code are "democratized," "deracialized," "decolonized," etc. Like challenged masters everywhere, the Arabs express nostalgia for the old order, when everyone knew his place. They invariably recall a happy past for all, stressing affective personal relations and ignoring political ones; the latter are subsumed, implied, and otherwise obscured. "We are not against the Jews," protested Yasser Arafat, head of the *Fatah*. "On the contrary we are all Semites and we have been living with each other in peace and fraternity, Moslems, Jews and Christians, for many centuries."[4] Or Ayoub Musallam, former mayor of Bethlehem and Jordanian minister: "For generations Arabs and Jews lived together peacefully in this country, bound by mutual interests and brought together by the factors of neighborhood and other aspects of life. The history of the main towns of Palestine—Jerusalem, Haifa, Safed, Tiberias, Hebron and other localities inhabited by both Jews and Arabs teems with instances of brotherhood and sincere cooperation."[5]

All this is quite beside the real point, which is Arab ascendancy, presumably so natural a condition as to make trite the bare mention of it. The elementary fact of Arab (or Muslim) superordination and Jewish subjection none seems able to recall—a curious amnesia in a civilization so keenly sensitive to politics, to secular dominion, as Islam. Not only is the past peculiarly devoid of politics but the vision of the future is also. In an advertisement in the New York *Times*, the Association of Arab-American University Graduates depicted the past of Palestine only in terms of coexisting religions, and urged the United States to help restore conditions "in which men will live *again* on a footing of equality and justice."[6]

As with code words in Arab usage in general, here too, there exists a basic consistency between foreign and domestic versions (note, the Arab-Jewish political relationship of the past is ignored, avoided, obscured, but not denied, although should the foreigner gain the impression that it was otherwise, that is *his* problem); the foreign versions are merely more vague than domestic ones, but not really inconsistent. When Sheikh Goshah, Supreme Judge (Grand *Kadi*) of Jordan, speaks to Americans, in search of support for the eviction of Israel from Jerusalem, he affirms affection for Jews, stressing the Mosaic roots of Islam, mentioning a happy past together.[7] Yet addressing Muslim theologians at Al-Azhar University, he is explicit: Muslims are free to war on Jews who renege their subjection; indeed, they must. ("Treachery was the business of the Jews throughout their ages and times," he said, explaining this last betrayal.)[8]

With the coming of Zionism, euphoria is lost to strain, enmity replaces brotherhood. "For many years, before the establishment of Israel, the Jews in our midst formed a very homogenous group. I have an uncle who is married to a Jewess, and their sons are now living among us," recalls Dr. Ibrahim Khaldi, a Jerusalem physician. "Now, after the rise of political Zionism, that homogenous Jewish group became very alien and the whole Arab population started to reject it."[9] According to King Hussein, "the relationship that enabled Arabs and Jews to live together for centuries as neighbors and friends has been destroyed by Zionist ideas and actions."[10] The attempt at radically changing ancient political relationships everywhere affects social and personal relations as well, and even the usual inclination to blame the disturbance on outside agitation has not been missing in this particular case. The pertinent literature abounds with distinctions between "our" Jews and the imported ones who cause the trouble: the *Ashkenazi* Jews have come to subvert the fraternity of Arabs and "Arab Jews," inciting the latter against their "brothers." The similarity with typical Southern rationalizations of Negro stirrings, as in the civil rights campaigns of the 1950's and 1960's, is inescapable: The trouble is caused by those who have gone North and returned perverted and in league with corrupt nonregional political forces; "our own" do not really want to change things; it is we who love and understand them, while their pretended liberators only debase and enslave them; and so on.

"Our brother has gone to Europe and to the West," the Secretary-General of the Arab League declared to the Anglo-American Inquiry Committee, "and has come back something else. He has come back a Russified Jew, a Polish Jew, a German Jew. He has come back with a totally different conception of things, Western and not Eastern. That does not mean that we are necessarily quarrelling with anyone who comes from the West. But the Jew, our old cousin, coming back with imperialistic ideas, with materialistic ideas. with reactionary or revolutionary ideas, and trying to implement them first by British pressure and then by American pressure, and then by terrorism of his own part—he is not the old cousin and we do not extend to him a very good welcome. The Zionist, the new Jew, wants to dominate . . ."[11]

More than two decades later a quite ordinary Arab repeats countless times nostalgia for "the peace that existed until foreign elements intervened and destroyed this region's calmness and brought disillusion to its inhabitants. . . . Oriental Jews still dream of the time when they lived side by side with their Arab neighbors and comrades, a feeling European Jews have never known."[12] Now Arabs and "their" Jews suffer together the arrogant dominion of their common foe, as witness complaints of discrimination by *Sephardic* Jews in Israel. The latest version presents Israel no longer so much a "Zionist" (read Jewish) state as an *Ashkenazi* dominion over Arabs and Arab-like Jews.[13] (While indeed feeling discriminated against by *Ashkenazis*, the actual feelings of the *Sephardic* mass for Arabs, as revealed in opinion polls, are about as warm as those of Southern Negroes for Dixiecrats.)

Some awareness of the abject nature of Jewish subjection in Islam enables one to fathom the anxieties behind this collective Arab failure of memory. The long historical encounter of Jew and Arab has been both a symbiotic as well as an antagonistic one, and historians have reflected the peculiar needs and perceptions of the last century in their emphasis on the favorable position of Jews in Muslim countries during the Middle Ages. More than one generation of scholars was nurtured on euphemized history, hence one naturally thought of past Muslim and Jewish corelationships as the fruition of a glorious civilization. Our more sober age allows us to see the gore behind the rosy façade. The collective record of Muslim dominion over Jews still looks better than Christendom's (the Nazi Holocaust makes virtually any other record look good by comparison, anyway). But enough is known of the Muslim record to lend a touch of irony to familiar protestations that the West has discharged its guilty conscience by supporting Zionism at the expense of righteous Islam—Toynbee's "cynical principle of making the defenceless pay," the West "compensating their victims at the expense of innocent third parties," which he termed "the most perverse of all the base propensities of Human Nature."[14]

In reality the whole sore gamut of conquest, massacre, subjection, spoliation in goods and women and children, contempt, expulsion—even the yellow badge—was not just Christian practice witnessed from afar by disapproving Muslims but rather authentic Muslim practice, from the days of the Prophet on in many cases, and in the case of the badge actually an original contribution to international discrimination. Islam regards Judaism standing at the inception of the Muslim era as an imperfect precursor of the faith, whose followers in Madina, although befriended by the Prophet, rejected and betrayed him most cowardly. Upon his return from triumph at the battle of Badr, Mohammed stormed the Beni Qainuka quarter of Medina, despoiled and forcibly exiled the Jewish tribe, only reluctantly sparing their lives (for they refused to fight); this fate was shared by the nearby Beni Nadheer, following his defeat by the Meccans at Uhud. Another such Muslim setback, at Hudeibiya, was followed by a veritable orgy with the blood of the Jewish Beni Quraidha, of whom perhaps as many as one thousand were ceremoniously slaughtered after surrender. The ritual shedding of Jewish blood thus served to solidify the still-wavering early community of believers, much as cohesion by shared complicity in bloodshed is deliberately sought in certain modern mass movements. The war against the Jews culminated in the conquest of wealthy Khaibar, the center of Jewish power in Arabia, where Mohammed imposed political subjection and economic exploitation (Caliph Omar later banished the Jews to Syria), a formula that, rather than extermination or forced conversion, was to be the model for the treatment of Jews, Christians, and Zoroastrians in the ensuing conquests outside Arabia. Jews continued to exist throughout Islam until the collapse of the Ottoman Empire within the appropriate self-administered religious community, or *millet*, which survives even now for purposes of civil law in many Middle Eastern countries.

The war of Islam on the Jews thus stands as a major confrontation at the very beginning of the faith, the Prophet himself leading the struggle against the mortal danger ("deadliest enemies")[15] subjecting them in cruel punishment to the humiliating subordination that is rightfully theirs. For the Jews are innately accursed from the beginning of time; persecuted by all in antiquity for their criminal corruption, they persisted in depravity. "Their own sufferings at the hands of ruthless persecutors had failed to teach them the value of humanity and peace. The atrocious cruelties which they committed in the cities of Egypt, of Cyprus and Cyrene, where they dwelt in treacherous harmony with the unsuspecting natives, take away all sense of pity for their future fate. The house of Israel was a total wreck [after the wars of Titus and Hadrian]; its members were fugitives on the face of the earth, seeking shelter far and wide, but carrying everywhere their indomitable pride, their rebellious hardness of heart, denounced and reprehended by an endless succession of prophets. The Jews, in their safe retreats in foreign lands, re-enacted the scenes of past times. The nation lived in hope, but the hope was mixed with rigid uncompromising bigotry on the one hand, and a voluptuous epicureanism on the other. Jesus had come and gone, without producing any visible effect upon them."[16]

Neither has Mohammed, despite an early offer of alliance. "No kindness or generosity, however, on the part of the Prophet would satisfy the Jews; nothing could conciliate the bitter feelings with which they were animated. Enraged that they could not use him as their instrument for the conversion of Arabia to Judaism, and that his belief was so much simpler than their Talmudic legends, they soon broke off, and ranged themselves on the side of the enemies of the new Faith. . . . They reviled him; they 'twisted their tongues' and mispronounced the Koranic words and the daily prayers and formulae of Islâm, rendering them meaningless, absurd, or blasphemous; and the Jewish poets and poetesses, of whom there existed many at the time, outraged all common decency and recognized code of Arab honour and chivalry by lampooning in obscene verse the Moslem women. But these were minor offences. Not satisfied with insulting the women of the Believers and reviling the Prophet, they sent out emissaries to the enemies of the State, the protection of which they had formally accepted. The Koreish, who had sworn Mohammed's death . . . knew . . . that the moment they showed themselves in the vicinity of Medina the worshippers of Jehovah would break away from him and join the idolaters. And now came the moment of severest trial to Islâm."[17]

"Thus the Jews rightfully deserved the wrath and the curse of Allah,"[18] branded with the stigma of humiliation and meanness. "Allah has sent among them those who torture them severely and will keep on persecuting them up to the Last Day. . . ." Among leading theologians of Islam, the slightly apologetic treatment of the Jews' punishment marking the above message to the outside world (think of the fury of battle, of the abominable nature of the Jews' crimes), gives way to sheer revelry in details of the Prophet's torment of his Jewish foe: how the assassination of a Jewish poet was accomplished—"The murder of Ibn Al Ashraf horrified the Jews'

poets and their adventurers"—how Jewish tribes were defeated—
"Therefore, the Jews of Fadk, Taimaa and Garba's were much
terrorized. . . ."[19]

The modern conflict with the Jews is seen by Muslims as part of
an ongoing struggle originating with the Prophet (whom, Muslims
believe, a Jewess had poisoned in the end). The last will of the
Prophet, on the verge of death, was to purge all Arabia of Jews. And
now the Jews are at it again: "The Jews followed the attitudes of
their ancestors towards the Prophet and the Muslims. The Jews kept
on sticking to their corrupt demoralized instinct and their vicious
wicked prejudice. They committed their treacherous oppressive
atrocities in Palestine and they paid no heed to honour, manliness or
truth."[20] (Arab knowledge of Judaism, even among Christians and
the educated, is characterized by just such belief in innate, un-
changeable traits, once and for all times revealed in antiquity.)[21]
Muslims are now warring on the same enemy, whose just deserts
have been shown by the Prophet himself and ordained by Allah. In
the October war, Egyptian troops carried official pamphlets explaining their campaign in this sense, while Syrian tanks carried the in-
scription "Death to the Infidels."

Against this background, grasped even better once one understands the full depth of the imprint of Islam on even contemporary
orientations, news items that may otherwise seem odd in the twentieth century suddenly assume serious connotations: Sadat affirming
"he would never hold direct negotiations with Israelis because they
were a mean, perfidious, conspiring people bent on treachery," that
"we will return them to the state in which the Koran described
them: to be persecuted, suppressed and miserable."[22] Or the President of Libya: "The Koran says that the Moslems' worst enemies
are the Jews," and citing divine injunctions to struggle against them
as well as prophecies of triumph ("We shall return; and We have
made Gehenna a prison for the unbelievers"[23]). (Colonel Kisch
cited this manifesto by Arab students in the wake of the 1929 massacres of Jews in Palestine: "O Arabs! Remember that the Jew is
your strongest enemy, and the enemy of your ancestors from earliest times. Do not let ourselves be seduced by his lies, for it was he
who tortured Christ—Peace be unto him—and poisoned Mohammed—Peace be unto him—whom we venerate. It is he who is
now trying to slaughter you, as he did in the past."[24])

There is nothing mysterious about the character and status of the
Jewish *millet*; as a tolerated group of outsiders, depending for its
protection on the goodwill of others, its position was always "utterly

precarious,"[25] for even periods of calm could precipitously abut in terror. The condition was not one of abused civil rights at all; it was one of no rights, just sufferance. "An Islamic state was part of or coincided with *dār al-islām,* the House of Islam. Its treasury was *māl al-muslimīn,* the money of the Muslims. Christians and Jews certainly were not citizens of that state, not even second-class citizens. They were outsiders under the protection of the Muslim state, a status characterized by the term *dhimma,* for which protection they had to pay a poll tax specific to them. They were also exposed to a great number of discriminatory and humiliating laws."[26] The Jews were generally safer in the first century of Islam than in the two following ones, when many restrictions appeared—in dress, housing, use of animals—and many outrages occurred, including the sacking of synagogues. In many areas throughout the centuries Jewish children were torn from their mothers in forced conversions of orphans; in Yemen, well into our own time, Jews were prohibited from using sidewalks lest their heads be higher than those of Muslims. It was generally sectarian Islam that was responsible for the worst persecutions of Jews, the actual position of the Jews depending also on their power and influence in various periods; the smaller their numbers, the more likely was Muslim outrage. And the lower the political fortunes of their Muslim masters, the less secure were the Jews among them.

The justification of the sheer existence of *dhimmis* (protected ones) was that their faiths, however imperfect. were precursors of Islam; their function was essentially twofold: Their humiliation served to exalt the Muslims; their economic exploitation supported the Muslims' state. The two were joined in the rendition of the *jizya* (the poll tax), arranged to be particularly outrageous and demeaning in public display; according to one regulation, cited in Baron and elsewhere, *dhimmis* appear before the designated emir, who does not allow them to render the tax, instead shaking it brutally from the offering palms by striking their necks—"taking it," as in rape—then evicting them in shame, before a public assembly.[27]

The basic regulation attributed to Caliph Omar provided the following limitations on *dhimmis:* the wearing of special, often grotesque, signs, to distinguish them from Muslims; stepping aside and yielding the right of way to Muslims, passing them only on their left, and remaining standing in their presence; not repairing their houses of worship or building new ones, nor residing in houses higher than the Muslims'; living in assigned quarters; celebrating their rites quietly and inconspicuously so as not to provoke Muslims (even their funereal lamentations must not annoy Muslims); paying higher taxes than Muslims, in addition to the special tax; traveling only with special permission; not being permitted to testify against Muslims; and many more. They could be put to death for mating with Muslim women, obliged to work without pay, and suffered many other discriminatory practices. Implementation varied, with some rulers offering lax implementation only and others zealously enforcing rules and contributing a large range of special innovative arrangements. Thus, after some laxness, the fabled Haroun al-Rashid renewed old restrictions vigorously; then the decree of Mutawakkil (A.D. 850) ordered the following, among others: the wearing exclusively of honey-colored (yellow; there were variations of color among *millets*) clothing, badges, etc. (except for hats, to be distinguished otherwise);[28] the transformation of spacious synagogues and churches into mosques; demon-shaped wooden figures to be affixed to the *dhimmis'* houses; the razing of their tombs to earth level, so as not to resemble Muslim tombs. This and additional persecution rendered in the High Middle Ages the condition of Jews in Islam not better than in Christendom, perhaps even worse, as might be indicated by the growing immigration in the period of Oriental Jews to Europe. (A sad dialectic of persecution is evident in the period, as persecution in the East triggers persecution in the West, invariably victimizing Jews, in various patterns; in one case, the Norman conquerors of Sicily made the profitable discovery of the *jizya* practiced by the previous, Muslim, rulers of the island; in another the religious persecutions of Caliph Hakim provoked attacks on the Jews in the West, where *they* were accused of having destroyed the churches in Egypt.)

Overall conditions turn worse for Jews in Christendom with the Crusades, not just for the animus they generate, but ironically also because of the adoption in large measure of discriminatory practices long congenial in the Orient, the large movement of the Crusades itself enhancing contact between East and West. (The ritual-murder accusation, a hoary Eastern practice, thus appears in England for the first time in 1144. Incidentally, the historical perception of Judaism in the Arab world is manifested here, too, in that ritual-murder accusations are treated seriously in the contemporary Arab press and government, for instance, as proof of the criminal character of the Israeli foe.) In the permanent pattern of the *dhimma* in the relatively more tolerant East now—alternate relative security and terror—one finds, among such things as continuing innovations in the arts of discrimination, the more basic bloodsheds *en masse* punctuating Jewish history in Islam: the three-day pogrom in Baghdad and other places in 1289;[29] the recurring massacres in Fez, 1032–33, claiming some six thousand Jewish lives;[30] and others.

To put in proper perspective the periods of efflorescence and reason in the Middle Ages one must take a closer look at Maimonides, the most famous of Jewish medieval leaders, at one time court physician to Saladin the Great, the figure often cited as symbol of the vaunted Muslim-Jewish symbiosis. Maimonides fled to Egypt—not from Christian persecution, but from Muslim terror in Spain—and was later forced to hide his Judaism from the Muslims of Arabia and other places so as not to endanger his safety. The topic of his famous Epistle to the Jews of Yemen was how to face the choice between death and forced conversion, asserting that the nation of Ismael torments, debases, and hates the Jews more than any other nation in history. Still, relative to the aggravation in the position of European Jewries as the West enters the prelude to the subsequent vast transformations, the declining East, as under the Mameluke rule in Egypt (1254–1517), appears as mere harassment, and the migration is toward it, particularly from militantly Christian Spain.

The uplift of the modern, emancipating West was absent from the Jewish *millet* in more recent centuries; within stagnating Islamic societies the overall lot of the Jew is a pattern of sporadic death and extortion punctuating the usual precariousness. For the most part the bottom of a backward society, the Jew comes close to experiencing the lot of his coreligionist in backward East European societies. Albert Memmi, brought up on the fresh memories of parents and grandparents of libels, hangings, extortions and atrocities perpetrated openly or covertly by the rulers of Tunis and their peoples, was struck by the similarity of the Jewish condition in tsarist Russia with his elders'.[31] Indeed, the systematic exertions against barbaric treatment of Jews by the various American presidents in the last century and in this were focused almost equally in just these two regions, Orthodox East Europe and Islam.

In Persia Jews were forced to wear distinctive patches as late as 1894, and the severity of persecution pushed many into conversion, but they were not spared even as Muslims. American diplomatic intervention in that period cited murders, looting, and other forms of persecution. One case, in Hamadan, involved a Jew who converted to Islam in the wake of the mob violence of 1892; still, the populace asked for his head; he was executed, and the mob looted his house and those of other Jews.[32] "As late as 1905, the Jews of Morocco were still subject to many restrictions because of their religion. There restrictions were especially severe in interior towns. Jews had to live in *mellahs*, or ghettos, the gates of which had to be closed at night. They had to wear a peculiar garb, and when outside of the *mellah* had to go barefoot and bareheaded as a sign of submissiveness. Jewish provision dealers were forced to offer their goods free to all officials. Jews were not permitted to testify in court, and the punishment for the murder of a Jew was a mere money fine. These are only a few of the many restrictions which the Jews of Morocco had to suffer and against which they dared not protest."[33]

Jews were singled out for especially "painful and injurious restrictions," wrote Secretary of State Elihu Root, who described the details of the Jewish condition in Morocco as "well-nigh incredible."[34] Some specific instances making American officials feel duty-bound "to protect a minority specially subject to outrages at the hands of barbarous tribes, ruled by weak and conscienceless government:"[35] a Jew, who in self-protection raised his hand against a Moor, had his hand cut off; Jews in Tangier, "falsely accused of the most fearful crimes, had been barbarously tortured and many executed"; at Saffi two Jews were falsely accused and executed; pogrom by ravaging bands in Arzila, August, 1878; pogrom in Laraiche, later; an eighty-five-year-old Jew burned alive in the streets of Fez. ("The vizier justified this atrocity on the alleged ground that the old Jew had insulted and threatened a crowd of Moors. He further charged that a Moor had previously been killed by another Jew." Evidence furnished by an American consular agent who was in Fez at the time led the American consulate in Tangier to term the explanation "ludicrous" and the other story a "fabrication.")

Of the Western influences dominating the most recent period, liberalism, weak in general in Islam, was mostly ineffectual in its impact on the Jewish condition. (Such citadels of Arab liberalism as Lebanon are also oases of relative peace for Jews, as was Egypt under the sway of the parliamentary—though corrupt—*Wafd* regime.) Modern anti-Semitism, stimulated by the conflict in Palestine, had much the more potent impact. Mussolini's fascism and Hitler's national socialism captivated much of the Arab world in the 1930's and 1940's; repeated attempts were made during World War Two to open the Middle East to the Axis, by plot and open rebellion (in Iraq, 1941, occasion for the worst pogrom in the modern East). And

Arab leaders, such as the acknowledged head of Palestine's Arabs, the Mufti of Jerusalem, openly allied themselves with the Nazis, particularly in respect to their solution of the Jewish problem. In more recent years the Arab world has been a haven for hunted Nazis and was virtually overrun with anti-Semitic literature, both of the authentic *Stürmer*-type variant and other European originals (*The Protocols of the Elders of Zion*, in several Arabic editions, has thus become a popular household article) and of some true Arab originals and more or less imaginative syncretizations of traditional Muslim and modern Western anti-Jewish lore. But only few Jews are left in Islamic countries.

The area that became Palestine after World War One had a relatively mild record of persecution, albeit this subsumes such outrages as the confiscation of the Jerusalem synagogue and its conversion into a mosque in the middle of the fifteenth century; the wave of terror launched against Jews in Jerusalem by Mohammad Ibn Farukh between 1625–27; the closing of synagogues in 1655 to enforce payment of confiscatory taxation; the pogroms in Safad in 1834 and 1838; the pogroms in Jaffa early in this century; etc. Karl Marx thus described the condition of the Jews of Jerusalem in his time, then already constituting the majority in the city: "The Mussulmans, forming about a fourth part of the whole, and consisting of Turks, Arabs and Moors, are of course, the masters in every respect, as they are in no way affected by the weakness of their Government at Constantinople. Nothing equals the misery and the sufferings of the Jews at Jerusalem, inhabiting the most filthy quarter of the town, called *hareth al-yahoud*, in the quarter of dirt, between the Zion and the Moriah, where their synagogues are situated—the constant objects of Mussulman oppression and intolerance, insulted by the Greeks, persecuted by the Latins, and living only upon the scanty alms transmitted by their European brethren."[36] Religious relations of Muslims and Jews in the Holy Land matched the political relations. Arab conquest had once again deprived the Jews of their holy shrines, which were revered also by Muslims, and Jewish access to them was precarious, discriminatory, or categorically denied. Jews were allowed to ascend only the first few steps of the Tomb of the Patriarchs in Hebron, and only at certain times; no Jew was ever permitted to enter the mosque of Nebi Musa, said to mark the burial place of Moses.

Though sharing *dhimma* status with Christians, the Jews were thus in Islam the object of particular contempt, in the words of the

Koran, "the most abominable of God's creatures."[37] Divinely accursed in the eyes of both Muslims and Christians, the Jews alone were powerless in this world, in both Muslim and Christian realms. Western visitors found the Jews even more demeaned than the Christians, as counting for almost nothing—in one early treatise on Egypt, "despised and oppressed"[38]—long before the word "Zionism," allegedly signifying the breach of amity, was even coined.

George Sale, the English translator of the Koran, wrote that Muslims then treated the Jews "as the most abject and contemptible people on earth."[39] In his classic work on Egypt Lane wrote in the early part of the nineteenth century of extraordinary hatred and contempt for Jews by Muslims, much more than for Christians; they were beaten in the streets by the most miserable Muslims for no real reason; he himself witnessed the execution of a Jew for the crime of a Muslim, observing that Jews are hung, never decapitated, for they are deemed so impure that their blood might pollute the executioner's sword.[40] A French observer wrote that Judaism was more demeaned among Muslims than in barbarian Europe of old.[41] "In the eyes of Muslims," wrote a consular official, "there exists no more contemptible race than the Jewish race," so much so, he pointed out, that in order to be admitted to Islam, Jews were required first to convert to Christianity.[42] In some areas Jews were even recently treated simply as pariahs, as a British official discovered in Afghanistan in 1937, where Muslims refused to travel with them in the same vehicle.[43] The contempt seems ageless: A.D., 644 when the Caliph Omar berated Amr Ibn al-Aasi, the conqueror of Egypt, the latter is said to have replied, "You could not have said more to a Jew of Khaibar. God forgive you and me."[44] Even now an Arab who feels he is being treated with contempt by another often says, "Am I a Jew to you?"

It is outrageous enough for any *millet* to jeopardize Muslim overlordship, as the fate of the Armenians and others in the Ottoman Empire has shown; the reaction was genocidal in even so Westernized an individual as Enver Pasha, the World War One Ottoman leader. That this most abject, Jewish *millet* should presume to rule over Muslims in the Arab heartland is a particularly unbearable thought, and is probably sufficient reason why it is not the shape or extent, but rather the fact, of Jewish statehood that most disturbs the Arabs.

The waging of war ruthlessly on any *millet* endangering Muslim overlordship is a categorical injunction in Islam. Even a presumption of equal status elicited stern response, as one of many reports indicates. "The attitude of the Moslems towards the Christians and Jews," wrote the British Vice-Consul in Mosul in 1909, "is that of a master towards slaves whom he treats with a certain lordly tolerance so long as they keep their place. Any sign of pretension to equality is promptly repressed."[45] The Armenian *millet* was accused of the betrayal of its master by a Turkish revolutionary leader, Enver, precursor of Nasserite radical officers, ruler of a state already pretending to norms of universal citizenship, and subjected to systematic extermination claiming more than one million lives during World War One.[46] The Greek *millet* suffered tens of thousands of fatalities for the same crime, as Kemal Ataturk, the secular revolutionary, mobilized for *jihad* the rural mass of Anatolia against them and their brother Hellenes in the encroaching armies. (Ambassador Morgenthau feared that the campaign against Armenians would be followed by one against Zionists and intervened to prevent it.)[47]

The pattern was to be repeated with yet another, Jewish, *millet* further to the south, as was, incidentally, a pattern of response in the West, where bureaucrats urged support for the "strong" as *Realpolitik*, and ecclesiastics and romantics apologetically represented Islamic atavism "as a strict unitarian version of Protestantism," to use Kedourie's phrase. The Muslim Arabs of southern Syria, part of the ruling community in the deceased Ottoman Empire, were not about to acquiesce in subjection to a despised *millet*; their posture remained throughout basically that of masters of the land faced by "an act of rebellion";[48] that the rule of even advanced Jews by backward Arabs was natural, that the subjection of the latter within even diminutive Jewish dominion was "obnoxious."[49]

In the past this was said clearly and widely understood. "It is true that part of the Palestinian problem is economic," explained Arthur Jeffery. "As peasants lose their land, as source after source of income is cut off by the Jewish infiltration, as young educated Arabs find it impossible to compete with Jewish youth for positions in the professions and official life, as immigration forces life to a pace to which they are not accustomed, the economic pinch becomes serious. It is true also that there is the natural resentment of the old established inhabitant against the newcomer—a resentment which tends to be fiercer in the Orient than we know it in the West. But deeper than either of these as a source of Arab resistance to Zionism is the feeling that Palestine is a Muslim land by divine right. Christians and oriental Jews feel equally the economic pinch and the resentiment against the newcomer, but the Muslim Arab's deepest sense of outrage is that a land given the Muslims by Allah in the early years of Islam as their inalienable possession is in grave danger of becoming a land where they live but no longer rule."[50]

Ottoman power had meant emphatically Muslim supremacy—*Sunni*, to be exact—and in the Levante, moreover, the area to be mandatory Palestine was the most compact and homogenous territory with a predominant *Sunni* majority (therefore the worst area, perhaps that could have been chosen for a Jewish national home, opined Kedourie).[51] As *Sunnis*, the Muslim Arabs of the land belonged to the dominant group in the empire; their leading families enjoyed preeminence in the empire, which they defended loyally in the war with the infidel. "Under the Ottoman Regime," the *Mufti* of Jerusalem testified before the Royal Commission on Palestine, "the Arabs formed an important part of the structure of the Ottoman Empire. It is wrong to say that the Arabs were under the yoke of the Turks and that their uprising and the assistance which was rendered to them during the Great War were merely intended to relieve them from such yoke. The fact is that under the Ottoman Constitution they enjoyed all rights and privileges, political and otherwise, on an equal basis with the Turks. . . . The Arabs had a complete share with the Turks in all organs of the State, civil as well as military. There were Arabs who held the high office of Prime Minister and Ministers, Commanders of Divisions and Ambassadors."[52] If they were of the Turk, it was for them alone to rule what he had abandoned —the *Sunni* presumption to rule thus devolved on Arab nationalism —certainly not to be ruled by the Jews. "It is very true," observed an American diplomat in the area at the close of the war, "that the Syrians and the Palestinians for the greater part are easily overawed by power, but that depends to a certain degree upon the source of the power; the Palestinians will not be intimidated by the Jews, whom for centuries they have looked down upon and despised and considered as inferiors."[53]

An important difference between the Jewish challenge to Muslim dominion and that of the Greeks, earlier, was pointed up by Lewis. "The emergence of Israel in 1948—or rather, the failure of the Arab armies to prevent it, was a climactic event in the history of the Middle East, comparable in many ways with the landing of the Greeks in Izmir in 1919. It was bad enough to be dominated by the Franks [Western Christians]—but they were after all the invincible masters of the world, who—on both occasions—had just defeated their enemies in a great war. It was a very different matter, and an intolerable humiliation, to submit to the Greeks or Jews—to local *dhimmis* whom Muslims had long been accustomed to despise as inferiors. The Franks, moreover, would, sooner or later, go back whence they came. The Greek Great Idea—*megalê idea*—of a revived Byzantine empire, and the Zionist idea of a revived Jewish state, were clearly intended to be permanent. The same sense of outrage colours the Kemalist reaction against the Greeks, and the Arab reaction against Israel. Some of the difference in the subsequent development of Turkey and the Arab states may be ascribed to the fact that the Turks won their war, whereas the Arabs lost theirs."[54]

A nightmarish quality attaches to the Arabs' shock, as if someone were perpetrating a cruel joke on them to boot, since the Jews are surely the least likely sovereign people on earth, being "the dregs of peoples," and "the weakest and most submissive" of peoples. Denied a claim to dominion in the holy scriptures and everywhere naturally subjected to all, the thought of the Jews as rulers suggests cosmic disorder.[55] (There is in Islamic eschatology a messianic belief in an Armageddon between Muslims and Jews on the threshold of final salvation.)[56] Hence, the common resort among Arabs to Jewish statehood as "abnormal," "unnatural," "artificial," and in similar terms: "Israel has never had, and never will have a *natural* sovereign existence that can easily and quickly adjust itself to the changing atmosphere. Israel has been, and still is an *artificial* state composed of poor-quality, brittle material, something like plaster, which can only change when it breaks up."[57] Or: "It is our duty to expose Zionism for what it really is, an international racist movement synthesized of religious prejudice, intellectual dishonesty and capitalist greed. This *anachronism* of a movement is much more inhuman than the Nazism it purports to have opposed."[58] Whatever the particulars, the essence is invariably expressed in synonymous terms: unnatural, however one puts it.

Hence, the resilient expectation that the Jewish state will naturally somehow dissolve; and the belief that Jewish statehood is a thoroughly factitious phenomenon held together by crafty means against all nature; and the insistence that the Jews are merely a religious group that cannot possibly constitute a nation.[59] One can hardly overstate the strength among Arabs of these beliefs; they appear genuinely puzzled that the Jews should act so totally out of character. "Why," exclaimed Azzam Pasha in 1948, "must it be necessary for the approximate number of 700,000 Jews who are at present in

Palestine to have a State of their own, when there are far larger numbers of Jews in other parts of the world without any question arising of establishing a separate State?''[60]

Affirmations, especially from Jewish sources, that Jews indeed are merely a religious group are gratefully accepted as reassurances of lingering sanity at least somewhere among the Jews; the others are invariably urged to return to sanity, for their own good above all. In one such plea, they are warned that their toleration as minorities around the world is jeopardized by the insistence on constituting the majority in one country.[61] It is in this light that one can make sense of the otherwise puzzling familiar Arab appeals to the Jewish state to dismantle itself voluntarily—as if to say, it is time to put an end to the charade, time to return to "normal" conditions ("to resume their historically positive relationships"[62] with Arabs, and many other variants).

The same applies to equally puzzling assertions that, in seeking the destruction of the Jewish state, the Arabs are also struggling to liberate the Jews who live in it—i.e., they will be enabled to exist once more as Jews naturally do. The *fedayeen* who put particular emphasis after 1967 on the Jews' liberation are also particularly insistent in denying them any basis for the organization of a political personality of their own; the Palestinian National Covenant explicitly denies them nationality, peoplehood, even a spiritual tie with the country as such basis, and international law insofar as it lends itself to such purpose. The ironclad premise for them also insures their eventual triumph: Since the Jews have no real nationalism, terror will induce them to relinquish statehood.

The strain between the Arabs' conceptualization of the Jew and the reality is psychologically demanding, both because the latter fails to live up to the stereotype and because Arabs do not quite measure up either to their cherished views of themselves. The Muslim heritage has invested self-esteem with extraordinary dependence on martial prowess and the weight of tradition leans heavily on the idea that war is a particularly appropriate and successful manner for assertiveness, just as it assumes the Jews to be naturally defenseless creatures. Having been drained of manly virtues by long servility to others, the Jews compensate for (and thereby further aggravate) their degeneracy by particular deviousness, a conception that allows one to see them as weak, while explaining upsetting outcomes in struggle with them.

The Arabs entered their struggle with the Jews firmly convinced that the latter may be victimized with impunity, as they had been, after all, in Islam for more than a thousand years (and almost with impunity, as the normal condition, approximating the German medieval status, *Vogelfrei*). A founder of *kibbutz* Degania, the first ever, recalled, "when we came we found that the Arabs despised us, they called us 'children of death,' meaning that we were soft, we couldn't defend ourselves, we were frightened."[63] (But by devious means, they could control the British and others, hence, Jewish inadvertent strength.) Jews were referred to in the Holy Land as "devils" (*shayatin*) and "dogs." (*Al-billad billadna, wa al-yahoud kellabna*—This land is ours and the Jews are our dogs—was a traditional chant in Arab demonstrations in Palestine.)[64] They were also referred to as *siknag,* meaning coward, a distortion of the word *Ashkenazi,* comparable to "kike."[65] By fateful coincidence the Jews imposed on themselves for a considerable period of time the policy of utmost restraint in the face of violence (*havlagah*), thus unwittingly confirming the Arab belief in Jewish vulnerability. The erosion of this policy in the late 1930's and later produced a psychological problem for Arabs at least as severe as the military one, some observers describing reaction to Jewish martial feats as shock. "Arabs in the streets," wrote a witness to an Israeli air raid in 1948, "couldn't get over the fact that the once lowly Jews—four thousand of whom were cooped up in their Damascus ghetto, afraid to venture out—had used four-engine bombers."[66] ("For an Arab to be beaten by the Jew," this observer was later told by a Christian Lebanese leader, "is a terrible insult.")

Arabs relate to Jewish martial power as Zionists earlier related to the Arabs' hostility: They are sensitive to its manifestations though dubious about its genuineness. Arabs thus are badly beaten, but they are never defeated; the Jew they fear is really a coward; acknowledged Arab weakness is a function of distant international powers. After their disastrous first war the Arabs felt betrayed by the British, cheated of victory by the United Nations, but not defeated by the Jews. After the second they felt stronger than before the Jews' pretense, for had they not been found hiding behind the British and the French, and, besides, within a few years Arabs implicitly believed that they had won the war, even on the battlefield. The June war has made for much more sobriety, yet faith in the *inherent* military superiority of the Arabs lingers on. Returning from a sojourn in the Arab world, Desmond Stewart offered a sampling of the perplexity reigning in the wake of the June war, as he listed a few explanations of the disaster heard in Iraq: a. Israel has a more liberal society; b. Israelis think of their country, while Arabs think of their pocketbooks; c. Israel's allies supported it ruthlessly, but the Arabs' ally got the jitters; d. Israel is better armed; e. the Syrians sold the Golan Heights; f. King Hussein, fearing his own people, never armed them; g. the Arabs had broken their alliance with Britain; etc. One Baghdadi explained why the Jews had to make it a lightning victory: "They were frightened what might happen if the Iraqis got there."[67] And in the traditional atmosphere of *kalam fadi* (empty words) and *hifaq* (two-facedness) it is often the same people who express contradictory views.

The explanation Arabs really want to believe is that which attributes the Jews' victory to others, which appears in many variations, the best known abroad being Anglo-American military intervention, no longer thought to be literally true by the literate, though true nonetheless in a more profound sense. In another version foreigners in the Jews' clothing did their fighting for them, either filling the ranks of their conquering armies or flying their deadly aircraft (American jets piloted by American airmen).[68] In yet another, Israeli power is generally somehow a function of American will, so that Israeli military superiority exists because Washington is determined to maintain it. In the October war Egypt's acceptance of the cease-fire was explained by Sadat and others as reluctant, since the Arabs could not fight America, having already defeated Israel— when in fact the joint American-Soviet move stopped the latter from completing the destruction of Egypt's military might, the Israelis standing before the gates of Cairo itself. The accusation was made, during the war and after, that Americans and the Dutch had done the fighting for Israel.

Though Arabs often say that only a radical change in their social order could redress the military disparity, there appears to be no real awareness of what exactly must be done; other than voicing the appropriate generalities, they manifest a distinct tendency to confuse collective capacity with sheer technique. Seemingly puzzled by the impersonal and mobile nature of the modern warfare the Israelis wage (their own ostensibly modern armies appearing inherently incapable of producing the same), Arabs express curious disbelief that the Jews have fought, indeed, that war had taken place at all. "We don't feel defeated," a young Arab told an Israeli journalist soon after the June war in Jerusalem, "because there was no war here,"[69] an attitude also assumed by King Hussein, among others.[70] Arabs have failed to see the foe fighting war as they know it (a blend of primitive and historical patterns of warfare) and feel deprived of the opportunity to show the world what the Jews really are and what the Arabs can do. (Many Arabs have complained that the Jews never show their faces in battle, expressing doubt that Arabs and Jews really had fought each other.)[71] The widespread disorientation, disbelief, and shock reported in Arab nations after the June war may thus represent simply anomic behavior, that is, deriving from the breakdown of a normative order governing action, when individuals lack clear guidelines for conduct. Arabs seemed genuinely at a loss at explicating what had happened; the events were both awesome and unintelligible, almost apocalyptic—like fire pouring down from heaven, as one Jordanian put it.[72] Terms Arabs have used to describe the war—hurricane, earthquake, lightning, calamity, catastrophe—would indicate that it is an act of nature over which they have no control.

Behind the horror, one strained mightily to discover the Jews as they must be, as cowards. Stripped of artificial and alien accouterments, they appear, as of old, in fear even of Arab children, trembling as ever. The Jordanian daily *Ad-Difaa* published a story from a West Bank special correspondent about an alleged incident in the market of Hebron. An eleven-year-old Arab boy was playing with two eggplants his mother had asked him to buy, and frightened a group of Israeli soldiers, who, when they saw him, were so shaken that they hardly had time to fall on the ground for safety. The Cairo daily *Al-Gumhuria* reported a fight between Arab prisoners and Israeli soldiers in Nablus, in which the unarmed Arabs naturally had the upper hand.[73] With his army in total collapse before the Israelis, after the June war, the Arab ruler, Hussein of Jordan, said that he refused to "protect" the Israelis when asked why he failed to control the *fedayeen* in his country.[74] A young officer in his army explained that his men crave to meet the Jew in battle, assured that they would have him, if only he would meet them face to face, not hide behind waves of fire and steel.[75] How badly Arabs need to be reassured of their manhood may be gathered from the jubilation that greets any martial feat, real or imagined, against the Jew; in the wake of the Lydda airport massacre, when three Japanese fired point blank into civilians, killing some two dozen, mostly gentile tourists, the Egyptian Premier, Aziz Sidky, remarked that the shooting proved that the Arabs were capable of achieving victory over Israel.[76] This is why Arabs see the initial and limited successes in the October war as victory, their subsequent rout seeming inconsequential.

An essential difference between knowledge of Jews in the West and in the Arab world is that such knowledge in the West, despite anti-Semitism, has a substantially contemporary character; but it is fundamentally archaic in the Arab world, hence, its overwhelmingly stereotypical nature. We have seen the Jews in the eyes of the Arab world as possessed of an immutable, fixed syndrome of (mostly demeaning) traits, divinely revealed in antiquity and seemingly unaffected by the passing of centuries. Such an ahistorical conception fits well the revelatory and prescientific character of thought processes, among Arabs, whose civilization did not participate in the revolutionary transformation of Western Christendom in past centuries. Hence, the archaic stereotype of the Jew is normative in Arab society, rather than merely a deviation found on its fringes or just purely propagandistic overlays. The Arab intelligentsia shares a knowledge of Jews strikingly archaic by Western standards, "updated" only to the level of nineteenth-century European pseudo-scientific racial theorists and some *fin-de-siécle* notions. A Westerner's personal experience of this phenomenon is always surprising, sometimes incredible, like witnessing a reversal of temporal sequence. "I do not consider it irrational that Arabs, Palestinians particularly, should hate Jews," observed an American with close ties to Arabs here and abroad. "What I do find surprising is that most Palestinians I have known, both in their country and outside, who are Western-educated, do not have the sort of perception of the Israelis which we, their 'counterparts' in the West, seem to have. These people, almost all Christians and from distinctively bourgeois backgrounds, view the Israelis as 'stereotypical Jewish' merchants and speculators who will, as a Palestinian member of another Arab country's UN mission put it to me, 'run in panic to be evacuated by the Sixth Fleet following the first significant Arab victory.'"[77]

Owing to the characteristic disregard of time among Arabs, in their imagination of things Jewish, fragments of contemporary and ancient periods, events, and beliefs freely mingle to form new sequences. A recent military operation would thus be mentioned and the allegation made that Israeli troops had intended to massacre Arabs. Massacres by ancient Israelites cited in the Bible are then adduced as evidence of the Israeli motive in this particular case only several thousands of years later. In an article in Beirut's *Al-Hawadath* on December 24, 1971, a description of Israeli relations with the Vatican includes reference to a medieval allegation of a Jewish need for the blood of Christian children for the manufacture of *matzot*, the unleavened bread of Passover.[78] The intellectual climate is one in which Nasser naturally recommended the nineteenth-century fabrication, *Protocols of the Elders of Zion*, to an Indian journalist in order that he may learn about the Jews today.[79]

An American journalist, Marshall Frady, witnessed in amazement a gathering in this country of distinguished men—"a cameo panorama of the whole Arab world"—discussing the nature of Jews. "Presently, they began passing down the table a worn volume published in the early nineteen-hundreds, written by some pundit philosopher of the time with a name like Hubbell or Hubbard, with passages, which they would pause to read aloud, describing the Jews as descendants of a tribe of slaves and squatters who had never suffered from any sense of other people's property ever since they had revolted against their masters some four thousand years ago and been led, by a runaway slave who himself had murdered one of his masters, on a trek of thieving and spoilage. They all listened to these readings with small wistful smiles and shakings of the head. One of them turned to the American finally and said, 'You know, it is very difficult to be an Arab in this country. Even though most of those you see around you tonight are citizens of this country, yet we are Arabs. You have no idea what it is like to be an Arab living in the United States. No one around us truly understands the situation. I must tell you, it is a very lonely feeling. . . .'"[80]

What is the conception of Jews of a *Fatah* commander, a Palestinian Christian educated in French and English schools, son of an intellectual father and of a Jewish-born mother? As expressed in an interview in captivity with Leonard Wolf, an American writer, the views of the man so directly involved in so many ways in the Arab-Jewish conflict are the same as those above. William Naguib Nassar never thought of Jews as individuals; even his mother—"I always thought of my mother as a Lebanese—an Arab"—or the Jews in the Jerusalem he knew as a boy. What did he imagine the Jews to be like? "Well, we had the image of the Ashkenazim, with *peyot* [sidelocks], and the big hat, but we never felt hatred against Jews as human beings. We used to consider them as cowards. We used to hate some of their leaders for the massacres like Deir Yassin [a village near Jerusalem where an attack by Jewish dissidents on April 8, 1948, resulted in more than 250 Arab dead]." But Nassar admires such leaders for teaching him the uses of inhumanity; he feels the

Jews are temporarily stronger, because they have more education and more money, especially the latter. "To find money," is what makes Jews immigrate to Israel. "Most of them. . . . Actually, Jews like money. . . ." The prosperous Jews who come from places where they make more money than they do in Israel seek a better climate, the sun, ease, and the honey and milk cited in the Bible. There is no mention whatever of national feeling pulling Jews to Israel; they, moreover, do not fight for it, either. Who does? "A lot of mercenaries."[81] The Prothro-Melikian study at the American University of Beirut indeed found that among Arab students from various countries and of various religious backgrounds the Jews (and Negroes) were the most definitely stereotyped, the least favorably regarded from among thirteen national groups surveyed.[82]

The idea that the past is prologue and omen has puzzled the many writers who accept the fraud of Arab-Jewish historical amity, for such beneficent base makes the present virulence of the Middle East conflict all the more mystifying. The Quaker Report, a widely acclaimed missionary effort at enlightening the public by those who "know" the region from within, thus introduces readers to the past: "The Jews and the Arabs are Semitic cousins, share many cultural traits and traditions, and through long centuries lived in relative peace with one another even during periods when Jews were subject to almost continuous persecution by the Christian West." Little wonder that on such foundation the Quakers thought the present conflict was "one of the great ironies of history."[83]

There certainly is irony here, but not in the sense intended by the Quakers. Rather, as George Orwell once observed in another context, the proposition they proffer is so patently absurd that only intellectuals would take it seriously. The popular mass intuitively opts for an essentially correct position; the *Gallup Report* for July 24, 1968, shows the largest segment of Americans who express an opinion on the root cause of the Arab-Israeli conflict to cite "ancient enmity"—not a particularly informative answer, but closer to reality than the alleged expertise. Conventional initiation in the finer aspects of the problem might have changed their views. One such effort, expressly designed for the general public by the prestigious American Assembly of Columbia University, thus disabuses the "almost totally ignorant" public of any thought that the conflict has anything to do with "the fact that [Israel's] population is Jewish. They are, after all, kin to the Semitic Arabs."[84]

(To appreciate the possibly unintended humor in the alleged Semitic kinship of Arabs and Jews one must remember that it is premised on the same racialist pseudoscientific theorizing common in the nineteenth century, which spoke of an Aryan race; in reality the two peoples are fellow Semites only in the sense that both speak Semitic languages, and to imply any further content, writes Lewis, is like describing the English and the Bengalis as fellow Aryans and to suggest that they share some common identity because of that. "Anti-Semitism" became a euphemism for anti-Jewishness, having nothing whatever to do with anti-Arab sentiment. "The argument is sometimes put forward that the Arabs and their friends, in opposing Israel or Zionism, cannot be anti-Semitic because the Arabs themselves are Semites. This argument is doubly flawed. First, the term Semite has no meaning as applied to groups as heterogenous as the Arabs or Jews, and indeed it could be argued that the use of such terms is in itself a sign of racialism. Secondly, anti-Semitism has never anywhere been concerned with anyone but Jews. The Nazis, who may be accepted as the most authoritative exponents of anti-Semitism, made it quite clear that their hostility was limited to Jews only, and did not include the other so-called Semitic peoples. On the contrary, the Nazis found and still find no difficulty in simultaneously hating Jews and courting Arabs; they made a considerable and on the whole successful effort to cultivate the Arabs, and won the friendship and support of many Arab leaders, including some who still hold high office."[85])

The myth of Semitic amity was fostered by Jews in nineteenth-century Europe in reaction to their rejection by gentile compatriots as "Oriental"; picking up the slander with pride, they spun a magnificent dream of closeness to their "brother" in the East. The latter rejected the relationship, yet found the myth invaluable, particularly in hitting the Jews with their own invention over the Palestine question. The myth fits only too well with the euphemization of Islam featured in the establishmentarian versions of Middle Eastern history in the English-speaking world (Chatham House Version in Britain; Missionary Version in the United States). The fraud of Semitic amity is thus fostered by knowledge institutions presumed to speak with unbiased authority on the Middle East, such as the Middle East Institute, to which less specialized institutions turn for "guidance" in that area. The likeminded members of the Anglo-American residential colonies in the Arab world endorse the fraud with the ring of particularly impressive authority. Thus, Dr. John S. Badeau proclaimed it to the American people at a crucial moment of Middle

Eastern history from the presidency of the American University at Cairo (where he went to an ambassadorship and to leadership of the Middle East Institute, having previously been a twice-ordained Protestant missionary in the Arab East). Another takes public issue with the notion that ancient hostility marks the contemporary Arab-Jewish relationship: "Nation-states at war with each other is a modern tragedy; the traditional relationships between Muslims and Jews is something very different indeed."[86] The typical text in American higher education repeats the canard as a matter of fact ("peace and harmony"),[87] and it is given further force by the peculiar social composition of the academic personnel involved in Middle Eastern studies in the North American colleges and universities, as indicated in Chapter One. Either as a consequence or surely as a further force for diffusion, one finds journalism harnessed to the effort for such enlightenment. Thus, a widely respected commentator on network radio from the Arab world: "Anti-Semitism exists in America and Britain, as in many western countries, but never in the Arab countries. The Arabs are Semites, too."[88]

This issue provides a further illustration of the fallacy of middlingness commonly applied to the Middle East problem; that is, that Truth is reached by the adversary method somewhere between Arab and Jewish positions. (The prevailing tendency is to discern not between good and bad analysis, but rather between such positions.) In actual fact on this issue both positions coincide with untruth; for among the Jewish writers one finds the same deception though practiced for somewhat different reasons. The reversal of the ancient ruler-ruled relationship among Arab and Jew is invested with anxiety and guilt for the ascending (Jewish) side as well. Psychological pressures to evade and obscure it thus appear on both sides, not just among the injured masters. The same effect is obtained in what appears as a deliberate effort at casting in positive terms the past of what is seen as an inevitably close relationship in the future, between Jews and Arabs, if only for the sake of a better future. Hence, the conventional explanation by some Jewish writers that the present Arab-Jewish conflict is *merely* political (as if to say "superficial"), with no suggestion as to how acutely political it really is.[89] Much of what the public perceives as pro-Israeli writing in the West simply voices the hoary clichés or simply ignores the real issue.[90] Israeli and Zionist notables frequently deliver themselves before foreign audiences of the same.[91] Some popular Jewish histories present the Islamic past simply as fairy tale. One of them depicts that past in glowing, romantic terms, suggesting that Muslims applied the contempt of the *dhimma* only to Christians, hardly to Jews. The spirit of the work may be gathered from the fact that it singles out the Jewish sage Judah Halevi as epitome of "the life of the Jews in the Islamic civilization,"[92] then gently losing his traces into nothingness, there being no mention that he was—like other Jewish sages, Saadiah Gaon, Joseph Hanassi—actually murdered in a Muslim pogrom.

Since the Israeli imagination of the conflict with the Arabs is dominated by the notion of two nationalist movements competing for Palestine in contemporary history, only little attention devolves on traditional antecedents of the clash, even when they are known, which is not always the case. The Israeli political writers to whom foreigners are especially likely to be exposed—the dissenting intellectuals—are also particularly unlikely to deviate from mythologized Arab-Jewish history. Elon's *The Israelis,* which has had substantial impact abroad, is actually notable for its insistent endorsement of the Toynbee thesis on the Arabs, as victimized innocent bystanders in Christendom's persecution of the Jews.

9

A VARIANCE OF ARABS

THE region variously described as the Arab world is very large and in some respects quite heterogenous. Islam and Arabic are major unifying bonds, but the several lands in that "world" have been rather poorly connected islands until the arrival of modern means of communication. Their pre-Islamic pasts vary greatly and even the processes of Islamization and Arabization of their pristine populations have not been the same throughout, sometimes displaying sharp discontinuities, particularly with regard to Arabization. Political unity existed mainly in cultural terms and even the large empires were rather loose aggregates of petty dominions, despite the authoritarian and personal character of central government, the scope of which was limited and the effectiveness of whose arms often waned at the very outskirts of principal cities. That part of the world thus emerged in our age as a veritable mosaic of ethnic, racial, religious, linguistic, and other diversity. The heterogeneity subsumed by the term "Arab" manifests itself also in relation to Israel, although the latter serves to unify the diverse and not usually cooperative Arabic-speaking peoples.

In relation to Israel, there appear to be different pressures on traditionalists and modernizers, nationalists and parochials, Palestinians and others, dominant groups and minorities. One variable would seem to be spacial proximity; as a general proposition the more geographically remote an Arab is from Israel, the more aloof he seems to be from the conflict with Israel. The classic dichotomy is that between the near Arab East (*Mashrek*) and the more distant Arab West, or the *Maghreb,* comprising Morocco, Algeria, Tunisia, and (part of)[1] Libya. A survey of *Maghrebi* diplomats in New York has indicated that, though reluctant to deviate from the more militant positions of their Eastern Arab colleagues in public, the former frequently assume more moderate stances in private. ("Militancy" refers to relentless pressure by all available means for the immediate elimination of Jewish statehood, while "moderation" indicates rejection of military means and support for an indefinite postponement of the [same] ultimate objective.) The *Maghrebi* moderates described their position as no less patriotic than the militants', but more realistic. In mixed groups with Eastern Arabs, *Maghrebis* often did little talking and most of the listening, occasionally asking questions of the others, much like sympathetic outsiders.[2] Before the 1967 war *Maghrebis* were much more likely to say that the conflict, as Bourguiba put it, "is not directly our business";[3] since the war, more *Maghrebis* say it is their business, while more Eastern Arabs say it is not theirs so much as the Palestinians'. Tunisia still displays aloofness even now (as does Morocco), its leader reiterating after the war the "geographical imperatives," that, after all, "The Middle East is far from Tunisia. . . ."[4]

Impressions to the contrary notwithstanding, the Algerians do not really deviate much from the other *Maghrebis'* essential aloofness. Their greater involvement in the conflict since the 1967 war reflected their own experience with Western colonialism rather than any real identification with Eastern Arabs or grasp of the actual dimensions of the conflict with Israel. Since that disaster of Arab regular armies appeared to justify both the Algerians' (at least theoretical) ultra-anti-Americanism—U.S. "intervention" in the war—and their earlier resort to irregular warfare against the French—Arab weakness in the regular kind—they seemed genuinely stirred by the war and inclined to offer their own experience as a model for the redemption of Palestine.[5] Their greater involvement was not necessarily related to a better acquaintance with the problem, even though the facile analogy with the Palestinians made Algerians think that they now indeed were intimately acquainted with the problem. The Tunisians, it turns out, did essentially the same, projecting *their* experience with the French on the Palestinians' with the Jews, which happened to yield, incidentally, a prescription that was radically different from the Algerians': gradualism and subtlety rid us of the French, preached Bourguiba;[6] the scorched earth and a people's war did it for us, asserted Boumedienne. The view that the Algerian war was the model for Palestine had become for a time the dominant one in Tunisia, too; the success of Sadat's phased approach has since 1973 swayed even Algeria to the old Bourguiba method. For the countries of the *Maghreb* the Palestine question is of great concern, yet not really their problem; their own interests come first, and they are not disinclined to foster these by using the Palestine question.[7]

The *Maghrebi-Mashreki* differences on the conflict with Israel have also been explained on grounds other than geographic distance, essentially as reflecting differences of mentality, the Arab West said to be more truly Western than the Arab East. Close contact with French civilization—Algeria is actually the only Arab country in which direct foreign rule and full integration with the metropolitan country ever was attempted—has made for congeniality with Western *esprit*, not just for acquaintance and ambivalence, as in the Arab East, grounded in classic Arabic. *Maghrebis* have been said to be more rational and realistic, as well as less emotional and ambiguous than *Mashrekis*. A Lebanese political commentator gave expression to this belief in these words: "French training has brought it about that the young Tunisian and Moroccan politicians have a sense of realities which their emotional colleagues in the East lack. We in the Near East should learn from them."[8] *Maghrebis* display annoyance with traits that Europeans and other Westerners usually associate with Arabs; in the case of so Western a man as Bourguiba, this reaches the point of public derision of much of Eastern Arab culture, and the tendency to differentiate oneself at times from "the Arabs" is marked. On various occasions Bourguiba thus accused "them" of collective schizophrenia; as being obsessed with destructive, negative purposes; as inefficient, substituting curses for deeds, daydreams for performance; as fanatical and illogical.[9] Like other *Maghrebis*, he seems comfortable with the French, sharing with them his impressions of the Eastern Arabs, as if speaking of odd and exotic peoples.[10] We encounter this same ambivalence toward Arab identity in the Arab East, notably among (also Frenchified) Lebanese Maronites (a Christian sect in communion with Rome, that retains the use of Syriac in its liturgy), where it also denotes relatively low hostility toward Israel.

The Islamic factor is more substantial than the Arab throughout the *Maghreb*, where the Arab conquest has failed fully to penetrate vast stretches of the hinterland until very recently, the Berbers still constituting the bulk of the population in many rural areas in Morocco, Libya, and Algeria. Urbanization and state education turns Berbers increasingly into Arabic-speaking citizens of nation states, in which Islam, Arabism, other *isms*, and parochial distinctions founded on pre-Islamic history (Phoenicia) vie for the loyalty of new

Moroccans, Algerians, Tunisians, and Libyans. While traditional society increasingly disintegrates, pressures are felt throughout the *Maghreb* (as in the Arab East's radical-revolutionary regimes) for emphatic reaffirmation of Islam itself with simultaneous strengthening of ties of solidarity to the Arab East. The process has been evident in revolutionary Algeria and the crusading secular regime of Bourguiba has lately relented, the tendency there seemingly being one of more accommodation with popular religious sentiment and with the excitement the Palestine *fedayeen* created in the streets.[11]

In the Arab East, however, even considerable geographic remoteness does not necessarily entail aloofness, as is indicated by the distant Iraqis' intensive involvement in the Palestine conflict. Their diplomatic involvement is as old as Iraqi independence; their military involvement goes back at least to the 1930's. Iraq had a leading role in bringing about the Arab invasion of Palestine in 1948 and has maintained almost continuous military confrontation with Israel on the Jordanian front ever since and on the Syrian in the October war. The earlier and perhaps even now more intense engagement of Iraq than of the more geographically proximate Egypt may be explained by the lateness of Egypt's identification with Arabism. (Iraq had been quite unambiguously Arab from the start, like Syria, Jordan or Saudi Arabia; on the other hand, substantial numbers of Egyptians have rejected the claim that Egypt was an Arab nation until quite recently, and some apparently still do.) Moreover, the more geographically remote Iraqis share a sense of regional community with the Arabs of Palestine, as part of a common effort in the First World War and after for Arab independence, unlike the nearer Egyptians, whose struggle for independence had until the 1940's been thought of as separate from the others'.

Despite considerable geographic remoteness, Kuwait, situated on the easternmost frontier of the Arab East, has in recent years increasingly sought involvement in the struggle with Israel, lending substantial financial and propagandistic backing to both moderate and militant groupings confronting the Jewish state. The sharply pan-Arab posture in so minute, oil-rich (West-linked), and distant state, one only recently "arrived" on the scene of Arab politics, may be explained by the prominence of the Palestinians in Kuwait, a considerable number of whom occupy sensitive positions in the ranks of professionals, technicians, and bureaucrats managing the tiny, backwater sultanate upon which petroleum has thrust extraordinary riches. The weighty and wealthy Palestinian diaspora stimulates the unusual activism of the Kuwaitis, and makes, by their sheer presence, the sultanate a focus of actions directed at Israel, as a site for conferences, fund-raising, etc. Kuwait, moreover, has perhaps been prepared for such a belligerent role by the very wealth that has devolved on it, curious though this may seem in the context of commonsense beliefs, linking poverty, not plenty, with contentious and hostile moods. Hottinger has suggested that the Kuwaitis have been deprived by their vast wealth of a sense of identity and purpose, a vacuum now being filled by militant pan-Arabism and engagement in the struggle for Palestine.[12] For the application of these riches on so tiny a sultanate has meant the installment from the ground up of an ultramodern environment—a world of up-to-date gadgetry wholly purchased abroad, the product of a civilization alien to the Kuwaitis, which they can buy and use because of the happenstance of petroleum under their feet, yet in which they do not creatively participate, in fact do not even really comprehend. Intellectual and moral nihilism ensues.[13] Pan-Arabism may help fill the need to know who one has become in this strange new world; fighting for Palestine may lend some meaning to a seemingly endless pursuit of indulgence in dazzling gimmickry now descending upon Kuwait from abroad by virtue of a bountiful Providence.

Distant Libya, on the opposite, westernmost, fringes of the Arab East, also manifesting acute hostility to Israel, parallels Kuwait in respect to the vastness of its oil bounty and (though to a lesser degree) in the importance of the Palestinians in its small professional and managerial class; but it has not yet produced a futuristic environment as in Kuwait. (Neither has Saudi Arabia, which features the largest oil wealth and also a substantial Palestinian contingent in its elite.) The extraordinary activism of Libya in the cause of Palestine began only with the coming to power in 1969 of the military junta, headed by Qadhafi, who clearly follows the Nasserite model and is thought to aspire also to inheriting the role of the deceased leader in the Arab world.[14] Hence, a possible linkage between oil wealth and militancy at variance with common Western expectations.

The territorial focus of the Arab-Israeli conflict coincides with the epicenter of militant modern Arabism. Palestine is part not just of *Sunni* Muslim compactness, as are some other regions in the Arab world, but of one in which the Christians actually joined *Sunnis* in promoting Arabism, indeed even initiated and led the struggle. (By comparison *Sunni* Egypt joined pan-Arabism only half a century later, the Egyptian Christians [mostly Copts] never showing much enthusiasm for that *ism.*) The Arabs of newly formed British Palestine viewed themselves as Syrians, who are distinguished by emphatic pan-Arabism and militance in pursuit of Arab causes. The involvement of Syrians in the Palestine conflict is second only in intensity to that of Palestinians themselves, and sometimes actually exceeds it. "They are not more mad than any other Arabs," an Israeli intelligence officer commented on Syrians to an American journalist, "but they have a special position in that they think of themselves as the original and the unique Arabs. Not only are they the best Arabs, but also the best socialists. Therefore they could not accept the U. N. November [1967] resolution. Therefore they had to nationalize more industries and be the only country to support El Fatah even before the 1967 war. They are not mad, but they are extremists."[15]

As for the other peoples in the larger Syrian region, the Muslim half of Lebanon may be said to be "Syrian" in this sense, while the bedouin to the east, mainly in Jordan's East Bank and in the desert, are on the whole intellectually remote from the conflict, though they can be engaged in it. They have little contact with the Jews and interact with them and other Arabs in almost purely parochial and particularistic terms, either fighting for King Hussein—against Jew or Arab—or looting Jew or Arab—for instance, preying on the shambles of the Egyptian armies in the Sinai wars—or joining Arab irregular warfare on Jews (and in at least one instance, in the Galilee in 1948, joining the Israeli army fighting other Arabs). Glubb Pasha distinguished the Arabic-speaking peoples of the region according to ethos or mentality, between the Arabs of the Eastern Mediterranean littoral (Levantines, including Egyptians), who are fanatical, subtle, voluble, and uncompromising, and the Arabs of the desert, who are more pragmatic. The latter would harm Israel as much as the former, if that were possible, but would cut their losses early, however painfully, if greater calamity can thus be avoided; the former would rather perish than acquiesce in even minor losses.[16]

Evolving Palestinian nationalism has shared with the Syrian variant a particularly high tension between parochial and Arab identities. So insistent have Syrians been on being Arabs, that they have repeatedly jettisioned separate sovereignty in order to secure wider Arab union. Nasser himself, the epitome of integral union, was rushed by them into a premature and troublesome United Arab Republic in 1958. They have since participated in all successive attempts at unification. What had been characteristic of the Palestine national movement throughout the British period was that it behaved rather like an arm of a larger Arab Nation; it seemed more intent on preventing Jewish encroachment on even the margin of the Arab homeland than on securing Palestinian sovereignty.

The Arab-first sentiment was furthered by the adoption, toward the end of World War Two, of the Palestine cause by the new Arab League as primary all-Arab cause, and the subsequent engagement of member states in open war in Palestine. Though disappointed by their sponsors, the Palestinians became after the 1948 defeat more intensely Arab: Their refugees were dispersed in many states—the camp dwellers now the symbol of the Arab cause, while the bourgeois, traveling and living in an Arab diaspora, were perhaps the only group in the entire Arab world that really felt cosmopolitan Arab. "Through their dispersion and wanderings many of the Palestinians became acquainted with Arab countries and sometimes even attached to them, whereas Egyptian, Syrian and Lebanese Arabs tend to know one country, and patriotism toward their homeland predominates over pan-Arab sentiments.[17]

The Arab loyalty may also be nursed by grievances Palestinians harbor against the individual Arab countries, both for their failure to liberate Palestine and for the disabilities and discriminatory regulations put on them by these countries. The role of the Palestinian bourgeois in their Arab diaspora had been obscured by the almost general focus abroad on the camp-dwelling refugees. Actually in their dispersion in the various countries the bourgeois Palestinians had assumed by their great educational and other attainments a significance greatly out of proportion with their numbers, in the press, the professions, the universities, business, government and even in diplomatic service abroad. Several years before the 1967 war one writer described them as "a sort of brotherhood of the like-minded spread over all the Arab countries,"[18] ever on the watch against waning enthusiasm against Israel, enthusiastic supporters of Nasser and of integral Arab union. The *Qawmiyun al-Arab* movement, which vied even with Nasserism in the pursuit of that goal, emerged from among the Palestinians. The conventional discourse on a "Palestinian personality," a "Palestinian nation" or "Palestinian entity," which has been the fashion since the June war ignores the immersion in Arabism both of the class the leaders of the Palestine movement come from (Arafat, Habash, Hawatmeh, and the others) and of their struggle.

It is in the educated class of Palestinians in their several diasporas that one finds the most intensive hostility to Israel. "The best measure of the irreconcilable hatred these circles have for Israel," Hottinger wrote before the June war, "is their treatment of their own compatriots, the Palestinian lower classes. These form the great bulk of the Palestinian refugees who now with their descendants are said to number more than a million and live in camps or improvised huts, and some too in the houses of relatives, in Jordan, the Gaza Strip, Syria and Lebanon. Most of them receive rations, primitive shelter and education from UNRWA. It is their own compatriots, the well-to-do Palestinians, who are loudest in their demands that they must continue to live under these conditions until they are able to return to Palestine. . . .

"One may ask what the seemingly inexhaustible sources of hatred are with which the Palestinian Arab intellectuals conduct their propaganda campaign. Material and political losses seem to play a smaller part than psychological factors, for the upper class Palestinians have acquired comparatively good positions in the other Arab countries.

"At the time when Zionism appeared the educated Palestinians were in the process of becoming 'westernized' and had every reason to be satisfied with their progress for Palestine was, along with Lebanon, in many respects the most advanced Arab country. Then the Zionists came to their country and proved themselves more able to use western, modern methods than the Arabs. To be sure, the Palestinians try to argue away this fact by pointing to the financial preponderance of the Zionists and 'international Jewry's control of the European press' but in their heart of hearts they know that they were beaten by the Zionists in the field of 'modern life', a field they were anxious to master and which they believed they had already mastered.

"The leading Palestinians refuse to admit their defeat, considering it merely a reverse, but they are also not sure of themselves and of the power over their own people. Today they feel that they are still inferior and want to gain time, for tomorrow, so they hope, they will perhaps be equal. Until that day there is only one thing for them to do: to engage in no contest, but rather to isolate and cut themselves off. This their hatred helps them to do.

"Behind this barrier of hatred to which the welfare of the great majority of the refugees is being sacrificed, they hope that in the long run they will have advanced so far with their own development that they will be able at last to resume the struggle with their dangerous opponent and bring it to a successful conclusion."[19] (Many of them, precipitously placed in the limelight of international attention by the June disaster, had vowed to pursue the struggle to the end, even if the Arab countries themselves must perish in the process.) The inclination among some to advance the struggle from a perhaps less sheltered base, a "National Authority" within part of Palestine itself, probably reflects a rise in confidence since the Arabs' successful use of oil and the "defeat" of Israel in October, 1973

The significance of attitudes toward Arabdom and modernity in shaping attitudes toward Israel has been recognized by several students, one of whom has offered his systematic categorization.[20] In respect to Arabdom two elements were discerned: *parochial nationalism*, whose primary terminal attachment is to a smaller community than the Arab nation, or which independent statehood is desired, and *Arab nationalism*, describing primary terminal attachment to just such nation. In respect to modernity there are three elements: *traditionalism*, describing attachment to the political, social, and economic institutions of the landowner-ascriptive system, and rejection of government control and planning of the economy; *transitionalism*, meaning preference for gradual transformation from the above to a technocratic-achievement system, with advocacy of governmental planning and restricted governmental investment programs; (*revolutionary) modernism* indicates desire for rapid elite alteration, removal of landowning groups, rapid transformation of social and governmental institutions, and extensive governmental planning and control of the economy.

The *traditional, parochial nationalists* could be expected to dislike Israel and to regard its imposition as an act of humiliation, but not to make further sacrifices to eliminate it as a Jewish state; typical examples would be a Maronite landowner in Lebanon and a conservative Egyptian landowner, member of the *Wafd* party, which was suppressed in 1952. The *traditional Arab nationalists* dislike Israel intensely but oppose it mainly rhetorically; examples are now rare, but historically would be men like Nuri-Said, premier of Iraq until 1958, and ex-King Saud of Saudi Arabia, both deceased. The *transitional, parochial nationalists* express a sense of outrage and shame with regard to Israel, but show little enthusiasm for the programs required to bring about the elimination of the Jewish state; examples are Camille Chamoun, formerly President of Lebanon, and King Hassan II of Morocco. *Transitional Arab nationalists* are willing to pay a considerable price for the elimination of Jewish statehood, but sensing that this aim may require their own removal from power, they might settle for less; examples are King Hussein of Jordan, King Faisal of Saudi Arabia, and former President of Syria, Quwatli. *Modernizing parochial nationalists* wish Israel were not in existence but have shown little desire to do much about it; Christian, particularly Maronite, socialists in Lebanon and perhaps even President Bourguiba of Tunisia fit in this category. Finally the *modernizing Arab nationalists* seem most uncompromising in their determination to eliminate Jewish statehood and appear ready to pay any price to reach this goal; the *Baath* Party exemplifies this category.

The fact that the peculiar dialectic between social change and Arabism has been pressing for increasingly heightened hostility to Israel may be gathered simply from the roster of those personifying the above categories; notice how often has-beens were used to personify the relatively low hostility categories. A survey of Israeli Arabs has disclosed this relationship; more modernized Arabs who have lived a considerable period of time, and in many instances from birth, under Jewish rule clearly tend toward more nationalistic—and anti-Israeli—orientations.[21] The relatively few Palestine Arab intellectuals who remained in Israel have been attracted strongly to the one political party that gave legal expression to a firm, Nasserite anti-state position, the Communist Party. Students, for instance, were found to be much more hostile to Israel than their parents. While about half their parents agreed that Israel had a right to exist, only a quarter of the students, most or all probably born under Israeli rule, expressed similar agreement (eight times more of the latter than of the former explicitly denied such agreement—24% versus 3%[22]). The relatively few Israeli Arabs who threw in their lot with Israel publicly in the nearly two decades before the June war of 1967 were largely traditionalist. The Israeli Arab community as a whole was characterized rather by a desire to avoid commitment, displaying the apathy and aloofness typical of those subject to strong cross-pressures (proximate Israeli power—distant Arab world), and considerable anxiety, much like hostages in a deadly duel. Only 14% of Israeli Arabs thought that the Israeli forces would defeat the Arab armies in their third major war; in the crisis just before the June war this community appears to have experienced the extremes of elated anticipation and mortal fear, as acts of open and provocative defiance (hoisting enemy flags) alternated with acts of solidarity with Israel (blood donations), and storekeepers reported a run, by Arabs, on butcher knives and other such deadly implements. After the defeat of Arab armies in the June war Israeli Arabs displayed greater respect for Israeli power than before, but also much more hostility toward the Jewish state and more eagerness to identify with the Arab world around it.[23]

The adoption of militant Arabism by a Middle Eastern regime, while affecting the official opinion of the state (because of the usual press control) and of its policies, does not necessarily describe real popular orientations, though sustained indoctrination surely has some effect in this respect. The sociological makeup of the population provides a better key to this than official pronouncements. Nor does actual identification with the Arab nation usually denote what national allegiance represents in Western societies. Largely rhetorical and emotive, the phenomenon resembles more affective ideologies than practical ones; weak in the production of such conduct as would engender cooperation in sustained efforts for collective goals, it does nonetheless entail acts—in the case of Israel and the West, for instance, acts of violence, defiance—though they tend to be sporadic. Even among declared Arab nationalists, however, the religion of an individual may still constitute the most reliable guide to political behavior, including conduct usually governed by national loyalties in the West. Some observers have been led by the above shortcomings to assume overly mechanistic and deprecating views of the Arab *ism;* because failed by Western standards, they regard it as altogether a fraud, or ghosts that crafty leaders make appear or disappear at will.

Egypt's commitment to Arab nationalism under Nasser has thus inspired superficial views of the phenomenon, particularly the notion that the change was artificial. It is true that Arab nationalism had been weak and late in coming to Egypt, and until 1953 the predominant theme in official communications was that of Egyptian nationalism. But then an increasingly marked shift toward Arab nationalism developed, exaggerating and encouraging further an already discernible process in that direction of the country.[24] The so-called Nilotic school of thought, founded on liberalism, a European orientation, and some appeal to the Coptic (Christian), pre-Islamic strand in Egypt's imagination, had already been in retreat for many years before the pan-Arab and anti-Western surge, rooted in the very authentic Islam of the popular masses. The acceptance of the Jewish state by an apostle of the Nilotic, liberal, pro-European movement, Salama Moussa, is part of a distinct minority syndrome in Egypt—Christianity, Western humanism.[25] Nasser, on the other hand, appealed to the more broadly based rejection of the West and related sentiments. His Arab socialist regime produced mosques at a rate exceeding even ambitious plans under the more traditional regime before it.[26]

The connection of Arab nationalism to Islam, pervasive social change, and antagonism to the West does not warrant sanguine expectations for drastic change in Egyptian attitudes toward the Jewish state in the event of an abandonment of the Nasserite commitment to integral Arab union. One popular theory thus views Egyptian hostility to Israel as only negligible until that commitment arose in the 1950's, and even then essentially only because Israel forms a physical barrier to the union of Egypt with the several Arab states to the east.[27] Because of the importance of Egypt in the Arab world, anything that would reduce its involvement in the conflict with Israel would certainly make the conflict more manageable, and removal or reduction of the commitment to integral union would probably have this effect. But it is difficult to see how such a step would seriously affect the other roots of hostility to Israel outside of Egypt and even within it. The presumed flimsiness of Arabism in Egypt had given rise to hope abroad for a sharp reversal to parochial nationalism following the catastrophic outcome in June, 1967, of the crusade for the Arab cause, hope the actual developments seem not to have matched. Given the extraordinary burden Egypt has continued to carry since the 1967 debacle for the Arab cause, perhaps one ought to wonder why parochial nationalism has yet proved so weak even where Arab nationalism is so recent. Even in lately Arab Egypt the appeal of Arabism is more considerable than many abroad suppose.

The variation introduced by social class would appear less significant than differences in attitudes toward the Jewish state associated with sectarianism. One, indeed, expects this to be the case in all traditional societies, in which vertical loyalties (religious, kinship, ethnic, regional) generally prevail over horizontal loyalties of social class. Observation in the Arab world confirms such expectations, and there is evidence that even university students there have not much detached themselves from traditional ties. A study of university students in Lebanon found social class not an important factor affecting attitudes toward the Palestine problem; yet citizenship ("proximity") and national identity were found to be highly significant variables. Palestinians expressed the highest degree of support for the Palestine Resistance Movement (*fedayeen*), followed by Jordanians, followed by other Arab students, the students from half-Christian Lebanon expressing the least support. Those identifying with Arab nationalism expressed the greatest support for the *fe-dayeen*, followed by those who identified with Syrian nationalism, the Lebanese nationalists showing the least support. Sectarianism emerged as the most highly significant determining factor of attitudes toward the *fedayeen*, the difference between Muslim and Christian attitudes appearing quite substantial, about half the former expressing strong support for a radical solution by armed struggle, and only about one-fifth of the latter sharing this stance.[28]

While Muslim attitudes toward Israel are conditioned by the posture of rulers facing rebellious subjects, Arab Christians, though once subjects themselves, tend to show solidarity with Muslims, whose culture they share and with whom they aspire to share full parity. Both great streams in Islam, *Sunnis* and *Shiis*, have ruled Jews throughout the many centuries, the latter appearing generally even more repressive than the former. Though viewed as heretics by *Sunnis*, the *Shiis* were less tolerant than they toward infidels, including Jews. On the other hand, *Shiis* themselves represented rebellion against established Islam from the first, and it was heretical Islam that appealed greatly to the early Muslim converts, deemed socially inferior by the Arab ruling class of conquerors, who relegated these nominally equal Muslims to the role of clients *(mawali)*. Though originating among Arabs, the *Shia* developed more affinity for non-Arab Islam than the *Sunna;* and though itself ruling in some domains of Islam, the *Shia* failed to develop the extraordinary presumption to overlordship characteristic of the *Sunna*. Fitting well with this trait is the markedly more "spiritual" nature of the *Shia*, less emphasis being placed in it on the place of Islam in the secular world, and, being less worldly than the *Sunna*, there has been more inclination in the *Shia* also toward chiliastic, utopian behavior.

The *Shia* is thought to accommodate more readily to non-Muslim rule than the *Sunna*. An Ottoman defeat in the First World War occasioned this comment by a British Arabist: "It is interesting, but not in the least unexpected, that the same Basra telegram, summarising reports from Persia and the Gulf, should draw a distinction everywhere between the Shiite attitude and the Sunnite. The Shias are stated to be delighted by the news at Bahrein and Bandar Abbas, and pleased in Arabistan and Southern Persia generally. Merchants foresee renewed and extended facilities for trade; the educated class hopes to enjoy office again in the Shiah Holy Cities; the common folk expect to be able once more to visit the Holy Shrines in life, and to have conveyance to hallowed earth in death. This last consideration, added to the comforting reflection that a Sunnite government, which has always shown itself contemptuous and oppressive towards the Shias, has ceased to sit astride the pilgrim roads, is enough to make the unorthodox section of Islam rejoice at the fall of Baghdad; and, further, it must be remembered that the Shias, though personally among the most fanatical Moslems, have not that sense of, or desire for, unity in Islam, or that deep craving for temporal dominion, which actuates Sunnis. Waiting for the appearance of the twelfth Imam, or detached from practical politics by transcendentalism, they care little if one great city, more or less, pass under Christian Government, so their religion and its observances remain unhampered. Not so the Sunnis. Whether they be friends or foes to us at this moment, to them Baghdad in our hands is one more dreary tide-mark of a receding flood. Even King Hussein, hearing the news at Mecca, commented upon it to his notables in a spirit of regretful warning. This was what came of suffering 'Turanians' in a seat of Moslem power! Probably no sincere Sunni in the world has received the news with any feeling more joyful than chastened acquiescence, or more salutary than a conviction that Turks have been backing the wrong horse. . . . When the news of Baghdad arrived, the present writer was in an Egyptian province far from Cairo. It was clear that a wide and profound impression was caused, and hardly less clear that some measure of sadness and disillusion was its immediate consequence."[29]

No substantial concentration of *Shiis* exists in the Near Arab East, with one exception. Only Iraq possesses a large *Shiite* population, perhaps more than half the nation's total, whose contribution to the Arab cause appears dubious. Feeling excluded from the government of Iraq, the *Shiis* gravitate politically toward (*Shiite,* non-Arab) Iran; many have Persian mothers and are formally banned from official posts by recent legislation. (*Sunnis* in Iraq look to Syria instead, and beyond to other Arab states.) Even among *Shiite* intellectuals a much weaker tendency toward identification with Arab nationhood obtains than among *Sunni* intellectuals in Iraq. *Shiis* are suspected to be unreliable Arab nationalists and are thought to fear the emergence of integral union, for in a large Arab nation, including Iraq, they would be reduced further in status to the insignificance characteristic of the Copts in Egypt, from half a nation to a negligible segment of another.[30] Fear of *Sunni* oppression among the *Shiis* of Turkey also weakens the Arab struggle against Israel; the Unity Party, representing the *Shiite* Alevis, has opposed a pro-Arab stance in Turkish policy on the assumption that the traditional *Sunni*-Arab affinity might turn such foreign involvement into domestic pressure for a *Sunni* revival in the secular Turkish state. [31]

A group of some significance in the proximate area of Arab-Israeli confrontation is the Druse community, a sect sprung from the *Shia*, Arabic-speaking and distinct in some manner and dress from their Muslim neighbors, concentrated on the Lebanon and Anti-Lebanon mountain ranges in Lebanon, Syria, and Israel. Though numerically weak, the Druse are important for their strategic location, on both sides of Israel's northern lines, their warlike reputation, and the variability of their loyalties in the conflict. They display the opportunism characteristic of minorities everywhere, the sharp fluctuations relative to dominant groups by insecure subjects: there is both safety and status to be gained by identification with the dominant group—and members of minorities frequently manifest the consequent self-hate, internalizing dominant norms against their own group, as well as excessive zeal in the pursuit of the values of the dominant group (''105 percenters'').[32] There is safety also in the reduction of the power and prestige of the dominant group and even satisfaction to be derived from the mishaps of the dominant group *(Schadenfreude).* (Language and culture generally provide, as with Arab Christians, obvious sources of solidarity for the Druse with the dominant *Sunnis.*)

The Druse thus participated with apparent ardor in the war of the Arab irregulars against the *Yishuv,* fighting with distinction and within their own formations in the Galilee in the spring of 1948; but ever since the turn of the tide of war, by midyear, they have taken their place with equal ardor on the side of the Jew. On the insistence of their leaders, they later have assumed the legal obligation of military service for their males, unlike Muslim and Christian Arabs in Israel; the Jerusalem government has granted them recognition as a separate, autonomous religious community and generally favors them with special consideration. The Druse leadership in Lebanon happens to support a military stance against Israel; but the great mass of the Druse population of the Syrian Golan Heights did not flee before the conquering Israelis in 1967, as did their neighbors, staying instead in their villages to collaborate with the new rulers. Pending a definitive disposition of the territory, they appear on the whole to withhold commitment either way, seeking to insure themselves against either eventuality. As for the properly *Shiite* minority in Lebanon, more sizable than the Druse, and known as *Metawilis,* they are aligned with the Christian half of the country in upholding a separate national identity from the mostly *Sunni* Muslim and ardently Arab Syria.

To the ambivalence and opportunism Christian Arabs share with the Druse and *Shiites* because of minority status, must be added their special relationship with the West, which further complicates matters. From it derives a peculiar tension between affection for the West, the sponsor in Arab eyes of the Jews' state, and hostility to the Jews molded by European anti-Semites. One encounters in the substantial Christian population in the Arab East extreme polarization on the Palestine problem—from unambiguous and public acceptance of the Jewish state to bitter rejection, and many other positions in between. What seems peculiar about Christian attitudes in this respect is not just their extraordinary range, but also a tendency to surpass Muslim extremism. One finds among the Christians bold pro-Zionism, like that displayed by the late Maronite Archbishop of Beirut, Ignatius Mubarak, though simple acquiescence is the much more common "pro-Israel" posture among them.[33] What is really surprising, however, is that among them one also finds hostility to Israel even exceeding the Muslims' in certain respects. Among Jordanian-Palestinian university students the Christians have been found to be more inclined to support the *fedayeen* and less inclined to endorse a peaceful solution to the Palestine problem than the Muslims.[34] There obtains in fact among the *fedayeen* a striking correlation between extremism (in the sense that the Habash-led PFLP is more extreme than *Fatah*) and incidence of Christians in the membership rolls.

The modern Arab national movement itself was begun by Syrian Christians, whose condition gave rise to seemingly erratic and contradictory behavior, yet altogether naturally flowing from Christian ambiguities in the Middle East. The generation that gave birth to modern Arabism had experienced terrible Muslim oppression and even slaughter at the hands of putative brother Arabs, whose punishment and humiliation by Western power they earnestly desired. The presence of Western power brought such exultation to Christian *dhimmis* as to obviate the need for words. "I was lounging one day, I remember, along 'the paths of the faithful,'" wrote an English visitor, "when a Christian Rayah (subject) from the bridle path below saluted me with such earnestness and craved so anxiously to speak and be spoken to that he soon brought me to a halt; he had nothing to tell, except only the glory and exultation with which he saw a fellow

Christian stand level with the imperious Mussulmans. . . . His joy was great; so strong and strenuous was England (Lord Palmerston reigned in those days), that it was a pride and a delight for a Syrian Christian to look up and say that the Englishman's faith was his too; if I was vexed at all that I could not give the man a lift, and shake hands with him on level ground, there was no alloy to *his* pleasure; he followed me on, not looking to his own path, but keeping his eyes on me; he saw, as he thought and said (for he came with me on to my quarters), the period of the Mahometan's absolute ascendancy—the beginning of the Christian's. He had so closely associated the insulting privilege of the path with actual dominion that, seeing it now in one instance abandoned, he looked for the quick coming of European troops. His lips only whispered and that tremulously, but his fiery eyes spoke out their triumph in long and loud hurrahs! 'I, too, am a Christian. My foes are the foes of the English. We are all one people, and Christ is our King.' "[35]

"Safely installed within walls protected by the Union Jack," an Arab writer recalls of the bombardment of Beirut in the Italian-Turkish war, "within hearing of the Italian guns doing their glorious work, I exulted over the defeat and terror of the Moslems. It was our turn at last to feel exultant; theirs to tremble and flee. The Christian God had after long ages heard His people's prayers."[36]

It was altogether fitting that nineteenth-century Beirut was to be the center of the renaissance of Arabic and Arab historiography, while Cairo felt the impulse toward religious reform; the first was a Christian city, the second an Islamic one. The zeal with which the Lebanese scholars sought reason and justification for their autonomy as "Arab" Christians, as opposed to the "Ottoman" Muslims (in the wake of the slaughter and under Western protection) was remarkable. "In those days it was easier for an Arab Christian than it was for an Arab Muslim to anticipate the birth of an Arab national state. The Christian felt no ties of religion to the Porte and to the (Turkish) Caliph."[37] When the Turks left, the *Sunni* Arabs took over Arab nationalism.

Intense hostility to Zionism has been associated with Christians in Palestine and with the Greek Orthodox in particular throughout the Arab East. Palestine was where Jewish pressure was strongest and where opportunism consequently had particularly great scope. Elsewhere Christians faced the Muslims alone and directly or with the uncertain buffer or intermediacy of foreign power and protection, but in Palestine the dynamic Jewish factor provided an unusual opportunity for assuring Christian safety from Muslims. Under attack, Muslims were eager for solidarity with Christians (all are Arabs, above all); Jewish power, on the other hand, made it unlikely that Christians would be left someday soon confronting alone the victorious Muslims. (In 1920, when rumors were spread in Palestine indicating that Faisal had been crowned king of Syria in Damascus and that the British were about to turn Palestine over to him, the Christians of Palestine were thrown into panic.)[38] While "self-protection" may have been the overwhelming reason for the intense anti-Zionism of Palestine's Christians, there certainly were additional reasons, some being peculiarly Christian ones. Thus, Christians had long exhibited in Palestine deprecating and even violent behavior toward Jews, the contemptible "Christ killers," whom they mistreated, subjected to blood-libels, and physically attacked on many occasions. (Certain Christian quarters of Jerusalem had been considered so dangerous for Jews under the Ottomans that at certain Christian holidays Jews could venture through them at mortal peril only.)[39] The intensive anti-Zionism, practically inseparable from anti-Jewishness, of Christian missionaries in Palestine—patrons and companions of the country's Christian communities—must be cited in this connection, particularly the stimulating function of American (and some British) Protestant missions, the so-called American Colony in Jerusalem being specially influential. (Founded on theological beliefs, among others, missionary anti-Zionism was addressed simply against the sheer existence of Jews in substantial numbers in the country, seen as desecrating its holy character, not to mention the Jews' attempted transformation of the picture-postcard biblical view of the land into a contemporary society.)

The Jews, moreover, were economically competitive with Palestine Christians, who, being more literate, more urban, more Westernized than the Muslims, regarded professional, clerical, commercial, and other valuable functions pretty much their own preserve. Given the Jews' educational and other achievements and resources, only the presence of some form of political or psychological barrier between the Jews and the Muslim mass could have protected Christian interests in lucrative and high-status activities.

While endorsing and even stimulating Muslim hostility, Palestine's Christians appear not to have participated in actual warfare with Jews and the British to the extent to which Muslims did. Their active participation in the several "disturbances" in the mandatory period apparently ran at a substantially lower rate than the Muslims'. In the extended unrest from 1936 to 1939 the Christians actually suffered as much or more than the Jews, and considerable sums were extorted by Arab fighters from wealthy Christians, just as the country's economy was grinding to a virtual halt.[40] (In 1928 a Protestant missionary conference in Jerusalem occasioned a general Muslim boycott of Christians in Palestine, which was effective and also accompanied by bloodshed.) In the great defeat of Palestine's Arabs in the war of 1948, the Christians lost much less than the Muslims, a lower proportion of Christians than Muslims departed for exile, some sects emerging from the disaster virtually unscathed when compared with the Muslim community.[41] (Community structure and the fortunes of war had something to do with this outcome, but also the sense of separateness animating Christian communities; among the overwhelmingly rural Muslims, wholesale evacuation was the typical mode of departure.)

The Greek Orthodox, who formed the bulk of Palestine's Christians, demonstrated a particularly great affinity for militant Arabism, within Palestine and outside as well. Among the Greek Orthodox prominent in the leadership of Arab Palestine were: George Antonius, author of *The Arab Awakening,* the classic exposition of modern Arab nationalism; Issa al-Issa, editor of an important newspaper, *Filastin;* Yakub Faraj, one of the members of the Arab Higher Executive Committee established in 1936 under the chairmanship of the *Mufti* of Jerusalem; Khalil Sakakini, a leader of the Arab Congress of Palestine, which functioned in the 1920's; and many others. (The Arab part of the Communist Party of Israel, which became the legal home of extreme Arab nationalism following the debacle of Palestine's Arabs in the 1948 war, was overwhelmingly Greek Orthodox as well.)

Kedourie has connected the potent Arabism of the Greek Orthodox to discordant clergy-laity relations in the church, contrasting it with the weak Arabism of the Maronites, that was tied to remarkable intracommunal solidarity in their church.[42] Unlike the latter, internally homogenous and linked to Europe's strong Roman Catholicism, the former was split between Greek-speaking patriarchate and higher clergy and Arabic-speaking lower clergy and laity. The linkages to the outside fell prey to imperialistic manipulation, leaving the Greek Orthodox after the First World War, with the collapse of tsardom in Russia, with only a weak reed beyond the Middle East. The grievances of the laity and the village clergy, impoverished and ignorant in most instances, against the patriarchate became crystallized already in the nineteenth century as the grievances of Arabs against Greeks, the Russians energetically promoting this antagonism. When the American Protestant missionaries were forced to shift from the fruitless attempt at proselytizing Muslims to ministering to Eastern Christians, they found the Greek Orthodox community ripe for penetration, while the Maronites strongly resisted their probing. The existence in the Greek Orthodox church of a secular communal organization alongside the ecclesiastical organization helps make it more accessible to external influence than the Maronite, which does not have it. The marked Russofilism of many contemporary Greek Orthodox in the Arab East would seem to reflect the above developments.

When the fall of tsardom deprived the Greek Orthodox of their imperial sponsor, they probably felt more acutely than other Christians the need for "self-protection" in alliance with Muslims against Zionism, being already inclined to identify as Arabs against other aliens (Greeks) anyway. Secularization, the process that generally enhanced acceptance of Arabism,[43] was probably more precipitous in a church so many deemed as worthy of desertion as the Greek Orthodox—weak, divided, and relegating Arabic-speakers to low status, both in the church and outside it. There was attraction for some Christians even in the more confident Maronite community in the strength of dominant Islam; when Greek Orthodox or Maronite threw overboard the traditions of his community as reactionary or superstitious, temptations to assume Islamic traditions were strong, in some cases secularization ironically abutting on conversion to the Faith.

Even among Americans from the Arab world, loosely called "Syrians," differences in self-identification and attitudes toward politics in the Middle East are based largely on religion, mirroring the above patterns.[44] Maronites and Catholics from Lebanon have thus been least affected by the growth of Arab unity in the Middle East and the anti-Western policies of some Arab states; the Orthodox from Syria proper, as well as from Palestine and Lebanon, tend to identify with that development, though appearing anxious lest the stance jeopardize their acceptance as Americans. The former express a sense of separateness, emphasizing their pre-Arab, Phoenician origins; the latter are more likely to trace their roots to the Arab period, appearing to be less estranged from the Muslims in general. The relatively few Muslims in America, quite a few from Palestine, manifest much stronger identification with Arab causes than the Christians, who seem on the whole quite remote from Middle Eastern politics and politics of any kind, because of the pronounced parochialism of the immigrants. With the exception of a hard core of activists, the "Syrians" in America thus merely dislike the Jewish state with varying degrees of intensity, a feeling that is usually weakest with Maronites, without doing much else about it, however.

Because of the sectarian structure of Lebanon, this discussion is particularly relevant to the politics of that northern neighbor of Israel. The distribution of attitudes toward the Jewish state and related problems in the country follows the indicated religious pattern closely, with the *Sunnis* and the Maronites, the two largest communities, about equal in numbers, confronting each other from opposite poles of the spectrum, and the smaller Islamic and Christian sects ranging themselves in between, usually near their coreligionists.[45] By the informal agreement worked out in 1943, known as the National Pact, the Christians abandoned the idea of a Lebanese state isolated from the Arab world in return for which the *Sunni* Muslims accepted Lebanese statehood, giving up their idea of union with Syria or other Arab countries. In essence Lebanese independence rests on the Maronites, who often apply the term "Arab" (sometimes derisively) to Arabic-speaking Muslims rather than to themselves, even though they empathize with the latter in some respects, at their humiliation at the hands of the Jews in the June war of 1967, for instance.[46]

With few exceptions their acceptance of Israel is only acquiescence or accommodation, not rousing reception; but the antagonism between them and the Muslims is profound. "Self-protection" requires the Maronites to distort their spontaneous feelings and pretend to the opposite, in what one observer termed "the law of asceticism" of Lebanese politics, i.e., denial of one's feelings for the sake of survival. In private Maronites or Orthodox express a certain sense of accommodation with Israel; but in some official capacity, members of even the best Christian families confront one with a gruffly negative attitude, which differs little from that encountered in Damascus.[47] But assuring Christian survival in a Muslim sea is clearly the mainspring of Lebanese politics, consistently the source of the seemingly contradictory policies of Beirut, leading to the invasion of Palestine in 1948 and to collaboration with *fedayeen* in the more recent past and to open war with their allies in both these enterprises, thus the civil war of 1958, the armed clashes with the *fedayeen* beginning in 1969, and the sporadic warfare with Syria throughout the years.[48]

The Lebanese Christians are under heavy pressure, and their response reflects both the genuine torment of this condition and their equally authentic Levantinism—the term Western visitors to the shores of the eastern Mediterranean have used to denote the peculiar blend of superficiality, sophistication, and perversity they felt dominated the intellectual climate there. To the Israelis' refusal to pay the price of Lebanon's Arab role, i.e., acquiesce in *fedayeen* warfare on them waged openly from Lebanon, President Hilu thus replied with—of all things—a recitation of their "expansionist plans" (which both anticipates Israeli reaction and absolves the Lebanese action that occasions it, while signaling to the "Arabs" in appropriate language the urgency of reducing pressure on Beirut on behalf of the *fedayeen*).[49]

As for differences of social class they were noted in the involvement of the Arabs of Palestine in the struggle with the Jews from the beginning of the conflict. A survey of the British period cites two urban categories as outstanding in their belligerence: the literate urban middle class, insofar as national feeling was concerned; the urban lower class, as far as volatility and excitability was concerned.[50] (The combination of "intelligentsia" and "urban rabble" occupies a familiar position in Middle Eastern political violence generally.) The latter category consists of artisans, unskilled laborers, urchins, and idlers and the assorted *Lumpenproletariats* in the *casbahs* and *bazaars* (native quarters and markets in the old parts of cities). Largely illiterate, "sociable, credulous, readily collecting in crowds at any moment when any cause of excitement arises,"[51] this *shebab* ("youth," as they were often termed) was always a lethal potentiality, easily ignited. "Fanaticism and excitability may turn the most quiet among them into a murderer. They tend to respect force and ruthlessness. . . . The number of their crimes, consisting of theft, beatings, stabbings and murder is greater than that of other classes."[52]

The equivalent in volatility and violence of the urban *shebab* in rural areas of British Palestine were the bedouin. Altogether twice as many as the mob in the large cities, (i.e., some 100,000), most were nomads in the Negev, with only about one-fifth scattered in the coastal plain and in the north as semi-sedentary. They lived almost completely outside the sway of governmental law and order, engaging permanently in bloody feuds, raids, robbery, random killing, and extortion; they quite randomly preyed on, and harrassed, Jewish farmers and participated often singly and in tribal groups in attacks on Jewish settlements in the several disturbances that rocked the country.

The great mass of Palestine's Muslims were *fellaheen,* or peasants, who lived an exceedingly poor and primitive life, by European standards, and mostly outside the realm of government law and order. Lying, thieving, and killing—the great bedouin values—were compelling norms also among the peasantry, as their folklore, demeanor, and criminal statistics amply bore out. As in other preindustrial societies, rural violence patterns were shared with urban dwellers. Thus, brigandage, which arises quite spontaneously among the *fellaheen*; the folk hero is a Robin Hood figure—in the Arab context he's the mythical Antara, poet and robber, epitome of mustachioed fierceness armed—straddling the uncertain line between highwayman preying on *fellaheen* and others or defender and avenger of his oppressed people. (*Fedayeen* are a variant of the phenomenon.) In characteristic modes of participation in war individual males would pick up their arms (there being almost universal male armament) and fire a few shots somewhere before returning to their daily routine; or small groups of males would cohere for longer periods of time and roam as brigands, sometimes attaching themselves briefly to other groups; or the whole village, including women and children, would be mobilized behind the armed males in attempts at storming a settlement, in a so-called *zafaa* (alarm).

The *fellaheen* of Palestine and adjacent areas of Syria and Transjordan participated in the struggle throughout, the intensity and frequency of their belligerence being uneven, however. There are many reports of sullen hostility among the *fellaheen* toward the Jewish settlers from the early periods onward, although a certain inclination toward good neighborly relations with Jewish farmers in many areas asserted itself quite frequently.[53] Some regions, such as Samaria and Judea, and quite a few villages, some near Jewish areas, such as Lifta in the Jerusalem area, were reputed to be implacably hostile and downright dangerous for Jews at any time. Jews avoided many Arab localities in daylight and virtually all after dark. Even rumors of impending trouble sufficed to transform all areas inhabited by Arabs and even adjacent areas into territory off limits to Jews.

Some notable occasions demonstrated the extraordinary frenzy that religious agitation could produce among *fellaheen*, yet they are said to have shared an acute political awareness of a struggle for the mastery of the land with the Jew from the beginning of the British period,[54] differences between the more and the less urbanized individuals being smaller than one might suppose.[55] Equally characteristic of the more tradition-bound Muslim peasants is acquiescence in the power of rulers, both Muslim and infidel. Those remaining under Israeli rule after the first war were notable for their quiescence, as were those in the previously notoriously militant regions of Samaria ("The Triangle") and Judea after the 1967 war. In both instances the *fellaheen* seemed greatly preoccupied with pursuit of the economic uplift accompanying Israeli dominion. Other than the heightened political sense typical of Islam, the rural mass displays the same psychological remoteness, parochialism, and preoccupation with concreteness found among peasantries around the world. Their world is small, and beyond its near borders even drastic events fail to move them much. (There is some evidence of only faint awareness of, and not much concern with, the struggle with Israel among Egyptian villagers and Saudi Arabian nomads even in the wake of the considerable excitement in the Arab world produced by the first Arab-Israeli war.[56])

Fellaheen and nomads can naturally be mobilized for the struggle in even distant areas; apart from the peasant conscripts of the army, a certain number of Egyptian peasants had actually served in the war of 1948 as irregulars (in the form of a private levy of a large landlord); many individuals and groups from nearby areas spontaneously joined the fray, nomads especially. The extraordinary resort to radio in more recent years has had the effect of enhancing the psychological mobilization in distant areas of even illiterates.[57] But their traditional world does not endow them with intellectual and emotional resources sufficient for active engagement in dynamic, protracted struggle; they tend to be passive and must be moved by others, and even then the span of activism is brief.

The traditionals' attitude is one of frank antagonism on religious and mythical grounds, rather free of complexes, which does recognize superior force and accommodates to it more readily than the transitionals' or modernizers'. The latter are vulnerable to the dilemmas of modernization and identity and the consequent malaise engendering obsessive concern with the Jewish state and the West. Education, even more than urbanization, replaces the psychological remoteness of traditionals with a capacity for empathy enabling intense involvement with distant factors. As a result, causes are "internalized," stimulation is *within* man, who is more likely to expose himself to further stimulation and involvement. Differences in attitude toward the Jewish state among its Arab citizens were only slight when residents of towns were compared with those of villages. But the change connected with education, even though under the aegis of an Israeli government department, was startling; only about half as many students as parents conceded legitimacy to the state and eight times as many students categorically denied it. (Other young respondents were intermediate, but closer to the students' positions.[58])

The former commander of the Arab Legion, Glubb Pasha, once observed that modern education in the Arab world had the surprising effect of enhancing irrationality; academic learning there is mostly rote learning, conferring high status to students, who thus become more haughty than knowledgeable. He thought the untutored bedouin were closer to the real world than the Arab intelligentsia.[59] Similar observations have repeatedly been made by other sources. In a survey done by Israeli authorities among Egyptian prisoners of war in 1967, the mostly illiterate *fellaheen* largely adhered more closely to the "reality principle" than their educated officers. The interviewed soldiers were asked whether they had seen United States aircraft participating in combat against their army with their own eyes, it being assumed that most of them then believed Nasser's claim of American intervention. While hardly any of the illiterates had actually seen such planes, a very high percentage of the officers testified that they had indeed seen the planes in action. A similar correlation between education and ideology-directed cognition emerged when the respondents were asked to describe the nature of Egyptian society. The illiterates showed awareness of Egypt as a polarized society of haves and have-nots, the powerful and the powerless, etc., while the educated described Egypt as a classless and egalitarian society.[60]

Rote learning dramatizes the premodern conception of knowledge still animating Arab higher education. The classic Islamic culture is an oral culture founded on revelatory theology, in which truth is the revealed word, and the impact of the Western-type university in that setting is to produce more of the same in appropriately adjusted idioms rather than spawn an experimental approach. The tools of modern Western civilization are appropriated eagerly and the underlying spirit rejected, indeed not really understood. The humanistic foundations of Western civilization have not taken hold in Islam. The scientific revolution could build on these bases when the West emerged from the tutelage of religion; the same emergence in Islam leaves mainly nihilism, intellectual activism bereft of the stern disciplines of mind respecting words and things. Knowledge is thus recognition of words, following fashion and power, rather than things to which they presumably refer; truth is learned, rather than understood. Thus the world of the words and the real world, as has so frequently been observed in the Arab world, tend not to have much in common.[61]

To the intellectual inclinations peculiar to the Arab world must be added the special form of obscurantism that does not just twist reality, but actually reverses it completely; thus the *fedayeen*, the egregious practitioners of primitive violence, claim to have learned such behavior from their Jewish foe, whose culture in reality is marked by profound anguish and restraint in this respect. A recent intellectual product makes the Israeli military reports mendacious and those of the *fedayeen* truthful[62]—as nearly perfect a reversal of a relationship as may be had in any contemporary conflict.

Education and exposure to radio and other media thus produce in the Arab world a large class of semi-educated literates, by Western standards, comsummately engaged in the production and consumption of intensely ideological verbiage, marking the consciousness and articulateness of increasingly larger parts of that world.

Because of the oral and revelatory character of truth in classic Islamic culture, the autonomy of ideology from the real world is extraordinary. (For a measure of its oral character, consider the Arab society had not felt the need to introduce the printing press before the 1830's, and even then Protestant missionaries imported it for their production of Arabic translations of the Bible, incredible though this sounds.) As for the intensity of ideological engagement, foreign observers have resorted to such terms as "ferocious," "restless," "obsessive," "psychotic" when describing it. Certainly the ideological fervor of the Arab intelligentsia is quite considerable, suggesting that compelling personal needs stand behind it. To the sense of shame and guilt shared with traditionals vis-à-vis the Jewish state are added tensions and painful ambiguities peculiar to those alienated from tradition. One has been described as a strain between belief and profession of belief: Increasingly more young Muslims fail to conform to Islamic practice, as has widely been noticed throughout the Arab world; yet accompanying the process of secularization is increasing self-assertion against the West, and religion, being the primary heritage of the Arabs, must be extolled with particular fervor by those who have no use for it in their own lives, indeed often are ashamed of it.[63] Whether or not such explanations are correct, the fact that the behavior of the Arab intelligentsia elicits theories of psychological pathology is certainly significant.

In the contemporary pattern of social change in the Arab world, the intelligentsia emerges earlier and more vigorously than the urban working class. There is as yet no industrial proletariat to speak of, as the number of workers in large industrial concerns is small and mostly not yet fully removed from peasanthood, in mentality and even way of life. The percentage of skilled craftsmen, who tend to think of themselves as workers, in the large urban propertyless mass is also small. The trade-union movement in the Arab world for the most part constitutes just an adjunct to the governing elites, particularly in the "socialist" regimes, serving essentially to harness the popular mass to domestic and foreign-policy needs of the ruling elites. Yet despite the conformity of the trade-union movement with the struggle with Israel, the class for which it speaks seems not particularly amenable to militancy in that respect.

In British-ruled Palestine the incipient Arab working class seemed prepared for a measure of cooperation, including political cooperation, with the *Yishuv* exceeding that of any other class and serious enough to provoke the Arab national movement in the country repeatedly to preemptive, remedial, and severe punitive measures. The overtures to Arab workers by the Jewish workers had met with success by the 1920's, few years after the latter established the *Histadrut* (General Confederation of Jewish Labor in Palestine). In 1925 the Haifa branch of the *Histadrut* opened a club for Arab workers ("General Workers' Club"). Soon Arab carpenters and tailors organized with *Histadrut* help and struck successfully for shorter hours and better pay, in what probably was the first such Arab labor dispute in Haifa, despite the public disapproval of the Arab press and of ecclesiastic authorities (many workers were Christian). Joint Arab-Jewish strikes took place in 1927 in Jaffa and Acre and in 1928 in Jerusalem. In the same year some two hundred Arab workers struck under *Histadrut* sponsorship a Haifa cigarette factory; some three hundred Arab workers, mostly skilled, were then associated with the Haifa branch, not counting the members of the binational railway workers' union, in existence since 1919.[64]

"Perhaps the area most fraught with potential for the establishment of an ongoing and deeply felt Arab-Jewish brotherhood was that of working-class unity," concluded an examination of Arab-Jewish relations in Palestine in the years preceding the 1929 riots.[65] From 1925 on Arab workers participated in the *Histadrut* Haifa May Day celebrations. An athletic club and a loan fund were formed under its sponsorship, and medical services were extended by it to

Arab workers and their families at nominal fees; Hebrew classes were organized. A Jaffa Arab workers' theater company performed for Jewish workers. In 1926 the *Histadrut* began publication of the first Arabic labor newspaper in the Middle East, *Ittihad al-Amal* (Unity of Labor).

The economic recession in the later 1920's and the riots of 1929 set this proletarian *rapprochement* back somewhat, without interrupting its course altogether. It is noteworthy that only in the bloody events beginning in 1936 was there any significant involvement of Arab workers in anti-Jewish violence.[66] Earlier a Palestine Arab Workers' Society had been set up by nationalist sources to counteract the growing influence of the *Histadrut*.

The trend was remarkable particularly in view of the rejection by the mainstream of the Jewish labor movement of the demand of its own left wing and of Arab workers for fully integrated binational unions, such as the one joining Jews and Arabs in the railway workers' union, and in the face of the movement's insistence on the policy of *avoda ivrit,* Jewish labor only in Jewish enterprises. Though animated also by proletarian fraternal leanings, the intensely nationalist majority of the Jewish labor movement cultivated the Arab workers, not in order to abandon the idea of a Jewish commonwealth, but to hasten its coming, regarding the emancipated Arab working class as a more amenable negotiating partner than the traditional elite. The 1927 decision for parallel, but separate, union organization for Jews and Arabs reflected this determination for proletarian cooperation within Jewish ascendancy—not true binational organization, but Arab organization connected to the much more powerful Jewish organization. The Arab section of the resulting Palestine Labor League claimed some one thousand active members in 1942, one-third of whom were clerical and skilled workers, and this, following several years of great unrest and violence (1936–39) in the course of which a show of Arab-Jewish proletarian solidarity was maintained despite assassinations of Arab unionists by Arab irregulars. Though not large, the number indicates the tendency of proletarian consciousness to conflict with nationalist feeling in Arab Palestine; of special interest in this respect was the failure of the Arab national movement, including the personal intervention of the *Mufti* of Jerusalem, to mobilize the Arab port workers of Haifa for their general strike in the above disturbances. Later, under Israeli rule, organized workers formed the segment in Arab society most closely linked to Jewish society (the *Histadrut* has been integrated in 1960). In the areas conquered in 1967, and notably in East Jerusalem, the pursuit of class interest has led Arab workers to deviate from national postures repeatedly. In East Jerusalem they participated in great numbers in the first municipal elections in the unified city held under Israeli aegis; in the Gaza Strip (and elsewhere) they defied lethal terror by *fedayeen* to protect their employment in Israeli enterprises.

One of the parties claiming to represent the workers in the Arab world, the Communist party, had signaled acceptance of a Jewish state, as provided in the abortive United Nations plan in 1947. One may question the significance of this position on several grounds: first, the social composition of the party is not notably proletarian, the intelligentsia and the several religious and other minorities being greatly overrepresented in its midst; second, the endorsement of the partition plan obviously followed the lead of Soviet policy needs— since the Kremlin at that time enthusiastically supported the plan— and not necessarily the spontaneous inclinations of party members in the Arab world, though compliance with the Soviet line was probably facilitated in the party by its large number of members drawn from minority groups. (Since 1949 the demand for a return to partition plan borders and demography has been used as an anti-Israel diplomatic instrument by various sources in the Arab world, and some Arab Communist leaders have even called for the annihilation of the state.)[67] Still, the programmatic acquiescence in Jewish statehood did indicate to Arab workers that the Communists expected them to deviate from the drift of Arab opinion in this respect; it constituted an ideological position that individual Arabs may have come to accept as appropriate for their new social status, as they began to think of themselves as proletarians. Occasional indications of spontaneous proletarian attitudes in the Arab world suggest relatively weak concern with Israel. An extensive survey in Egypt disclosed that urban workers subordinated national symbols to class demands for economic and social welfare.[68] More recently, in a survey of student opinion in Lebanon, contrary to some expectations (since the *fedayeen* frequently identify with leftist movements and causes), among Muslims (though not among Christians) children of manual workers expressed less support for the *fedayeen* and were more likely to support a peaceful solution to the Palestine conflict than others, including sons of big businessmen and professionals.[69]

10

IMAGINING THE FUTURE

THERE are forces at work, in the ubiquitous challenge of modernity and the inexorable decay of the old order, independent of any of the factors usually discussed in connection with a settlement with the Jewish state, that tend to incline Arab peoples toward its rejection. This alone bodes ill for any facile presumption of conciliation. Deeply rooted in the distant past and in profound historical transformation, the conflict of Arabs and Jews in the Middle East resembles more the religious struggles of Europe (which seemed to take forever to "work themselves out") than, say, industrial struggles amenable to quick solution by contrived, intricate formulations. Besides material interests and genuine emotion, the struggle with the Jews has been embedded in the currents of ideology sweeping the Arab world, which, like other societies striving to recast themselves through development into dynamic and just commonwealths, experiences a particularly compelling need for ideological expression. Emerging from tradition, the abhorrence of Jewish statehood has been propelled into the center of the collective consciousness that Arabs expect to guide them in the new world born of the machine. Not the base sentiment to be pandered by demagogues, as we perceive it in the West, it is actually one inscribed in national charters and constitutions with the same pride with which Americans once asserted Jeffersonian verities in their hallowed parchments. To disown it is much like disowning one's soul. Indeed, not a few observers have said that for the Arabs really to accept the Jewish state in this period of their history, they would have to cease being Arabs, as they understand the term.

Embedded in the depth of consciousness and ideology, hostility to the Jewish state thus assumes a certain functional autonomy—a life all its own—which is further strengthened by the substantial emotional investment in its persistence, resulting both from basic personality traits peculiar to Arab peoples and from mechanisms associated with the prosecution of the struggle against the foe. In the opinion of foreign observers, and by their own admission, Arabs are a fiercely vengeful people. "With Arabs, to be implacable and revengeful is the sign of a proud and noble man. 'He who takes revenge after forty years is in a hurry,' says a Bedouin proverb."[1]

The manner in which Arabs make the outrage of Jewish statehood psychologically bearable also serves to strengthen intransigence. They naturally resort to the same apologias, self-indulgence, and nostalgic reveries of distant glories with which they had earlier learned to endure their humiliation by the resurgent West. They consequently have a large and emotionally comforting stake in uncompromising rejection of Israel. The problem with these mechanisms is not simply that their abandonment would constitute painful self-denial, which is not likely to happen anyway within a civilization so marked by self-indulgence as the Islamic; the implications of really coming to terms with Jewish statehood are so damaging to Arab self-esteem as to be virtually intolerable, certainly at this phase of Arab history. Temporary accommodations with (an instrument of) imperialism may be justified on the grounds of *force majeure*, in the sense that, though the Arabs are again important in this world, the world still would not allow them to remove a moribund entity altogether.

But what are the Arabs really worth if the small Jewish state represents a legitimate, and even superior, antagonist? Thus, the grounds for some accommodation acceptable to Arabs are predicated on continuing struggle. War is thus built into the very structure of the peace Arabs can tolerate with the Jewish state. Though absurd in Western terms, this is precisely how Arabs conceive of the "peace" (*salaam*) they now offer in return for submission to all their demands at this time.

Intransigence on Jewish statehood may thus well be the margin between a world that is tolerable for an Arab's existence and one that is not, though the stance need not always be translated into effective action, or else be denied but rather leans on "an Eastern reliance on time," as Barbara W. Tuchman put it, "to wait is to win in the end."[2] The utter inability of Arab masses to face their world without this crutch had been dramatically demonstrated in the wake of the gravest defeat, in June of 1967, when Nasser, the symbol of hopes for redemption and triumph, indicated that he was removing himself from politics. While some feel that the public frustration of his "resignation" was not entirely left to chance, there can be little doubt that the mass hysteria of Egyptians was quite genuine. Both official and oppositional Egyptian voices interpreted this incredible spectacle as the masses' insistence on victory.[3] An Israeli diplomat has acknowledged this consequence of the Arabs' painting themselves psychologically into a corner: "This psychological condition has turned the Arabs into more formidable foes of Israel than they were: they have entrenched themselves ever more deeply in their enmity—for lack of a better way out."[4]

More likely than a redefinition of the Arab national ethos to accommodate the outrage of Jewish statehood is actual accommodation with it in a frustrating and imperfect world. In fact, the reluctant coexistence with the Jewish state in the past was paralleled by a general rise in hostility toward it, rather than the opposite. Time itself thus forms an important variable: in one sense, because of the advancing disarray in traditional Islam, entailing more painfully antagonistic attitudes toward Israel; in another, because of the accumulation of military defeats over the years, entailing rising pressure to resolve the dissonance between the Arab heroic self-image and the actual results of the fighting—and when they restore the image, as in the October war, they become overly confident, thus pushing once more in the same direction; in yet another sense, time forms a variable because of the accumulation of secondary problems arising at different turns of the ongoing conflict (refugees, more refugees, water rights, boundaries, new conquests, divided Jerusalem, unified Jerusalem, etc.).

As the conflict lingers, various opportunities for wider involvement arise, as for the Algerians, both before the outbreak of the June war and after, when the disaster of Arab regular forces shifted Arab hopes to the *fedayeen*, with whom the Algerians could identify more closely than with other Arab forces. Another illustration of wider involvement over time is the increasing exposure of previously isolated individuals to official anti-Israeli propaganda. Long exposure to propaganda was said to have had a certain effect even among Maronites; among nearby *Sunnis* the change can be from near apathy to obsessive concern.[5]

The Arab-Jewish conflict has involved over time increasingly more Arabs and greater intensity of feeling, but not uniformly. The same individuals were not always more hostile than before, at least not overtly; reports of foreign observers on attitudes in certain Arab communities suggest the existence of substantial fluctuation in this regard.[6] For one thing, much manifest hostility tends to appear prior to war itself and soon after. From this, the impression flows that war itself aggravates hostility, but the connection between the two is quite complex. To begin with, while defeat in war has indeed been accompanied by an apparent intensification of hostility (even so, reports are far from unanimous in every case)[7] in Arab countries, a rise in hostility clearly preceded war in the first place. Sources other than war first escalate sentiment, then war itself may affect it further, though not necessarily in the same direction. One effect of the 1967 defeat among Israeli Arabs was to estrange them from the state and intensify revanchist sentiment among them; on the other hand, overt hostility seems to have decreased after 1967 among the Arabs of the previously Jordanian West Bank. The personal contact with the Arab world made possible by the Israeli conquests in the war was said to have made the former more reckless in relations with the Israeli Jews, while similarly sudden contact with the latter made West Bank Arabs more prudent in relations with them.[8] Repeated military defeats could well make the Arab cause look hopeless, thus actually facilitating accommodation. We cannot really know what the effect of yet another crushing defeat in 1973 would have been, because American interventions in the war were quite candidly poised to avoid just such an outcome, on the premise that only humiliation in war prevented the Arabs from making peace with Israel.

Another popular assumption, that Arab hostility is directly related to the extent of Jewish dominion is equally open to question.[9] We just do not know whether the Jewish state was really more acceptable to Arabs in its pre-1967 shape than in the much larger expanse since the June war; by urging it to abandon new territory, the great powers seem to imply that it was, or can be in future. Yet they are suggesting at the same time that the larger shape itself had made Arab acceptance more likely, or even possible in the first place. If Arab acceptance has indeed emerged or grown only as Israel expanded, why should one believe that the opposite would still have the same effect on it? One trouble with the popular idea of trading Israeli conquests for Arab acceptance—the essence of the Security Council Resolution Number 242—is that Arab concessions made under pressure would also be present in the absence of pressure. Why would words uttered in order to recover land be honored once it is recovered? Surely not out of gratitude. Besides, the record of adherence to treaty obligations by the Arab governments concerned is among the worst in the world. And it is difficult to see how the international community would assure compliance, even if it wanted to. For the record of international guarantees in the Middle East conflict is simply dreadful, and for very good reasons, since the very idea of enforcing an onerous condition on the numerous and wealthy Arab states and their many allies on behalf of a diplomatically insignificant Jewish state is an absurdity in international politics.

By phasing it into several steps, the Kissinger version of "territory for peace" does not escape the essential fallacy, but merely obscures it. Its rationale is that successive Israeli withdrawals linked to new Arab concessions would build a durable structure of peace, in that each agreement would further good faith between the antagonists. This assumes that what really divides them is distrust and that piecemeal concessions are somehow invulnerable to the obvious deficiency—unilateral repudiation—one as dubious as the other. What the variously disguised Israeli retreats ("disengagement," in the first phase) do provide is trade-off for various American short-term needs. They produce public-relations successes for the Secretary of State ("miracles," in the case of the first withdrawals in 1974); they purchase eclipses of Soviet influence in Egypt and elsewhere; they serve as chips in bargaining with Arab oil-producing countries.

Previous experience with Israeli withdrawal does not support the prevailing wisdom either. In the war with Egypt in the fall of 1956, Israel acquired the Gaza Strip and virtually the whole of the Sinai, then withdrew under international pressure against certain diplomatic assurances concerning the virtual demilitarization of the abandoned territory and the protection of the right of passage through the Gulf of Aqaba. Israel's return to narrower territorial confines did not substantially affect hostility to it in the Arab world. If it were expansionism, rather than sheer existence, that Arabs rejected in the Jewish state, then withdrawal should have markedly alleviated hostility to it. As it was, withdrawal was credited not to non-expansionism, but rather to Israeli weakness before Arab diplomatic power. Since their loss of land in 1967, the Arab states have sought anew to regain it by similar means; even voluntary return of territory is certain to be interpreted by them as successful enforcement. They indeed interpret in this wise what withdrawals have already taken place.

Arab hostility may actually grow as Israel diminishes, or appears to diminish. In the crisis preceding the June war, the initially restrained mood in Arab capitals escalated quickly to what foreign observers described as a lynching frenzy, as Israel, taken by surprise by Nasser's diplomatic coups, seemed on the run and worse. While many abroad believe that Israel's salvation lies in some narrow and grotesque shape, it is the latter that Arabs actually cite in their invective against it; a common reference to Israel within the armistice lines of 1949 was "the *dwarf* gangster state." Given the political orientations of Islamic peoples, accommodation to an imperious outrage is actually more likely than to a pitiful one.

In the general frustration with the seemingly endless conflict, much hope has been placed on the Palestinians, to whom both the Arab world and the world outside are looking for relief from the quandary, though each envisions the cutting of the knot in rather contradictory ways. The Arab disaster in June of 1967 set the stage for this role. On the one hand, failure itself removed the Arab states from their previous place of pride in the struggle with Israel in the popular Arab imagination, shifting hopes for redemption to the Palestinian *fedayeen* and a people's war; on the other hand, the disaster unified all of Cisjordania under Israeli rule, bringing more Palestinian Arabs than there were at the close of the British period together with the Jews (now four times as many as in 1948), and thus suggesting, particularly in Israel and the West, the possibility of a new start at coexistence. Whether the Palestinians' past political record revealed capacities and traits commensurate with these expectations was not among the concerns of the more hopeful observers.

The years of unsuccess since their romantic emergence from the ashes of Arab defeat have tarnished the *fedayeen* glitter in much of the Arab world, even in the pages of Western journals, where they had scored their greatest triumphs. On the other hand, in part because of this disillusionment, hopes had grown that the Palestinians would accept sovereignty in only part of Palestine, thus ending their conflict with the Jewish state and that of the other Arab states as well. The controversy over such a solution by a Palestinian "entity" or "state" has been confused by partisanship and wishful thinking. To begin with, the controversy arose as an internal Israeli debate in which some Arabs and some Westerners happened to participate, not as an Arab or even Arab-Jewish debate. The implications of this fact are obvious. Whom does the matter preoccupy? Whose needs does it answer? A leading Israeli student of Arab affairs, who had been engaged in the administration of the West Bank, a region envisioned for such "entity," contrasted the Arabs of the region with the way "some Israelis wish them to be." He told a London symposium: "I don't know how acquainted you are with the quite busy debate which is going on in the Israeli, Jewish, Hebrew press among two camps, those who are for a Palestinian entity, among them very well known Israeli professors, members of our university as well, and those who are against a Palestinian entity. There were very interesting and important arguments by both camps; the only remark I should add to this debate is that Arabs as such, West Bankers, did not take part, not only in this debate, but have not paid much attention to it."[10]

As an essentially Israeli preoccupation, the controversy naturally enough reflected beliefs peculiar to some Israelis.[11] For what is so enticing to them about the "entity" idea is the promise of an elegant escape from the seemingly hopeless struggle with the Arab world, in the form of a syllogism founded on conceptions of the Arab-Jewish conflict prevailing in Israel. Since the conflict originated as a clash of Jewish and Palestinian national movements over the same land, goes the argument, accommodation between them would remove the seed of contention for other Arabs, thus terminating the whole struggle altogether. Yet even if such was the origin of the conflict, the suggested conclusion need not follow. Furthermore, the origin of the conflict was clearly not what many Israelis believe, in the first place.

One cannot take issue with the proposition that some sort of accommodation may sometime emerge as between Israelis and Palestinians—it may already be in the process of emerging—or that such accommodation might have a cooling effect on the Middle East conflict. But that is not what the Israeli proponents of a Palestine entity were demanding. They asked prompt commitment to a proposition that was patently not acceptable to the overwhelming mass of Palestine's Arabs and not likely to produce peace with the other Arabs, either.

In discussing the preferences of Palestine's Arabs, observers usually accord special importance to one of the three major groupings forming that community since the June war, namely the West Bankers and the Gaza Strip residents. (Frequently, in fact, references to "Palestinians" mean only West Bankers, with the Arabs of East Jerusalem included, since they form the larger and more settled segment, the majority of the Gaza Strip residents being refugee camp dwellers.) The other two major groupings are the Palestinians who had been Israelis before the June war and those outside Palestine, not under Israeli rule of any kind. What had made the first grouping, particularly the more than 600,000 West Bankers, especially intriguing was their seemingly conciliatory stance toward Israel, their denunciation of war, and their marked reluctance to back the *fedayeen* actively. For a guide to the West Bankers' attitudes to the Middle East conflict one must look above all to the fact of their subjection to Israeli rule. The variable ("situation") is a familiar one, for we know a good deal about Arab behavior in the circumstance. After all, a sizable number of other Palestinians, the Israeli Arabs, have been observed over a considerable period of time in this condition before. A typical variation of attitude was shown by Archbishop Hakim, for many years leader of the Melchite Catholic community in Israel. While in that capacity, the Egypt-born prelate was seen by some Israelis as almost a patriot; militant in pursuit of the interests of his flock, he ostentatiously participated in the national life, busily socializing with Israel's leading personages, seemingly a model of cooperation with the state. Elected a patriarch of his church, he departed for his see, in Syria, and soon delivered himself publicly of bitter recrimination against Israel, with thinly veiled endorsement of its elimination.[12]

If an Arab's acceptance of Israel, when under its rule, is not a reliable guide to subsequent behavior, when under Arab rule, neither does the experience of Israeli rule leave him wholly unaffected, particularly where personal exposure to the foe is substantial. Personal realization of the nature of the foe, without necessarily diminishing the sense of injustice felt by Arabs, would seem at least to remove from their conception of him some demonic qualities he assumes when his strength must be explained from a distant Arab perspective.[13] The standard imagination of Israel in the Arab world often seems fantastic to the more sensitive Arab who experiences it from within, irritating and overwhelming though it seems even then. Many realize the social roots of Israeli power and the autonomy of the political system from Western power. Some even develop awareness of the pugnacity of the Israeli national will, as the manifestation of a "natural" polity, not simply a foreign colony, an artificial conglomerate, or an imperial extension. The widely diffused expectation abroad in the Arab world that the Jewish state would disintegrate under *fedayeen* pressure strikes many on the West Bank as absurd. Before the October war, some even risked reprisal by openly deriding *fedayeen* ideology, not for Israel's sake, but as a threat to the last remnants of Arab Palestine.[14] For the large mass, random contact with Israeli officials and soldiers has generated not unfavorable comparison with experiences under Jordanian or Egyptian equivalents.

"Four years of forced proximity with Israel," wrote a West Bank journalist, "revealed it to be a vibrant state with its own goals and its own aspirations independent of any power outside the area. To be sure this state was set up at the expense of the Palestinian Arab and is therefore an arch enemy, but an enemy that must be evaluated honestly if he is to be defeated at all. . . . Reality revealed the Jew to be a cultivated man with higher values than those of the Arab. In fact, his occupation of Palestinian lands was not a simple matter of a military invasion as often depicted, but a cultural invasion whose success on the battlefield was one indication of its technological superiority. Superb organizational planning at all levels of society has provided it with an internal cohesion rarely encountered in the western world. Perhaps there is the real reason for the Arab's morbid fear of Israel: it has undermined his belief in his own culture, in his blind faith that Allah's people possess superior qualities to those of the infidels; it has shown Arab civilisation, evaluated in twentieth-century terms, to be technologically backward, culturally deprived, and politically impotent."[15]

But a sober reading of the Arabs' predicament did not legitimize it even before the October war. Experience does not carry the same measure of chastising discipline in their intellectual milieu as in the humanistic West. This has only sometimes been recognized abroad, as when Barbara W. Tuchman put it, "they cannot be counted upon to act in their own best interest."[16] In so strongly oral a tradition as the Arab, "facts" are less compelling than in the Western context. The definition of a situation in terms that suggest some action as the logical remedy does not necessarily entail such action at all, a popular pattern known among Arabs as *hifaq* (two-facedness).[17] In discussions of their predicament Palestinian Arabs under Israeli rule thus often delivered themselves of seemingly contradictory statements, perhaps reflecting different layers of consciousness, alternately coming to the fore, now one, now the other, according to circumstance or mood. One could, to cite one colloquium, deliver oneself of a bitter indictment of Israel as a crime against mankind, urging its elimination at all cost; only to describe somewhat later the same as a self-defeating exercise, indicating resignation to Israel's being; then actually to speak in admiration of the grandeur of Jewish nationhood; and finally to revert to fear of being slaughtered by Jews (the moderator interpreted this to mean fear of punishment by *fedayeen* for the previous statement).[18]

Characteristic of the Palestinians under Israeli rule since 1967, and even after 1973, is *attentisme,* or procrastination as policy. It assumes the form of passively marking time under occupation, or of avoiding responsibility for their own fate, or of seeking to postpone indefinitely a definitive settlement of the Israeli phenomenon.[19] *Attentisme* fits well with the weakness of the Palestinians in sustaining cooperative ventures and is compatible with caution and safety—thus, they will not unduly provoke the Israelis, nor really betray to them the Arab cause. The abhorrence of war they often expressed before the October war, while perhaps not devoid of genuinely ethical foundation in many cases, likewise reflected their fear, that as hostages they were certain to suffer most regardless of the outcome of another war (the fear earlier of the Israeli Arabs). The fear is reflected even after 1973 in a marked preference for political solutions to their problems.

Having emerged from shock in the wake of the June war, when the Israeli conqueror failed to exact the bloody revenge they had expected from him, the Palestinians first passed through a phase of enthusiastic cooperation with the *fedayeen* (not having massacred, the Jew was taken to be weak), only to settle, in 1969, into *attentisme,* a posture more appropriate to their real condition. They were guided in this by the Dayan occupation policy, blending the carrots of minimal interference with local government, economic prosperity, and continued open channels to the Arab world with the stick of ruthless suppression of *fedayeen* action. The large majority on the West Bank persisted in identifying as "Jordanians under occupation," including many who really regarded themselves as Palestinians first, in many cases because of habit or affection, and above all, perhaps, for this was expected to deliver them from Israeli rule.[20] Disillusionment with both the Jordanian and the *fedayeen* paths to that cherished goal even gave rise to a small West Bank faction favoring the "entity" idea that so preoccupied Israeli opinion, as a third option.[21]

The imperative of liberation by political means had aligned most West Bankers before 1973 with the moderate tendency in the Arab world. They eagerly welcomed Egyptian overtures to the great powers, international involvement, and in particular American peace initiatives. They assumed a concomitant posture of toleration toward Israel but an Israel in a much diminished shape which they understood to be the price of deliverance from their immediate predicament, occupation. Some demanded just a return to the *status quo ante bellum* (1967), others hinting at still more retreat, to the partition lines envisaged in 1947. Yet on closer scrutiny one could see virtually all envisaging peace with a restricted Jewish state as actually an armistice of variable duration, categorically put at only ten years, in one case,[22] and appearing less definitive in most others. But a certain realization was developing among some West Bankers that statehood might not be just a passing aberration in the Jewish *millet*, after all. And even the others had acquired awareness of the Israeli reality rarely matched elsewhere in the Arab world.

We can see now that the international campaign in the wake of the June war to patch up quickly the debris of war by forcing a precipitate Israeli withdrawal against some paper arrangements, would, if successful, simply have returned masses of Palestinians to Arab rule, just as they emerged from their great shock—only to further strengthen their earlier conceptions of the Jew as contemptible—or, if occurring somewhat later, in the phase of their "active struggle," to produce the myth that the *fedayeen* had defeated Israeli military might. Little thought has been given abroad to the impact on Arab behavior in the struggle with Israel by similar delusions of power nurtured by earlier diplomatic legerdemain, as in 1957, when a shocked and momentarily sobered Arab world was pushed directly into diplomatic triumph over Israeli victors subdued for them by the superpowers. The curious "lesson" of defeat taught by international diplomacy is reflected in the ideology of the Arabs, who, having been hit by a juggernaut, awakened to see it suddenly turned, by great-power intervention, into a mere toy train. *Realpolitik* abroad does not much enhance the reality principle in the Middle East; its failure after 1967 had at least allowed substantial numbers of Israelis and Arabs to begin facing up to unpleasant realities as never before. The period has been one of gestation, fraught with predicament and opportunity, on the way to an uncertain destination.

Events since October, 1973, appear to have slowed the emergence of new orientations among Arabs under Israeli occupation without wholly reversing recent learning or changing basic political behavior. While hopes for an end to the occupation have sharply risen, *attentisme* has merely adjusted to new circumstances: The Jordanian identity has become less fashionable than the Palestinian, but they still expect others to deliver them.[23] Arab regular armies and the *fedayeen* have won new respect, chiefly because of the sanguine broadcasts from abroad, but glimpses of the Israeli juggernaut tempers judgment as it cannot among Arabs across the front lines.

When a Palestinian solution to the Arab-Israeli conflict became an issue of real concern to the Arabs as well, after the October war, it was in terms quite different from the earlier Israeli and Western controversy. Whereas in foreign eyes the Palestinians close the conflict for all by settling in their "entity" or "state" alongside the Jewish state, in Arab eyes they advance the struggle nearer conclusion to an internationally protected base at the foe's very heartland. Western media suppress the Arab vision by systematic "translation" into the other. In just one egregious case the front-page report by America's leading newspaper's man on the spot speaks of the solemn, all-Arab decision for a "national authority" in "any liberated area of Palestine"—the term "state" is invariably rejected for its implication of finality and limitation, "authority" being dynamic and expansionist—as if it asked for a "state" limited to the West Bank and the Gaza Strip; the headline spoke of a "state," and the introduction put the term alongside the authentic text, presumably for authenticity.[24] A rational public discussion of the Middle East would seem under these circumstances well nigh hopeless.

A consideration of the practical possibilities of accommodation between the Jewish state and the Arabs, Palestinians and others, requires clarification of arrangements attainable at this time and of circumstances affecting their durability in future. What Arabs prepared for an arrangement with Israel are in fact offering is a return to the armistice in effect before the June war for an indefinite period; they are prepared to accept slight semantic alteration in the description of that condition ("peaceful agreement" or "contractual undertaking" or similar words) and possibly some minute modification in the armistice line; other details might be discussed, so long as the essential restoration of the *status quo ante bellum* is assured. The recent rise in Arab confidence has led to the further formal demand that the *fedayeen* replace the more quiescent Jordanians along Israel's longest and most vulnerable lines to the east.

When one considers the incredible obfuscation, deliberate and otherwise, accompanying the diplomatic maneuvering since 1967, the laymen's confusion about what really is at stake is only natural. But among serious students of the Middle East the consensus on the essential character of the Arab offer has been as solid as one may reasonably expect on any complex issue of international affairs. The author of a standard history of the Palestine dispute wrote after the June war: "As politically unrealistic as the position of the *fidaiyun* may now appear, it is at least frank. By accompanying an implicit rather than explicit endorsement of the 1949 armistice lines with a categorical rejection of direct negotiation, the Arab states confirm their adamant refusal to accept the reality of Israel and lack candor, thus outraging Israel.''[25] Arab statements on the recognition of Israel's existence, which usually excite journalists and diplomats, have been understood as either plainly tactical or rendered nearly worthless by a mass of *arrierès-pensées*. "As long as the Arabs cannot or will not accept the existence of Israel *as final and immutable*," wrote another historian of the long conflict, "the best that can be expected is an uneasy truce maintained by Israeli strength."[26] The Kissingerian euphoria after the Arab attack of October 6, 1973, has not spread to this group.

This consensus often manifests itself in discreet form, because of the peculiar sociological composition of the academic study of the Middle East and the need for continued access to the region. There may be deliberate obscurantism in some cases by public-relations-conscious writers, but the ephemeral nature of the "peace" the Arabs are offering and the inconclusive character of the "recognition" of Israel they talk about are so generally taken for granted in the profession that most simply do not bother to make the appropriate qualifications when using the terms in question. The real contention among serious students concerns the viability and fate of the new armistice, under whatever name, offered by Arab sources in return for the territory surrendered to Israel in the June war, the more hopeful among them thinking that the momentum of even a disingenuously concluded accord might prevail or that the international community could somehow enforce it. So this is the crucial question, for the worth of even a formal peace treaty concluded with the best of intentions would still depend on durability.

If the past is prologue in the Middle East, the environment for Arab-Israeli peaceableness must be deemed unpromising. More than just the unhappy impression to this effect gained over many years, there are in this case specific precedents of a particularly relevant nature that are just as unpromising. After all, armistice agreements had once before been concluded between Israel and Arab states. Negotiated under United Nations mediation (and much more directly than the Kissinger disengagements) and endorsed by the great powers, they banned all belligerency and provided a host of security and other arrangements, "in order to facilitate the transition from the present truce to permanent peace. . . ."[27] While historical situations are never perfectly parallel, the one in 1949 seemed more promising than the present. Thus, the present claim that Egypt wanted out of an unwanted conflict, if only the national patrimony were restored, was voiced then with as much cogency, at least, as after 1967. The regime was then much less committed to Arabism than later or now; the army had gone into Palestine only reluctantly, and the younger officers (Nasser included) had sought domestic Egyptian politics and development as their battlefield, just as Sadat is said to desire now. Moreover, no substantial *fedayeen* force existed to challenge the armistice agreement; neither Libya nor others existed as potential unbalancers of such agreement. The point here is not to blame anyone for the degeneration of the 1949 armistice agreements into almost incessant warfare; rather, it is to clarify some anti-peace dynamics of the Middle Eastern setting, in which any armistice with Israel must survive.

The first of these may be termed the dynamics of stalemate, deriving from contradictory asymmetries of power in the Middle East and in the international community. On the one hand, Israeli military power in the area of conflict has grown to the point where it reduces the adversary to helplessness before it; left alone to face Israel, the Arab position would be virtually hopeless. While conventional wisdom persists in the assumption that Israeli military ascendancy is temporary, the consensus of students of the power disparity in the Middle East points to its continuation in the foreseeable future, the October war not changing their judgment at all.[28]

But outside the area of conflict, in the international community, altogether a different asymmetry of power obtains: there the Arabs are on top. The Arabs thus escape overwhelming Israeli military power by recourse to the international community; for it is there that they obtain immediate succor and draw hope for continued confrontation. Since they greatly outweigh Israel in resources and alliances, the Arabs constitute highly desirable diplomatic factors, whose goodwill the powers court, the diplomatic insignificance of their foe becoming even greater by contrast than might otherwise be the case. The international community shields the Arabs from the consequences of Israeli power. They are relieved of facing up to the foe or seeking accommodation before wars; after wars they are relieved of the customary necessity of seeking terms by means of going to the powers and international organizations for nullification of the wars' outcome. The international community is eager to intervene in this sense, although the powers are moved only by the purest of intentions, naturally. These dynamics are well understood and widely and candidly discussed in the Arab context. The October war confirmed this proposition once again.

International involvement in the Middle East conflict results also in a dynamics of violence quite peculiar to that environment. Facing the Arabs' reluctance to accept Jewish statehood is the profound insecurity of the other side; and while one is a response to the other, insecurity goes much deeper in the Jewish psyche. An extraordinary history of victimization and martyrdom has given rise to Jewish anxiety, which is particularly heightened in Israel, even as it is vindicated. Against this anxiety, the Arab threats and deliberately provocative acts become amplified, because the Jewish reaction to them cannot be severed from the European Holocaust and earlier traumas with Christendom. But if peaceableness in the immediate framework of the conflict requires allaying Israeli anxiety and discouraging Arab harassment of the foe, the behavior of the international community toward the region has the opposite effects. In the small-scale warfare of provocation and reprisal that fills much of the interwar periods in the Middle East, the constant pattern of international intervention is acquiescence in provocation and rejection of reprisal. Within the United Nations there has in fact obtained an automatic premium for Arab harassment of the foe in the region: If he responds in kind to harassment, which the international organization is often reluctant even to acknowledge, the foe brings on himself as well the censure and threat and punishment that the organization produces against him as a matter of routine. The impact of the international peacekeeping machinery on the spot was in the past similar to that of the parent organization in New York: quite useless as far as preventing the irregular warfare that the Arabs produce spontaneously (marauding, hit-and-run attacks, sniping, etc.) it did, however, manage to deepen the anxiety and frustration of the other side, the one possessing really serious military capacity.

The continuation of the pattern of international intervention in the Middle East conflict would seem assured by the tendency of individual foreign powers to protect and promote what they regard as their national interest, even in pursuit of collective goals in concert with other powers. While the usual cant of diplomats obscures the elemental function of international intervention in the conflict, their motives for intrusion need not always be cynical. They may genuinely wish to allay instability and war, but their perceptions of the requisite actions cannot escape the influence of Arab resources and connections, which their competition usually exaggerates as well. Thus, a persistent and compulsive tendency toward destabilization obtains in the environment for future Arab-Israeli relations.

Now, agreement between Israel and some Arab states must stand up, in the Arab context, to dynamics of incoherent coalition characterizing the Arab forces confronting Israel. If the usual inability of the Arabs to combine their forces weakens them in war with Israel, it does not follow that it must also enhance peace. Disunity actually sabotages peaceableness as much as warfare, as the record of the past several decades amply shows. For the familiar references in the histories of the conflict (that this or the other Arab factor was "dragged" into war despite lack of preparation and even the desire to fight) only advertise the great vulnerability of intended abstemiousness. Tied by emotional solidarity, yet without much discipline, the Arab coalition tends to place the effective commitment and fate of the stable members in the hands of the more volatile. The Egyptians and Jordanians have experienced this peculiar power of the Palestinians and Syrians repeatedly throughout the conflict with Israel, as the immediate antecedents of the June war make especially clear. Members of the Arab coalition may not actually commit other members to war immediately and inescapably; their pull has been resisted, at least temporarily, on several occasions, and sometimes only with great difficulty. But on some occasions they can be said to have virtually committed others in this fashion.

As a perpetual provocation and insult to the Arabs, Israel exerts a certain spell upon the more volatile or desperate among them, some rising from time to time to meet the challenge, for this is a noble cause in the Arab context, however regrettable it may appear abroad. Opportunities are not wanting: Before the June war there was a long and vulnerable border, with large numbers of Israelis easily within range of even light arms, a situation now obtaining only in the north and northeast, but that would once again obtain everywhere should Israel withdraw from conquered territory as the Arabs and the foreign powers demand. There are vulnerable sea lanes, where Israeli shipping may be harassed, in the Red Sea or in the Mediterranean (the recent threat to the former and Libyan moves to secure a base in Malta may indicate the shape of things to come). The same applies to the wide network of air traffic with even more urgency. Then there are always Israelis (and in the last resort just Jews) scattered around the globe, who provide easy targets if all else fails. Opportunities for diplomatic harassment seem unlimited; a relatively small investment of Libyan oil wealth in Uganda had shown before the October war what havoc can be wrought with Israel's meager economic and political resources by the use of growing Arab oil revenues. An additional incentive for seizing such opportunities is the competition for leadership and prestige in the Arab world, in which recklessness is more amply rewarded than nonbelligerency.[29]

Israel is thus under siege even as some members of the Arab coalition withdraw from active confrontation, and since the international community tends not to provide relief from harassment, the Jewish state's own response to particularly unnerving provocation tends to activate the more quiescent members of the Arab coalition. This occurs in two ways: Israeli attack on activist members elicits feeling of solidarity in the more quiescent; and when seeking the cooperation of the latter (and their foreign patrons) in curbing their more militant Arab brethren, Israel may apply pressure directly on them as well. Military pressure on Jordan and Lebanon illustrates this proposition.

But withdrawal from active confrontation with the Jewish state is vulnerable above all else because of the dynamics of opportunism. In practical terms whether or not Arabs translate their feelings about the foe into deeds is, in the last resort, a function of opportunity. Moderation on Israel in the Arab world is essentially a fair-weather phenomenon: The greater the opportunity to liquidate Israel, the weaker moderation becomes. This is altogether normal in a society whose highest values actually demand such liquidation; thus, the quarrel between moderates and militants is really over the choice of means, not ends. Moderates evaluate the price of immediate liquidation as excessive or the chances too poor and turn militant as their evaluation changes.

An Israeli writer has reminded us that during the crisis preceding the June war, when Israel seemed on the run, or worse, not a single voice called for moderation in the Arab world, not publicly, at any rate. He argued that the tenuous nature of moderation is aggravated by the excessive power of rhetoric in contemporary societies that, like the Arab societies, lack the social structure of modern nationhood. Where rhetoric *is* politics, the more demagogic appeal is in general likely to displace the less demagogic, in situations of great stress in particular. The operation of this version of Gresham's Law was made manifest in the meteoric rise of Ahmed Shukeiry in the Arab world in the course of the pre-June war crisis. "And whereas Shukeiry's tiny Palestine Liberation Army hardly constituted a threat to Israel, his rhetoric became a threat to the whole Arab world, for nobody was able to stand up to him, stop him, shut him up, or shut him in. As tempers began to rise, one feat of rhetoric followed another; pro-Western Jordan became as belligerent in egging

Nasser on as 'leftist' Syria; nobody was able to prevent Shukeiry from granting TV interviews in which he invited all concerned to be his guests for coffee 'next week in Tel Aviv.' Under this kind of stress, the distinction between 'moderate' and 'radical' Arab governments evaporated. . . ."[30]

In Tunisia, the epitome of moderation, Bourguiba voiced his support for "the struggle of the Palestinians to regain their usurped fatherland," and amid mass hysteria and anti-Jewish riots, in anticipation of the soon-to-come demise of the Jewish state, the regime announced that Tunisian troops would join other Arab forces at the front.[31] René Aggiouri, the voice of reason in Beirut's *L'Orient,* was jubilant. (Maronite leaders voiced solidarity with the Arabs in public, but a sense of unease over the train of events was discernible in their community.)[32] Further demonstration of its opportunistic character soon came with the startling resurgence of moderation, as suddenly as the reversal of the fortunes of war; the defeated Arabs, now at the mercy of foreign powers, tried it again. "In the Middle East capitals," wrote one observer soon after the war, "moderation meant no more than cessation of provocative attacks on Israel during the diplomatic campaign to force the Zionist aggressors to disgorge conquered territory."[33] After the October war moderation meant dismantling the rest of Israel in stages.

Another manifestation of the opportunism governing Arab behavior in the struggle with Israel is the spontaneous escalation of objectives in keeping with perceived possibilities. Whatever the reason for his initial involvement in the crisis (said to be Syrian anxiety) in the middle of May, 1967, Nasser soon proceeded much beyond it, to restore the *status quo ante bellum* 1956; and having effected this by the quick eviction of the United Nations peacekeeping force from Sinai and the imposition of a naval blockade at Sharm el Sheikh, the issue suddenly became the existence of Israel itself. Though prepared to discuss modalities legitimizing the coup in Western eyes, the agenda proposed by Egypt to the international community urgently featured no less than the restoration of the rights of the Palestinian people. In Nasser's own metaphor the task now was to return to (the eve of) 1948, the year of the establishment of the Jewish state. Despite the doubts and fears some Egyptians nursed in those exciting days—whether the foe would actually acquiesce in all this—the dominant mood was fatalistic abandon, a sense that one must not, cannot, escape the fated confrontation. Nasser's earlier cautious determination not to confront Israel militarily until fully prepared for the crunch had come to this within a matter of days. No Arab leader was said to equal his power over the masses throughout the Arab world, and even he could not resist the dynamics of opportunism. And Sadat, after him, having given before the October war the impression that all he sought was recovery of land lost in 1967, proceeded to press hard for *fedayeen* goals as soon as the former seemed within reach.[34]

How well could a future determination to avoid military confrontation with Israel stand in the conditions prevailing in the Arab world? One Arab, who has urged just such a course of action for his people, has himself expressed doubt concerning their ability, as he put it, to distinguish between containment and conquest, especially when temptations are acute.[35] The basic difficulty with a policy to end military confrontation with Israel indeed lies in understanding precisely how it would differ from a policy aimed at merely delaying it. In the absence of appropriate moral inhibitions (the moral imperative in the Arab world actually demands the liquidation of the Jewish state), restraint hinges mainly on a shifting calculus of the feasibility of military action. If the past is any indication of future behavior, the calculus of feasibility can be expected to incline toward overstatement; the tendency will be to exaggerate, even wildly exaggerate, future improvements in the Arabs' military position. They will be encouraged in this, as in the past, by their Western friends, whose estimates of the Arabs' progress are as bloated as their fondness for Arabs is indeed genuine; by scholars and writers who mistake heroic posture for revolutionary change; by military experts who wonder aloud every few years after each war whether the Arabs are ready again to take on the foe.

While a more pronounced realization of the military weakness of the Arabs had come about after the June war, no real change occurred in their faith in ultimate ascendancy over the Jewish state. After 1967 they talked in terms of ten, eighteen, or more years on overtaking the foe, rather than just several, as before. Some envisaged such fortuitous global developments in the future as to obviate any need for reliance on military might. That the Arabs will sooner or later overtake their foe in even this respect was treated as axiomatic even before 1973. As an offense against nature,[36] Jewish statehood was and is regarded as only a temporary aberration.

The Arabs eagerly scanned the Israeli landscape for signs of fatal "contradictions" heralding the future demise of the Jewish state; thus, they saw the young Israelis as rejecting their elders and preparing to throw off the yoke of repressive, exclusivist, and racist Zionism (i.e., Jewish statehood). *Sephardi* protests against the preferential treatment of *Ashkenazi* immigrants were hailed as the opening of an internecine struggle, the beginning of the end of Israel. Abroad, the United States appeared as the last prop of Israel's existence; how long before that power discovers where its true interests lie? When the United States abandoned Taiwan for the sake of Peking, Arab publicists immediately perceived a parallel with the future desertion of Israel. As soon as an American dependence on Middle Eastern oil was anticipated for the 1980's, they immediately discerned the writing on the wall.

The future of Arab-Israeli relations is affected by the manner in which the Arabs' crisis since the June war is evolving. Six years of frustration in attempts at getting the international community to recover, as before, their losses in that war and their military impotence were beginning to threaten the Arabs' confidence, when the energy crisis and the October war suddenly lifted it to perhaps unprecedented heights. They finally can see the beginning of the end of Zionism. Yet with all their ascendancy the Arabs still require others to do their work for them. The enormous wealth that buoys them must be extorted from the creativity and productivity of others, for they have hardly any themselves. Lacking the capacity to wage a war of movement, as before, they cannot conquer the foe, but bleed him in extravagant waste, expecting one superpower to threaten him with direct intervention and the other to restrain him from crushing them. Hence, the imperative of international diplomacy, mediators, and peacemakers.

The drift of international diplomacy is to spare the Arabs the agony of a serious reappraisal of their posture toward Israel. It is founded on the peculiar proposition that one creates the greatest departure from previous, undesirable conditions in the Middle East by reproducing them as nearly as possible, that one moves forward by turning the clock back. Its nostrum for all ills has all along been to force Israel to give up vital territory for empty promises—and after a quarter of a century of application, the vaunted Kissingerian breakthrough was to discover it anew. The greater the success of international diplomacy in imposing its ideas on the peacemaking process, the greater the likelihood of the old patterns to prevail in future. The more nearly satisfied the Arabs will be with their achievement in "eliminating the traces of aggression," the greater will be the vindication of their struggle, the less urgent will become the need for its sober reconsideration. Why cease playing a game in which one never really loses, for

losses are always restored by diplomatic referees, and need win but once for final triumph? The greater the involvement of third parties in peacemaking—mediators, great powers, international organizations—the less the need for Arabs to really face up to Israel, the stronger their conviction that they indeed face a factitious phenomenon, to be handled, like the pest, from a safe distance, through foreign manipulation, not a partner worthy of national coexistence.
ner worthy of national coexistence.

Although the Arab-Israeli conflict is unlike any other in many respects, we are not entirely without models for its future course. The Indo-Pakistani conflict, starting at about the same time, and involving also incompatibility of claims, insofar as India viewed Pakistan's pretention to Islamic unity as a threat to Indian national unity, would appear as an adequate parallel. But unlike the Arab-Israeli conflict, the antagonists in the Indian subcontinent were more nearly matched in military and diplomatic power and, more important, accepted each other's existence as sovereign states; neither severe culture gap nor anti-West animus separated them. Their relationship from the beginning was, moreover, marked by such diplomatic and economic intercourse as cannot be expected to govern Arab-Israeli relations even in the event of peaceful agreement based on Israeli withdrawal from conquered territory: formal diplomatic relations, trade, cooperation within regional and other international organizations, etc. Yet the record of the past quarter century does not inspire sanguine hopes for the future of conflicts similar to the Indo-Pakistani, for at least three major military confrontations between India and Pakistan were reckoned up to 1972. These hostilities involved antagonists whose relationship was from the first better than the relationship likely to be established between Israel and the Arabs, if they were to conclude a peaceful agreement tomorrow.

Resolution of conflict in the Middle East, for so long as Jews insist on sovereignty and Arabs reject it, clearly cannot flow from compromises over territory, water rights, refugees, or semantics. Compromise under these circumstances may actually have the opposite effect from that usually anticipated. The real tragedy in the Middle East is not the conflict, bad as it is, as many think, but the rigid determination of the rest of the world to meddle and aggravate an already sad situation there, by forcing upon it the nostrum of compromising the uncompromisable. Resolution of conflict in the Middle East, if it is to come, must come despite the good efforts of the foreign peacemakers.

Assuming that the Jews will successfully maintain their sovereignty, the Arabs will be left to live a way of life founded on contradictory principles: on a moral commitment to the demise of the outrage and on the imperative to order one's existence as though there is no chance of fulfilling that commitment. In order to resolve the contradiction between the two, apart from compartmentalization and other devices, a mechanism frequently resorted to in similar circumstances in history might be resorted to here as well, namely messianic or millenarian expectations, beliefs in redemption from without.[37] While orthodox Islam (as opposed to Christianity) has not been congenial to millenarian movements, such movements have in the past gained considerable momentum on its fringes, most notably in the form of the Sudanese Mahdiya in the late nineteenth century, but also in Morocco earlier, and elsewhere.[38] We may actually be witnessing at this time incipient messianism, in both active and passive variants; the latter may be disguised as a form of moderation, the former may be represented by aspects of the *fedayeen* movement. In passive messianism redemption cannot be doubted, but is transported into the indefinite future; even if it is slow in coming, one must not despair, but neither need one consider its eventuality seriously when managing one's affairs from day to day. The familiar and reassuring analogy of Israel and the Crusades in the Arab world would seem to contain the seed of such defiant acquiescence to the intolerable. Active messianism tends toward brevity and explosiveness; there are visions of instantaneous apocalypse, of redemption by monstrous destructiveness, not a withdrawal from history, or its indefinite protraction and postponement, but insistence on its immediate fulfillment by any means. Disappointment may heighten fanaticism still more in such movements, to the point of suicidal fervor, at least for a while; the tendency afterward is to engender religious sectarianism. The *fedayeen* movement, with visions of utter redemption by purgatory, would seem to belong in this category; and if it does, much terrible, and futile, outrage yet may lie in store for sorely tried Arabs and Jews and even others.[39]

One of the oldest ideas in the burgeoning literature and controversy on Arab-Jewish relations may yet contain the seed of a formal resolution of the conflict. This is the idea of confederation, which has in one form or another been brought to the fore from the beginning of the confrontation, first mainly by Jews, but lately also by Arabs. Its appeal for Jews derived from the widespread myth of the Golden Age of fraternity and partnership of Muslims and Jews, the idea of confederation appearing in this context as a return to normalcy, marking an end to strife. Its appeal for Arabs was founded on a more accurate reading of the Muslim-Jewish past. By confederation Arabs understood spontaneously some variation on the old *millet* system, meant to assure their political primacy in the last resort; for the idea connotes a linkage of some Jewish autonomy to Muslim overlordship. But adapted to the reality of modern Palestine, even several decades ago, this would have implied, not a meek Jewish religious community, but a politically assertive *Yishuv*, in effect a state within a state, a nation merely acknowledging nominal Arab overlordship. Hence, those Arabs who, like Abdallah of Transjordan, reckoned that efforts at crushing the Jews were more wisely spent at exploiting them peacefully were likely to entertain ideas of confederation with them. Why strain with truculence, when one can harness it? The *Yishuv* had the power with which to rule a great empire (the Fertile Crescent was his favorite design), while *he* had the power to legitimize it in the Arab world, as long as the Jews acknowledged him nominal master. Islamic tradition had always cherished gentle exploitation of the subjects' services. "Significant of this situation is the title borne by the Jewish doctor of a later Muslim ruler of Egypt who was called al-Haqir an-Nafi, the Despised and Useful One."[40]

But Islamic tradition insists also on the severe chastisement of rebel *dhimmis*, protected ones. As long as Arab opinion tends to view coercion of the Jews as possible, ideas of confederation remain weak in its realm; only the creeping fear that the Jews' political achievement may, indeed, be irreversible would give them strength. Within some form of federal union, there may be found the last opportunity for the assertion of Arab ascendancy over them, however nominal. But time does not stand still on the other side; President Bourguiba of Tunisia, who has urged a federation between Israel and her Arab neighbors as the "only positive solution" to the Middle East conflict, understood that the longer the Jews have occasion to practice sovereignty, the less likely they are to renounce any part of it, though apparently still trusting that they will ultimately shed the unnatural, for them, status.[41] The generational change among Israelis indeed produces a growing shift to statism, or *memlachtiut*, an attachment to sovereignty, pragmatic and power-oriented, and away from the classic Zionism, which was earlier amenable to less politically assertive objectives for the movement, such as a merely cultural home for the Jewish people.[42] Characteristically the drift of Arab opinion is to perceive this shift in Israeli opinion in accordance with wishful thinking and in complete opposition to ascertainable fact. And in this they get encouragement from friends abroad, some of whom, incredibly, speak even now of the future solution of the Middle East conflict in terms of dissolving the Jewish state into lots of refugees, to be dispersed through international charity in new countries of immigration.[43] So what may now be attainable in reality is only a most superficial pretense of Arab primacy in some loose Middle Eastern confederation. But if the past is prologue, even this may well be what the Arabs ignore only to clamor for it when no longer available.

Notes

CHAPTER ONE

1. See especially John G. Stoessinger, *Nations in Darkness: China, Russia, America* (New York: Random House, 1971) and Ole R. Holsti, "Cognitive Dynamics and Images of the Enemy: Dulles and Russia," *Enemies in Politics*, eds. David J. Finlay *et al.*, Chicago: Rand McNally, 1967.

2. Kenneth E. Boulding, "National Images and International Systems," *Comparative Foreign Policy: Theoretical Essays*, ed. Wolfram F. Hanrieder (New York: David McKay, 1971), p. 91.

3. Rony E. Gabbay, *A Political Study of the Arab-Jewish Conflict: The Arab Refugee Problem (A Case Study)* (Geneva: E. Droz, 1959), p. 30.

4. The author is Dr. Ismail Sabri Abdullah. Cited in Nissim Rejwan, "Impact of June War on Arab Intellectuals," *New Outlook*, Vol. 14, No. 8 (October-November, 1971), p. 26.

5. This model was suggested by Don Peretz in "Israel and the Arab Nations," *Journal of International Affairs*, Vol. 19, No. 1 (1965), p. 101.

6. George Sternlieb, reported in The New York *Times*, November 19, 1971, p. 49.

7. American Professors for Peace in the Middle East, *The Middle East in the Contemporary World*, Proceedings of the First Annual Conference, December, 1967 (New York, 1968), p. 80.

8. The American Friends Service Committee, *Search for Peace in the Middle East* (Philadelphia, 1970), p. 1.

9. Harry Hopkins, *Egypt the Crucible: The Unfinished Revolution of the Arab World* (London: Secker & Warburg, 1969), p. 468. (Italics added.)

10. See, for example, Michael Reisman, *The Art of the Possible: Diplomatic Alternatives in the Middle East* (Princeton: Princeton University Press, 1970), pp. 38, 62, 85, and *passim*.

11. Nahum Goldmann, "The Future of Israel," *Foreign Affairs*, Vol. 48, No. 3 (April, 1970), p. 458. He is more explicit in "The Failure of Israeli Foreign Policy," *New Outlook*, Vol. 13, No. 5 (June, 1970), p. 11 ("the Arab psychology").

12. J. Bowyer Bell, "Looking Through a Glass Darkly: Illusion and Reality in the Arab-Israeli Crisis," mimeographed paper, Center for International Affairs, Harvard University, June, 1970, p. 1.

13. Jon Kimche, *The Second Arab Awakening* (London: Thames and Hudson, 1970), pp. 209, 234–36.

14. *Op. cit.*, pp. 340, 273.

15. Kennett Love, *Sinai: The Twice-Fought War* (New York: McGraw-Hill, 1969).

16. Elmo Hutchison, *Violent Truce: A Military Observer Looks at the Arab-Israeli Conflict, 1951–1955* (New York: Devin-Adair, 1956), pp. 95, 120.

17. Arthur Lall, *The UN and the Middle East Crisis, 1967* (New York: Columbia University Press, 1970), p. 279.

18. *The News from the Middle East*, International Press Institute, Survey No. 3 (Zürich: IPI, 1954), p. 73 and *passim*.

19. *Time*, Vol. 96, No. 3 (July 20, 1970), p. 19.

20. George Kirk, "United States Policy in the Middle East: An Historical Approach," *Forces of Change in the Middle East*, ed. Maurice M. Roumani (Worcester, Mass.: Worcester State College, 1971), p. 6. See also John A. DeNovo, *American Interests and Policies in the Middle East 1900–1939* (Minneapolis: University of Minnesota Press, 1963); David H. Finnie, *Pioneers East: The Early American Experience in the Middle East* (Cambridge: Harvard University Press, 1967); Frank E. Manuel, *The Realities of American-Palestine Relations* (Washington: Public Affairs Press, 1949).

21. Elie Kedourie, *The Chatham House Version and Other Middle Eastern Studies* (London: Weidenfeld and Nicolson, 1970), pp. 2–3. The chapter from which this quotation is drawn had previously been published in *Commentary*, Vol. 25, No. 1 (January, 1958), as "Western Illusions About the Middle East."

22. The roster of officers as per listing in *Middle East Journal*, Vol. 25, No. 2 (Spring, 1971); the essential source of biographical data is *Who's Who in America*, for which data are supplied by the subjects themselves.

23. Sources for the following are the *Middle East Studies Association Roster of Fellows*, October, 1971; and Seymour Martin Lipset and Everett Carl Ladd, Jr., "Jewish Academics in the United States: Their Achievements, Culture and Politics," *American Jewish Year Book* (New York: The American Jewish Committee, 1971), p. 96 and *passim*.

24. Joseph Kraft, "Those Arabists in the State Department," *The New York Times Magazine* (November 7, 1971).

25. *American Interests in the Middle East* (Washington: The Middle East Institute, 1969), p. 6.

26. Don Peretz, "The Coming Decade in the Middle East: A Symposium, Part II," *Interplay*, Vol. 3, No. 15 (December, 1970), p. 46.

27. From an editorial, "The Quaker Way," *Christianity and Society*, Vol. 15, No. 1 (Winter, 1949–50), p. 6.

28.   Hugh Davis Graham and Ted Robert Gurr, *Violence in America: Historical and Comparative Perspectives,* Vol. I (Washington: U.S. Government Printing Office, 1969), p. xii.

29.   Harry Eckstein, "Introduction. Toward the Theoretical Study of Internal War," *Internal War: Problems and Approaches,* ed. Harry Eckstein (Princeton: Princeton University Press, 1964), p. 1.

30.   Nora Beloff, "The Kiss-and-Make-Up Delusion," *Encounter,* Vol. 30, No. 2 (February, 1968), p. 36.

CHAPTER TWO

1.   The New York *Times,* March 14, 1923, p. 8.

2.   The New York *Times,* March 11, 1924, p. 7.

3.   The New York *Times,* December 4, 1923, p. 21.

4.   The New York *Times,* September 11, 1923, p. 36.

5.   The New York *Times,* October 29, 1923, p. 10.

6.   Cited in Amos Elon, *The Israelis: Founders and Sons* (New York: Holt, Rinehart and Winston, 1971), pp. 149–50.

7.   Yaacov Ro'i, "The Zionist Attitude to the Arabs 1908–1914," *Middle Eastern Studies,* Vol. 4, No. 3 (April, 1968), p. 206; see also pp. 224 *ff.*

8.   Fred M. Gottheil, "Arab Immigration Into Pre-State Israel: 1922–1931," University of Illinois, College of Commerce and Business Administration, 1971 (mimeo).

9.   Ro'i, *op. cit.,* pp. 203–4.

10.   Elon, *op. cit.,* p. 155; italics in the source.

11.   Colonel R. Meinertzhagen, *Middle East Diary, 1917–1956* (London: Cresset, 1959), p. 7.

12.   *New Palestine,* Vol. 1, No. 23 (June 17, 1921), p. 2.

13.   Kenneth W. Bilby, *New Star in the Near East* (Garden City: Doubleday, 1950), p. 88.

14.   *Siege in the Hills of Hebron: The Battle of the Etzion Bloc,* ed. Dov Knohl (New York: Thomas Yoseloff, 1958), pp. 53, 38, 162, 167, 340.

15.   Dov Joseph, *The Faithful City: The Siege of Jerusalem, 1948* (New York: Simon and Schuster, 1960), p. 190.

16.   *Underground to Palestine* (New York: Boni and Gaer, 1946), pp. 238–39.

17.   See Morroe Berger, *The Arab World Today* (New York: Doubleday, 1964), pp. 272–76.

18.   See Harry Eckstein, *A Theory of Stable Democracy,* Center of International Studies, Research Monograph No. 10 (Princeton, Princeton University Press, 1961).

19. Bernard Lewis, "The Pre-Islamic Jews," *Judaism*, Vol. 17, No. 4 (Fall, 1968), p. 403.

20. Ro'i, *op. cit.*, pp. 214–15.

21. See especially George E. Kirk, " 'The Arab Awakening' Reconsidered," Appendix II, *A Short History of the Middle East: From the Rise of Islam to Modern Times* (New York: Frederick A. Praeger, 1964).

22. Elon's *The Israelis*, cited earlier, is an illustration of these orientations.

23. Max I. Dimont, *Jews, God, and History: A Modern Interpretation of a Four-Thousand Year Story* (New York: Simon and Schuster, 1962), pp. 208–9. For a similar treatment by an Israeli writer, see Aharon Cohen, *Israel and the Arab World* (New York: Funk and Wagnalls, 1970), especially Chapter One, "Initial Encounters in the Distant Past."

24. Gottheil, *op. cit.*, pp. 1–2.

25. As cited in Elon, *op. cit.*, p. 161.

26. Dov Joseph, *op. cit.*, p. 194. See also *The Memoirs of Sir Ronald Storrs* (a high official in early British Palestine) (New York: G.P. Putnam's Sons, 1937), p. 393. The *Mufti*, a high religious official, was head of the Arab national movement.

27. Netanel Lorch, *The Edge of the Sword: Israel's War of Independence, 1947–49* (New York: G.P. Putnam's Sons, 1961), p. 48.

28. *Palestine Disturbances in May, 1921* (London [Command 1540], 1921), pp. 52–54.

29. *Ibid.*, p. 12; Ro'i, *op. cit.*, p. 231.

30. Meinertzhagen, *op. cit.*, p. 85.

31. Command 5479, pp. 50, 68–69, 370.

32. Command 1540, pp. 13, 43.

33. This translation from Herzl's *Altneuland* is from Elon, *op. cit.*, p. 161.

34. Erskine B. Childers, "Palestine: The Broken Triangle," *Journal of International Affairs*, Vol. 19, No. 1 (1965), p. 87.

35. For a typical early Zionist view, see N.I. Stone, "The Arab Question: Our Present and Future Policy," *New Palestine*, July 22, 1921.

36. Rose Zeitlin, *Henrietta Szold: Record of a Life* (New York: Dial, 1952), pp. 107–8.

37. Joseph B. Schechtman, *The United States and the Jewish State Movement. The Crucial Decade: 1939–1949* (New York: Herzl Press, 1966), p. 99.

38. Elon, *op. cit.*, p. 168.

39. Esco Foundation for Palestine, *Palestine: A Study of Jewish, Arab, and British Policies* (New Haven: Yale University Press, 1952), p. 571.

40. *Ibid.*, pp. 587–92.

41. Richard Crossman, *Palestine Mission: A Personal Record* (New York: Harper and Brothers, 1947), p. 148.

42. Margaret Larkin, *The Six Days of Yad-Mordechai* (Tel Aviv: Ma'aracheth, Israel Defense Forces Publishing House, 1965), pp. 48, 210, 268.

43. See, for instance, *New Outlook*, Vol. 13, No. 4 (May, 1970), p. 56.

44. Menachem Begin, leader of the *Irgun*, military arm of the movement, in secret testimony before the United Nations Special Committee on Palestine (1947), in Itzhak Gurion, *Triumph on the Gallows* (New York: Brit Trumpeldor of America, 1950), pp. 176–77.

45. *Ibid.*, p. 177.

46. Crossman, *Palestine Mission*, p. 149.

47. Anny Latour, *The Resurrection of Israel* (Cleveland: The World Publishing Company, 1968), pp. 185–86.

48. Although obviously partial to Zionism, Colonel Meinertzhagen's detailed exposition of British instigation and complicity at the highest level in Palestine in 1920 stands unchallenged. The information was obtained by an intelligence unit under his command and passed on to his superior, General Allenby (Meinertzhagen, *op. cit.*, pp. 56, 82).

49. Schechtman, *op. cit.*, pp. 76–77. See also, Menachem Begin, *The Revolt: Story of the Irgun* (Tel Aviv: Hadar, 1964), p. 296.

50. Ben-Gurion thus told the *Knesset*, Israel's national legislature, on November 7, 1956, "We had no dispute with the people of Egypt. It was Nasser who had brought catastrophe upon them by inciting them to war against us." David Ben-Gurion, *Israel: Years of Challenge* (New York: Holt, Rinehart and Winston, 1963), p. 133.

51. See especially, Ben Halpern, "Zionist Conceptions of Sovereignty," Chapter Two, *The Idea of the Jewish State* (Cambridge: Harvard University Press, 1969).

52. Folke Bernadotte, *To Jerusalem* (London: Hodder and Stoughton, 1951), pp. 8 *ff.*

53. Cited in Schechtman, *op. cit.*, p. 86.

CHAPTER THREE

1. The paraphrases refer to works by Reinhold Niebuhr, Denis Brogan, and Eric Hoffer.

2. Thus, the *Ichud* notable Haim Kalvarisky, cited in Gabbay, *A Political Study of the Arab-Jewish Conflict*, p. 33.

3. Michael Brecher, "Ben Gurion and Sharett: Contrasting Israeli Images of 'the Arabs,' " *New Middle East*, No. 18 (March 1970), p. 33. An elaboration of this proposition is contained in his *The Foreign Policy System of Israel: Setting, Images, Process* (New Haven: Yale University Press, 1972).

4. Susan Hattis, "The Bi-National State and the Challenge of History," *New Middle East*, No. 35 (August, 1971), p. 26.

5. *The Times Literary Supplement* (London), October 23, 1970, p. 1209.

6. "Dayan and Ruppin: A Soldier Reflects on Peace Hopes," *The Jerusalem Post Weekly*, September 30, 1968, p. 6.

7. As cited in Elon, *op. cit.*, p. 179; a somewhat different translation appears in the above article.

8. "Dayan and Ruppin: A Soldier Reflects on Peace Hopes," *The Jerusalem Post Weekly*, September 30, 1968, p. 7.

9. Eisa al-Sapri argued in 1937 that the agreement was a forgery; in 1938 George Antonius explained that Faisal was induced by Lawrence to sign a document he did not understand.

10. Joseph, *The Faithful City*, pp. 116–17.

11. Command 5479, p. 145.

12. Lukasz Hirszowicz, *The Third Reich and the Arab East* (London: Routledge and Kegan Paul, 1966), p. 37.

13. Palestine Partition Commission, *Report* (London, [Command 5854], 1938), p. 265.

14. *Time*, Vol. 97, No. 15 (April 12, 1971), p. 31.

15. Charles Yost, "Israel and the Arabs: The Myths that Block Peace," *Atlantic*, Vol. 223, No. 1 (January, 1969).

16. Elon's *The Israelis*, one of the most popular books on Israel in many years, distorts the situation both explicitly and implicitly (see especially p. 260 and *passim*). For examples of acceptance of the myth, see the reviews of *The Israelis* and *Don't Ask Me If I Love* (by Amos Kollek) in *National Jewish Monthly*, Vol. 85, No. 10 (June, 1971), pp. 50–54. In an advertisement for the Kollek book, James A. Michener is quoted, among others: "The American reader will derive from this book a vital insight into what the typical young Israeli is thinking these days. . . ." (p. 52).

17. Command 5479, p. 110. Italics in the source.

18. *Op. cit.*, p. 244.

19. Hadley Cantril, *The Pattern of Human Concerns* (New Brunswick: Rutgers University Press, 1965), p. 156.

20. Cited in Brecher, *The Foreign Policy System of Israel*, p. 283.

21. Cantril, *op. cit.*, pp. 308, 99–118.

22. Charles D. Cremeans, *The Arabs and the World: Nasser's Arab Nationalist Policy* (New York: Frederick A. Praeger, 1963), pp. 187 *ff*.

23. The Israel Institute of Applied Social Research, *Popular Reactions to Current Problems* (Hebrew), Jerusalem (June, 1971), p. 8.

24. S.D. Goitein, "Arab Nationalism—As Viewed From Israel," *The Arab Nation*, William Sands, ed. (Washington: Middle East Institute, 1961), p. 65.

25. *Ibid.*, pp. 68–69.

26. Eliahu Elath, "Arabs and Jews in Israel," *New Outlook*, Vol. 11, No. 2 (February, 1968), p. 29 and *passim*. Urging total Israeli withdrawal from

occupied territory (except for East Jerusalem), David Ben-Gurion envisaged peace between Arabs and Jews, "as in the time when we were all sons of Abraham" (The New York *Times*, April 20, 1969, p. 2).

27.   Peretz Merhav, "Is De-Zionization the Answer?" *New Outlook*, Vol. 12, No. 2 (February, 1969), p. 31. Emphasis added.

28.   Thus, for late reaffirmation of the thesis of the spoiling of inherent Arab-Jewish harmony by local and foreign incitement, see *The Jewish Quarterly*, Vol. 16, No. 1 (Spring, 1969), especially pp. 27–30; also *New Outlook* (special issue, *To Make War Or Make Peace*), Vol. 12, Nos. 5–6 (June, July, August, 1969), especially p. 163.

29.   The excerpt is from the essay "Meaning of Homeland," first published in the Israeli press, an English version of which appeared in *New Outlook*, Vol. 10, No. 8 (December, 1967), and reprinted in part in *The Jewish Quarterly*, Vol. 16, No. 1 (Spring, 1968). Citation from p. 32. Italics in the source.

30.   The confidence of the military in their ability to rout the Arab armies seems not to have been impaired even in the crisis.

31.   See Simon N. Herman, *Israelis and Jews: The Continuity of an Identity* (New York: Random House, 1970).

32.   Samuel Merlin, *The Search for Peace in the Middle East: The Story of President Bourguiba's Comparison for a Negotiated Peace Between Israel and the Arab States* (South Brunswick: Thomas Yoseloff, 1968), pp. 234 *ff.*, presents the prewar lineup, strikingly similar to that obtaining after the war.

33.   Yael Dayan, "Security, Yes, Peace, No," *Hadassah* magazine, Vol. 49, No. 10 (June, 1968), p. 4.

34.   At a symposium at Hebrew University, in *Israel* magazine, Vol. 2, No. 8 (May, 1970), pp. 63, 69.

35.   *Op. cit.*, p. 4.

36.   Martin Lakin *et al.*, *Arab and Jew in Israel: Case Study in Human Relations Training Approach to Conflict* (New York: American Academic Association for Peace in the Middle East, 1969), p. 122.

37.   The Israel Institute of Applied Social Research, *Popular Reactions to Current Problems*, pp. iv, 62.

38.   The Israel Institute of Applied Social Research, *Telephone Poll of August 2–3, 1970* (Hebrew), Jerusalem (August, 1970), p. 2.

39.   The Israel Institute of Applied Social Research, *Attitudes Toward Policy, Security and Public Morale* (Hebrew), Jerusalem (May, 1970), p. 21.

40.   The Israel Institute of Applied Social Research, *Telephone Poll of August 2–3, 1970*, p. 2.

41.   The Israel Institute of Applied Social Research, *Attitudes Toward Policy, Security and Public Morale*, p. 9.

42.   The Israel Institute of Applied Social Research, *Popular Reactions to Current Problems*, p. 47.

43.   *Ibid.*, p. 49.

44. *Ibid.*, p. iv.

45. *Ibid.*, p. 66.

46. *Ibid.*, p. 65.

47. *Ibid.*, p. 54.

48. *Ibid.*

49. *Ibid.*

50. *Ibid.*, p. 59.

51. The Israel Institute of Applied Social Research, *Attitudes Toward Policy, Security and Public Morale,* pp. 7–8. See also Alan Arian, "Stability and Change in Israeli Public Opinion and Politics," *Public Opinion Quarterly*, Vol. 35, No. 1 (Spring, 1971), pp. 24 *ff.*

52. Georges R. Tamarin, *The Leap Forwards—Into the Past: An Essay on Middle Eastern Irrationalism: Mysticism and Activism as Sources of the Israeli Annexationist Movement,* Institute for Socio-Psychological Research, Giwatayim, 1971 (mimeo).

53. Merlin, *op. cit.*, pp. 237–38.

54. Melford E. Spiro, *Kibbutz: Venture in Utopia* (New York: Schocken, 1970), pp. 187, 189.

55. Haim Darin-Drabkin, in *New Outlook*, Vol. 12, No. 3 (March-April, 1969), p. 9.

56. See, for example, Danah Zohar, "Israeli Left in Disarray as Labour Moves to Right," *New Middle East,* Nos. 42–43 (March-April, 1972).

57. Sol Stern, "The Russian Jews Wonder Whether Israel Is Really Ready for Them," *The New York Times Magazine* (April 16, 1972), p. 98. See also *Hadassah* magazine, Vol. 53, No. 9 (May, 1972), p. 24.

58. Uri Avneri, "Fighting for Peace: The Silent Minority," *New Middle East,* Nos. 42–43 (March-April, 1972).

59. Ande Manners, *Poor Cousins* (New York: Coward, McCann & Geoghegan, 1972). p. 68.

60. Tamarin, *The Leap Forwards—Into the Past,* p. 32.

61. *Ibid.*, p. 79.

62. *Ibid.*, p. 80.

63. *Time,* Vol. 97, No. 15 (April 12, 1971), p. 31.

64. *Ibid.*, p. 32. Contemporary attitudes of Israeli Jews toward Arabs are discussed in Tamarin, *Two Essays on Jewish-Arab Relations,* Institute for Socio-Psychological Research, Giwatayim, 1972 (mimeo), pp. 69–80, 117, and *passim.*

65. See Ehud Ben-Ezer's survey of modern Hebrew literature, in *Keshet,* Vol. 10, No. 4 (Summer, 1968).

66. See Elon, *op. cit.*, pp. 267 *ff.*

67. Yehoshafat Harkabi, "Reflections on our Policy in the Conflict," *Maariv*, May 10, 1970, mimeo. Trans. Y. Karmi.

68. Shimon Shamir, "The Myth of Arab Intransigence," *Israel and the Palestinians: Reflections on the Clash of Two National Movements*, ed. Shlomo Avineri (New York: St. Martin's Press, 1971), pp. 29–30.

69. The Israel Institute of Applied Social Research, *Popular Reactions to Current Problems*, p. iv.

70. For example, in Jacob Talmon, "Israel Among the Nations," *Commentary*, Vol. 45, No. 6 (June, 1968), especially pp. 49 *ff.*; or, in the Arieli (pp. 83–84) and Yalin-Mor (p. 192) contributions in *New Outlook*, Vol. 12, Nos. 5–6 (June, July, August, 1969).

71. *Newsweek*, Vol. 74, No. 13 (September 29, 1969), p. 56.

72. Erich and Rael Jean Isaac, "The Siren Song of Peace: Israel's Dissenting Intellectuals," *Conservative Judaism*, Vol. 26, No. 3 (Spring, 1972).

73. *Israel* magazine, Vol. 2, No. 8 (May, 1970), pp. 74, 76.

74. From Shmuel B'ari's review of Elon's *The Israelis*, in *New Outlook*, Vol. 14, No. 8 (October-November, 1971), p. 59.

75. Professor Shalom Abarbanel, see *Histadrut Foto News*, Vol. 31, No. 4 (May-June, 1974), p. 9.

76. Amos Oz; see *Hadassah* magazine, Vol. 55, No. 8 (April, 1974), p. 37.

77. Cited in James R. Adams, "Amos Oz; Disillusioned Dove," *Crossroads*, Vol. 5, No. 3 (July, 1974), p. 3.

78. The New York *Times*, August 15, 1974, p. 2.

79. The New York *Post*, November 9, 1973, p. 31.

80. Israel Institute of Applied Social Research data, cited in *Time*, Vol. 102, No. 24 (December 10, 1973), p. 58.

81. Survey by the above institute, reported in The New York *Times*, April 19, 1973, p. 19.

82. Bernard Reich, *Israel and the Occupied Territories*, a study prepared for the Department of State under its External Research Program (August, 1973), p. 36.

83. *Middle East Intelligence Survey*, Vol. 1, No. 19 (January 1, 1974), p. 151.

CHAPTER FOUR

1. Nadav Safran, "N.K., K.G.B., or C.I.A.? Khrushchev's Reminiscences on the Middle East," *New Middle East*, No. 30 (March, 1971), p. 45.

2. *Congressional Record—Senate*, August 24, 1970, p. S14038.

3. See Uri Ra'anan, "The Changing American-Soviet Strategic Balance: Some Political Implications," memorandum prepared at the request of the Subcommittee on National Security and International Operations of

the Committee on Government Operations, United States Senate (Washington: U.S. Government Printing Office, 1972), pp. 9–10; "Arab 'Moderates' and the 'American Fallacy,'" *Congress Bi-Weekly*, Vol. 38, No. 6, (April 30, 1971), p. 3; Fred Charles Iklé: *How Nations Negotiate* (New York: Harper and Row, 1964), pp. 238–53.

4.   Lyndon B. Johnson, *The Vantage Point: Perspectives of the Presidency 1963–1969* (New York: Holt, Rinehart and Winston, 1972), p. 484.

5.   Arthur Lall, *The UN and the Middle East Crisis.*

6.   Charles W. Yost, *"The Arab-Israeli War: How it Began,"* *Foreign Affairs*, Vol. 46, No. 2 (January, 1968), p. 304.

7.   Charles W. Yost, *The Insecurity of Nations: International Relations in the Twentieth Century* (New York: Frederick A. Praeger, 1968), p. 21.

8.   Charles W. Yost, "Israel and the Arabs: The Myths that Block Peace," *Atlantic*. Vol. 223. No. 1 (January, 1969).

9.   The term in this sense is used in Hans J. Morgenthau, *Politics Among Nations: The Struggle for Power and Peace* (New York: Alfred A. Knopf, 1960), p. 5.

10.   Thus, Michael Reisman, Roger Fisher, Gidon Gottlieb, and many others.

11.   Robert Alter, "Rhetoric and the Arab Mind," *Commentary*, Vol. 46, No. 4 (October, 1968), p. 61.

12.   As late as February 16, 1970, the *Times* termed his reported backing of *fedayeen* aims as "apparent endorsement" and described it as "extraordinary" (p. 36).

13.   The New York *Times*, March 16, 1972, p. 10. Editorial comments below appeared on p. 46.

14.   Compare The New York *Times*, June 12, 1971, p. 28, and July 23, 1971, p. 32; also March 23, 1972, p. 42.

15.   In the *Times* editorial comments (December 15, 1971, p. 34; January 20, 1972, p. 42), the issue appeared as Israel's alleged desire for just "security arrangement," the deadlock being represented as merely rhetorical.

16.   Nora Beloff, "The Kiss-and-Make-Up Delusion," *Encounter*, Vol. 30, No. 2 (February, 1968), p. 37.

17.   Hearings before the Subcommittee on National Security and International Operations of the Committee on Government Operations, United States Senate (Washington, D.C.: U.S. Government Printing Office, March 17, 1971), pp. 92–93.

18.   International Press Institute Survey No. 3 (1954), p. 73.

19.   Thus, Moshe Menuhin, "A Tribute to Count Folke Bernadotte," *Arab World*, Vol. 14, No. 9 (September, 1968), p. 4.

20.   Thus, letter by Ragaei Mallakh, The New York *Times*, August 11, 1967, p. 30.

21.   The New York *Times*, December 8, 1971, p. 10.

22. The New York *Times*, April 16, 1970, p. 10.

23. The New York *Times*, November 27, 1971, p. 1.

24. Lieutenant General E.L.M. Burns, *Between Arab and Israeli* (New York: Ivan Obolensky, 1962), p. 177.

25. Eric Rouleau, Jean-Francis Held, Jean and Simonne Lacouture, *Israël et les Arabes: Le 3ᵉ Combat* (Paris: Éditions du Seuil, 1967), p. 44.

26. Bernard Lewis, "Semites and Anti-Semites: Race in the Arab-Israel Conflict," *Survey*, Vol. 17, No. 2 (Spring, 1971), p. 179.

27. On the characteristic modes of violence of this genus of warfare, see 1) Harry Holbert Turney-High, *Primitive War: Its Practices and Concepts* (Columbia: University of South Carolina Press, 1949).
2) *Jewish Observer and Middle East Review*, Vol. 18, No. 35 (August 29, 1968), p. 11.
3) The New York *Times*, March 4, 1969, p. 18.
4) Sources on Arab contemporary practices of mutilation in its various forms are usually foreign observers. On Palestine: J. Bowyer Bell, *The Long War: Israel and the Arabs Since 1946* (Englewood Cliffs, N.J.: Prentice Hall, 1969), pp. 79, 84; R.M. Graves, *Experiment in Anarchy* (London: Victor Gollancz, 1949), pp. 133, 157, 167–68; Bilby, *New Star in the Near East*, p. 30; John Roy Carlson, *Cairo to Damascus* (New York: Alfred A. Knopf, 1951), pp. 172, 347; Gerold Frank, *The Deed*, (New York: Simon and Schuster, 1963), pp. 39, 69.

On Egypt and Syria: Brigadier Peter Young, *The Israeli Campaign, 1967* (London: William Kimber, 1962), p. 89.

On Iraq and South Arabia: Erik Verg, *Halbmond um den Davidstern: Die Arabische Welt und Israel* (Berlin: Ullstein, 1964), pp. 94, 166, 171; Carl Mydans and Shelley Mydans, "The Violent Peace: A Report on Wars in the Postwar World" *Atlas*, Vol. 18, No. 5 (November, 1969), p. 32.

28. Richard Aldington, *Lawrence of Arabia: A Biographical Enquiry* (London: Collins, 1955), p. 306.

29. See, for instance, Clement Henry Moore, "On Theory and Practice Among Arabs," *World Politics*, Vol. 24, No. 1 (October, 1971).

30. Thus, in Burns, *op. cit.*, and Hutchison, *Violent Truce*.

31. See Rona Randall, *Jordan and the Holy Land* (London: Frederick Muller, 1968), esp. Ch. 14; Hutchison, *op. cit.*, pp. 31–32, 72–73, and esp. Ch. 17; Bilby, *op. cit.*, p. 13; Lieutenant Colonel Peter Young, *Bedouin Command: With the Arab Legion, 1953–1956* (London: William Kimber, 1956), pp. 16, 78.

32. In the account of one Briton a poor (wild-looking) Lebanese herdsman "had only one standard: that of a prince." John Sykes, *The Mountain Arabs: A Window on the Middle East* (London: Hutchinson, 1968), p. 211.

33. As Peter Young assumed command in 1953 of the Ninth Regiment of the Arab Legion he, as is customary, also took over a group of retainers and servants attached to the previous commander, James Wilson. "All of mine are in the Regiment," he said, "and will naturally become yours" (*Bedouin Command*, p. 16).

34.   See Erskine B. Childers, *The Road to Suez: A Study of Western-Arab Relations* (London: MacGibbon and Kee, 1962), p. 49; also note 63 below.

35.   S.D. Goitein, *Jews and Arabs: Their Contacts Through the Ages* (New York: Schocken, 1955), p. 16.

36.   *Op. cit.*, p. 89.

37.   *Ibid.*

38.   See T.R. Fyvel, "Reporter in Palestine—Sheean Looks Back," *New Middle East*, No. 19 (April, 1970).

39.   *Op. cit.*, p. 13.

40.   *Ibid.*, p. 151.

41.   Harry Levin, *I Saw the Battle of Jerusalem* (New York: Schocken Books, 1950), pp. 119–20.

42.   The New York *Times*, January 31, 1972, p. 7.

43.   Elon, *The Israelis,* p. 237.

44.   *Ibid.*, p. 309.

45.   Thus, Emanuel Feldman, in *The 28th of Iyar* (New York: Bloch Publishing Company, 1968).

46.   *Middle East Diary*, p. 362.

47.   C.R. Ashbee, *A Palestine Notebook, 1918–1923* (Garden City: Doubleday, Page and Company, 1923), pp. 106–8.

48.   V.D. Segre, *Israel: A Society in Transition* (London: Oxford University Press, 1971), p. 99.

49.   Thus, by the Peel Commission, 5479, p. 163.

50.   Latour, *The Resurrection of Israel,* p. 195.

51.   Bartley C. Crum, *Behind the Silken Curtain: A Personal Account of Anglo-American Diplomacy in Palestine and The Middle East* (New York: Simon and Schuster, 1947), p. 289.

52.   Richard H.S. Crossman, *A Nation Reborn: A Personal Report on the Roles Played by Weizmann, Bevin and Ben-Gurion in the Story of Israel* (New York: Atheneum, 1960), p. 56.

53.   *Op. cit.*, p. 88, for subsequent quotations.

54.   Schechtman, *The United States and the Jewish State Movement*, p. 90.

55.   Crossman, *A Nation Reborn*, p. 79, for this and subsequent quotations, also pp. 80–82.

56.   Arnold Hottinger, *The Arabs: Their History, Culture, and Place in the Modern World*, (Berkeley: University of California Press, 1963), pp. 237–40.

57.   *Palestine Mission*, p. 102.

58.   *Ibid.*, p. 103.

59.   *Ibid.*, pp. 33–34.

60. On frictions peculiar to relations with European Catholic diplomats, see Joseph, *The Faithful City*, pp. 272 *ff*.

61. Oscar I. Janowksy, *Middle Eastern Affairs*, Vol. 4, No. 11 (November, 1953), p. 372.

62. For example, Major General Carl von Horn's *Soldiering for Peace* (New York: David McKay, 1967).

63. George W. Ball, "Nixon's Appointment in Peking—Is This Trip Necessary?" *The New York Times Magazine* (February 13, 1972), pp. 50–51.

64. For instance, Kenneth T. Young, *Negotiating with the Chinese Communists: The United States Experience, 1953–1967* (New York: McGraw-Hill, 1968); also Ikle, *op. cit.*

65. John C. Haughey, "A Vindication of the Truth of Islam," The New York *Times*, December 11, 1971, p. 31.

66. George Kirk, in Roumani, *Forces of Change in the Middle East*, p. 6.

67. Berger, *The Arab World Today*, pp. 141–42.

68. Luigi Barzini, *The Italians* (New York: Bantam Books), p. 236.

69. *Ibid.*, p. 349.

70. *Ibid.*, p. 350.

71. *Ibid.*, p. 236.

72. *Ibid.*, p. 105.

73. Marshall Frady, "An American Innocent in the Middle East," *Harper's*, Vol. 241, No. 1445 (October, 1970), p. 75.

74. *Op. cit.*, p. 77.

75. Sania Hamady, *Temperament and Character of the Arabs* (New York: Twayne, 1960), pp. 67–68.

76. *Ibid.*, p. 66.

77. Nissim Rejwan, "Culture and Personality: Building the New Egyptian Man," *New Middle East*, No. 41 (February, 1972), pp. 16–17.

78. J. Bowyer Bell, *The Myth of the Guerrilla: Revolutionary Theory and Malpractice* (New York: Alfred A. Knopf, 1971), p. 282.

79. Edward R.F. Sheehan, "Colonel Qadhafi—Libya's Mystical Revolutionary," *The New York Times Magazine* (February 6, 1972), p. 56.

80. *Ibid.*

81. Winston Burdett, *Encounter with the Middle East: An Intimate Report on What Lies Behind the Arab-Israeli Conflict* (New York: Atheneum, 1969), p. 20.

82. The New York *Times*, December 6, 1971, p. 14.

83. Burdett, *op. cit.*, p. 21.

84. Frady, *op. cit.*, p. 60.

85. An example is mentioned in Merlin, *The Search for Peace in the Middle East*, p. 314.

86.   *Time*, Vol. 97, No. 18 (May 3, 1971), p. 24.

87.   Walter Eytan, "To Cut the Gordian Knot—An Assessment of Israel's Foreign Policy and the Search for Genuine Peace," *New Middle East*, No. 36 (September, 1971), p. 17.

88.   See The New York *Times*, October 12, 1968, p. 3, and October 13, 1968, Section E, p. 5.

89.   Thus, Bertram Johansson, of *The Christian Science Monitor*, in conversation with Joel S. Bloom, cited in the latter's "The Middle East Crisis in *The Christian Science Monitor*," New York, Hunter College, 1969 (mimeo), p. 6.

90.   Amnon Rubinstein, "Why the Israelis Are Being Difficult," *The New York Times Magazine* (April 18, 1971), p. 114.

91.   Frady, *op. cit.*, pp. 76–77.

92.   Colonel Meinertzhagen, *Middle East Diary*, p. 163.

93.   Bilby, *op. cit.*, p. 88.

94.   Lester Velie, *Countdown in the Holy Land* (New York: Funk and Wagnalls, 1969), pp. 39–40.

95.   For some recent cases, see The New York *Times*, May 6, 1971, p. 8 (on Foreign Secretary Home); and May 6, 1971, p. 6 (on President Ceausescu); also, *To The Point*, Vol. 1, No. 4 (February 26, 1972), p. 13.

96.   *Time*, Vol. 95, No. 26 (June 29, 1970), p. 29.

97.   Frady, *op. cit.*, p. 77.

98.   *Der Spiegel*, Vol. 22, No. 37 (September 9, 1968), p. 123.

99.   *Survey*, Vol. 17, No. 2 (Spring, 1971), p. 179.

100.   *Op. cit.*, p. 21.

101.   Embassy of Israel, Washington, D.C., Policy Background, "How Radio Cairo Carried the Nasser Interview in *Time* magazine, May 16, 1969," May 22, 1969.

102.   King Hussein of Jordan, *Uneasy Lies the Head* (New York: Bernard Geiss, 1962), p. 234. Emphasis added.

CHAPTER FIVE

1.   Crum, *Behind the Silken Curtain*, p. 249.

2.   Marvin Kalb, on WCBS Radio (New York), May 2, 1971, 7:00 P.M.

3.   John Bagot Glubb, *The Great Arab Conquests* (London: Hodder and Stoughton, 1963), p. 317.

4.   Hottinger, *The Arabs*, p. 84.

5.   Inge Deutschkron, *Bonn and Jerusalem: The Strange Coalition* (Philadelphia: Chilton, 1970), p. 219.

6.   Walter Laqueur, *The Road to War 1967: The Origins of the Arab-Israel*

Conflict (London: Weidenfeld and Nicolson, 1968), pp. 309, 336.

7.   A large part of this output is meticulously analyzed in Yehoshafat Harkabi, *Arab Attitudes to Israel* (New York: Hart, 1972).

8.   Cecil A. Hourani, "The Moment of Truth," *Encounter*, Vol. 39, No. 5 (November, 1967).

9.   Bernadotte, *To Jerusalem*, p. 33.

10.   Verg, *Halbmond um den Davidstern*, p. 21. Trans. Gil Carl AlRoy.

11.   *Brief (Middle East Highlights)*, No. 5 (March 1–15, 1971), p. 2.

12.   Verg, *op. cit.*, p. 65. Trans. Gil Carl AlRoy.

13.   *New Star in the Near East*, p. 99.

14.   Merlin, *The Search for Peace in the Middle East*, p. 94.

15.   *Ibid.*, p. 103.

16.   Bernard Lewis, *The Middle East and the West* (New York: Harper and Row, 1966), p. 125.

17.   Dr. Ahmed Mounif Razzaz, cited in Merlin, *op. cit.*, p. 170.

18.   Dan Wakefield, "Incident in Jerusalem," *Commentary*, Vol. 41, No. 2 (February, 1966), pp. 50, 53. Emphasis in the source.

19.   The New York *Times*, June 26, 1967, p. 3.

20.   Merlin, *op. cit.*, pp. 37, 38, 41, 42, 47.

21.   Cited in Arnold M. Soloway *et al.*, *Truth and Peace in the Middle East: A Critical Analysis of the Quaker Report* (New York: Friendly House, 1971), p. 43.

22.   The New York *Times*, July 4, 1970, p. 5.

23.   Radio Cairo, April 10, 1968, as cited in Soloway *et al.*, *op. cit.*, p. 43.

24.   The New York *Times*, July 28, 1968, Section E, p. 14.

25.   Cited in Joseph Neyer, *Middle East Happenings, Colloquies, Images, Mythologies: A Response in Perspective to Some Current Positions* (New York: American Academic Association for Peace in the Middle East, 1971), p. 8.

26.   *Al-Ahram*, August 2, 1970, as cited in *Bulletin of the American Professors for Peace in the Middle East*, Vol. 1, No. 2 (May 19, 1971), p. 4.

27.   *Brief*, No. 5 (March 1–15, 1971), p. 2, for this and the following citation. The slightly different translation here appears in Neyer, *op. cit.*, p. 8.

28.   The New York *Times*, November 12, 1971, p. 9.

29.   The New York *Times*, January 14, 1972, p. 6.

30.   For the language of the statement, see the report from Washington, in The New York *Times*, August 24, 1971, p. 12; for the correspondent's report from Cairo, see the issue for September 2, 1971, p. 3.

31.   Arnaud de Borchgrave described this typical evasion an "unprecedented concession" (*Newsweek*, Vol. 77, No. 8 [February 22, 1971], p. 39; for the text of his talk with Sadat, see pp. 40–41).

32. The New York *Times*, April 7, 1972, p. 1.

33. An Egyptian official at the United Nations, in conversation with this writer, intimated that as many as eighteen years might intervene.

34. By Yost, October 25, 1971, p. 33; by Copeland, April 16, 1971, p. 37.

35. *Congressional Record—Senate,* August 24, 1970, p. S14032.

36. Joseph C. Harsch, of *The Christian Science Monitor,* in an exchange with a reader, in *Jewish Post and Opinion,* October 1, 1971, p. 1.

37. George Saunders, "Sadat's Inheritance: Remnants of a Half-Revolution," *National Jewish Monthly,* Vol. 85, No. 9 (May, 1971), p. 32.

38. The New York *Times,* October 29, 1971, p. 4.

39. The New York *Times,* July 4, 1970, p. 5.

40. For the text of the National Covenant, see Yehoshafat Harkabi, "The Position of the Palestinians in the Israeli-Arab Conflict and their National Covenant (1968)," *New York University Journal of International Law and Politics,* Vol. 3, No. 1 (Spring, 1970).

41. Yehoshafat Harkabi, "Liberation or Genocide?" *Transaction,* Vol. 7, Nos. 9–10 (July-August, 1970), p. 65.

42. In "The 'Liberated' State," *Maariv,* July 10, 1970, Harkabi cites such distortion by Yusif Sayigh, of the Palestine Liberation Organization in Beirut, in a letter in The *Times* of London (February 28, 1970), and another by Hisham Sharabi, in *Palestine and Israel: The Lethal Dilemma* (New York: Pegasus, 1969), p. 201.

43. *Transaction,* Vol. 7, Nos. 9–10 (July-August, 1970), p. 66.

44. Leonard Wolf, "Interview With a Fatah," *National Jewish Monthly,* Vol. 85, No. 8 (April, 1971), pp. 37–38, 44.

45. Arnold Hottinger, *10 Mal Nahost* (Munich: R. Piper, 1970), p. 414.

46. *Ibid.,* p. 415; translation by Gil Carl AlRoy.

47. Haikal wrote in *Al-Ahram,* February 26, 1971, "The elimination of the traces of the aggression (recovery of the territory lost in the June war, in the Arab idiom) is a limited objective. But if the war for that objective ends in victory, the results will not be limited" cited in *Brief,* No. 5 (March 1–15, 1971), p. 2:

48. "Mohammed Hassanein Heykal Discusses War and Peace in the Middle East," *Journal of Palestine Studies,* Vol. 1, No. 1 (Autumn, 1971), pp. 6–7.

49. Georgiana G. Stevens in *The United States and the Middle East* (Englewood Cliffs: Prentice-Hall, 1964), p. 7; letter to the editor of The New York *Times* by Frank Harris of Beirut, March 14, 1969, p. 40.

50. Cited in *The United States and the Middle East,* p. 136.

51. *Violent Truce,* p. 117. And in a similar vein, Childers, in *Journal of International Affairs,* Vol. 19, No. 1 (1965); Maxime Rodinson, *Israel and the Arabs* (New York: Pantheon, 1968); General Thomas A. Lane, "Our Friends, The Arabs," The New York *Times,* October 4, 1971, p. 39.

52. Bernard Lewis, *Survey,* Vol. 17, No. 2 (Spring, 1971), pp. 178–79.

53. We follow here closely the exposition of Robert E. Lane and David O. Sears, *Public Opinion* (Englewood Cliffs: Prentice-Hall, 1964), Ch. 5.

54. Other factors may press in the same direction; Soloway and his associates thus report that Dr. Landrum Bolling, editor of the Quaker report *(Search for Peace in the Middle East)*, cited anxiety lest Arab displeasure "barred a return to Cairo and the continuation of the dialogue" *(op. cit., p. 58)*.

55. *Op. cit.*, p. 130.

56. Grant C. Butler, *Kings and Camels: An American in Saudi Arabia* (New York: Devin-Adair, 1960), p. 202. Emphasis added.

57. Leo Mates, Director of the Institute of International Politics and Economics, Belgrade, formerly Secretary-General to the President of Yugoslavia and Undersecretary of State for Foreign Affairs, in a conversation with this writer, at Princeton, April 2, 1968.

58. I.L. Kenen *et al.*, *A Just Peace in the Mideast: How Can It Be Achieved?* (Washington: American Enterprise Institute for Public Policy Research, 1971), pp. 107, 129.

59. Arnold J. Toynbee, *A Study of History,* Vol. 8, (London: Oxford University Press, 1954), p. 301.

60. Millar Burrows, "Jewish Nationalism," *The Christian Century,* Vol. 66, No. 13 (March 30, 1949), p. 401.

61. Elmer Berger, *Who Knows Better Must Say So* (New York: American Council for Judaism, 1955), p. 100.

62. Alfred M. Lilienthal, *There Goes the Middle East* (New York: Devin-Adair, 1957), p. 288. Emphasis added.

63. The New York *Times,* November 29, 1973, p. 16.

64. *Newsweek,* Vol. 82, No. 24 (December 10, 1973), p. 56.

65. Peter Grose, The New York *Times,* May 21, 1974, p. 41.

66. Henry Tanner, The New York *Times,* June 1, 1974, p. 8.

67. For first citation, The New York *Times,* June 8, 1974, p. 4; for the second, see the issue for May 18, 1974, p. 12.

68. See especially, Edward N. Luttwak and Walter Laqueur, "Kissinger and the Yom Kippur War," *Commentary,* Vol. 58, No. 3 (September, 1974).

69. In a meeting with several Jewish intellectuals in December, 1973, widely reported in the press, a transcript having been shown to this writer by a participant.

70. Egyptian Youth Minister Kamal Abu al-Magd at Beirut news conference on April 17. 1974.

71. *The Voice of Palestine,* Cairo, as translated in the BBC Summary of World Broadcasts, IV, A, p. 2, June 11, 1974. A front-page report in the New York *Times,* June 9, 1974, interprets the Council decision as defining "national rights as the right of Palestinians to establish a state in the West Bank or Gaza area."

72. *Brief,* No. 80 (April 16–30, 1974), p. 2.

73.   The New York *Times*, June 3, 1974, p. 13.

74.   The New York *Times*, June 9, 1974, p. 11.

CHAPTER SIX

1.   Hal Lehrman, "Is An Arab-Israeli War Inevitable?" *Commentary*, Vol. 21, No. 3 (March, 1956), p. 210.

2.   William R. Polk, *What the Arabs Think*, No. 96, Headline Series, Foreign Policy Association, (November-December, 1952), p. 37.

3.   Bilby, *New Star in the Near East*, p. 82.

4.   Lakin *et al.*, *Arab and Jew in Israel*, pp. 121–22.

5.   General Mohammed Neguib, on April 18, 1953, as cited in Gabbay, *A Political Study of the Arab-Jewish Conflict*, p. 425.

6.   *Liwa al-Istiklal* (Baghdad), August 18, 1952, as cited in Polk, *op. cit.*, p. 40.

7.   *New Middle East*, No. 34 (July, 1971), p. 3.

8.   *To The Point*, Vol. 1, No. 4 (February 26, 1972), pp. 13–14.

9.   Richard W. Cottam, "Arab Nationalism," *Attitudes Toward Jewish Statehood in the Arab World*, ed. Gil Carl AlRoy (New York: American Academic Association for Peace in the Middle East, 1971), p. 175.

10.   *Baghdad Observer*, March 6, 1968, p. 4.

11.   Thus C.A.S. Sanders, "From a History of the Fourth Millenium," *The Middle East Newsletter*, Vol. 2, No. 7 (August-September, 1968), p. 12.

12.   *Israel* magazine, Vol. 2, No. 8 (May, 1970), p. 65.

13.   *Arab World*, Vol. 14, Nos. 10–11 (special issue, 1969), p. 36.

14.   Source unknown. Graphic demonstrations are quite common in Arab presentations; one in an advertisement by the Arab Information Center in The New York *Times*, November 29, 1971, p. 43, shows the outlines of the 1947 abortive partition plan; then the 1949 armistice lines (captioned in the source simply as 1948); finally, the cease-fire lines following the June war of 1967.

15.   Hisham Sharabi "Prelude to War: The Crisis of May-June 1967," *Arab World*, Vol. 14, No. 10–11 (special issue, 1969), pp. 26–27.

16.   *The New York Times Magazine* (February 6, 1972), p. 70.

17.   Bilby, *op. cit.*, pp. 52–53.

18.   *Op. cit.*, p. 120.

19.   Sir John Bagot Glubb, *A Soldier with the Arabs* (New York: Harper and Brothers, 1957), p. 152.

20.   *Encounter*, Vol. 39, No. 5 (November, 1967), pp. 4–5.

21.   Anthony Nutting, *The Arabs: A Narrative History from Mohammed to the Present*, (New York: Clarkson N. Potter, 1964), p. 337.

22.   Kenen *et al.*, *A Just Peace in the Mideast*, pp. 45–46.

23.   Schechtman, *The United States and the Jewish State Movement*, p. 168.

24.   In Burdett's words, "they always remained at least one war behind the facts" (*Encounter with the Middle East*, p. 58).

25.   Thus, Cremeans, writing in that period, before the June war (*The Arabs and the World*, pp. 193, 198 *ff.*).

26.   Ibrahim D'Eibis, "What Future is There for the Arab People of Palestine?" *New Middle East*, No. 29 (February, 1971), p. 36.

27.   Mervyn Harris, "From Nile to Euphrates: The Evolution of a Myth," *New Middle East*, Nos. 42–43 (March-April, 1972), p. 46.

28.   Merlin, *The Search for Peace in the Middle East*, p. 31.

29.   *Encounter*, Vol. 39, No. 5 (November, 1967), pp. 4–5; emphasis in the source.

30.   Muhammed Abu Shilbaya, "An Appeal to Palestinian Leaders," *New Middle East*, No. 29 (February, 1971), p. 37.

31.   R.E. Robinson and J. Gallagher, "The Partition of Africa," *New Cambridge Modern History*, Vol. 11 (Cambridge: Cambridge University Press, 1962), p. 609.

32.   See Cremeans, *op. cit.*, p. 190.

33.   Thus, Matityahu Peled, in *Maariv*, February 4, 1972, cited in *Palestine Digest*, Vol. 2, No. 1 (April, 1972), pp. 14–15.

34.   Georges R. Tamarin, "The Israeli-Arab Conflict in Terms of Non-Communication," *Attitudes Toward Jewish Statehood in the Arab World*, pp. 86–87.

35.   *The Leap Forwards—Into the Past*, p. 16, and on the effect of war on annexationist sentiment in general, pp. 15, 36, and *passim*.

36.   George F. Hourani, "Palestine as a Problem in Ethics," *Arab World*, Vol. 15, Nos. 3–4 (March-April, 1969), p. 7.

37.   The New York *Times*, November 29, 1971, p. 43.

38.   Derk Kinnane, *The Kurds and Kurdistan* (London: Oxford University Press, 1964), p. 75. Also Dana Adams Schmidt, *Journey Among Brave Men* (Boston: Little, Brown, 1964), *passim*: René Mauriés, *Le Kourdistan ou la Mort*, (Paris: Robert Laffont, 1967), pp. 113 *ff.*; and press reports, for instance, The New York *Times*, March 15, 1965, p. 10. Also, see *Brief*, No. 64 (August 16–31, 1973), p. 4 and No. 79 (April 1–15, 1974), p. 4.

39.   *New Middle East*, No. 34 (July, 1971), p. 21.

40.   The New York *Times*, September 23, 1969, p. 14, and September 24, p. 2.

CHAPTER SEVEN

1.   Wilfred Cantwell Smith, *Islam in Modern History* (New York: The New American Library, 1959), pp. 17, 23, 39–40.

2.   Arthur Jeffery, "The Political Importance of Islam," *Journal of Near Eastern Studies*, Vol. 1, No. 4 (October, 1942), p. 384.

3.   *The Arabs*, p. 28.

4.   *Op. cit.*, p. 385.

5.   Polk, *What the Arabs Think*, p. 19.

6.   Ayad Al-Qazzaz, "Political Socialization in Iraq" (Paper delivered at the Fifth Annual Meeting of the Middle East Studies Association, Denver, November 11–13, 1971).

7.   Barzini, *The Italians*, pp. 260, 225. The parallels extend to other traits, as we read (p. 122) of "national reliance on make-belief as an instrument of policy" in Italy.

8.   Berger, *The Arab World Today*, pp. 272–76.

9.   Bernard Lewis, *Race and Color in Islam* (New York: Harper and Row, 1971), p. 19.

10.   Hottinger, *The Arabs*, p. 49.

11.   Polk, *op. cit.*, pp. 7, 9.

12.   D.G. Hogarth, "Arabs and Turks," *The Arab Bulletin*, No. 48 (April 21, 1917), reprinted in Elie Kedourie, *England and the Middle East: The Destruction of the Ottoman Empire 1914–1921* (London: Bowes and Bowes, 1956), p. 226.

13.   The words of an Egyptian Muslim Brotherhood leader, cited by George Kirk, in American Academic Association for Peace in the Middle East, *The Anatomy of Peace in the Middle East* (Proceedings of the Annual Conference, February 15–16, 1969), p. 31.

14.   Wolfgang Bretholz, *Aufstand der Araber* (Munich: Kurt Desch, 1960), p. 160.

15.   Father Haughey, in The New York *Times*, December 11, 1971, p. 31.

16.   Marshall Frady, "On Jordan's Banks," *Harper's*, Vol. 241, No. 1446 (November, 1970), p. 105.

17.   See Haughey, above, and Hottinger, *10 Mal Nahost*, p. 422.

18.   Fayez A. Sayegh, *Understanding the Arab Mind* (New York: The Organization of Arab Students in the United States, 1953), pp. 35–36.

19.   *Op. cit.*, p. 119.

20.   *Halbmond um den Davidstern*, p. 183.

21.   Michael W. Suleiman, "Mass Media and the June Conflict," *Arab World*, Vol. 14, Nos. 10–11 (special issue, 1969), p. 63. Thomas Thompson's report, "U.S. Humiliation—A Diary from Cairo," appeared in *Life* (special edition, "Israel's Swift Victory," 1967), pp. 70–71.

22. Kermit Roosevelt, *Arabs, Oil and History: The Story of the Middle East* (New York: Harper, 1949), pp. 83–84.

23. *Op. cit.*, pp. 122–23.

24. Polk, *op. cit.*, p. 32.

25. Lewis, *The Middle East and the West*, pp. 135–36.

26. Abdullah Kannoun, member of the Academy of Islamic Research at Al-Azhar University, *Arab Theologians on Jews and Israel; Extracts from the Proceedings of the Fourth Conference of the Academy of Islamic Research*, ed. D.F. Green, (Geneva: Éditions de l'Avenir, 1971), p. 49.

27. Shadhel Taga, in *Baghdad Observer*, March 7, 1968, p. 4 (This thesis is axiomatic in the Arab world; thus, a future president of Egypt, writing over a decade earlier: "Exhausted by two world wars, the Western powers realised that they were powerless to maintain their position by force, and evolved another means to attain their ends: namely, to place the industrial power and energy of Israel at the service of imperialism. It was imperialism's last fling." Colonel Anwar El Sadat, *Revolt on the Nile* (London: Allan Wingate, 1957), p. 87.

28. From the summary of a study of Arab textbooks by Hava Lazarus Yafeh, in *Hamizrah Hehadash* [Jerusalem], Vol. 17, Nos. 3-4 (1967), p. ii. Subsequent citation from p. iii.

29. *New Star in the Near East*, p. 85.

30. "The success of Israel in becoming an advanced industrial society only highlights the failure of the Arab states in their own quest for modernization," *Conflict in the Middle East*, ed. James Chace (New York: H.W. Wilson, 1969), p. 12. For variants of this proposition, see Ernst Trost, *David und Goliath: Die Schlacht um Israel 1967* (Vienna: Fritz Molden, 1967), pp. 240–41; Eliahu Ben Elissar and Zeev Schiff, *La Guerre Israëlo-Arabe 5–10 Juin 1967* (Paris: Julliard, 1967), p. 272.

31. Dan Avni-Segre, "Pre-Risorgimento and Post-Risorgimento Zionism," *New Middle East*, No. 15 (December, 1969), p. 26.

32. "Guerrilla Movements and the Arab Dilemma," *Attitudes Towards Jewish Statehood in the Arab World*, pp. 184–85.

33. The widely observed phenomenon has been borne out by systematic surveys; thus, Peres, in *Attitudes Toward Jewish Statehood in The Arab World*, p. 162.

34. Amnon Rubinstein, "No Man's Land Remains in Jerusalem," *The New York Times Magazine* (May 11, 1969), p. 130.

35. J. Gaspard, "Must Israel Assimilate?" *New Middle East*, No. 13 (October, 1969), p. 25.

36. Peres, in *Attitudes Toward Jewish Statehood in the Arab World*, p. 152.

37. In the Jerusalem newspaper's issue of August 23, 1952, as cited in Polk, *op. cit.*, p. 25.

38.   Ahmed Baha ed-Dine's "Returning to Palestine," translated and reprinted in *New Outlook*, Vol. 11, No. 5 (June, 1968), p. 35.

39.   The New York *Times*, April 20, 1969, p. 14.

40.   Hottinger, *10 Mal Nahost*, p. 421, translation by Gil Carl AlRoy. Hottinger suggests (p. 420) that the less well Arabs grasp the real source of Israel's competence the more absurd it seems, the more convinced they are it is merely some bridgehead of imperial power.

41.   Raphael Patai, *Cultures in Conflict: An Inquiry into the Socio-Cultural Problems of Israel and Her Neighbors* (New York: Herzl Press, 1961), especially Chs. 1, 2.

42.   Command 5479, pp. 116–17. See also Ashbee, *A Palestine Notebook*, Ch. 20, "Allah and the Machines."

43.   Cited in Herman F. Reissig, "Another Look at the Arab-Israeli Problem," *Christianity and Crisis*, Vol. 16, No. 5 (April 2, 1956), p. 45.

44.   Bilby, *op. cit.*, pp. 87–88.

45.   "The Bridge on the River Jordan," *The New York Times Magazine* (November 26, 1967), pp. 100, 102.

46.   *Arab News and Views*, Vol. 14, No. 11 (November, 1968), p. 2.

47.   Rubinstein, *The New York Times Magazine* (May 11, 1969), pp. 128–29.

48.   *Race and Color in Islam*, pp. 4–5.

49.   In *Harper's*, Vol. 241, No. 1445 (October, 1970), p. 75.

50.   *Brief*, No. 89 (September 1–15, 1974), p. 1.

CHAPTER EIGHT

1.   Though perhaps not for want of trying; in negotiations with the Axis powers, the Committee for the Co-ordination of Arab Policies, founded in Baghdad in 1940 by the *Mufti* of Jerusalem, formally asked them to acknowledge the Arabs' right "to settle the question of Jewish elements in Palestine and other Arab countries in accordance with the national and racial interests of the Arabs and along lines similar to those used to solve the Jewish question on Germany and Italy" (Kimche, *The Second Arab Awakening*, p. 150; also Hirszowicz, *The Third Reich and the Arab East*, p. 83). The *Mufti* and other Arab leaders later pressed the Nazis to accelerate the process of their "final solution" of Europe's Jewry.

2.   Thus, Burrows, in *The Christian Century*, Vol. 66, No. 13 (March 30, 1949), p. 401.

3.   Thus Suleiman, in *Arab World*, Vol. 14, Nos. 10–11 (special issue, 1969), p. 65.

4.   The New York *Times*, December 3, 1968, p. 6.

5.   Ayoub Musallam, "Peace Depends Upon Israel," *New Outlook*, Vol. 11, No. 6 (July-August, 1968), p. 28.

6.   November 2, 1969, Section 4, p. 9; emphasis added.

7.   CBS-Radio (New York), May 28, 1972, 12:20 P.M.

8.   Green, *Arab Theologians on Jews and Israel*, pp. 60–61.

9.   *Israel* magazine, Vol. 1, No. 8 (special edition, 1968), p. 20.

10.   *Uneasy Lies the Head*, p. 91.

11.   Cited in Crossman, *A Nation Reborn*, p. 67.

12.   Yusuf Al-Waddah, in *New Outlook*, Vol. 11, No. 8 (October, 1968), p. 61.

13.   Thus, Eugene M. Fisher and M. Cherif Bassiouni, *Storm over the Arab World: A People in Revolution* (Chicago: Follett, 1972), pp. 242–49 and *passim*.

14.   *A Study of History*, Vol. 8, pp. 259, 291; also p. 292.

15.   The words of Sheikh Abdul-Hamid 'Attiyah al-Dibani, Rector of the Libyan Islamic University (Green, *Arab Theologians on Jews and Israel*, p. 35).

16.   Ameer Ali, *The Spirit of Islam: A History of the Evolution and Ideals of Islam with a Life of the Prophet* (London: Methuen, 1967), p. xxxvii.

17.   *Ibid.*, pp. 59–60.

18.   Muhammad Azzah Darwaza of Syria, in Green, *Arab Theologiana on Jews and Israel*, p. 27.

19.   *Ibid* ., pp. 28–29. (For the apologetic treatment, see Ali, *op. cit.*, p. 80.)

20.   *Ibid.*, p. 30.

21.   A representative version is contained in the *Le Jour* (Beirut) columns of the celebrated Christian journalist Michel Chiha: From antiquity the Jews, with their extraordinary talents and riches, aspire to dominate the world; they are innately poised in that direction through the ages; are currently using Israel as center of their international conspiracy, and both capitalism and communism, both of which they invented as instrumentalities for that historic purpose of domination (*Palestine*, pp. 137–39 and *passim*).

22.   The New York *Times*, April 26, 1972, p. 5; and *Brief*, No. 32 (April 16–30, 1972), p. 1.

23.   *Brief*, No. 12 (June 16–30, 1971), p. 3; and *New Middle East*, No. 33 (June, 1971), p. 34.

24.   Cited in Latour, *The Resurrection of Israel*, p. 182. A cartoon in the Cairo weekly *Akhbar al-Yom* (January 22, 1972) depicts the Jews as deicides, Nixon as Pilate.

25.   Goitein, *Jews and Arabs*, p. 84.

26.   S. D. Goitein, "Minority Self-Rule and Government Control in Islam," *Studia Islamica*, Vol. 31 (1970), p. 105.

27.   *Op. cit.*, p. 167; also A.S. Tritton, *The Caliphs and Their Non-Muslim Subjects: A Critical Study of the Covenant of 'Umar* (London: Frank Cass, 1970), p. 227.

28.   On some variation among *millets*, see *ibid.*, Tritton, pp. 118–19 and *passim*.

29.   W.J. Fischel, *Jews in the Economic and Political Life of Mediaeval*

Islam (London: Royal Asiatic Society, 1968), p. 116.

30.   Salo Wittmayer Baron, *A Social and Religious History of the Jews*, Vol. 3 (New York: Columbia University Press, 1957), p. 108.

31.   Albert Memmi, *Portrait d'un Juif* (Paris: Gallimard, 1969), pp. 44, 298.

32.   Cyrus Adler and Aaron M. Margalith, *With Firmness in the Right: American Diplomatic Action Affecting Jews, 1840–1945* (New York: The American Jewish Committee, 1946), pp. 14–15.

33.   *Ibid.*, pp. 35–36.

34.   *Ibid.*, p. 37.

35.   *Ibid.*, p. 19; and for subsequent references, pp. 19, 21–24, 28.

36.   Cited in *Karl Marx on Colonialism and Modernization: His Despatches and Other Writings on China, India, Mexico, The Middle East and North Africa*, ed. Shlomo Avineri (Garden City: Doubleday, 1968), p. 142.

37.   Passage cited in the Friday sermon at the al Masjid al-Haram Mosque in Mecca on June 17, 1969, according to 'Sarih,' "Frankly Speaking," *New Middle East*, No. 13, (October, 1969), p. 10.

38.   Johann Adam Bergk, *Aegypten in historischer, geographischer . . . Hinsicht* (Gera: W. Heinsius, 1799), p. 198, translation by Gil Carl Al-Roy.

39.   *The Koran: Commonly Called The Alcoran of Mohammed* (London: William Tegg, 1850), p. 25 ("The Preliminary Discourse").

40.   E.W. Lane, *Manners and Customs of the Modern Egyptians* (Paisley: Alexander Gardner, 1895), pp. 557–61.

41.   A.B. Clot-Bey, *Aperçu général sur l'Egypte*, Vol. 1 (Paris: Fortin, Masson, 1840), p. 243.

42.   Edmond Combes, *Voyage en Egypte, en Nubie . . .* , Vol. 2 (Paris: Desessart, 1846), p. 367, translation by this writer.

43.   Meinertzhagen, *Middle East Diary*, p. 163.

44.   Glubb, *The Great Arab Conquests*, p. 264.

45.   Cited in Lewis, *Semites and Anti-Semites*, p. 176.

46.   Franz Werfel, *The Forty Days of Musa Dagh* (New York: Random House, 1934), p. 132. (Based on the historical records of a conversation between Johannes Lepsius and Enver Pasha.)

47.   Adler and Margalith, *op. cit.*, p. 65.

48.   As stated with special emphasis on the occasion of the establishment of the Jewish state, see The New York *Times*, May 16, 1948, pp. 1, 5. The Premier of Egypt, Nokrashi Pasha, said soon after to the United Nations mediator that "the Arabs would continue to regard Palestine as Arab territory and the Jews as rebels" (Bernadotte, *To Jerusalem*, p. 202).

49.   Command 5854, pp. 263 *ff*.

50.   *Journal of Near Eastern Studies*, Vol. 1, No. 4 (October, 1942), p. 389.

51. *England and the Middle East*, p. 152.

52. *Ibid.*, p. 153.

53. William Yale, special agent of the Department of State in the Near East, 1917–1919, *ibid.*, p. 154.

54. *The Middle East and the West*, p. 126.

55. Hottinger, *10 Mal Nahost*, p. 422.

56. Sheikh Nadim al-Jisr of Lebanon, in Green, *Arab Theologians on Jews and Israel*, p. 45.

57. Haikal, in *Al-Ahram* (June 2, 1967), as cited in Laqueur, *The Road to War 1967*, p. 100. Emphasis added.

58. From a Palestine National Liberation Movement publication, cited in Bell, *The Myth of the Guerrilla*, p. 182; emphasis added.

59. Hence the Arab code "secular" Palestine. Since a Jewish state is by definition religious, secularizing it is to abolish it.

60. Bernadotte, *op. cit.*, pp. 32–33.

61. *Arab World*, Vol. 14, Nos. 7–8 (July-August, 1968), p. 12.

62. The words of Ibrahim Abu-Lughod, in *Arab World*, Vol. 16, No. 2 (February, 1970), p. 39.

63. Joseph Baratz, *A Village by the Jordan: The Story of Degania* (London: Harvill, 1954), p. 117.

64. Thus, Douglas V. Duff, *Sword for Hire* (London: John Murray, 1934), as cited in Latour, *op. cit.*, p. 151.

65. Saul S. Friedman, "Arab-Jewish Bi-Nationalism," *Jewish Frontier*, Vol. 39, No. 3 (April, 1972), p. 16.

66. Carlson, *Cairo to Damascus*, p. 292; p. 427 for subsequent citation.

67. "Arabian Notebook," *Encounter*, Vol. 32, No. 6 (June, 1969), p. 90.

68. For instance, *Progrès Dimanche*, May 12, 1968, p. 1.

69. *Jerusalem Post Weekly*, September 16, 1968, p. 14.

70. Vick Vance and Pierre Lauer, *Hussein de Jordanie: Ma "guerre" avec Israël* (Paris: Albin Michel, 1968). Note the quotation marks in the title.

71. Nasser, in a speech on April 29, 1968; see Carlson (*op. cit.*, p. 350) on his experience in the 1948 war.

72. Former Prime Minister Saad Jumaa, cited in *New Middle East*, No. 16 (January, 1970), p. 41.

73. Cited in *Jerusalem Post Weekly*, August 4, 1969, p. 9.

74. Cited in *Hadassah* magazine, Vol. 50, No. 4 (December, 1968), p. 4.

75. In conversation with Aizaz Sarfraz, a Pakistani visitor, who reported it to this writer on March 5, 1970.

76. The New York *Times*, June 3, 1972, p. 3.

77. Robert St. Cyr, "Arab Perceptions of the Jew and Zionist: Do they Differ?" unpublished paper, Hunter College, 1969, p. 13.

78.   *Brief,* No. 25, (January 1–15, 1972), p. 3.

79.   In an interview with R.K. Karanjai, on September 28, 1958 (Laqueur, *op. cit.*, p. 22).

80.   *Harper's,* Vol. 241, No. 1445 (October, 1970), p. 60.

81.   *National Jewish Monthly,* Vol. 85, No. 8 (April, 1971), pp. 34, 36, 38–39.

82.   *The Journal of Social Psychology,* Vol. 40, No. 2 (November, 1954), pp. 240–43.

83.   *Search for Peace in the Middle East,* p. 1.

84.   Stevens, *op. cit.*, p. 7.

85.   *Semites and Anti-Semites,* pp. 170, 172.

86.   Louise E. Sweet, in *Peoples and Cultures of the Middle East,* ed. Louise E. Sweet (Garden City: The Natural History Press, 1970), I, p. xv.

87.   Khouri, *The Arab-Israeli Dilemma,* p. 353.

88.   Howard K. Smith, on CBS radio from Amman in 1956, as cited in Lilienthal, *There Goes the Middle East,* p. 290.

89.   In Nissim Rejwan, "Why the Arabs Reject Anti-semitism," *New Middle East,* No. 10 (July, 1969), p. 19.

90.   Thus, Dan Kurzman, *Genesis 1948: The First Arab-Israeli War* (New York: The World, 1970), p. 27; or Nadav Safran, "A Critique of Jewish Skeptics: Arabs and Peace," *Hadassah* magazine, Vol. 55, No. 9 (May, 1974).

91.   For instance, Elath, in *New Outlook,* Vol. 11, No. 2 (February, 1968), p. 29.

92.   Dimont, *Jews, God, and History,* p. 202.

CHAPTER NINE

1.   The provinces of Tripolitania and Fezzan are closer by culture to Tunisia to the West, while Cyrenaica has more such affinities with Egypt, on the other side.

2.   George Kahale III, "Arabs in the United States," unpublished paper, Hunter College, 1969.

3.   In conversation with Jean Daniel, April 15, 1965, as cited in Merlin, *The Search for Peace in the Middle East,* p. 256.

4.   *Ibid.*, p. 401.

5.   Richard A. Roughton, "Algeria and the June 1967 Arab-Israeli War," *Middle East Journal,* Vol. 23, No. 4 (Autumn, 1969).

6.   Merlin, *op. cit.*, pp. 325 ff.

7.   J. Gaspard, "Algerian Mentor Gives a Helping Hand," *New Middle East,* No. 33 (June, 1971).

8. Cited in Hottinger, *The Arabs*, p. 172. See also his *10 Mal Nohost*, p. 410.

9. Merlin, *op. cit.*, pp. 318, 317, 92.

10. *Ibid.*, p. 317.

11. Gaspard, *New Middle East*, No. 33 (June, 1971), p. 34.

12. Hottinger, *10 Mal Nohost*, pp. 285 *ff*.

13. Classic Islamic culture is unhumanistic—"revelatory, which mistrusts man's power of judgement and is inclined to confine itself to the mysteries of revelation and to rely on them"—and its breakdown differs sharply from the crumbling of the sacred tradition in Westen Christendom, where secular man rediscovered the autochthonous humanistic, philosophic tradition, "which is built on human reason and speculates from those premises" (Hottinger, *The Arabs*, p. 79).

14. See Arnold Hottinger, "Colonel Ghadhafi's Pan-Arab Ambitions," *Swiss Review of World Affairs*, Vol. 21, No. 3 (June, 1971).

15. John Scott, "The Middle East at War," a report to the publisher of *Time*, 1970, p. 80.

16. *A Soldier With the Arabs*, pp. 151, 152, 153, 258, 286.

17. Yehoshaphat Harkabi, "The Palestinians in the Israel-Arab Conflict," *Midstream*, Vol. 17, No. 3 (March, 1970), p. 7.

18. Hottinger, *The Arabs*, p. 245.

19. *Ibid.*, pp. 245, 247.

20. Richard W. Cottam, in *Attitudes Toward Jewish Statehood in the Arab World*, pp. 167–71.

21. Peres, *ibid.*, pp. 162–63.

22. *Ibid.*, p. 162.

23. Yochanan Peres and Nira Yuval-Davis, "Some Observations on the National Identity of the Israeli Arabs," *Human Relations*, Vol. 22, No. 3 (June, 1969), pp. 227–28.

24. R. Hrair Dekmejian, *Egypt Under Nasir: A Study in Political Dynamics*, (Albany: State University of New York Press, 1971), pp. 96, 90.

25. See Eliahu H. Khazoum, "Salama Moussa: An Egyptian with a Message for Today," *New Middle East*, No. 3 (December, 1968).

26. Morroe Berger, *Islam in Egypt Today: Social and Political Aspects of Popular Religions* (Cambridge: Cambridge University Press, 1970), p. 15.

27. Thus, Nadav Safran, in *From War to War: The Arab-Israeli Confrontation, 1948–1967* (New York: Pegasus, 1969), pp. 83–88.

28. Halim Barakat, "Social Factors Influencing Attitudes of University Students in Lebanon Towards the Palestine Resistance Movement," *Journal of Palestine Studies*, Vol. 1, No. 1 (Autumn, 1971).

29. Extract from a note in *The Arab Bulletin*, No. 47 (April 11, 1917), reprinted in Kedourie, *England and the Middle East*, pp. 230–31.

30. Hottinger, *10 Mal Nahost*, pp. 218–19.

31. Andrew Mango, "Turkey and the Arabs," *Arab Nationalism and a Wider World*, ed. Sylvia G. Haim (New York: American Academic Association for Peace in the Middle East, 1971), p. 48.

32. The Syrian *Baath* party, epitome of militant Arab nationalism, was founded by a Christian and reached a particularly militant phase in the mid-1960's when led by a military junta dominated by *Alawites*, members of a *Shia*-related sect.

33. Crum, *Behind the Silken Curtain*, pp. 245–46. Also, Bilby, *New Star in the Near East*, p. 95; Carlson, *Cairo to Damascus*, pp. 427–29.

34. Barakat, *op. cit.*, p. 95.

35. Hottinger, *The Arabs*, p. 145; emphasis in the source.

36. *Ibid.*, pp. 212–13; citation from Edward S. Atiyah's *An Arab Tells His Story: A Study in Loyalties.*

37. *Ibid.*, p. 213.

38. Esco, *Palestine*, p. 551.

39. Kedourie, *The Chatham House Version*, p. 336.

40. Esco, *op. cit.*, p. 552.

41. The Christians, who had constituted less than ten percent of Palestine's Arab population shortly before the war (and probably just slightly over ten percent in those parts of the country that became Israel), were nearly seventeen percent of the Arabs remaining in the Jewish state at the close of the fighting.

42. See the chapter on "Religion and Politics," in *The Chatham House Version*, and p. 155 in *England and the Middle East*. Also, Aharon Laish, "The Arab Minority in Israel," paper presented to the Institute of Jewish Affairs symposium, "The Arabs and Palestine" (London, March 19, 1972), p. 4.

43. Barakat found in Lebanon that "the less religious a student is, the more likely he is to support the commandos and their popular struggle" (*op. cit.*, p. 95).

44. Morroe Berger, "Americans from the Arab World," *The World of Islam: Studies in Honour of Philip K. Hitti*, ed. James Kritzeck (London: Macmillan, 1960), pp. 357 *ff.*

45. Halim Barakat, "Social Class, Religion and Voting Behavior of University Students in Lebanon," paper presented to the Middle East Studies Association meeting in Denver, November, 1971. A survey of the Lebanese Christian press in another paper presented at the meeting (William W. Haddad, "The Christian Arab Press and the Palestine Question: A Case Study of Michel Chiha of Bayrūt's *Le Jour*") disclosed a similar range, the Green Orthodox tending strongly toward Arabism, the Catholic emphasizing Lebanese separateness, and the Maronite strongly insisting on the latter.

46. Some of these intricacies of Arab-Maronite relations are perceptively reported in John Sykes, *The Mountain Arabs*. See especially pp. 26, 44, 52,

91, 154, 194, 220. Also, Stewart, in *Encounter*, Vol. 32, No. 6 (June, 1969), p. 92; and Carlson, *Cairo to Damascus*, pp. 427–29.

47. Hottinger, *10 Mal Nahost*, p. 22.

48. For a sketch of a Maronite village at war with Muslims, see Alfred Friendly, Jr.'s report in The New York *Times*, November 4, 1969, p. 3.

49. Cited in John P. Entelis, "Palestinian Revolutionism in Lebanese Politics: The Christian Response," Fordham University, 1971 (mimeo), pp. 15–16.

50. Esco, *op. cit.*, pp. 500 *ff.*

51. *Ibid.*, pp. 514–15.

52. *Ibid.*, p. 515. Hottinger believes that the urban lower-middle class forms a particularly appreciative public for official propaganda of the acutely anti-Zionist, anti-imperialist variety common in so-called revolutionary regimes and identifies that class also a social base for the enlarged managerial group of etatistic enterprise that those regimes promote (*The Arabs*, pp. 292, 295).

53. T.E. Lawrence, *Seven Pillars of Wisdom* (Garden City: Doubleday, Doran and Company, 1935), p. 332. Meinertzhagen, *Middle East Diary*, p. 7.

54. Command 1540, pp. 52–54.

55. Peres, in *Attitudes Toward Jewish Statehood in the Arab World*, p. 163.

56. Ilse Lichtenstadter, "An Arab-Egyptian Family," *Middle East Journal*, Vol. 6, No. 4 (Autumn, 1952), p. 398; Butler, *Kings and Camels*, pp. 52, 146-47.

57. Daniel Lerner, *The Passing Of Traditional Society: Modernizing the Middle East* (Glencoe: The Free Press, 1958), pp. 52–69 and *passim*.

58. Peres, in *Attitudes Toward Jewish Statehood in the Arab World*, pp. 162–63.

59. *A Soldier with the Arabs*, p. 152.

60. Shlomo Avineri, "Modernization and Arab Society," *Modernization and the Middle East*, ed. I. Robert Sinai (New York: American Academic Association for Peace in the Middle East), 1970, p. 19.

61. Hottinger, *The Arabs*, pp. 79, 155, and *passim*, and *10 Mal Nahost*, pp. 425–27. See also note 13 above.

62. Hisham Sharabi, *Palestine Guerrillas: Their Credibility and Effectiveness* (Washington: The Center for Strategic and International Studies, Georgetown University, 1970).

63. Goitein, *Jews and Arabs*, p. 16.

64. Esco, *op. cit.*, pp. 587–92.

65. Fred S. Sherrow, *The Arabs of Palestine As Seen Through Jewish Eyes: A Study, 1925–1929*, unpublished master's thesis, Columbia University, p. 87.

66.   Nathaniel Brody, "Palestine Conflict: 1921, 1929, 1936," unpublished paper, Hunter College, 1969.

67.   Thus the Secretary-General of the Moroccan party, Ali Yata, on June 5, 1968, at Casablanca. On divisions on this issue in the Syrian party, see The New York *Times*, June 30, 1972, p. 6.

68.   Lerner, *op. cit.*, pp. 229–31.

69.   Barakat, in *Journal of Palestine Studies*, Vol. 1, No. 1 (Autumn, 1971), pp. 99, 103.

CHAPTER TEN

1.   Goitein, *Jews and Arabs*, p. 232.

2.   "In the Wake of War: Time and Reality in the Middle East," *Atlantic*, Vol. 220, No. 5 (November, 1967), p. 65.

3.   Thus, Anouar Abdel-Malek, *Egypt: Military Society. The Army Regime, the Left, and Social Change under Nasser* (New York: Random House, 1968), pp. viii–x. See also Hottinger, *10 Mal Nahost*, pp. 158–59.

4.   Eytan, in *New Middle East*, No. 36 (September, 1971), p. 17.

5.   On the Maronites, see J. Gaspard, "The Mystery of Chéhabisme— How Lebanon Survives," *New Middle East*, No. 7 (April, 1969), p. 35; on the Egyptian mass, see Hal Lehrman, "Three Weeks in Cairo," *Commentary*, Vol. 21, No. 2 (February, 1956), pp. 105, 108.

6.   On Egypt, for example, reports on the period of the first Arab-Israeli war spoke of mass hysteria (Carlson, *Cairo to Damascus*, 76–77, 138, and *passim*); in the early 1950's reports spoke of "little talk of Palestine outside the government" (Polk, *What the Arabs Think*, p. 38) and in similar terms; by early 1956, however, it was reported that "Israel has become a national mania in Egypt" (Lehrman, above).

7.   Thus, a report by "Ibn el-Assal" (supposedly one who has special knowledge of Egypt), contradicting the usual journalistic evaluation of public opinion in the wake of the 1967 war: "Return to Cairo," *Encounter*, Vol. 33, No. 2 (August, 1969).

8.   On the postwar deterioration of Israel's Arabs' relationship to the state, see Peres and Yuval-Davis, in *Human Relations*, Vol. 22, No. 3 (June, 1969), pp. 228 *ff*.

9.   In 1937, before Jewish statehood and especially any Arab humiliation in war and the conquests and the refugee problem, on which the escalation of hostility is commonly blamed, the Peel Commission had already concluded: "The conflict has grown steadily more bitter. It has been marked by a series of five Arab outbreaks, culminating in the rebellion of last year. In the earlier period hostility to the Jews was not widespread among the *fellaheen*. It is now general" (Command 5479, p. 371). The escalation may be related to the increase in the size of the Jewish community in Palestine (i.e., immi-

gration), regarded as a threat to Arab rule of all Palestine, however minuscule its territorial basis. At the outbreak of the most violent disturbances, which occasioned the Peel Commission, Jews occupied no more than four to five percent of Palestine.

10. Amnon Cohen, "The Arabs and Palestine," speaking at the symposium of the Institute of Jewish Affairs, London, March 19, 1972.

11. See, for instance, Shlomo Avineri, "The Palestinians and Israel," *Commentary*, Vol. 49, No. 6 (June, 1970).

12. See *Arab World*, Vol. 14, Nos. 7–8 (July-August, 1968), pp. 3, 15.

13. Hottinger, *10 Mal Nahost*, p. 420.

14. Thus, Mohammed Abu Shilbaya; see The New York *Times*, November 14, 1971, p. 22.

15. Jamil Hamad, "Palestinian Future—New Directions," *New Middle East*, No. 35 (August, 1971), p. 19.

16. *Op. cit.*, p. 65.

17. Stewart, in *Encounter*, Vol. 32, No. 6 (June, 1969), p. 90.

18. Maurice Carr, "Comment," *Israel* magazine, Vol. 1, No. 8 (1968), pp. 38–39.

19. A typical plea, by Ayoub Musallam, featuring wholly blameless but betrayed Palestinians, is appropriately titled, "Peace Depends Upon Israel," *New Outlook*, Vol. 11, No. 6 (July-August), 1968.

20. Colonel David Farhi, "The West Bank: 1948–1971. Society and Politics in Judea and Samaria," *New Middle East*, No. 38 (November, 1971).

21. The New York *Times*, November 14, 1971, p. 22.

22. See Naomi Shepherd's interview with Youssef Nasser, *New Outlook*, Vol. 14, No. 3 (April, 1971), especially p. 42.

23. The New York *Times*, January 29, 1974, pp. 1, 4.

24. Henry Tanner, from Rabat, in The New York *Times*, October 29, 1974, pp. 1, 6.

25. J.C. Hurewitz, *Changing Military Perspectives in the Middle East* (Santa Monica: The Rand Corporation, 1970), p. 36.

26. Bell, *The Long War*, pp. 428–29; emphasis added. Concerning the matter of finality, consider Haikal's reply to the question, assuming that Israel withdrew under American pressure from Arab territory conquered in 1967, as demanded by Egypt, how does he conceive of Arab-Israeli relations under a resulting peaceful settlement?: "I do not believe that even if we reached a peaceful settlement under the conditions you have just mentioned, it would be humanly possible or natural to move from a state of war to a state of complete harmonious peace. I do not envision, either in my generation or my children's, that it is possible to develop full normal relations between us and Israel. I cannot discuss the future beyond that, but with my generation, which witnessed 1948, 1956, and 1967, it is not possible. Why is it not possible? There must be basic changes in Israeli thinking. It is not enough to return to the borders of 1967. Adjustments are needed

which it is unlikely that Israel will make" (*Journal of Palestine Studies,* Vol. 1, No. 1 (Autumn, 1971), pp. 18–19).

27.   From the Preamble of the Israel-Jordan General Armistice Agreement of April 3, 1949: the phrase appears in the agreements with the other Arab states as well.

28.   Bell, *The Long War,* especially p. 393; see also his "National Character and Military Strategy: The Egyptian Experience, October 1973," unpublished paper, Institute of War and Peace Studies, Columbia University. Safran, *From War to War,* especially pp. 198–204; see also his "The War and the Future of the Arab-Israeli Conflict," *Foreign Affairs,* Vol. 52, No. 2 (January, 1974). AlRoy, "The Prospects of War in the Middle East," *Commentary,* Vol. 47, No. 3 (March, 1969). Hurewitz, *op. cit.*

29.   See also Malcolm H. Kerr, "The United Arab-Republic: The Domestic, Political, and Economic Background of Foreign Policy," *Political Dynamics in the Middle East,* ed. Paul Y. Hammond and Sidney S. Alexander (New York: American Elsevier, 1972), p. 207.

30.   Shlomo Avineri, "The New Status Quo," *Commentary,* Vol. 45, No. 3 (March, 1968), p. 50.

31.   Merlin, *The Search for Peace in the Middle East,* pp. 379–80.

32.   Sykes, *The Mountain Arabs,* p. 52.

33.   Bell, *The Long War,* p. 427.

34.   Hourani, in *Encounter,* Vol. 39, No. 5 (November, 1967), p. 4.

35.   In the words of President Sadat: "Our enemies, the Israelis, must understand, if they want to understand, that the path is long and nature is with us and so is history" (The New York *Times,* July 27, 1972, p. 12).

36.   See Peres and Yuval-Davis, *op. cit.,* p. 232.

37.   See Michael W. Dols, "The Muslim Reaction to the Black Death: An Interpretation," paper presented to the Middle East Studies Association meeting at Denver, 1971, especially p. 4.

38.   Harkabi, *Maariv,* April 17, 1970, a translation of the revised text of which appears in the author's *Three Articles on the Arab Slogan of A Democratic State* (n. p., n. d.), as "Arab Reconsiderations Pointing to a Change?"

39.   Goitein, *Jews and Arabs,* p. xii.

40.   Merlin, *op. cit.,* p. 351; also The New York *Times,* November 18, 1971, p. 6.

41.   Tamarin, *The Leap Forwards—Into the Past,* Ch. 5.

42.   John H. Davis, *The Evasive Peace: A Study of the Zionist-Arab Problem* (New York: New World, 1970), p. 126.

BIBLIOGRAPHY

Listed below are books and papers in European languages (the daily press and digests excepted) cited in this work or used in its preparation.

Abdel-Kader, Rezak. *Le Conflit judéo-arabe.* Paris: Maspero, 1961.

Abdel-Malek, Anouar. *Egypt: Military Society. The Army Regime, the Left, and Social Change under Nasser,* trans. Charles Lam Markmann. New York: Random House, 1968.

Adams, James R. "Amos Oz: Disillusioned Dove." *Crossroads.* Vol. 5 (July, 1974).

Adler, Cyrus, and Aaron M. Margalith. *With Firmness in the Right: American Diplomatic Action Affecting Jews, 1840–1945.* New York: The American Jewish Committee, 1946.

Aggiouri, René. *Le Conflit de Palestine dans le jeu des puissances (1950–1967).* Beirut: Editions les cahiers de l'est, 1968.

Aldington, Richard. *Lawrence of Arabia: A Biographical Inquiry.* London: Collins, 1955.

Ali, Syed Ameer. *The Spirit of Islam: A History of the Evolution and Ideals of Islam with a Life of the Prophet.* London: Methuen, 1967.

AlRoy, Gil Carl. "Patterns of Hostility." *Attitudes Toward Jewish Statehood in the Arab World,* ed. Gil Carl AlRoy. New York: American Academic Association for Peace in the Middle East, 1971.

———"The Prospects of War in the Middle East." *Commentary,* Vol. 47 (March, 1969).

Alter, Robert. "Rhetoric and the Arab Mind." *Commentary,* Vol. 46 (October, 1968).

American Interests in the Middle East. Washington: Middle East Institute, 1969.

The Arab Heritage, ed. Nabil Amin Faris. Princeton: Princeton University Press, 1946.

An Arab Philosophy of History: Selections from the Prolegomena of Ibn Khaldun of Tunis (1332–1406), trans. and arranged Charles Issawi. London: John Murray, 1950.

Arab Theologians on Jews and Israel: Extracts from the Proceedings of the Fourth Conference of the Academy of Islamic Research (Al-Azhar), ed. D. F. Green. Geneva: Editions de l'avenir, 1971.

Arian, Alan. *Ideological Change in Israel.* Cleveland: The Press of Case Western Reserve University, 1968.

———. "Stability and Change in Israeli Public Opinion and Politics." *Public Opinion Quarterly,* Vol. 35 (Spring, 1971).

Ashbee, C. R. *A Palestine Notebook, 1918–1923.* Garden City: Doubleday, Page, 1923.

Avineri, Shlomo. "Modernization and Arab Society," *Modernization and the Middle East,* ed. I. Robert Sinai. New York: American Academic Association for Peace in the Middle East, 1970.

———. "The New Status Quo." *Commentary,* Vol. 45 (March, 1968).

———. "The Palestinians and Israel:" *Commentary,* Vol. 49 (June, 1970).

Avneri, Uri. "Fighting for Peace: The Silent Minority." *New Middle East* (March–April, 1972).

Avni-Segre, Dan. "Pre-Risorgimento and Post-Risorgimento Zionism." *New Middle East* (December, 1969).

Badeau, John S. "The Arabs, 1967." *Atlantic,* Vol. 220 (December, 1967).

Barakat, Halim. "Social Factors Influencing Attitudes of University Students in Lebanon Towards the Palestine Resistance Movement." *Journal of Palestine Studies,* Vol. 1 (autumn, 1971).

Baratz, Joseph. *A Village by the Jordan: The Story of Degania.* London: Harvill, 1954.

B'ari, Shmuel. Review of Amos Elon's *The Israelis. New Outlook,* Vol. 14 (October-November, 1971).

Baron, Salo Wittmeyer. *A Social and Religious History of the Jews,* Vol. 3. New York: Columbia University Press, 1957.

Barzini, Luigi. *The Italians.* New York: Bantam Books, 1969.

Bar-Zohar, Michel. *Ben Gourion: le prophète armé.* Paris: Librairie Fayard, 1966.

Begin, Menachem. *The Revolt: Story of the Irgun,* trans. Samuel Katz. Tel Aviv: Hadar, 1964.

Bell, J. Bowyer. *The Long War: Israel and the Arabs Since 1946.* Englewood Cliffs: Prentice-Hall, 1969.

———. "Looking Through a Glass Darkly: Illusion and Reality in the Arab-Israeli Crisis." Center for International Affairs, Harvard University, 1970.

——. *The Myth of the Guerrilla: Revolutionary Theory and Malpractice.* New York: Knopf, 1971.

Beloff, Nora. "The Kiss-and-Make-Up Delusion." *Encounter,* Vol. 30 (February, 1968).

Ben-Elissar, Eliahu, and Zeev Schiff. *La Guerre israelo-arabe 5–10 juin 1967.* Paris: Julliard, 1967.

Ben-Gurion, David. *Israel: Years of Challenge.* New York: Holt, Rinehart and Winston, 1963.

——. *Letters to Paula,* trans. Aubrey Hodes. London: Valentine, Mitchell, 1971.

——. *My Talks With Arab Leaders,* ed. Misha Louvish and trans. Aryeh Rubinstein and Misha Louvish. New York: The Third Press, 1973.

Berger, Elmer. "How Can Palestine Be Explained to the West." *Middle East Newsletter,* Vol. 2 (December, 1968).

——. *Who Knows Better Must Say So.* New York: American Council for Judaism, 1955.

Berger, Morroe. "Americans from the Arab World," *The World of Islam: Studies in Honour of Philip K. Hitti,* ed. James Kritzeck and R. Bayly Winder. London: Macmillan, 1960.

——. *The Arab World Today.* New York: Doubleday, 1964.

——. *Islam in Egypt Today: Social and Political Aspects of Popular Religion.* Cambridge: Cambridge University Press, 1970.

Bergk, Johann Adam. *Aegypten in historischer, geographischer . . . Hinsicht.* Gera: W. Heinsius, 1799.

Bernadotte, Folke. *To Jerusalem.* London: Hodder and Stoughton, 1951.

Bilby, Kenneth W. *New Star in the Near East.* Garden City: Doubleday, 1950.

Binder, Leonard. "The Middle East Crisis: Background and Issues." Center for Policy Study, University of Chicago, 1967.

Bloom, Joel S. "The Middle East Crisis in *The Christian Science Monitor.*" Department of Political Science, Hunter College, New York, 1969.

Boulding, Kenneth E. "National Images and International Systems," *Comparative Foreign Policy: Theoretical Essays,* ed. Wolfram F. Hanrieder. New York: David McKay, 1971.

Brecher, Michael. "Ben Gurion and Sharett: Contrasting Israeli Images of 'the Arabs.'" *New Middle East* (March, 1970).

——. *The Foreign Policy System of Israel: Setting, Images, Process.* New Haven: Yale University Press, 1972.

Bretholz, Wolfgang. *Aufstand der Araber.* Munich: Kurt Desch, 1960.

Brody, Nathaniel. "Palestine Conflict: 1921, 1929, 1936." Department of Political Science, Hunter College, New York, 1969.

Burckhardt, J. L. *Notes on the Bedouins and Wahabys, Collected During his Travels in the East.* London: Henry Coburn and Richard Bentley, 1831 (2 vols.).

Burdett, Winston. *Encounter With the Middle East: An Intimate Report on What Lies Behind the Arab-Israeli Conflict.* New York: Atheneum, 1969.

Burns, E. L. M. *Between Arab and Israeli.* New York: Ivan Obolensky, 1962.

Burrows, Millar. "Jewish Nationalism." *Christian Century,* Vol. 66 (March 30, 1949).

Butler, Grant C. *Kings and Camels: An American in Saudi Arabia.* New York: Devin-Adair, 1960.

Campbell, John C., and Helen Caruso. *The West and the Middle East.* New York: Council on Foreign Relations, 1972.

Cantril, Hadley. *The Pattern of Human Concerns.* New Brunswick: Rutgers University Press, 1965.

Carlson, John Roy. *Cairo to Damascus.* New York: Knopf, 1951.

Carmichael, Joel. *The Shaping of the Arabs: A Study in Ethnic Identity.* New York: Macmillan, 1967.

Carr, Maurice. "Comment." *Israel,* Vol. 1, No. 1 (1968).

Chace, James. "Editor's Introduction," *Conflict in the Middle East,* ed. James Chace. New York: H. W. Wilson, 1969.

Chiha, Michel. *Palestine.* Beirut: Éditions du trident, 1957.

Childers, Erskine B. "The Other Exodus." *Spectator,* Vol. 206 (May 12, 1961).

——. "Palestine: The Broken Triangle," *Modernization of the Arab World,* ed. J. H. Thompson and R. D. Reischauer. Princeton: Van Nostrand, 1966.

——. *The Road to Suez: A Study of Western-Arab Relations.* London: MacGibbon and Kee, 1962.

Clot-Bey, A.-B. *Aperçu général sur l'Égypte,* Vol. 1. Paris: Fortin, Masson, 1840.

Cohen, Aharon. *Israel and the Arab World,* trans. Aubrey Hodes *et al.* New York: Funk and Wagnalls, 1970.

Cohen, Amnon. "The Arab Population in the Israel-Administered West Bank and Gaza Strip." London: Institute of Jewish Affairs, 1972.

Combes, Edmond. *Voyage en Égypte, en Nubie . . . ,* Vol. 2. Paris: Desessart, 1846.

Coon, Carleton S. *Caravan: The Story of the Middle East.* New York: Henry Holt, 1951.

Copeland, Miles. *The Game of Nations: The Amorality of Power Politics.* London: Weidenfeld and Nicolson, 1969.

Cordtz, Dan. "But What Do We Do About the Arabs?" *Fortune,* Vol. 76 (September 1, 1967).

Cottam, Richard W. "Arab Nationalism," *Attitudes Toward Jewish Statehood in the Arab World,* ed. Gil Carl AlRoy. New York: American Academic Association for Peace in the Middle East, 1971.

Cremeans, Charles D. *The Arabs and the World: Nasser's Arab Nationalist Policy.* New York: Praeger, 1963.

Crossman, Richard. *A Nation Reborn: A Personal Report on the Roles Played by Weizmann, Bevin and Ben-Gurion in the Story of Israel.* New York: Atheneum, 1960.

————. *Palestine Mission: A Personal Record.* New York: Harper, 1947.

Crum, Bartley C. *Behind the Silken Curtain: A Personal Account of Anglo-American Diplomacy in Palestine and the Middle East.* New York: Simon and Schuster, 1947.

Darin-Drabkin, Haim. "Realism Instead of Fatalism." *New Outlook,* Vol. 12 (March-April, 1969).

Davis, John H. *The Evasive Peace: A Study of the Zionist-Arab Problem.* New York: New World, 1970.

"Dayan and Ruppin: A Soldier Reflects on Peace Hopes." *Jerusalem Post Weekly* (September 30, 1968).

Dayan, Yael. "Security, Yes. Peace, No." *Hadassah,* Vol. 49 (June, 1968).

de Gaulle, Charles. *Memoirs of Hope: Renewal 1958–62, Endeavour 1962–,* trans. Terence Kilmartin. London: Weidenfeld and Nicolson, 1971.

D'Eibis, Ibrahim. "What Future is There for the Arab People of Palestine?" *New Middle East* (February, 1971).

Dekmejian, R. Hrair. *Egypt Under Nasir: A Study in Political Dynamics.* Albany: State University of New York Press, 1971.

DeNovo, John A. *American Interests and Policies in the Middle East 1900–1933.* Minneapolis: The University of Minnesota Press, 1963.

Deutschkron, Inge. *Bonn and Jerusalem: The Strange Coalition.* Philadelphia: Chilton, 1970.

Dickson, H. R. P. *The Arab of the Desert: A Glimpse into Badawin Life in Kuwait and Sau'di Arabia.* London: George Allen and Unwin, 1951.

Dimont, Max I. *Jews, God, and History: A Modern Interpretation of A Four-Thousand-Year Story.* New York: Simon and Schuster, 1962.

ed-Dine, Ahmed Baha. "Returning to Palestine." *New Outlook,* Vol. 11 (June, 1968).

Dodd, C. H., and M. E. Sales. *Israel and the Arab World.* New York: Barnes and Noble, 1970.

Dols, Michael W. "The Muslim Reaction to the Black Death: An Interpretation." Department of History, California State College, Hayward, 1971.

Dov, Joseph. *The Faithful City: The Siege of Jerusalem, 1948.* New York: Simon and Schuster, 1960.

Duff, Douglas V. *Sword for Hire.* London: John Murray, 1934.

Eckstein, Harry. "Introduction: Toward the Theoretical Study of Internal War," *Internal War: Problems and Approaches,* ed. Harry Eckstein. Princeton: Princeton University Press, 1964.

———. *A Theory of Stable Democracy.* Princeton: Center of International Studies, Princeton University, 1961.

Edelstein, Lily. "Conversation with Amos Oz." *National Jewish Monthly,* Vol. 87 (September, 1972).

Elath, Eliahu. "Arabs and Jews in Israel." *New Outlook,* Vol. 11 (February, 1968).

Elazar, Daniel J. "Arab 'Moderates' and the 'American Fallacy.'" *Congress Bi-Weekly,* Vol. 38 (April 30, 1971).

Elon, Amos. *The Israelis: Founders and Sons.* New York: Holt, Rinehart and Winston, 1971.

Entelis, John P. "Palestine Revolutionism in Lebanese Politics: The Christian Response." Department of Political Science, Fordham University, New York, 1972.

Esco Foundation for Palestine. *Palestine: A Study of Jewish, Arab, and British Policies.* New Haven: Yale University Press, 1947 (2 vols.).

Eytan, Walter. "To Cut the Gordian Knot—An Assessment of Israel's Foreign Policy and the Search for Genuine Peace." *New Middle East* (September, 1971).

Farhi, David. "The West Bank: 1948–1971: Society and Politics in Judea and Samaria." *New Middle East* (November, 1971).

Feldman, Emanuel. *The 28th of Iyar.* New York: Bloch, 1968.

Feron, James. "Time Stands Still in an Israeli-Occupied Town." *New York Times Magazine* (May 17, 1970).

Finger, Seymour M. "The Arab-Israeli Problem and the United Nations." *Middle East Information Series* (February, 1972).

Finnie, David H. *Pioneers East: The Early American Experience in the Middle East.* Cambridge: Harvard University Press, 1967.

Fischel, W. J. *Jews in the Economic and Political Life of Mediaeval Islam.* London: Royal Asiatic Society, 1968.

Fisher, Eugene M., and M. Cherif Bassiouni. *Storm over the Arab World: A People in Revolution.* Chicago: Follett, 1972.

Frady, Marshall. "An American Innocent in the Middle East." *Harper's,* Vol. 241 (Part I: October, 1970; Part II: November, 1970).

Frank, Gerold. *The Deed.* New York: Simon and Schuster, 1963.

Friedman, Saul S. "Arab-Jewish Bi-Nationalism." *Jewish Frontier,* Vol. 39 (April, 1972).

Friedmann, Georges. *The End of the Jewish People?* trans. Eric Mosbacher. Garden City: Doubleday, 1967.

Fulbright, J. William. "Old Myths and New Realities—II: The Middle East." *Congressional Record—Senate* (August 24, 1970).

Fyvel, T. R. "Reporter in Palestine—Sheean Looks Back." *New Middle East* (April, 1970).

Gabbay, Rony E. *A Political Study of the Arab-Jewish Conflict: The Arab Refugee Problem (A Case Study).* Geneva: Librairie Droz, 1959.

Gaspard, J. "Algerian Mentor Gives a Helping Hand." *New Middle East* (June, 1971).

———. "Must Israel Assimilate?" *New Middle East* (October, 1969).

———. "The Mystery of Chehabisme—How Lebanon Survives." *New Middle East* (April, 1969).

Glubb, John Bagot. *The Great Arab Conquests.* London: Hodder and Stoughton, 1963.

———. *A Soldier with the Arabs.* New York: Harper, 1957.

———. *The Story of the Arab Legion.* London: Hodder and Stoughton, 1948.

Goitein, S. D. "Arab Nationalism—As Viewed From Israel," *The Arab Nation: Paths and Obstacles to Fulfillment,* ed. William Sands. Washington: Middle East Institute, 1961.

———. *Jews and Arabs: Their Contact Through the Ages.* New York: Schocken, 1955.

———. "Minority Self-rule and Government Control in Islam." *Studia Islamica,* Vol. 31 (1970).

Goldmann, Nahum. "The Future of Israel." *Foreign Affairs,* Vol. 48 (April, 1970).

Gottheil, Fred M. "Arab Immigration into Pre-State Israel: 1922–1931." College of Commerce, University of Illinois, Urbana, 1971.

Graham, Hugh Davis, and Ted Robert Gurr. *Violence in America: Historical and Comparative Perspectives, Vol. 1.* Washington: U. S. Government Printing Office, 1969.

Graves, R. M. *Experiment in Anarchy.* London: Victor Gollancz, 1949.

Gurion, Itzhak. *Triumph on the Gallows,* prep. Konrad Bercovici. New York: Brit Trumpeldor, 1950.

Hadawi, Sami. "The Arab States: Why Won't They Negotiate?" *Arab World,* Vol. 14 (May-June, 1968).

Haddad, William W. "The Christian Arab Press and the Palestine Question: A Case Study of Michel Chiha of Bayrūt's *Le Jour.*" Department of History, Illinois State University, Normal, 1971.

Haim, Sylvia G. "The 'Lesson of Japan' Put to a New Use," *Arab Nationalism and a Wider World,* ed. Sylvia G. Haim. New York: American Academic Association for Peace in the Middle East, 1971.

Halpern, Ben. *The Idea of the Jewish State.* Cambridge: Harvard University Press, 1969.

Hamad, Jamil. "Palestinian Future—New Directions." *New Middle East* (August, 1971).

Hamady, Sania. *Temperament and Character of the Arabs.* New York: Twayne, 1960.

Hanna, Sami A. "Tunisian Socialism Revisited." Middle East Center, University of Utah, Salt Lake City, 1971.

Harkabi, Yehoshafat. *Arab Attitudes to Israel.* New York: Hart, 1972.

———. "Liberation or Genocide?" *Transaction,* Vol. 7 (July-August, 1970).

———. "The Palestinians in the Israel-Arab Conflict." *Midstream,* Vol. 17 (March, 1970).

———. "The Position of the Palestinians in the Israeli-Arab Conflict and their National Covenant (1968)." *New York University Journal of International Law and Politics,* Vol. 3 (spring, 1970).

Harris, Mervyn. "From Nile to Euphrates: The Evolution of a Myth." *New Middle East* (March-April, 1972).

Hatoum, Karin. "Israel's Lost Identity: A New Theory." *Arab World,* Vol. 14 (March-April, 1968).

Hattis, Susan. *The Bi-National Idea in Palestine During Mandatory Times.* Haifa: Shikmona, 1970.

———. "The Bi-National State and the Challenge of History." *New Middle East* (August, 1971).

Herman, Simon N. *Israelis and Jews: The Continuity of an Identity.* New York: Random House, 1970.

Hirszowicz, Lukasz. *The Third Reich and the Arab East.* London: Routledge and Kegan Paul, 1966.

Hogarth, D. C. "Arabs and Turks." *Arab Bulletin* (April 21, 1917).

Holsti, Ole R. "Cognitive Dynamics and Images of the Enemy: Dulles and Russia," *Enemies in Politics,* ed. David J. Finlay *et al.* Chicago: Rand McNally, 1967.

Hopkins, Harry. *Egypt the Crucible: The Unfinished Revolution of the Arab World.* London: Secker and Warburg, 1969.

Horn, Carl von. *Soldiering for Peace.* New York: David McKay, 1967.

Hottinger, Arnold. *The Arabs: Their History, Culture and Place in the Modern World.* Berkeley: University of California Press, 1963.

―――. "Colonel Ghadhafi's Pan-Arab Ambitions." *Swiss Review of World Affairs,* Vol. 21 (June, 1971).

―――. *10 Mal Nahost.* Munich: R. Piper, 1970.

Hourani, Cecil. "The Moment of Truth." *Encounter,* Vol. 39 (November, 1967).

Hourani, George F. "Palestine as a Problem in Ethics." *Arab World,* Vol. 15 (March-April, 1969).

Housepian, Marjorie. *The Smyrna Affair.* New York: Harcourt Brace Jovanovich, 1971.

Hurewitz, J. C. *Changing Military Perspectives in the Middle East.* Santa Monica: Rand, 1970.

―――. *The Struggle for Palestine.* New York: W. W. Norton, 1950.

Hussein, King of Jordan. *Uneasy Lies the Head.* New York: Bernard Geis, 1962.

Hutchison, E. H. *Violent Truce: A Military Observer Looks at the Arab-Israeli Conflict, 1951–1955.* New York: Devin-Adair, 1956.

Ibn el-Assal. "Return to Cairo." *Encounter,* Vol. 33 (August, 1969).

Ikle, Fred Charles. *How Nations Negotiate.* New York: Harper and Row, 1964.

Isaac, Erich, and Rael Jean Isaac. "The Siren Song of Peace: Israel's Dissenting Intellectuals." *Conservative Judaism,* Vol. 26 (spring, 1972).

Janowsky, Oscar I. Review of Folke Bernadotte's *To Jerusalem. Middle Eastern Affairs,* Vol. 4 (November, 1953).

Jeffery, Arthur. "The Political Importance of Islam." *Journal of Near Eastern Studies,* Vol. 1 (October, 1942).

Johnson, Lyndon Baines. *The Vantage Point: Perspectives of the Presidency 1963–1969.* New York: Holt, Rinehart and Winston, 1971.

Kahale, George III. "Arabs in the United States." Department of Political Science, Hunter College, New York, 1969.

Karl Marx on Colonialism and Modernization: His Despatches and Other Writings on China, India, Mexico, the Middle East and North Africa, ed. Shlomo Avineri. Garden City: Doubleday, 1968.

Kedourie, Elie. *The Chatham House Version and other Middle-Eastern Studies.* London: Weidenfeld and Nicolson, 1970.

————. *England and the Middle East: The Destruction of the Ottoman Empire 1914–1921.* London: Bowes and Bowes, 1956.

Kerr, Malcolm H. "The United Arab Republic: The Domestic, Political, and Economic Background of Foreign Policy," *Political Dynamics in the Middle East,* ed. Paul Y. Hammond and Sidney S. Alexander. New York: American Elsevier, 1972.

Khazoum, Eliahu H. "Salama Moussa: An Egyptian with a Message for Today." *New Middle East* (December, 1968).

Khouri, Fred J. *The Arab-Israeli Dilemma.* Syracuse: Syracuse University Press, 1968.

————. *The Second Arab Awakening.* London: Thames and Hudson, 1970.

Kimche, Jon, and David Kimche. *A Clash of Destinies: The Arab-Jewish War and the Founding of the State of Israel.* New York: Praeger, 1960.

Kinnane, Derk. *The Kurds and Kurdistan.* London: Oxford University Press, 1964.

Kirk, George E. "Comments," *The Anatomy of Peace in the Middle East.* New York: American Academic Association for Peace in the Middle East, 1969.

————. *A Short History of the Middle East: From the Rise of Islam to Modern Times.* New York: Praeger, 1964.

————. "United States Policy in the Middle East: An Historical Approach," *Forces of Change in the Middle East,* ed. Maurice M. Roumani. Worcester: Worcester State College, 1971.

Kraft, Joseph. "Those Arabists in the State Department." *New York Times Magazine* (November 7, 1971).

Kurzman, Dan. *Genesis 1948: The First Arab-Israeli War.* New York: World, 1970.

Laish, Aharon. "The Arab Minority in Israel." London: Institute of Jewish Affairs, 1972.

Lakin, Martin, *et al. Arab and Jews in Israel: Case Study in Human Relations Training Approach to Conflict.* New York: American Academic Association for Peace in the Middle East, 1969.

Lall, Arthur. *The U. N. and the Middle East Crisis, 1967.* New York: Columbia University Press, 1970.

Lane, E. W. *Manners and Customs of the Modern Egyptians.* Paisley: Alexander Gardner, 1895.

Lane, Robert E., and David O. Sears. *Public Opinion.* Englewood Cliffs: Prentice-Hall, 1964.

Laqueur, Walter Z. *Communism and Nationalism in the Middle East.* New York: Praeger, 1956.

———. *The Road to War 1967: The Origins of the Arab-Israeli Conflict.* London: Weidenfeld and Nicolson, 1968.

Larkin, Margaret. *The Six Days of Yad-Mordechai.* Israel: Ma'arachoth, 1965.

Latour, Annie. *The Resurrection of Israel,* trans. Margaret S. Summers. Cleveland: World, 1968.

Lawrence, T. E. *Seven Pillars of Wisdom.* Garden City: Doubleday, Doran, 1935.

Lehrman, Hal. "Is An Arab-Israeli War Inevitable?" *Commentary,* Vol. 21 (March, 1956).

———. "Three Weeks in Cairo." *Commentary,* Vol. 21 (February, 1956).

Lenczowski, George. "Conditions and Prospects for Tranquility in the Middle East," *United States Interests in the Middle East,* ed. George Lenczowski. Washington: American Enterprise Institute, 1968.

Lerner, Daniel. *The Passing of Traditional Society: Modernizing the Middle East.* Glencoe: The Free Press, 1958.

Levenberg, Alisa. "The War and the Sabras." *New Outlook,* Vol. 11 (January, 1968).

Levin, Harry. *I Saw the Battle of Jerusalem.* New York: Schocken, 1950.

Lewis, Bernard. *The Middle East and the West.* New York: Harper and Row, 1966.

———. "The Pro-Islamic Jews." *Judaism,* Vol. 17 (fall, 1968).

———. *Race and Color in Islam.* New York: Harper and Row, 1971.

———. "Semites and Anti-Semites: Race in the Arab-Israel Conflict." *Survey,* Vol. 17 (spring, 1971).

———. Statement, *Hearings Before the Subcommittee on National Security and International Operations of the Committee on Government Opera-*

Peled, Matityahu. "Golda Meir Draws Boundary Lines." *Palestine Digest,* Vol. 2 (April, 1972).

tions, United States Senate (March 17, 1971). Washington: U. S. Government Printing Office, 1971.

Lias, Godfrey. *Glubb's Legion.* London: Evans Brothers, 1956.

Lichtenstadter, Ilse. "An Arab-Egyptian Family." *Middle East Journal,* Vol. 6 (autumn, 1952).

Lilienthal, Alfred M. *There Goes the Middle East.* New York: Devin-Adair, 1957.

Lipset, Seymour Martin, and Carl Ladd, Jr. "Jewish Academics in the United States: Their Achievements, Culture and Politics," *American Jewish Year Book.* New York: American Jewish Committee, 1971.

Lorch, Netanel. *The Edge of the Sword: Israel's War of Independence, 1947–1949.* New York: Putnam, 1961.

Love, Kennett, *Sinai: The Twice-Fought War.* New York: McGraw-Hill, 1969.

Luttwak, Edward N., and Walter Laqueur. "Kissinger and the Yom Kippur War." *Commentary,* Vol. 58 (September, 1974).

Mango, Andrew. "Turkey and the Arabs," *Arab Nationalism and a Wider World,* ed. Sylvia G. Haim. New York: American Academic Association for Peace in the Middle East, 1971.

Mann, Jacob. *The Jews in Egypt and in Palestine under the Fatimid Caliphs . . . ,* Vol. 1. London: Oxford University Press, 1920.

Manners, Ande. *Poor Cousins.* New York: Coward, McCann, and Geoghegan, 1972.

Manuel, Frank E. *The Realities of American-Palestine Relations.* Washington: Public Affairs Press, 1949.

Masriya, Yehudiya. *Les Juifs en Égypte: Aperçu sur 3000 ans d'histoire.* Geneva: Éditions de l'avenir, 1971.

Mauriès, René. *La Kourdistan ou la mort.* Paris: Robert Laffont, 1967.

Mayhew, Christopher. "Fourth Lecture," *A Just Peace in the Mideast: How Can It Be Achieved?* I. L. Kenen *et al.* Washington: American Enterprise Institute, 1971.

Meinertzhagen, R. *Middle East Diary, 1917–1956.* London: The Cresset Press, 1959.

Memmi, Albert. *Portrait d'un Juif.* Paris: Gallimard, 1969.

The Memoirs of Sir Ronald Starr. New York: Putnam, 1937.

Menuhin, Moshe. "A Tribute to Count Folke Bernadotte." *Arab World,* Vol. 14 (September, 1968).

Merhav, Peretz. "Is De-Zionization the Answer?" *New Outlook*, Vol. 12 (February, 1969).

Merlin, Samuel. *The Search for Peace in the Middle East: The Story of President Bourguiba's Campaign for a Negotiated Peace Between Israel and the Arab States.* South Brunswick: Thomas Yoseloff, 1968.

The Middle East in the Contemporary World. American Professors for Peace in the Middle East, New York, 1968.

Millard, David. *A Journal of Travels in Egypt, Arabia Petrae, and the Holy Land During 1841–2.* Rochester: Erastus Shepard, 1843.

"Mohammed Hassanein Heykal Discusses War and Peace in the Middle East." *Journal of Palestine Studies*, Vol. 1 (autumn, 1971).

Moore, Clement Henry. "On Theory and Practice Among Arabs." *World Politics*, Vol. 24 (October, 1971).

Moorhouse, Geoffrey. *The Missionaries.* Philadelphia: Lippincott, 1973.

Morgenthau, Hans J. *Politics Among Nations: The Struggle for Power and Peace.* New York: Knopf, 1960.

Mussalam, Ayoub. "Peace Depends Upon Israel." *New Outlook*, Vol. 11 (July-August, 1968).

Mydans, Carl, and Shelley Mydans. *The Violent Peace: A Report on Wars in the Postwar World.* New York: Atheneum, 1968.

Neill, Stephen. *Colonialism and Christian Missions.* New York: McGraw-Hill, 1966.

Newnham, J. D. "Arab-Israeli Relations: A Pilot Study of International Attitudes," *Proceedings of the International Peace Research Association, Second Conference,* Vol. I. Assen: Van Gorcum, 1968.

The News From the Middle East. International Press Institute, Zurich, 1954.

Neyer, Joseph. *Middle East Happenings, Colloquies, Images, Mythologies.* New York: American Academic Association for Peace in the Middle East, 1971.

Nicholson, R. A. *A Literary History of the Arabs.* Cambridge: Cambridge University Press, 1969.

Nutting, Anthony. *The Arabs: A Narrative History from Mohammed to the Present.* New York: Clarkson N. Potter, 1964.

Oz, Amos. "Meaning of Homeland." *Jewish Quarterly*, Vol. 16 (spring, 1968).

Patai, Raphael. *Cultures in Conflict: An Inquiry into the Socio-Cultural Problems of Israel and Her Neighbors.* New York: Herzl Press, 1961.

Pearlman, Moshe. *Ben Gurion Looks Back.* New York: Simon and Schuster, 1965.

Peled, Matityahu. "Golda Meir Draws Boundary Lines." *Palestine Digest*, Vol. 2 (April, 1972).

Peoples and Cultures of the Middle East, ed. Louise E. Sweet. Garden City: Natural History Press, 1970 (2 vols.).

Peres, Yochanan. "Modernization and Nationalism in the Identity of the Israeli Arab," *Attitudes Toward Jewish Statehood in the Arab World*, ed. Gil Carl AlRoy. New York: American Academic Association for Peace in the Middle East, 1971.

———, and Nira Yuval-Davis. "Some Observations on the National Identity of the Israeli Arabs." *Human Relations*, Vol. 22 (June, 1969).

Peretz, Don. "The Coming Decade in the Middle East: A Symposium, Part II." *Interplay*, Vol. 3 (December, 1970).

———. "Israel and the Arab Nations," *The Middle East: Selected Readings*, ed. Don Peretz. Boston: Houghton Mifflin, 1968.

Polk, William R. *What the Arabs Think*. New York: Foreign Policy Association, 1952.

Porat, Jehoshua. *The Genesis of the Palestinian Arab Nationalist Movement, 1918–1928*. Institute for Afro-Asian Studies, Hebrew University, Jerusalem, 1971.

Prothro, E. Terry, and Levon H. Melikian. "Studies in Stereotypes: III. Arab Students in the Near East." *Journal of Social Psychology*, Vol. 40 (November, 1954).

Pundik, Herbert. "Israel's Arabs Establish Their Identity." *New Middle East* (August. 1969).

al-Qazzaz, Ayad. "Political Socialization in Iraq." Department of Political Science, Sacramento State College, Sacramento, 1971.

"The Quaker Way." *Christianity and Society*, Vol. 15 (winter, 1949–50).

Ra'anan, Uri. *The Changing American-Soviet Strategic Balance: Some Political Implications*. Washington: U. S. Government Printing Office, 1972.

———. *The USSR Arms the Third World: Case Studies in Soviet Foreign Policy*. Cambridge: MIT Press, 1969.

Randall, Rona. *Jordan and the Holy Land*. London: Frederick Muller, 1968.

Reich, Bernard. *Israel and the Occupied Territories*. Department of State, Washington, 1973.

Reisman, Michael. *The Art of the Possible: Diplomatic Alternatives in the Middle East*. Princeton: Princeton University Press, 1970.

Reissig, Herman F. "Another Look at the Arab-Israeli Problem." *Christianity and Crisis*, Vol. 16 (April 2, 1956).

Rejwan, Nissim. "Culture and Personality: Building the New Egyptian Man." *New Middle East* (February, 1972).

————. "Egypt's Second Thoughts on Pan-Arabism." *National Jewish Monthly*, Vol. 85 (May, 1971).

————. "Impact of June War on Arab Intellectuals." *New Outlook*, Vol. 14 (October-November, 1971).

————. "Israeli Attitudes to the Arab World." *New Outlook*, Vol. 9 (June, 1966).

————. "Why the Arabs Reject Antisemitism." *New Middle East* (July, 1969).

Report. Palestine Partition Commission, Command 5854, London, 1938.

Report. Palestine Royal Commission, Command 5479, London 1937.

Richter, Julius. *A History of Protestant Missions in the Near East*. Edinburgh: Oliphant, Anderson and Ferrier, 1910.

Robinson, R. E., and J. Gallagher. "The Partition of Africa," *New Cambridge Modern History*, Vol. 11. Cambridge: Cambridge University Press, 1962.

Rodinson, Maxime. *Israel and the Arabs*, trans. Michael Perl. New York: Pantheon, 1968.

Ro'i, Yaacov. "The Zionist Attitude to the Arabs 1908–1914." *Middle Eastern Studies*, Vol. 4 (April, 1968).

Roosevelt, Kermit. *Arabs, Oil and History: The Story of the Middle East*. New York: Harper, 1949.

Roughton, Richard A. "Algeria and the June 1967 Arab-Israeli War." *Middle East Journal*, Vol. 23 (autumn, 1969).

Rouleau, Eric, *et al. Israël et les Arabes: Le 3^e combat*. Paris: Editions du seuil, 1967.

Rubinstein, Amnon. "No Man's Land Remains in Jerusalem." *New York Times Magazine* (May 11, 1969).

————. "Why the Israelis Are Being Difficult." *New York Times Magazine* (April 18, 1971).

Sabin, Albert B., *et al. The Arabs Need and Want Peace, But—: Impressions. . . .* New York: American Professors for Peace in the Middle East. 1968.

Sadat, Anwar El. *Revolt on the Nile*, trans. Thomas Graham. London: Allan Wingate, 1957.

Safran, Nadav. "Arabs and Peace: A Critique of Jewish Skeptics." *Hadassah*, Vol. 55 (May, 1974).

————. *From War to War: The Arab-Israeli Confrontation, 1948-1967*. New York: Pegasus, 1969.

————. "N. K., K. G. B., or C. I. A.? Khruschev's Reminiscences on the Middle East." *New Middle East* (March, 1971).

————. "The War and the Future of the Arab-Israeli Conflict," *Foreign Affairs*, Vol. 52 (January, 1974).

Sale, George. "The Preliminary Discourse," *The Koran: Commonly Called the Alcoran of Mohammed*, trans. George Sale. London: William Tegg, 1850.

Sanders, C. A. S. "From a History of the Fourth Millennium." *Middle East Newsletter*, Vol. 2 (August-September, 1968).

"Sarih." "Frankly Speaking." *New Middle East* (October, 1969).

Saunders, George. "Sadat's Inheritance: Remnants of a Half-Revolution." *National Jewish Monthly*, Vol. 85 (May, 1971).

Sayegh, Fayez A. *The Arab-Israeli Conflict*. New York: Arab Information Center, 1956.

————. "The Encounter of Two Ideologies—Zionism and Arabism," *The Arab Nation: Path and Obstacles to Fulfillment*, ed. William Sands. Washington: Middle East Institute, 1961.

————. *Understanding the Arab Mind*. New York: Organization of Arab Students in the United States, 1953.

Schechtman, Joseph B. *The United States and the Jewish State Movement. The Crucial Decade: 1939–1949*. New York: Herzl Press, 1966.

Schleifer, Abdullah. *The Fall of Jerusalem*. New York: Monthly Review Press, 1972.

Schmidt, Dana Adams. *Journey Among Brave Men*. Boston: Little, Brown, 1964.

Scott, John. *The Middle East at War: A Report to the Publisher of* Time, *the Weekly Newsmagazine*. New York: Time, 1970.

Search for Peace in the Middle East. American Friends Service Committee, Philadelphia, 1970.

Segre, V. D. *Israel: A Society in Transition*. London: Oxford University Press, 1971.

The Seventh Day: Soldiers' Talk about the Six-Day War, ed. Avraham Shapira *et al.* and trans. Dvorah A. Sussman *et al.* New York: Scribner, 1970.

Shaban, M. A. "Maalesh! Inshallah!" *Encounter*, Vol. 30 (February, 1968).

Shamir, Shimon. "The Myth of Arab Intransigence," *Israel and the Palestinians: Reflections on the Clash of Two National Movements*, ed. Shlomo Avineri. New York: St. Martin's Press, 1971.

Sharabi, Hisham. *Palestine and Israel: The Lethal Dilemma.* New York: Pegasus, 1969.

―――. *Palestine Guerrillas: Their Credibility and Effectiveness.* Washington: Center for Strategic and International Studies, Georgetown University, 1970.

―――. "Prelude to War: The Crisis of May-June 1967." *Arab World,* Vol. 14 (special issue, 1969).

al-Shati, Bint. "The Historical Dimensions of this War." *Midstream,* Vol. 15 (June-July, 1969).

Sheehan, Edward R. F. "Colonel Qadhafi—Libya's Mystical Revolutionary." *New York Times Magazine* (February 6, 1972).

Shepherd, Naomi. "Palestine Profiles." *New Outlook,* Vol. 14 (April, 1971).

Sherrow, Fred S. "The Arabs of Palestine As Seen Through Jewish Eyes: A Newspaper Study, 1925-1929." MA Thesis, Columbia University, 1966.

Shilbaya, Muhammed Abu. "An Appeal to Palestinian Leaders." *New Middle East* (February, 1971).

Shouby, E. "The Influence of the Arabic Language on the Psychology of the Arabs." *Middle East Journal,* Vol. 5 (summer, 1951).

Siege in the Hills of Hebron: The Battle of the Etzion Bloc, ed. Dov Knohl. New York: Thomas Yoseloff, 1958.

Singer, Howard. *Bring Forth the Mighty Men: On Violence and the Jewish Character.* New York: Funk and Wagnalls, 1969.

Sleeper, James A. "Israeli Arabs: Israel's Peaceful Frontier?" *The New Jews,* ed. James A. Sleeper and Alan L. Mintz. New York: Vintage, 1971.

Smith, Terence. "The First Israeli Revolution." *New York Times Magazine* (December 30, 1973).

Smith, Wilfred Cantwell. *Islam in Modern History.* New York: New American Library, 1959.

Soloway, Arnold M., *et al. Truth and Peace in the Middle East: A Critical Analysis of the Quaker Report.* New York: Friendly House, 1971.

Spiro, Melford E. *Kibbutz: Venture in Utopia.* New York: Schocken, 1970.

St. Cyr, Robert. "Arab Perceptions of the Jew and Zionist: Do they Differ?" Department of Political Science, Hunter College, New York, 1969.

Stern, Sol. "The Russian Jews Wonder Whether Israel Is Really Ready for Them." *New York Times Magazine* (April 16, 1972).

Stevens, Georgiana G. "Middle East Perspectives," *The United States and the Middle East,* ed. Georgiana G. Stevens. Englewood Cliffs: Prentice-Hall, 1964.

Stewart, Desmond. "Arabian Notebook." *Encounter,* Vol. 32 (June, 1969).

Stock, Ernest. *From Conflict to Understanding: Relations Between Jews and Arabs in Israel Since 1948.* New York: Institute of Human Relations Press, 1968.

Stoessinger, John G. *Nations in Darkness: China, Russia, America.* New York: Random House, 1971.

Stone, I. F. *Underground to Palestine.* New York: Boni and Gaer, 1946.

Stone, N. I. "The Arab Question: Our Present and Future Policy." *New Palestine* (July 22, 1921).

Suleiman, Michael W. "Mass Media and the June Conflict." *Arab World,* Vol. 14 (special issue, 1969).

Swados, Harvey. "The Bridge on the River Jordan." *New York Times Magazine* (November 26, 1967).

Sykes, John. *The Mountain Arabs: A Window on the Middle East.* London: Hutchinson, 1968.

Talmon, Jacob. "Israel Among the Nations." *Commentary,* Vol. 45 (June, 1968).

Tamarin, Georges R. "The Israeli-Arab Conflict in Terms of Non-Communication," *Attitudes Toward Jewish Statehood in the Arab World,* ed. Gil Carl AlRoy. New York: American Academic Association for Peace in the Middle East, 1971.

————. *The Leap Forwards—Into the Past. An Essay.* . . . Giwatayim: Institute for Socio-Psychological Research, 1971.

————. *Two Essays on Jewish-Arab Relations.* Giwatayim: Institute for Socio-Psychological Research, 1972.

Tensions in the Middle East, ed. Philip W. Thayer. Baltimore: Johns Hopkins University Press, 1958.

Themes of Islamic Civilization, ed. John Alden Williams. Berkeley: University of California Press, 1971.

Thompson, Thomas. "U. S. Humiliation—A Diary from Cairo." *Life* (special edition, 1967).

Toynbee, Arnold J. *A Study of History,* Vol. 8. London: Oxford University Press, 1954.

Tritton, A. S. *The Caliphs and their Non-Muslim Subjects: A Critical Study of the Covenant of 'Umar.* London: Frank Cass, 1970.

Trost, Ernst. *David und Goliath: Die Schlacht um Israel.* Vienna: Fritz Molden, 1967.

Tuchman, Barbara W. "In the Wake of War: Time and Reality in the Middle East." *Atlantic,* Vol. 220 (November, 1967).

Turney-High, Holbert. *Primitive War: Its Practices and Concepts.* Columbia: University of South Carolina Press, 1949.

Vance, Vick, and Pierre Lauer. *Hussein de Jordanie: Ma "guerre" avec Israël.* Paris: Albin Michel, 1968.

Velie, Lester. *Countdown in the Holy Land.* New York: Funk and Wagnalls, 1969.

Verg, Erik. *Halbmond um den Davidstern: Die arabische Welt und Israel.* Berlin: Ullstein, 1964.

al-Waddah, Yusuf. Letter. *New Outlook,* Vol. 11 (October, 1968).

Wakefield, Dan. "Incident in Jerusalem." *Commentary,* Vol. 41 (February, 1966).

Werfel, Franz. *The Forty Days of Musa Dagh.* New York: Random House, 1934.

"Whose Country is Palestine? The Predicament of the Zionist Left." *Times Literary Supplement* (October 23, 1970).

Windsor, Philip. "Guerrilla Movements and the Arab Dilemma," *Attitudes Toward Jewish Statehood in the Arab World,* ed. Gil Carl AlRoy. New York: American Academic Association for Peace in the Middle East, 1971.

Wolf, Leonard. "Interview With a Fatah." *National Jewish Monthly,* Vol. 85 (April, 1971).

Yafeh, Hava Lazarus. Summary of Articles. *Hamizrah Hehadash,* Vol. 17, Nos. 3–4 (1967).

Yost, Charles W. "The Arab-Israeli War: How it Began." *Foreign Affairs,* Vol. 46 (January, 1968).

———. *The Insecurity of Nations: International Relations in the Twentieth Century.* New York: Praeger, 1968.

———. "Israel and the Arabs: The Myths that Block Peace." *Atlantic,* Vol. 223 (January, 1969).

Young, Kenneth T. *Negotiating with the Chinese Communists: The United States Experience.* New York: McGraw-Hill, 1968.

Young, Peter. *Bedouin Command: With the Arab Legion, 1953–1956.* London: William Kimber, 1956.

Zaher, Shafiq. "Reflections on the Arab Disaster." *New Outlook,* Vol. 13 (February, 1970).

Zeine, Zeine N. *The Struggle for Arab Independence: Western Diplomacy and the Rise and Fall of Faisal's Kingdom in Syria.* Beirut: Khayat, 1960.

Zeitlin, Rose. *Henrietta Szold: Record of a Life.* New York: Dial, 1952.

Zohar, Danah. "Israeli Left in Disarray as Labour Moves to Right." *New Middle East* (March-April, 1972).

INDEX

INDEX

A

Al-Aasi, Amr Ibn, 188
Abdallah, King of Jordan, 16, 54, 55–56, 93, 102; death of, 58
Achdut Haavoda, 47, 72
Aggiouri, René, 238
Al-Ahram (newspaper), 91, 119, 124, 128, 139
Al-Akhbar (newspaper), 139
Alami, Musa, 51
Aliya Hadasha, 72
Alter, Robert, 86
American Assembly of Columbia University, 198
American Council for Judaism, 73
American Friends of the Middle East, 19
Ammar, Hamed, 107
Anglo-American Committee of Inquiry, 116, 178
Antonius, George, 51, 95, 220
Antonius, Katy, 31, 171
Arab Awakening, The (Antonius), 31, 220
Arab-Israeli conflict, views of, 81–115; African views, 82; and Arab character, 106–14; and Arab courtesy, 94–97, 101–104; and Arab homicide rate, 109; and Arab leaders, 110–15; and "Arab psychology," 105; and Arab rhetoric, 92–94; and Arab subterfuge, 112–14; and British anti-Semitism, 96–101; diplomacy and diplomats' views, 81–86, 101–104, 111; early conflicts, 25–46; and Islamic attitudes toward non-Muslims, 107, 161–64; journalists' views, 86–92
Arab-Israeli relations, 176–201 passim; and "Arab bravery" concept, 195–96; and Christian attitudes toward Jews, 179–80; dual attitude of Arabs to Jews, 177–78; and ethnic affinities, 198–201; and "Jewish cowardice" concept, 195–96; and Jewish stereotype, 196–98; and Muslim subjection of Jews, 176, 179–201; and Zionism, 176–79, 189–92
Arab-Israeli relations, future of, 231–54; and Arab oil revenues, 246, 250; and Arab procrastination, 240; and changing Israeli opinion, 253–54; and fluctuations in Arab feeling, 233–36; Indo-Pakistan comparison, 251; prospects for peace, 243–54
Arab-Israeli War of 1948, 16, 54, 64, 94, 120, 122, 147, 150–51, 154, 205, 220
Arab-Israeli War of 1956, 65, 235
Arab-Israeli War of 1967, 16, 45, 59, 61, 64, 66, 122–23, 128, 141, 164, 193, 194, 203, 209, 211, 213, 216, 232, 236, 237, 240, 241, 247, 249, 250
Arab-Israeli War of 1973, 12, 16, 38, 77, 137, 138, 140, 150, 155, 182, 194, 196, 205, 210, 233, 238, 239, 240, 244, 246, 248, 250
Arab League, 119, 164, 178
Arab World (magazine), 111
Arafat, Yasser, 127, 177, 208
Ashraf, Ibn Al, 181
Association of Arab-American University Graduates, 177

Ataturk, Kemal, 189
Attitudes and orientations, Israeli,
  50–80; and American Jewish
  organizations, 60–61; and "Arab
  psychology," 75; and Arab-Zionist
  contacts, 51–59; of Ashkenazi, 73–74;
  and concept of Arab-Israeli
  compatibility, 50–51; and
  immigration/emigration trends, 79;
  and intentions of Arabs, 79–80; from
  opinion polls, 59–60, 62, 67; of
  Oriental Jews, 72–73; of sabras, 66,
  68, 73–74; of Sephardim, 72–73;
  toward U.S.S.R., 69–70; and war
  casualties, 78; of writers, 74–75; and
  Zionism, 50
Attlee, Lord, 99
Avneri, Uri, 71
"Awakening, Arab," 165–75
Azury, Neguib, 12
Azzam Pasha, 102, 190

B

Baath party, 122
Badeau, John S., 199
Al-Bairak (newspaper), 140
Barzini, Luigi, 105–106
Bell, J. Bowyer, 16
Beloff, Nora, 22, 23
Ben-Gurion, David, 28–29, 40, 47, 51,
  62, 145
Ben-Yehuda, Eliezer, 26
Ben-Zvi, Isaac, 28
Berger, Elmer, 136, 148
Bernadotte, Count Folke, 48, 102
Bernadotte Plan, 147, 149
Bethman, Erich W., 19
Bevin, Ernest, 99, 100
Bilby, Kenneth W., 58, 95, 96, 111, 120,
  166
Biltmore Program, 47
Borochov, Ber, 40
Boumedienne, Houari, 203
Bourguiba, Habib, 121, 124, 203, 204,
  211, 253
Boycotts, Arab, 31
Brit Shalom, 46–48, 51, 53

British Mandate, 12, 29–31, 46, 55, 77,
  223; and British anti-Semitism, 42–44,
  96–101; and labor unions, 228–29
Bunche, Ralph J., 82
Burdett, Winston, 109, 113
Burrows, Millar, 136
Butler, Grant, 135

C

Caradon, Lord, 23
Cassar, Anton, 27
Casualties of war, Israeli, 78
Chamoun, Camille, 210
Character, Arab, 106–14; Western views
  of, 133–36
Chatham House. See Royal Institute of
  International Affairs
Christian Arabs, 27, 28
Christian attitudes toward Middle East,
  18–20
Christian-Jewish relations, 179–80,
  184–85; and ritual-murder accusations,
  184
Christianity and Islam, 104
Churchill, Sir Winston S., 93
Cohen, Aharon, 52
Cohen, Gerson, 171
Cohn, Dr., 102
Compatibility, Arab-Israeli, 50–51
Conflict, Arab-Israeli. See Arab-Israeli
  conflict
Confrontation with Israel (Abdullah), 13
Conspiracy and the Battle of Destiny,
  The (Jumaa), 144
Cooperation, Arab-Israeli, 31–35
Coote, Captain, 93
Cottam, Richard W., 143
Courtesy, Arab, 94–97, 101–104
Crossman, Richard, 98–100
Crum, Bartley C., 98

D

Davis, John H., 133
Dayan, Moshe, 53, 54, 74
Dayan, Yael, 65, 66.

Diaspora, 25, 26
Ad-Difaa (newspaper), 170, 195
Diplomacy and diplomats, 81–86,
101–104, 111 passim
Djemel, Ahmed, 28
Druses, 216

E

Earl of Louisiana, The (Liebling), 174
Eckstein, Harry, 22
Elon, Amos, 61, 201
Emigration, Israeli, 79
Enver Pasha, 188
Ethnic affinities, of Jews and Arabs,
198–201

F

Faisal I, King of Syria and Iraq, 54–55,
219
Faisal, King of Saudi Arabia, 211
Faisal, Prince, 24
Faisal Agreement of 1918, 54–55
Faraj, Yakub, 220
Farukh, Mohammad Ibn, 187
Al Fatah, 177, 197, 207
Fedayeen, 128–31, 140, 151, 223–28
Fellaheen, 223–28
Filastin (newspaper), 220
Foot, Sir Dingle, 23
Frady, Marshall, 174, 197
Frangieh, Hamid, 102
Freedom Fighters of Israel, 45, 47
Fulbright, James W., 82, 127

G

Gabbay, Rony, 16
Gaon, Saadiah, 201
Genocide, 139. *See also* Holocaust
Ghareeb, Edmund, 132
Glubb, Sir John B., 56, 148, 226
Gohar, Salah, 110
Goitein, S. D., 62
Goldmann, Nahum, 48, 102

Goshah, Sheikh, 178
Guerrilla warfare, Arab propensity for,
94
Al-Gumhuria (newspaper), 195
Gumplowicz, Ludwig, 36

H

Habash, George, 208, 217
Haikal, Yusuf, 91, 125–26, 132
Hakim, Archbishop, 238
Hakim, Caliph, 184
Halevi, Judah, 201
Hammarskjöld, Dag, 16
Hanassi, Joseph, 201
Haolam Haze, 71
Hapoel Hatzair, 40
Harkabi, Yehoshafat, 130
Hashomer Hatzair, 40–42, 47, 48, 69
Hassan II, King of Morocco, 210
Haughey, Father, 104
Al-Hawadath (newspaper), 196
Hawatmeh, Naif, 140, 208
Haycraft Commission of 1921, 37
Hayes, Rutherford B., 73
Hazan, Yakov, 71
Herzl, Theodor, 36, 38
Heterogeneity, of Arabs, 202–230; and
attitudes, 210–12; and Christian
hostility to Zionism, 218–22; and
fedayeen and *fellaheen*, 223–28; and
Islamic divisions, 214–17; and
Mashrek and *Maghreb* dichotomy,
202–205; and nationalism, 212–14; and
reaction to Zionism, 209
Hillel, Rabbi, 48
Histadrut, 228–29
History, Arab, 159–75
History, Jewish, 179–201
Hitler, Adolf, 186
Holocaust, the, 47, 49, 64, 149, 176, 179
Holy Land Center, 19
Homicide rate, Arab, 109
Hottinger, Arnold, 131, 206, 209
Hourani, Cecil A., 119, 148, 151
Hussein, King of Jordan, 55, 56, 86,
114–15, 122, 127, 128, 148, 178, 194,
195, 207, 211, 215

Al-Husseini, Fauzi Darwish, 52
Al-Husseini, Haj Amin, *Mufti* of
  Jerusalem, 46, 95
Hutchinson, Commander, 133, 135
Hutchison, Elmo, 16

I

Ichud. See *Brit Shalom*
Immigration, Arab, 27, 38
Immigration, Israeli, 35–36, 79
Indo-Pakistan conflict, 251
Intentions, Arab, 79–80
Irgun. *See* National Military
  Organization
Islam, 159–75; and Arab history, 159–75;
  and "Arab awakening," 169–75; and
  Israeli manners and customs, 172–75;
  attitude toward Jews, 31–35, 176,
  179–201; attitude toward
  non-Muslims, 161–64; attitudes to
  politics and religion, 104; and
  Christianity, 104; divisions of, 214–17;
  and Israeli nationalism, 168–71; and
  missionaries, 18–21; modernization of
  Islam, 169–72; philosophy, 117; and
  role playing, 32; sociopolitical
  character of, 104, 160–62; Western
  attitudes toward, 18–21
Israel and the Arab World (Cohen), 52
Israel, early days of, 24–49; and
  anti-Jewish violence, 36–38, 45; and
  Arab immigration, 27, 38; and
  Arab-Israeli conflict, 31–35; and
  Arab-Israeli cooperation, 31–32; and
  Arab politicization, 39; British
  Mandate, 29, 31, 42–44, 46; and
  Christian Arabs, 27, 28; and early
  Arab-Israeli conflict, 25–46; Jewish
  immigration, 35–36; Jewish
  politicization, 40–49; and
  "revisionism," 42–45; and Turkey, 28;
  and Zionism, 25. *See also* Palestine,
  partition of
Israel, explanations of Arab hostility to,
  15–16
Israel, foundation of: and British
  Mandate, 12, 29–31, 42–44, 46, 55, 77,

96–101, 223; and Zionism, 24–26. *See
  also* Palestine, partition of
Israeli-Arab wars. *See* Arab-Israeli War
  of . . .
Israelis, The (Elon), 201
Al-Issa, Issa, 220

J

Jabotinsky, Vladimir, 47, 48
Jarring, Gunnar, 59, 87, 125–26, 127
Jeffery, Arthur, 160, 189
Jewish Agency, 52
Jewish-Arab relations. *See* Arab-Israeli
  relations
Jewish-Christian relations. *See*
  Christian-Jewish relations
Jewish World Congress, 16
Jews, history of, 179–201
Joseph, Dr., 102
Journalists, views of, 86–92
Jumaa, Saad, 144
June War. *See* Arab-Israeli War of 1967

K

Kalvarisky, Hayim, 52
Kaplan, Eliezer, 47
Kaplansky, Shlomo, 28
Kedourie, Elie, 18, 189
Khaldi, Ibrahim, 178
Khrushchev, Nikita, 82
King-Crane Commission, 24
Kisch, Col., 182
Kissinger, Henry M., 16, 83, 103, 108,
  131, 137, 138, 235
Koestler, Arthur, 97

L

Labor unions, Israeli, 228–29
Lall, Arthur, 16, 83–84
Land of Israel Movement, 45
Lane, E. W., 188
Lawrence, T. E., 170
Leaders, Arab, 110–15

League for Jewish-Arab Rapprochement and Cooperation, 52
Lerner, Abba P., 14
Lewis, Bernard, 88, 92, 113, 161, 173, 199
Lewis, Flora, 140
Lichtheim, Dr., 33
Liebling, A. J., 174
Lilienthal, Alfred, 136
Lorch, Netanel, 36
Love, Kenneth, 16
Luke, Harry, 43

M

Mack, Julian W., 25
Maghreb and *Mashrek* dichotomy, 202–5
Magnes, Judah L., 51–52
Maimonides, 185
Maki, 71
Manchester Guardian, 111
Manners, Arab, 94–97, 101–4
Manners, Israeli, 94–97, 101–4
Mapai, 47, 72
Mapam, 60, 69–71, 72
Marshall, George C., 44
Marx, Karl, 187
Mashrek and *Maghreb* dichotomy, 202–5
Massacre, of Palestinian Jews, 182
Matzpen, 129
Mayhew, Christopher, 135
Meinertzhagen, Col., 96, 111
Meir, Golda, 62
Merhav, Peretz, 63
Middle East Center, 19
Middle East Institute, 21
Middle East situation, Zionist perceptions of, 24–49; and founding of Israel, 24–26; and Jewish policy of *havlagah* (passivity), 45–46
Middle East, Western misconceptions about, 11–23; Arab hostility to Israel, 12–16; "Arab psychology," 15–16; crucial stages in Arab-Israeli relations, 16–17; and educational and research institutes, 19–20; resolvability of problem, 21–22; and Western missionaries, 18–20; and Western partisanship, 17–20; and Western religious attitudes, 18–20.
Missionaries, 18–20
Moderation, Arab, 121–40
Mohammed, Prophet, 180–82; death of, 182
Molki Pasha, 102
Morgenthau, Henry, 189
Morris, James, 111
Morrison-Grady Plan, 149
Moussa, Salama, 212
Moynihan, Daniel P., 83
Mubarak, Ignatius, 217
Musallam, Ayoub, 177
Muslims. *See* Islam
Al-Mussawar (magazine), 123, 138, 170
Mussolini, Benito, 186
Mutawakkil, decree of, 184

N

Nadheer, Beni, 180
Al-Nashashibi, Muhammad Isaf (quoted), 135
Nassar, William N., 197
Nasser, Gamal Abdel, 46, 82, 86, 91, 108–9, 111–12, 113, 114, 117, 125, 132, 135, 137, 197, 207, 208, 212, 232, 236, 244, 248
National Commission on the Causes and Prevention of Violence, 22
National Military Organization, 45
Nationalism, Arab, 212–14, 217–28; and rhetoric, 121–58
Neguib, Mohammed, 16
New Palestine (magazine), 95
New York *Times*, 86–88, 90, 91, 124, 126, 127, 137
Nixon, Richard M., 137
Nuri-Said, 210
Nutting, Anthony, 148

O

October War. *See* Arab-Israeli War of 1973
Oil revenues, Arab, 246, 250

Omar, Caliph, 180, 183, 188
Opinion, Israeli, 59–73, 253–54
Opinion polls, 59–73
L'Orient (newspaper), 248
Oz, Amos, 63, 78

P

Pace, Eric, 170
Palestine, partition of, 118, 148–49, 151,
    156. See also Israel, foundation of
Palestine Arab Workers' Society, 229
Palestine Development Council, 25
Palestine Liberation Organization, 51,
    129
Palestine National Council, 140
Palestine National Covenant, 129, 192
Palestine Resistance Movement, 213
Palmerston, Lord, 218
Passivity, traditional Jewish policy of,
    45–46
PDFLP, 129–30
Peace, prospects for, 243–54
Peace settlement, concepts of, 138–39
Pearson, Lester B., 81
Peel Commission, 61; Plan, 149; Report,
    37, 57
PFLP, 217
Philosophy, Islamic, 117
PLO, 51, 129
Poalei Zion Smol, 40, 41
Political parties, Israeli, 40–49
Political violence, lack of study of, 22
Politicization, Arab, 39
Popular Democratic Front for the
    Liberation of Palestine, 129–30, 217
Promise and Fulfillment (Koestler), 97
Pronouncements, Arab, complexity of,
    116–40; and Arab moderation, 121–40;
    concepts of peace settlement, 138–39;
    and elimination of Israel, 118–21; and
    fedayeen, 128–31, 140; and Islamic
    philosophy, 117; on Jewish genocide,
    139; and refugee problem, 133; and
    Western view of Arab character,
    133–36. See also Rhetoric, Arab
Protocols of the Elders of Zion, 90, 100,
    187
"Psychology, Arab," 15–16, 75, 105

Q

Al-Qadhafi, Muammar, 108, 139, 147,
    206
Quaker Report, 198

R

Rafi, 72
Rakah, 71
Rashid Bey, 38
Al-Rashid, Haroun, 184
Refugees, 133
Religious attitudes, Western, 18–20
Return Ticket (Nashashibi), 135
"Revisionism," 42–45
Rhetoric, Arab, 92–94, 141–58; and
    fedayeen, 151; and feeling of betrayal,
    142–44; and Israeli occupations, 155;
    and "Jewish conspiracy," 144–58; and
    subjection of non-Arabs, 157–58; and
    variability of feelings toward Israel,
    141; and Zionism, 141–58. See also
    Pronouncements, Arab
Ritual murder accusations, 184
Rodinson, Maxime, 16
Rogers, William, 108, 150
Roosevelt, Franklin D., 48
Roosevelt, Kermit, 164
Root, Elihu, 186
Rouleau, Eric, 92
Royal Institute on International Affairs,
    18
Rubinstein, Amnon, 170
Ruppin, Arthur, 53–54, 61

S

Sabras, views of, 66, 68, 73–74
Al-Sadat, Anwar, 104, 108, 126–27
Safran, Nadav, 82
Sakakini, Khalil, 220
Saladin the Great, 185
Sale, George, 188
Salem, Salah, 119
Samuel, Herbert L., 93
Saud, King of Saudi Arabia, 116, 210
Sayegh, Fayez A., 163

Sharett, Moshe, 48
Shaw Report, 37
Sheean, Vincent, 95
Shertoke, Moshe. *See* Sharett, Moshe
Shiite Muslims, 214–17
Shukairi, Ahmed, 51, 92
Shukeiry, Ahmed, 247
Siah, 71
Sidky, Aziz, 195
Sirhan, Sirhan B., 93
Sisco, Joseph, 108
Smith, Wilfred C., 159, 164
Stalin, Joseph, 70
Stereotypes, Arab and Jewish, 195–98
Stern Gang. *See* Freedom Fighters of Israel
Stewart, Desmond, 193
Stone, I. F., 32
Strauss, Leo, 117
Subjection of Jews, 157–58
Subterfuge, Arab, 112–14
Sunni Muslims, 34, 75, 157, 190, 206, 214–17
Swados, Harvey, 172
Szold, Henrietta, 38

T

Talmon, Jacob, 148
Tamarin, Georges R., 68, 72, 74
Tanner, Henry, 137, 140
Thieves in the Night (Koestler), 97
Thompson, Thomas, 164
Thon, Joseph, 28
Time (magazine), 114
Tito, Marshal, 135
To Jerusalem (Bernadotte), 102
Toynbee, Arnold J., 18, 136, 179, 201
Tuchman, Barbara W., 232, 239

U

U.N. Plan (for partition), 149, 156
U.N. Security Council. Resolution No. 242, 16, 23, 82, 88, 91, 110, 123, 124–25, 126, 127, 234
U.S.S.R., 69–70

U.S. Senate. Foreign Relations Committee, 16
U.S. State Department, 19

V

Van Paassen, Pierre, 43
Verg, Erik, 164
Violence, anti-Jewish, 36–38, 45
Violence, political, 22
Von Hentig, Otto, 58

W

War casualties, Israeli, 78
Weizmann, Chaim, 25, 46, 48
Wilson, Woodrow, 24
Windsor, Philip, 168
Wingate, Orde, 98
Wise, Isaac M., 73
Wolf, Leonard, 197
Woodhead Commission, 58, 148–49
World Zionist Organization, 25, 45
Writers, Israeli, 74–75

Y

Yost, Charles W., 85
Young Turk Revolution of 1908, 28

Z

Zionism, 50; Arab reactions to, 209; and Arab rhetoric, 141–58; and Arab-Israeli relations, 51–59, 176–79, 189–92; definitions of, 176–77; and "division of labor," 25; hostility of Christians to, 218–22; and "revisionism," 42–45, 153
Zionism, modern 46–49; and attitudes toward Arabs, 47–49; British attitude toward, 47–48; "monolithic" Zionism, 46, 47; "organic" Zionism, 46, 47; and perceptions of Middle East situation, 24–49